Donated by

Jane Moses

In Memory of

Mrs. Joseph Brown

THE DOOM OF
RECONSTRUCTION

The Doom of Reconstruction

The Liberal Republicans in the Civil War Era

Andrew L. Slap

FORDHAM UNIVERSITY PRESS
NEW YORK   2006

Library of Congress Cataloging-in-Publication Data

Slap, Andrew L.
    The doom of Reconstruction : the liberal Republicans in the Civil War era / Andrew L. Slap.—1st ed.
        p.   cm.— (Reconstructing America series ; no. 12)
    Includes bibliographical references and index.
    ISBN-13: 978-0-8232-2709-9 (cloth : alk. paper)
    ISBN-10: 0-8232-2709-X (cloth: alk. paper)
    1. Presidents—United States—Election—1872.   2. Grant, Ulysses S. (Ulysses Simpson), 1822–1885.   3. Greeley, Horace, 1811–1872.   4. Liberal Republican Party—History.   5. Reconstruction (U.S. history, 1865–1877)   6. United States—Politics and government—1849-1862.   7. United States—Politics and government—1861–1865.   8. United States—Politics and government—1865–1877.   I. Title.
    E675.S56   2006
    324.2732—dc22

                                                                            2006036539

Printed in the United States of America
08 07 06   5 4 3 2 1
First edition

Contents

Acknowledgments   *vii*

Introduction   *xi*

1   Rehearsal in Missouri for the Liberal Republican Movement, 1865–1870 | 1

2   The Liberal Republican Conception of Party, 1848–1872 | 25

3   Preserving the Republic while Defeating the Slave Power, 1848–1865 | 51

4   The Liberal Republican Dilemma over Reconstruction, 1865–1868 | 73

5   Legacies of the Civil War Threaten the Republic, 1865–1872 | 90

6   Grant and the Republic, 1868–1872 | 108

7   The National Phase of the Liberal Republican Movement, 1870–1872 | 126

8   The Experience of a Third Party in the Nineteenth Century | 164

9   The Lasting Effect of 1872 Campaign Rhetoric | 199

10   The Liberal Republicans Try Again, 1872–1876 | 222

Conclusion   *238*

Notes   *241*

Bibliography   *279*

Index   *295*

Acknowledgments

This project took longer and involved more people than the liberal republican movement it studies. While I liked getting to know the liberal republicans, the real pleasure of the last decade has been experiencing the intellect, support, generosity, and friendship of so many people. I owe countless debts to those who made this book possible.

The history department at Pennsylvania State University provided years of financial support, including a Hill Dissertation Fellowship that allowed me to spend a semester at the Library of Congress. The archivists at the Library of Congress and the many other places I visited made the research possible with their enthusiastic and patient help. The Richards Civil War Era Center at Penn State, directed by William Blair, gave me a James Landing Fellowship, enabling me to have an uninterrupted semester of thinking and writing.

The people at Penn State helped with this project and made my time in State College a pleasure. Fellow graduate students Jonathan Berkey, Barbara Gannon, Tristan Jolivette, Robert Sandow, David Smith, Mike Smith, and Jim Weeks all read a chapter of the dissertation—and provided hours of thoughtful conversation and years of friendship. Charles Holden supplied a place to stay on a research trip to North Carolina. Amy Greenberg, Paul Harvey, William Pencak, and James Rambeau all served on my dissertation committee and gave valuable comments that improved this manuscript. Joanne Reitano of LaGuardia Community College read a chapter on republican ideology and Paula Baker of Ohio State commented on a paper delivered at the American Historical Association Meeting about the party system and the election of 1872.

Three historians deserve special mention. Michael F. Holt served as an outside dissertation committee member and generously drove to State College for the defense. He gave my dissertation a meticulous reading and made hundreds of written comments that immeasurably improved the manuscript. I was a relative Civil War novice upon arriving at Penn State, but that quickly changed under the guidance of Gary W. Gallagher. He taught me a great deal about the war and how to use primary sources, and he supervised the beginnings of my dissertation. He remained on my dissertation committee after leaving Penn State and still provides support and advice. Mark E. Neely Jr. became my advisor just as I started writing the dissertation and he read numerous drafts without complaint, each time prodding me for sharper analysis and writing. He has been a wonderful mentor, setting an example of both outstanding scholarship and character. Studying with Mark has fundamentally changed how I think.

My colleagues at East Tennessee State University have helped in many ways, including offering me a teaching schedule that provides time to research and write. Steve Fritz has been a role model, and has given constant encouragement and advice on publishing. Paul A. Cimbala at Fordham University Press took an early interest in this project and made sure that it would be published. Anne Miller edited the manuscript for Fordham University Press with great care, correcting many errors and making stylistic improvements. As an outside reader for Fordham University Press Michael Green gave the manuscript a Holtesque reading, saving me from numerous factual and interpretive mistakes. Mike understood what I wanted to do with the manuscript and pushed me to do it better, for which I owe him a huge debt.

Friends and family made this project both possible and enjoyable. Mark and Daniel Oppenheimer hosted me while visiting archives in their cities. Tammy Murphy has been a friend since our first semester as undergraduates and has shared the academic journey. Roger and Judy Duffala are the perfect in-laws. Charles Slap's keen intellect and Elizabeth Menist's good heart have served as inspirations. Jackie Shanti has provided a lifetime of motherly encouragement and Carl McCargo has always been ready for a good debate. Derek Slap has been both a great brother and a best friend.

Though she would prefer not to be mentioned at all in something that will be published, Nicole deserves my greatest thanks. For years she has read manuscript drafts, organized research notes, and listened to me talk about the liberal republicans. She has displayed more patience, understanding, and faith than I deserve. In my last months of revising the manuscript she gave birth to our daughter, Abigail Elizabeth. Nicole has made my life happy and complete.

The Doom of Reconstruction

Introduction

The liberal republican movement doomed Reconstruction in 1872.* Given the background of the men who started the movement this is extremely ironic, for in the previous decade many of them had led efforts to reconstruct the South and help African Americans. For example, early in 1862 Massachusetts economist Edward Atkinson became secretary of the New England Freedmen's Aid Society, an organization that assisted recently freed slaves in South Carolina. As the war ended in 1865, journalist William Grosvenor publicly argued that the Union needed a continued military presence in the South because "we cannot justly leave the rights of the freedmen at the mercy of those who so long held them in slavery." Most of the liberal republicans agreed with Grosvenor. Newspapers sympathetic to the movement—*The Nation,* the *Springfield Republican,* the *New York Evening Post,* and the *Chicago Tribune*—all endorsed the First Military Reconstruction Act in Congress, while Lyman Trumbull drafted the 1866 Civil Rights Bill.[1]

Carl Schurz, senator from Missouri, explained the liberal republicans' long-standing desire to reconstruct the South in a speech about how to create peace after the Civil War. Insisting that it was first necessary to remove the cause of the strife, Schurz proclaimed that the South had caused the conflict because "in the South there existed a peculiar interest and institution—namely, slavery and the aristocratic class government inseparable from involuntary labor, which in its very nature was antagonistic to the fundamental principles upon which our democratic system of government rests." He identified these fundamental principles in classical republican terms; they included public virtue, independent citizenship, and vigilance against tyranny. Such ideological expressions were not unusual for these men. For decades they had believed that the Southern slave system endangered republican government in the United States and had fought against it, helping to start the Free Soil Party in the 1840s and then the Republican Party in the 1850s.[2]

Although they were members of the Republican Party during the Civil War, the liberal republicans only grudgingly compromised their republican ideology

---

* I use *liberal republican* in lowercase to indicate the movement and *Liberal Republican* in uppercase to indicate the political party that was formed at the Cincinnati Convention on May 1–3, 1872.

to secure victory. When Abraham Lincoln used patronage to unify the heterogeneous Republican Party in 1861, they assailed him for corrupting public virtue. Throughout the course of the war they regularly opposed war measures, such as the Legal Tender Act of 1862 and the Morrill Tariff Act, that they thought dangerously enlarged the power of the federal government and corrupted the nation's virtue. Horace White, an abolitionist who idolized John Brown, disliked legal tender so much that he compared it to slavery, insisting in the *Chicago Tribune* that "if the present war shall teach the American people the double lesson that they cannot make chattels of human beings, and that they cannot make money out of paper, it will be cheap at any price."[3]

The end of the Civil War drove the liberal republicans in seemingly contradictory directions. The long-perceived threat of the Southern slave system to republican government led them to support reconstruction of the South. Reconstruction, however, required uses of federal power that they admitted could be seen as tyrannical. While they ironically supported military rule to safeguard republican government, by the late 1860s they also increasingly feared that wartime changes in the North threatened that very system. In 1869 Charles Francis Adams Jr. argued that federal grants of land to build railroads had created a "railway power" more dangerous than the old Slave Power, and others of the liberal republicans worried that the protective tariff promoted corruption and plunder in the government. They soon formed a movement to counteract these threats. While many of them eventually criticized some aspects of reconstructing the South, ending Reconstruction was a minor part of their agenda. Most of the liberal republicans from the West thought that among their concerns, civil service reform was the most easily understood by the public, while those from the East had already demonstrated their primary interest by forming the Free Trade League in 1865. Thus, the first national liberal republican meeting decided initially to restrict the movement to the issues of revenue and civil service reform.

The impetus to form the national liberal republican movement came from the success of a local group in Missouri that in 1870 had captured the states' governorship and open U.S. Senate seat. The liberal republicans decided to try replicating this local triumph nationally, either by taking control of the Republican Party or by starting a new party. While it may now seem unrealistic for a small reform movement to contemplate taking control of a major political party or starting their own, the liberal republicans' expectations reflected their experiences with political parties as temporary organizations during the Civil War era. Many of them had helped create the Free Soil Party in the 1840s and the Republican Party in the 1850s, and they were ready to form a new party by 1870. They saw parties as creations organized around a great idea; they believed that when a party's objective was accomplished, new political parties should organize around the next great idea. The liberal republicans' achievement in Missouri, combined with their conception of the nature of political parties, led them to a reasonable hope of success. But while the political experiences of the liberal republicans provided reasons for optimism, lack of political talent soon destroyed their movement. At their first national convention, held in Cincinnati in May 1872, personal rivalries and mistakes allowed outsiders to take control of the new Liberal Republican Party and nominate Horace Greeley as its presidential candidate. When the regular Republicans had added War Democrats to their coalition in 1864, they had managed to maintain their ideology in the process. But the nomination of Greeley, a renowned supporter of the protective tariff and the patronage system, stripped the new Liberal Republican Party of the movement's republican ideology. Many original members of the movement refused to support Greeley and eventually either campaigned for the reelection of Republican President Ulysses S. Grant or left politics altogether. The Republican Party also affected the nature of the coming campaign by appropriating most of the Liberal Republican issues, such as civil service reform and legal tender. The combination of Greeley's nomination and the Republicans' appropriation of their issues forced the new Liberal Republican Party to focus the election of 1872 on the dangers of Reconstruction policies and the misdeeds of President Grant—minor issues for the liberal republican movement at its origin and for most of its short life.

The dynamics of the 1872 presidential campaign directed increasingly negative attention toward Reconstruction. Many of the new converts to the Liberal Republican Party had recently been among the most prominent Radical Republicans, such as Charles Sumner and George Julian, and had joined the new party because of differences with Grant. The presence of Radical Republicans helped to legitimize the Liberal Republicans' assault on Reconstruction. Many of the party's campaign speakers made it clear that they were Republicans and abolitionists, not Democrats or ex-rebels, attacking Reconstruction. In response to Liberal Republican assaults, the regular Republicans grudgingly defended Reconstruction. At the same time, however, they passed a sweeping amnesty act that restored the right to hold public office in the South to all but a few former Confederates, thereby co-opting one of the Liberal Republicans' main criticisms of Reconstruction: its denial of self-government to many citizens of the Southern states.

The circumstances of the 1872 campaign made it politically expedient for the Republican Party to begin undoing the work of Reconstruction. Though Grant won the election, the campaign fatally weakened Reconstruction by estranging important members of the party's ideological core, increasing the negative image of Reconstruction nationally, and beginning the party's retreat from its commitment to protecting the rights of Southern freedmen. During the next four years the Republicans supported Reconstruction primarily for political reasons and were constantly on the defensive. By 1876 the party had decided not to renominate Grant and was willing to end Reconstruction in the compromise that settled the disputed presidential election of that year. The liberal republican movement, started for other purposes, ended up playing a large role in the destruction of what its members had helped create.

The election of 1872 not only doomed Reconstruction, but its campaign rhetoric also permanently damaged the reputation of the liberal republicans themselves. To deal with the awkward situation of having many of the movement's original members campaigning against the Liberal Republican Party's presidential nominee, the party's campaigners and newspapers regularly ridiculed the disaffected reformers. Many of the former liberal republicans who were campaigning for Grant, needing some way to defuse their having left the regular Republican Party only to return to it after the Liberal Republican Convention in Cincinnati, made self-deprecating remarks that only added to this image. This contemporary portrayal would find a receptive audience among historians in the anti-elitist atmosphere of the 1950s and 1960s. In *The Age of Reform: From Bryan to F.D.R.*, an influential and Pulitzer Prize–winning book, Richard Hofstadter established the paradigm for interpreting the liberal republicans. He advanced the theory that the liberal reformers were a displaced elite class trying to regain power and contended that "they made their first organized appearance in the ill-fated Liberal Republican movement of 1872." Other historians soon began referring to the liberal reformers as the "best people" and arguing that they abandoned Reconstruction and formed a stop-Grant movement because of "status anxiety."[4]

This interpretation of the liberal republicans as disgruntled, anti-Grant elitists was codified in 1968 when John G. Sproat coined the pejoratively intended phrase "The Best Men" as the title for his study of liberal reformers in the Gilded Age. Picking up on 1872 campaign rhetoric, Sproat contended that "Liberal Republicanism essentially was a movement to rid the Republican party of Grantism." Following Sproat's lead, other historians similarly insisted that "the Liberals were more united in their opposition to Grantism than unified on a program." Dismissal of liberal republicanism as simply a movement to defeat Grant became so pervasive and automatic that two historians in the mid-1980s wrote that the liberal republicans responded to the Republicans' renomination of Grant by nominating Horace Greeley for president—when the Liberal Republican Party actually nominated Greeley six weeks *before* Grant's renomination. As for why the liberal republicans opposed Grant, Sproat asserted that "most liberal reformers suffered from a melancholy feeling of social displacement," thus promoting their portrayal as ineffectual elitists. According to Sproat, "the typical reformer possessed neither the inclination to 'get down' among the masses or voters nor the proper equipment for reaching them from afar," and he concluded that the liberal republicans "contributed little of lasting significance." Despite Sproat's dismal assessment of the liberal republicans and other Gilded Age reformers in *The Best Men*," Mark W. Summer recently suggested that Sproat "may give [Edwin L.] Godkin and the talkers—as opposed to the doers—far more weight than they deserve."[5]

The characterization of the liberal republicans as ineffectual elites trying to regain power lacks credibility, however. Historians advocating the displaced-class theory explicitly state that they rely on social psychology, a dubious historical method. In maintaining that the liberal republicans' public policy positions were ultimately concerned with fulfilling a psychological need rather than meeting an objective social or political problem, the theory is also reductionist. Most importantly, however, the liberal republicans simply were not a displaced class when they began advocating many of their reforms. According to Ari Hoogenboom, "Fervor for civil service reform grew from 1867 to 1869," yet during that time Senator Lyman Trumbull remained chairman of the powerful Senate Judiciary Committee, Carl Schurz became a United States senator, Murat Halstead owned and edited one of the most powerful Western newspapers and was president of the Western Associated Press, and Jacob D. Cox became secretary of the Interior. Far from being a displaced elite, the liberal republicans were men with powerful positions in government and the press, and by the time Grant began trying to limit their influence, civil service reform and free trade were well-established issues.[6]

Explanation of liberal republicanism as simply an anti-Grant movement also fails. While the Liberal Republican Party that was created at the Cincinnati Convention supported Greeley against Grant in the fall of 1872, the liberal republican movement that had already existed for several years was not primarily an anti-Grant movement. First, liberal republicanism arose long before Grant became involved in politics. Second, many of the liberal republicans strongly supported Grant in 1868. Carl Schurz gave speeches across the country proclaiming that "no fitter man than General Grant could be found," and Horace White served as an insider in the Grant campaign. Third, even as the liberal republicans prepared to break with the Republican Party in early 1872, they continued to insist in private correspondence that they did not want to participate in a merely anti-Grant movement. William Grosvenor commented, "Whether the attacks upon Grant in a personal sense have been successful, or not, I do not care a button. From the beginning I have urged that they were of little

consequence, and as likely to do harm as good." Jacob D. Cox repeatedly maintained, "I am not anxious to be in a movement designed only to beat Grant."
Finally, after Greeley was nominated at the Liberal Republican Convention,
many liberal republicans like Cox returned to the regular Republican Party and
supported Grant. Above all, the liberal republicans are historical victims of the
electoral campaign of 1872. The practical positions embraced in that awkward
canvass forever afterward dogged their reputations. Liberal republicanism may
have *ended* as an anti-Grant movement, but it did not *begin* that way.[7]

The misinterpretation of the liberal republicans was exacerbated by the rise
of the New Political History. This approach to history, which arose in the 1960s
as an attempt to use social-science methods in the study of the past, has served
ever since as the dominant paradigm for understanding nineteenth-century
politics. Using voter analysis as their primary methodology, New Political historians developed two interrelated arguments that reinforced the earlier anti-
elitist interpretation of the liberal reformers. First, these historians have contended that since 1788 there have been five distinct "party periods" within
which voters aligned themselves with one of the major political parties, shifting
parties only during one of the few "critical elections" in American history. Joel
Silbey, one of the founders of the New Political History, has argued that voters
aligned themselves with political parties "repeatedly and predictably, regardless
of short-term excitements, great personalities and events, or powerful induce-
ments to shift their allegiances." One of these periods is considered to have
stretched from 1856 to 1898; since the birth of the liberal republican movement
did not coincide with a critical election, it is deemed insignificant. Looking at
history through the lens of this party-system paradigm makes its participants
appear foolish for having challenged an established "period"; thus the paradigm reinforces the image of the liberal republicans as politically naïve.[8]

The New Political historians' assumption of party stability in the 1870s also
limits their understanding of Republican and Democratic actions. While members of both parties had seen much party reorganization in the preceding decades, the fear of another political upheaval affected how Republicans and
Democrats reacted to the liberal republicans. Michael F. Holt has recently suggested that in the nineteenth century, "The perception of the real possibility of
effecting partisan reorganization and voter realignments was arguably every bit
as important as the central role of political parties in distinguishing the so-
called party period." The Liberal Republicans, Democrats, and regular Republicans shared the expectation that at least one of the existing parties would disappear in 1872—a consideration that puts in question both the value of the party-
system paradigm and the prevailing interpretation of the liberal republicans.[9]

A second argument of the New Political historians has been that ethnocultural values, not ideology or issues, dominated nineteenth-century American politics. This assumption distorts the image of the liberal republicans by overlooking their motivations for starting their reform movement. In their discussions of the spoils system, protective tariffs, and Reconstruction, the liberal republicans relied heavily upon republican language and ideology, regularly citing the effects of corruption, threats to liberty, and the role of citizens. Some liberal republicans even expressed the ultimate republican fear—that a tyrant would destroy liberty. During President Andrew Johnson's fight with the Republican Congress in 1867, Carl Schurz repeatedly wrote to his wife about the potential for a coup, worrying that "the way Johnson is carrying on with his creatures raises the fear that he may be thinking of a *coup d'etat.*" By the spring of 1872, David Wells and J. D. Cox discussed in private correspondence whether Grant "could be the man for a political *coup d'etat.*" After the election in November, Schurz privately explained to Godkin that he had supported Greeley because "Grant's reelection appeared to me so heavily fraught with danger to the future of our republican institutions, that I could not, even indirectly, favor his success." The widespread use of republican rhetoric shows the importance of ideology in understanding both the liberal republicans and nineteenth-century politics.[10]

The stress on voter analysis, party periodization, critical-election theory, and the ethnocultural thesis in the New Political History has de-emphasized issues, platforms, ideologies, candidates, and individual elections. The concentration on political parties and voting has also come at the expense of those groups not fitting the traditional definition of politics, such as reform movements. Many accounts mention the liberal republicans only when they formed a political party in 1872. But the distinction between the liberal republican movement and the Liberal Republican Party is important, since a majority of the movement's members refused to support the party, and the party's presidential candidate was never a part of the movement. While some historians have explored part of the liberal republican's reform-movement phase, they have started only in 1870, thus missing the origins and first several years of the movement.

By the late 1990s, historians were increasingly questioning the paradigms of the New Political History, particularly the ideas of a rigid party system, the limited importance of ideology, and the strict definition of politics. In 1997 and 1999 the *Journal of American History* sponsored two roundtables to discuss the shifting constructs in political history, with scholars who had established the New Political History openly questioning its continued value. Michael F. Holt called for reforming it, and Jean Harvey Baker complained that "having established the paradigm for nineteenth-century political history, historians of this period currently lament the stagnation of the field, its fragmentation, its failure to provide a synthesis of the new social history and the old political history." Mark Voss-Hubbard, a leading young scholar, asserted two years later that "as both an organizing concept and an interpretative device, the party period is still the field's most powerful concept. Nonetheless, the concept may have exhausted its welcome."[11]

In just the last few years several young scholars have published books challenging the paradigms of the New Political History. In *Beyond Party: Cultures of Antipartisanship in Northern Politics before the Civil War*, Voss-Hubbard breaks down the traditional boundaries of politics, arguing that historians must examine "the forms and styles of political practice that existed outside the framework of national two-party competition" to more fully understand "the series of organizational and political innovations that fueled the political crisis of the 1850s." In *The Death of Reconstruction: Race, Labor, and Politics in the Post–Civil War North*, Heather Cox Richardson combines social and political history to examine why the North abandoned Reconstruction. She contends that "the relationship between freedpeople and white Northerners during Reconstruction was not only about race but also about the clash between two concepts of political economy." Nancy Cohen explicitly asserts the importance of ideology, declaring that "Gilded Age liberal reform was both a political and an intellectual movement." Her book, *The Reconstruction of American Liberalism, 1865–1914*, examines "the reconstruction of liberal political ideology, its causes and consequences, and its deeper implications for American governance and culture in the late nineteenth century and beyond."[12]

While historians have been publishing exciting new work on the nineteenth century, however, they have continued to rely on old, flawed interpretations of the liberal republicans. Heather Cox Richardson states, "The classic work on Liberal Republicanism remains John G. Sproat's '*The Best Men.*'" Not surprisingly, she classes them among the Gilded Age reformers "who saw themselves as members of what they called the better classes." Nancy Cohen similarly depends upon "*The Best Men.*" She concludes, "The Liberal Republican electoral campaign of 1872 was an utter disaster for the 'Independents,' and as John G. Sproat, one of its ablest chroniclers, has pointedly argued, it was of doubtful importance in American political history."[13]

Difficulty defining exactly who and what the liberal republicans were has been a major impediment to understanding their significance. Though numerous historians have studied "the liberal republicans," none has precisely defined exactly who was, and who was not, a liberal republican. Most studies of the movement fall into the category of either political or intellectual history, and both types of work have used flawed methodologies to determine the movement's membership. The mainly political studies, such as William Gillette's *Retreat from Reconstruction,* start with the Cincinnati Convention in 1872 to identify participants and then move backward to examine the origins of the movement, thus never distinguishing between the liberal republican movement and the later Liberal Republican Party. Gillette exemplifies the standard political interpretation of the liberal republicans when he describes the movement as "having been formed between 1870 and 1872 as an opposition to various policies and patronage decisions of the administration." The primarily intellectual studies, such as Sproat's, consider the liberal republicans part of the more general liberal-reform movement of the Gilded Age and extrapolate membership from that group, describing the liberal republicans merely as "liberal reformers." Some historians, such as Earle D. Ross and Eric Foner, see at least some distinction between the "liberal reformers" and the Liberal Republican Party, but still provide no exact membership for either one. In a recent study, Robert W. Burg explicitly conflates the liberal republican movement with the Liberal Republican Party, stating, "Liberal Republicans are defined in this article simply as Republicans who played prominent, official roles in the movement or in the party it spawned prior to the demise of both." Without a more precise sense of the players involved in the liberal republican movement, it has been impossible to analyze it accurately.[14]

I started this project with the broad definition of the liberal republicans that most political historians use. The problem, I discovered, was that there was little overlap between the group who started the national liberal republican movement in 1870 and the group who were part of the Liberal Republican Party's political campaign in 1872. In addition, I needed a more precise way to define who was a member of the movement, since it is impossible to analyze something until you have actually defined it. I tried many different methodologies for determining membership with little satisfaction, until my colleague Robert Sandow asked, "Well, who did the liberal republicans consider liberal republicans?" Thereafter I did what all historians are supposed to do—I followed the primary sources. In this book I am guided by the liberal republicans' own definition of themselves, as revealed in primary documents. As a national movement, the liberal republicans were a small, elite group that met regularly from 1870 to 1872 and considered themselves an organization. During a campaign speech in 1872, Charles Francis Adams Jr. described the liberal republican movement that emerged out of Missouri in 1870 as a small movement. Though letters indicate that between thirty to forty men may actually have attended some meetings, according to Adams, "Certain men met together at Washington, and subsequently in New York—editors, economists, politicians and men of business—few in number, being not more than fifteen or twenty in all, but wielding an enormous power through the press."[15]

This strict self-definition of "liberal republicans" excludes many men traditionally considered to have been part of the movement, such as George William Curtis and George Julian, who may have associated with the liberal republicans and expressed similar sentiments to theirs, but for whom there is no evidence of attendance at their meetings. It would have made my task much easier to use a more liberal definition of the liberal republicans, for Curtis and Julian wrote passages that would make wonderful pieces of evidence with which to buttress my thesis. The distinction between the liberal republican movement and the later Liberal Republican Party is a cornerstone of my work, and, I believe, a significant reinterpretation.

Using the liberal republicans' own strict self-definition of membership, I consider the movement to have consisted of twenty-three identifiable members. They were, in alphabetical order: Charles Francis Adams, Charles Francis Adams Jr., Henry Adams, Edward Atkinson, William Cullen Bryant, Jacob Dolson Cox, Samuel Bowles, Jacob Brinkerhoff, Roeliff Brinkerhoff, David Dudley Field, Edwin L. Godkin, William M. Grosvenor, Murat Halstead, George Hoadly, Henry Demarest Lloyd, Charles Nordhoff, Don Piatt, Mahlon Sands, Carl Schurz, Johann B. Stallo, Lyman Trumbull, David Ames Wells, and Horace White. These twenty-three men form the basis of this study.

The liberal republican movement existed officially for only a few years, but in this book I examine these men from 1848 to 1876. While I acknowledge that it is somewhat anachronistic to refer to them as "liberal republicans" before the late 1860s, I allow myself the use of the term to avoid the awkwardness of referring to them always as "future liberal republicans" or "proto–liberal republicans" when discussing their formative periods. I do not consider the liberal republicans a discrete group before the late 1860s, and when I refer to them as "liberal republicans" while discussing events before that time, the term should be understood to mean "future liberal republicans."[16]

My emphasis on the early lives and careers of the liberal republicans is an important part of this study. Political histories of the Liberal Republican Party concentrate on the few years surrounding the election of 1872 and thus focus on pragmatic political reasons for the liberal republicans' problems with the Republican Party. For example, Jacqueline Tusa has contended that in 1872, "While intra-party conflicts publicly focused on issues and principles, the real struggle between Republicans centered around control of party machinery." The intellectual histories place the liberal republicans among the Gilded Age reformers and thus consider them classical liberals devoted to *laissez-faire* policies in the economy and government. Sproat describes them as "an aristocracy

of brains, education, and talent" whose "political economy was orthodox liberalism, idealistic and sternly inflexible." Other historians have reiterated Sproat's
thesis, arguing that the liberal republicans advocated "political reform in the
tradition of laissez-faire liberalism," or insisting that their ideology, in a word,
"was liberalism, nineteenth-century variety." Many of the liberal republicans'
arguments on economic issues, however, focused on the traditional republican
fears that tyranny and corruption would destroy the nation's republican institutions. No study, with the exception of a dissertation from the 1960s, has
examined the liberal republicans in light of their past.[17]

Failure to analyze the liberal republicans in terms of their own chronologies
and to understand the flexibility of Civil War–era politics has led to numerous
interpretive mistakes. Civil service reform, for example, has been commonly
described as "the liberals' favored means of breaking the power of party
machines and opening positions of responsibility to men like themselves," yet
they displayed concern for corruption and public virtue decades before civil
service became a major issue after the Civil War. They are often labeled "insurgents" in the 1870s, even though their decades of political independence show
that they never knelt before the "shrine of party." Criticism of the liberal
republicans as elitists or inept politicians for creating a small movement instead
of a widespread political party does not match their experience in forming new
parties in the Civil War era, for at that time it was not unreasonable to assume
that a tiny movement could realign the major parties. It is strange that historians have not taken into consideration how the experience of the Civil War—
which many consider the formative event in the nation's history—affected the
liberal republicans.[18]

I began this project convinced that researching the liberal republicans' past
would help explain their actions in the late 1860s and early 1870s. I also started
with the thought that they were Burkean conservatives. After my first months
in the archives reading the liberal republicans' letters, I realized that my original
hypothesis was wrong, but I was intrigued by the numerous private references
to corruption, tyranny, and republican government. The liberal republicans'
papers convinced me that classical American republicanism was one of the primary prisms through which they saw and interpreted the world. I would certainly not suggest that republicanism is the only explanation for these men's
views and actions. As I mention throughout the book, personal feuds, class
issues, political ambition, abolitionism, classical liberalism, racism, and many
other factors motivated the liberal republicans and influenced the course of
their movement. Still, after years of primary research, I have found that classical
republicanism best explains their thoughts and actions.

Defining American republicanism is problematic, however. Even before historians from various fields began appropriating the term, Robert E. Shalhope proclaimed it "a difficult concept for historians to define." Since then labor historians, gender historians, Southern historians, and many others have taken republicanism out of its original political context to analyze relationships in the family or factory. Daniel T. Rodgers explains that "the sphere of classical republicanism was the public and the political" and that "its social thought was bent to the problem of finding a set of social arrangements . . . that would secure civic liberty against the corruptions of time." The liberal republicans' use of republican ideology fits within the classical context, for they clearly dealt with "the public and the political." Returning to the original, basic political conceptions of republicanism embodied by the liberal republicans allows us to focus on two dominant strains of republicanism as it emerged as a modern historical concept. In the late 1960s Bernard Bailyn argued that Americans revolted from England in 1776 because of the fear of centralized power. A few years later J. G. A. Pocock focused on the colonists' fear that corruption and luxury would destroy the conditions necessary for republican government. Republicanism is best understood as combining fear of centralized power and fear of corruption.[19]

Republicanism's lifespan, as well as its definition, has become controversial. For a generation, historians debated when liberalism replaced republicanism as the dominant political ideology in America, with many agreeing that this transition occurred well before the mid-nineteenth century. Jean Harvey Baker insists, "Certainly by the 1830s, the republican doctrine that had underwritten the American Revolution and shaped the new nation was rarely vented. Indeed few leaders of antebellum society drew their inspiration from that cluster of ideas defined by a suspicion of power, [and] a fear of tyranny. . . . Nor was there a need to recall the anticorruptionist core of classical Roman . . . ideology." William E. Gienapp finds that instead of fading away, republicanism changed with the times, losing its distrust of political parties and business corporations, and that "to mid-century Americans, the continuing survival of republican society depended upon the preservation of liberty and equality, against which aristocratic privilege and concentrated power were the principal threats." Republicanism was certainly not a static ideology; three generations of political and economic changes had altered it between the Revolution and the post–Civil War era. In addition, republicanism's dominance probably did weaken as the nineteenth century progressed. The strong classical education of the liberal republicans and their links to the Revolution, however, probably helped them maintain a more traditional republicanism than most of their contemporaries.[20]

Education made these men more likely than most to be familiar with both the classical Roman and Revolutionary concepts of republicanism. During the early and mid- nineteenth century, most American colleges concentrated on the classics. While few people went to college then, the vast majority of the liberal republicans attended some of the country's best colleges and universities. Their letters during college refer to classical authors such as Cicero and discuss the difficulty of learning French and German while still studying Greek and Latin. Years after graduating from Williams, a college that produced several of the liberal republicans and required the classic languages through the end of the junior year, David Wells complained that he still could not read French fluently because he had spent too much of his youth on Greek and Latin. Horace White graduated from Beloit College, which was created by New Englanders in the Yale mold and stressed a classical curriculum. The son of a college professor, Stanley Matthews graduated from Kenyon College—renowned for its classical education—two years before his kinsman Rutherford B. Hayes, whose presidential election in 1876 signaled the official end of Reconstruction. George Hoadly Jr. graduated from Case Western College in Ohio, where students were required to know Latin and Greek before being admitted, and the classics-heavy curriculum included Sallust and Livy in the freshman year. Charles Francis Adams and his sons Charles Francis Adams Jr. and Henry Adams, of course, all graduated from Harvard, and Henry Adams would eventually return to the university as a history professor.[21]

Even those liberal republicans who could not afford college displayed impressive erudition. Although the German-born Johann B. Stallo was unable to continue his formal education past age sixteen, he had become fluent in classical languages by age thirteen with the help of his schoolmaster father, and at twenty-one became a professor at St. John's College (now Fordham University) in New York City. According to his most recent biographer, Lyman Trumbull was unable financially to attend Yale, but as a teenager "he read widely, and was particularly fond of Latin and Greek, and read Virgil, Cicero, and Homer in the original." The liberal republicans' grounding in classical texts that discussed political philosophy reinforced for them America's fading tradition of republicanism.[22]

The liberal republicans were exceptional, however, even among the educated elite of America at the time. David Wells wrote a short history of Williams College his senior year; upon graduation he started working for Samuel Bowles's *Springfield Republican* and while at the newspaper invented a power printing press; he then taught at Harvard, and by his late twenties was publishing scientific works, including a chemistry textbook adopted by West Point—all this before writing numerous books on political economy and becoming special commissioner of revenue for the United States government in 1867. During the hectic political year of 1856, Carl Schurz wrote to a friend that "you may be surprised that I should turn again to the Roman classics in the middle of the material activities of this Western life. This is due less to the fact that I do not wish to forget my Latin than that I believe that one can learn from such authors much that has a bearing on American politics." Some even found the classics a leisure activity; William Cullen Bryant, regarded by contemporaries as one of the nation's preeminent literary figures, translated the *Iliad* and the *Odyssey* as a hobby during Reconstruction. During the Civil War, Henry Adams corresponded with his brother "upon theoretical reasoning as to the forms of government." The majority of the liberal republicans wrote in-depth articles and books on history, politics, and economics, establishing themselves among the leading intellectuals in America.[23]

The liberal republicans also had many ties with the American Revolution. A large number had relatives who had served in the Continental Army. Don Piatt's and David Dudley Field's grandfathers were both officers, while one of Samuel Bowles's uncles had served as a captain and another as a sergeant. Lyman Trumbull's grandfather, the Yale-educated clergyman Benjamin Trumbull, served as a volunteer and chaplain during the Revolution. The Adams family added to the intellectual foundation of the liberal republicans and provided a close link to the republicanism of the American Revolution. Charles Francis Adams and his sons Charles Jr. and Henry spent their summers organizing and editing the papers of Revolutionary-era giant John Adams. While studying abroad in 1860, Henry Adams echoed Carl Schurz's thoughts, writing to his mother that "here in Rome politics are suggestive, for precisely the same battle went on here between the aristocracy and the people as there is now with us; here in Rome more than two thousand years ago, the people, the plebs, in spite of several victories greater than we Republicans ever got, were kept disunited, by intimidation, bribery and the other usual means, and were beaten." The result, according to Adams, was "an aristocratic government for a century and half, [which] brought Rome down to anarchy and brought a military despotism in. . . . It is wonderfully striking how close the parallel can be drawn from between that fight and ours."[24]

While many Americans expressed some republican sentiments during the mid-nineteenth century, the liberal republicans were unusual in their persistent fears that corruption and centralized power threatened republican institutions. For most of the Civil War era their fears led them to fight against slavery—forming the Free Soil Party in 1848, helping to create the Republican Party in 1856, advocating strong measures to fight the Civil War, and leading efforts immediately after the war to reconstruct the South. Soon after the Civil War, though, the same ideology compelled them to begin a reform movement against perceived threats to republican government that had sprung up during the conflict. Relying on their antislavery political experience, in which a series of temporary organizations eventually led to the Republican Party and the end of slavery, the liberal republicans expected to be able to effect a party reorganization and carry out their reforms. A combination of mistakes, rivalries, and bad luck allowed the outsider Horace Greeley to capture control of the new Liberal Republican Party in 1872 and change its character. Stripped of its republican ideology, the new party concentrated on attacking Grant and Reconstruction, staining the reputations of both for generations. More importantly, the dynamics of the 1872 election estranged the ideological core of the Republican Party and undermined the political viability of Reconstruction. Thus unintentionally, the liberal republicans doomed Reconstruction.

1

Rehearsal in Missouri for the Liberal Republican Movement, 1865–1870

On December 15, 1870, Carl Schurz of Missouri rose before the U.S. Senate to "submit some observations upon the political movements in Missouri, which seem to have attracted unusual attention and have acquired more than local interest." The country was focused on Missouri because Schurz had led a group of self-named "Liberal Republicans" against the Republican Party in the state during the fall elections to advocate amnesty for former Confederates, civil service reform, and free trade—all positions that were unpopular with the national Republican Party. The bolt was particularly interesting because it was successful; Liberal Republican candidate B. Gratz Brown was elected governor, and parts of the state constitution disenfranchising ex-rebels were amended. President Ulysses S. Grant correctly feared that the Missouri bolt signified a challenge to his Republican administration. Just days after Brown's election, the American Free Trade League wrote Schurz to congratulate him on the success in Missouri. "There may be ulterior consequences resulting from it of even greater importance than its immediate advantages," noted the League; the group was "of the opinion that the time is near at hand when a new political movement in favor of Revenue and Civil Service Reform may be started with success. It is there for proposed to hold a conference of the leaders of these reforms." Two weeks later, the proposed conference met in New York and created a new national political organization, the liberal republican movement.[1]

The Liberal Republican bolt in Missouri did more than start the national liberal republican movement, for the events leading up to the bolt foreshadowed many of the same plots and themes the movement would act out on the national stage during the next two years. Just like Schurz's Liberals in Missouri, the national liberal republican movement advocated amnesty, civil service reform, and free trade. Both used classical republican arguments—that dependent citizens, corruption, and centralized power endangers liberty—to contend that the policies of the current party in power, the Republicans, threatened the country's future. Both relied on the support of German Americans and planned to use Democratic votes to gain control of the Republican Party. The events in Missouri leading up to the 1870 bolt not only demonstrate how the liberal republican movement began, but how the movement would develop, for the

success of the Missouri bolt led Schurz and others to try consciously to repro-
duce it on a national scale. Missouri politics from 1865 to 1870 were a dress
rehearsal for the national liberal republican movement, providing insights into
the movement's composition and ideology.[2]

Politics in Missouri had been byzantine since the beginning of the Civil War,
when Governor Claiborne Jackson tried to lead the state out of the Union and
into the Confederacy. The threat of secession disrupted the state's existing
Democratic-Republican party structure, as citizens realigned into Secessionist
and Unionist factions. Francis P. Blair Jr., a member of the powerful Blair family that dominated Maryland and Missouri politics throughout the mid-
nineteenth century, led the Unionists against the pro-Confederate state government. Blair arranged for a staunch Unionist to command the federal arsenal at
St. Louis, converted Republican "Wide Awake" election clubs into paramilitary
organizations, and invited Illinois volunteer regiments into Missouri. With
these military forces he effectively led a *coup d'etat* by attacking the pro-
Confederacy state militia camped outside of St. Louis, allowing the Unionists
to gain control of the state and prevent its secession. Since many Missouri
Secessionists refused to take the loyalty oath that was made a requirement to
vote in the state, the Unionists faced minimal political opposition. The absence
of the Secessionist Democrats from the state political scene—first by martial
law, and then by legal disenfranchisement—left the Unionist Republicans in
undisputed control and essentially destroyed the two-party system in Missouri.
This temporary collapse of the two-party system in Missouri demonstrates the
fluid and changing nature of the national political party "system" of the day
and the peculiar environment in which liberal republicanism originated.[3]

Despite almost completely excluding the Democrats from power for a while,
the Missouri Republicans were a politically heterogeneous group that quickly
divided into factions. Those known as Conservative Unionists wished to maintain the status quo with regard to slavery in the state, while the Radical Unionists, under the leadership of Charles D. Drake, pressed for speedy emancipation.
Drake, a St. Louis lawyer, had followed a circuitous route to the Republican
Party and earned the description "a skilled demagogue and opportunist." He
started the 1850s as a Whig, became a Know-Nothing, and then joined the
Democrats, supporting Stephen A. Douglas in 1860. By 1862 Drake had become
a Republican, and he assumed leadership of the Missouri Radicals at the 1863
state convention. Drake organized a new Radical Union Party in the late summer of 1863 and fought a number of close battles with the Conservatives for the
next year. The conflict between the two Unionist factions continued right up
until the election of 1864, when Drake and the other Radicals used the threat of
a Democratic resurgence in Missouri to coerce many Conservatives into sup-

porting them instead of splitting the Unionist vote. The Radical Unionists won a decisive victory in the election, obtaining the governorship and both houses of the legislature, and took firm control of the state. More importantly, the Radicals won the referendum for a constitutional convention and elected nearly three-fourths of its delegates from their own ranks.[4]

This unusual political situation, in which a small minority of citizens controlled the government, influenced the framing of Missouri's new constitution. Drake feared that the Democrats would eventually recapture the Missouri legislature, and he therefore sought to make the new constitution a bulwark even against a future Democratic majority. "We intend to erect a wall and barrier in the shape of a constitution," proclaimed Drake, "that shall be as high as the eternal heavens, deep down as the very center of the earth, so that they [the Democrats in the legislature] shall neither climb over it nor dig under it." The convention built Drake's "wall and barrier," limiting the power of the legislature to pass legislation and restricting its ability to amend the constitution or call a new constitutional convention. To prevent the Democrats from gaining control of the legislature, Drake persuaded the convention to pass an article concerning elections and voter qualifications. In an attempt to disenfranchise all Confederate sympathizers—that is, the Democrats—the constitution required individuals to swear under oath they had never committed any one of eighty-six disloyal acts, ranging from serving in the Confederacy to expressing sympathy for the enemy cause. The oath was not only mandatory for voters, but was also required of jurors, lawyers, corporation officers, teachers, and ministers. The constitution prohibited the Missouri legislature from revoking the oath before 1871, and even then it would need an absolute majority in each house to do so.[5]

Drake's new constitution, carefully designed to preserve Radical power, exacerbated divisions already existing within the Unionist Party. Radical strength came from two sources: the rural border areas that had suffered most severely from the guerrilla war that had been raging for years between proslavery and abolitionist irregulars, and the German community in St. Louis. Drake, though leader of the Radical Union Party and from St. Louis, had never enjoyed the full support of the German community. Despite cooperating with him to keep Missouri in the Union, the Germans had distrusted Drake since the 1850s, when he had belonged to the anti-immigrant Know-Nothing Party. The German community saw new signs of Drake's prejudice in several of the proposals for the constitution, particularly restrictions on churches, exclusion of immigrant suffrage, and realignment of voting districts in St. Louis. Not only would priests and ministers be forced to take a loyalty oath to preach, but Drake wanted to give the state the right to tax churches. He singled out the Catholic

Church, to which many Germans belonged, as a "money-making machine" that was generally disloyal during the Civil War. Drake also fought a proposal allowing immigrants who declared their intention to become citizens to vote immediately and suggested requiring the legislature to establish single-member districts in order to limit German influence in St. Louis. At one point during the constitutional convention a delegate mentioned the Know-Nothing Party, to which Drake replied, "I thought that party was dead and buried." The delegate shouted back at Drake, "You are living proof that it is not." Germans soon began referring to the constitution as "Drake's Code" or the "Draconian Code."[6]

The German community in Missouri looked to Radical Unionist Senator B. Gratz Brown to lead the opposition against ratification of the new constitution. Like Drake, Brown had an odd political history, even for that chaotic time. He grew up a Whig in a wealthy Kentucky family. As a twenty-one-year-old Yale Law student in 1847, he wrote home that he would remain a Whig despite spending time with his Democratic relatives, the Blairs. Brown assured his uncle that "I scarce think General Jackson could himself—if he were to rise bodily from the grave, could win me from the true cause. I am sure no lesser satellite could do so." Within a few years, though, Brown had moved to Missouri, begun working closely with the Blairs, and become a Democrat. As the Missouri Democratic Party disintegrated in the mid-1850s, Brown and the Blairs jumped to the Republican Party. Brown had led one of the militia regiments in the coup that had secured Missouri for the Union in 1861, and he had served as a general in the Union Army before becoming a United States senator in 1863. According to his biographer, "For the most part Brown's actions were based on the expediency of the moment. He followed the trend of the times and associated himself with whatever group appeared to be growing in power."[7]

Brown knew that his power base, the German American community in Missouri, disliked the proposed new constitution. In addition, he had some problems with it personally. As one of the earliest advocates of African American suffrage, Brown was disappointed that the constitution did not give them the right to vote. He also worried that some of its provisions were incompatible with the U.S. Constitution, particularly the loyalty oath. Despite many rumors that he would come back from Washington to oppose the new constitution, Brown reluctantly supported its ratification when Drake made it a question of party loyalty. "While I may have heretofore expressed antagonism to the New Constitution on some points," Brown explained in a printed letter, "a more mature consideration convinces me that the facility of amendment through the Legislature, which it provides, holds out infinitely more hope . . . than the old Constitution." Throughout the rest of the campaign Brown remained silent, refusing either to endorse or criticize the constitution again, which won ratification by a mere 2 percent margin in July 1865, despite losing in St. Louis by a two-to-one margin.[8]

The ratification of the constitution did not ease the growing tension within the Radical Union Party. The enforcement of the provision requiring ministers and priests to take a loyalty oath particularly upset Brown and the Germans. A minister wrote to Brown refusing to recognize the right of the state to extract loyalty oaths from clergy and suggesting an amendment eliminating this provision. Brown sent the letter to the governor of Missouri with a cover letter endorsing the position. "I am devoted to civil and religious liberty on principle, and cannot consent to violations of either," he insisted, "no matter how dear they may be to the ruling prejudices of the time." The loyalty-oath controversy soon centered around Catholics, after a young priest, arrested for preaching without having taken the oath, refused to post bond. He demanded an immediate trial and would not allow anyone to pay the fine when the court found him guilty. The priest spent a week in jail and over a year in the headlines as his case advanced to the United States Supreme Court, which eventually, in 1867, did find Missouri's test oaths for professionals unconstitutional. The refusal of Missouri's Radical Party to support amendments for black suffrage or to remove political disqualifications for whites also increasingly upset Brown. In addition, his experience with party pressure to support the constitution led him to sponsor a civil service reform bill before the U.S. Senate in June 1866. He warned that "the great danger of this Government—one that probably threatens its life within the next ten or fifteen years—consists in the use of public patronage for party purposes." At the same time Brown announced that because of ill health he would not seek reelection. In a public letter he declared the Missouri constitution "unworthy of a free people," and insisted that "the capacity of voting is the protection against class legislation, the oppression of race, the intolerance of party, and all those antagonisms which threaten to wreck and engulf liberty." He admitted that "disfranchisements resting on the crime of treason have been found necessary," but argued, "All this is temporary, and only defensible as being temporary." Brown's constant references to liberty and threats to liberty show an early inclination, typical of the liberal republicans, to frame arguments in classical republican terms. Throughout the rest of the 1866 campaign he remained silent.[9]

Just after the November election Brown invited leading Radicals to meet at Planters House in St. Louis to discuss the future of the party in Missouri. Brown offered the assembled group a series of resolutions to amend the recently ratified constitution, including giving blacks the vote, eliminating the loyalty oaths, and providing amnesty for all. "That in as much as the Republican Party of Missouri has won an unprecedented triumph in the latest election," argued Brown, "it is now right that the Constitution of this State should be made to conform more nearly to the requirements of a general freedom, by so amending it in several sections, as that Universal suffrage shall attend upon, and herald in Universal Amnesty." Ten of the twenty-nine Radicals stormed out of the meeting as soon as Brown presented the resolutions. Sixteen of the remaining nineteen Radicals, however, supported his resolutions for universal suffrage and universal amnesty. Charles Drake, who stayed at the meeting out of curiosity and voted against the resolutions, was not cowed. "I will not back down," declared Drake, as he instructed Radicals to "stand by your Constitution just as it is." The Planter House meeting transformed the existing tensions among the Radicals into intraparty warfare.[10]

One of the Radicals who supported Brown's resolutions was William M. Grosvenor, the new editor of the powerful *Missouri Democrat*. According to a contemporary, Grosvenor was "the active force which led this movement in this state with so much energy," and he personally wrote the call for the national Cincinnati Convention in 1872 that launched the Liberal Republican Party. Before the convention, Horace Greeley's lieutenant and assistant editor at the *New York Tribune*, Whitelaw Reid, sent a reporter to compile information on Grosvenor in case they needed to discredit him—and they certainly got enough. In a letter labeled "Strictly Confidential," Reid wrote that Grosvenor "was expelled from Yale somewhere around 1850—for the grossest immorality. Introduced a prostitute to his room, kept her there for days and sublet her to collegemates." Reid also reported that during the Civil War, Grosvenor "was court martialed + dismissed from service in disgrace in 1864, for 'conduct unbecoming an officer and gentleman.' Among other charges for keeping *two* prostitutes in his tent on Ship Island, one of them being the wife of his brother." After leaving the army, Grosvenor worked as a journalist in New England and soon thereafter moved to Missouri. According to Reid, "wherever he has lived he has been known as an utterly unprincipled, thoroughly rotten man, whose ability as a writer, and shrewdness as a demagogue only make him so much more the dangerous." Reid concluded that Grosvenor "has all of Aaron Burr's vices, with only a small portion of his genius." Other than the fact that Grosvenor was dishonorably discharged, it is difficult to know how much of Reid's report is reliable, particularly since at the time Grosvenor worked for the American Free Trade League, the nemesis of the protectionist *New York Tribune*. Ironically, when the League fired Grosvenor after the Cincinnati Convention because they thought he had betrayed them, Reid quickly hired him. By the mid 1870s Grosvenor was one of Reid's principal lieutenants, and in 1889 Grosvenor presided over the dinner celebrating Reid's appointment as minister to France. In addition, two United States senators came to think highly of Grosvenor. Carl Schurz relied on him for almost a decade starting in the late 1860s, and Lyman Trumbull gave him a glowing letter of introduction, proclaiming that "Mr. Grosvenor is a Gentleman of great intelligence."[11]

The Planter House call for universal amnesty made Grosvenor and Brown appear vulnerable to charges of demagoguery, since both men had advocated vindictive measures against Confederate sympathizers during the course of the Civil War. In 1863, Brown had demanded that rebels, whether in open arms or just sympathetic to the South, be denied the right to vote. "Franchise," he insisted, "is not for such—cannot be for such—will not be for such." Grosvenor repeatedly expressed similar opinions in 1865. No constitutional obligations limited the federal government in dealing with the South, according to him, because "rising to the standards of a civil war, it has placed in the hands of the nation not only the remedial agencies of the courts, but the torch and sword of the conqueror." He maintained, "To defeated rebels the Constitution gives no political right whatever. The Union has the absolute and untrammeled power of the conqueror." Grosvenor argued that the Union should use its power to disfranchise rebels.[12]

The Planter House resolution for universal amnesty makes sense, however, when it is remembered that the Civil War was over in 1866. Brown had justified political disabilities in 1863 by arguing, "Power and position belong only to the loyal, for self-preservation knows no 'higher law!'" By November 1866—with the Civil War's threat to national preservation ended and with Congress having passed the Thirteenth Amendment, the Freedman's Bureau Bill, the Civil Rights Bill, and the Fourteenth Amendment—Brown's reasons for the disfranchisement of rebels were gone. Grosvenor likewise perceived the differences between war, immediate postwar Reconstruction, and a permanent Reconstruction. Like Brown, he had used preservation of the Union to justify temporary disfranchisement, arguing that "schemes of reconstruction which make possible immunity for the great conspirators, or instant return to all political privileges for traitors as well as loyalists, will not be such as the people will approve or the nation can safely adopt." The Southern states had lost their rights through rebellion, according to Grosvenor, but once readmitted to the Union they were constitutionally entitled to all the rights and privileges of states. He thought that "a government kept alive only by military force is a civil authority only in name, and can confer only the shadow of benefits." Ultimately, Grosvenor predicted, "The military power must cease to protect when the work of reconstruction is complete, and the work is pressed with haste." He recognized, however, that white Southerners would harm the newly freed slaves and contended that "while the present state of feeling lasts, to withdraw the protecting power of the nation, and restore the rebel states to full control over their domestic affairs, would be a deed the most heartlessly cruel." According to Grosvenor only two remedies existed—"to continue the military or provisional government until a different state of feeling is developed, or to give the blacks an invulnerable shield of self-protection in the right of suffrage." Brown's and Grosvenor's resolutions for universal suffrage and universal amnesty at the Planter House meeting rested on the same reasoning as their wartime calls for rebel disfranchisement. In both instances they sought to balance protecting the safety of the republic with the liberty of its citizens. They both thought black suffrage would secure the results of the Civil War, making it safe to return the vote to former rebels.[13]

Uninvolved in Missouri politics, Carl Schurz came to the same conclusions as Brown and Grosvenor while touring the South in 1865. Schurz had emigrated from Germany after the Revolution of 1848, and his revolutionary ideals quickly led him to the Republican Party. He soon became a prominent member of the party as the representative of the German American community. After rallying German Americans for Lincoln in 1860, Schurz was appointed minister to Spain, and he later served as a major general in the Union Army. Schurz has often been accused of office-seeking, a charge that could be leveled at most nineteenth-century politicians, but even his admirers admitted he was ambitious. It did not help his reputation that he became one of famed cartoonist Thomas Nast's favorite targets in the early 1870s. Still, Schurz's biographer Hans L. Trefousse insists that "uncompromisingly honest, little given to the usual prejudices of the time, and always in the forefront of the fight for political and social justice, he remained true to the liberal and democratic ideals of his youth." Part of the perception problem arose because, while Schurz was extraordinarily smart, he was not as clever as he thought himself, and while he was a national figure, he was never as important as he thought himself. These misconceptions led him to invariably misjudge political situations. It also did not help that he seemed perfectly happy to play the political Don Quixote, content to champion lost causes so long as he could follow his convictions and lead others.[14]

Schurz's faith in his convictions soon led him to break with President Andrew Johnson. At the end of the Civil War he decided to travel through the South and make a report on the progress of Reconstruction, which he submitted to Congress in December 1865. Schurz's conception of Reconstruction rested on two principles. First, he thought "that as speedily as possible all the attributes of our democratic system should be restored." Restoring the nation's democratic system did not mean expanding the role of the federal government, for Schurz specifically explained that "the political system of this Republic rests upon the right of the people to control their local concerns in their several States by the operations of self-government." Schurz did not, however, advocate immediately returning local government to the South. During his travels Schurz had found white Southerners resistant to accepting the results of the war, particularly the emancipation of slaves and the introduction of the free-labor system, and feared they would overturn the Union's accomplishments if given a chance. Schurz's second principle of Reconstruction was thus "that the rebel States could not be reinstated in the full control of their local affairs . . . until, by the imposition of irreversible stipulations, it should be rendered impossible for them to subvert or impair any of the results of the war." Until the fruits of victory were secured, Schurz insisted that the national government must remain in control of the South, for "the spirit of persecution has shown itself so strong as to make the protection of the freedman by the military arm of the Government in many localities necessary—in almost all desirable."[15]

Schurz worried, though, how long the federal government could keep rebels disfranchised and maintain a military presence. Loyalty oaths in particular, he argued, "can be very serviceable in certain emergencies and for certain objects, but they have never insured the stability of a government." Ultimately, Schurz warned, "we cannot long continue to control the great transformation in all its details, without seriously changing the character of our government." According to Schurz, the solution to the problem of securing the results of the war while quickly returning to a democratic form of government lay in black suffrage. Allowing blacks to vote would cement the results of the Civil War, and "the interference of the National authority in the home concerns of the Southern States would be rendered less necessary." Many liberal republicans, Schurz in particular, remained committed to state-centered federalism and hostile to centralization of power during Reconstruction. Some of Brown, Grosvenor, and Schurz's early concerns about increasing the authority of the federal government demonstrate a classical republican anxiety that a centralized power would threaten liberty.[16]

Schurz soon faced living with, not just visiting, the problems of Reconstruction. He was losing money running a paper in Detroit when Emil Preetorius, a fellow Forty-Eighter and editor of the *Westliche Post*, St. Louis's largest German newspaper, offered to make him co-editor and co-owner. With the help of a loan arranged by Preetorius, Schurz joined the paper and moved to Missouri in April 1867, just months after the Planter House meeting. The move to Missouri helped not only Schurz's finances but also his political prospects. The conflict within the Radical Party and Drake's departure for Washington after being elected senator in January had left a power vacuum into which Schurz stepped. During his first spring in Missouri he toured the state's German communities every weekend, often giving speeches. With the advantages of being a nationally recognized German leader and a newcomer not involved in old political feuds, Schurz soon became a leading figure in the Radical Party. Preetorius arranged for Schurz's election as delegate to the Republican National Convention in 1868, where he was elected temporary chairman, served on the platform committee, and delivered the keynote address. While serving on the platform committee Schurz pressed for universal amnesty and universal suffrage. The committee refused his plea for an unqualified endorsement of black suffrage, but did allow him to author a plank calling for the end of political disabilities for former rebels as soon as public safety would permit. Increasingly prominent after the convention, Schurz stumped across the North for the Republicans, but reserved the last six weeks of the campaign for Missouri.[17]

Two major issues dominated Missouri politics in the fall of 1868—a new voter-registry law and black suffrage. Anxious to maintain their power, the Radicals had pushed a new, harsher registry law through the legislature in early 1868. The law created new appointed positions—superintendents of registration—in each senatorial district to control the elected county supervisors of elections. Each superintendent had virtually unlimited power in determining the electorate, for the new law forbade courts from issuing writs of mandamus compelling additions to the voter lists. While passing the new voter-registration law, Radicals in the legislature had also pushed through an amendment to the state constitution enfranchising blacks. Though all of the Radical leaders endorsed the black suffrage amendment, differences continued to emerge on the policy toward former rebels. Charles Drake defended the new registry laws and "waved the Bloody Shirt"—a phrase used to describe Republican campaigners' use of Civil War allusions to sway their audiences—telling crowds, "This then is the one solitary issue: Shall the people that saved the country rule it, or shall rebels and traitors?"[18]

Schurz took a more moderate tone in a campaign speech. He excused the federal government's role in Reconstruction, explaining that the only excuse for military rule was the necessity to transition from the slave-labor to a free-labor system "surrounded by the political institutions necessary to guarantee its existence." Because of the republic's constitutional system, though, the national government "could only start and give direction to this movement, then turn it over with certain restrictions to the local majorities in the several states, to the operation of local self-governments." Schurz spent the last half of his speech arguing that the key to guaranteeing free labor lay in black suffrage. Schurz's political allies in Missouri echoed his arguments. In a published address to the people of Missouri, Grosvenor and Preetorius contended that "either the revolted States must be kept under military rule for an indefinite time . . . or the government must be placed in the hands of the whole people."[19]

The Radicals won a huge victory at the polls in 1868—electing their state ticket by an almost 15 percent margin—but failed to secure ratification of the amendment for African American suffrage. According to William E. Parrish, "prejudice among the Radical rank and file overcame all the moral and political arguments advanced by their leaders." The failure of voters to ratify black suffrage undercut one of the core principles of Schurz, Brown, and Grosvenor's plan for Reconstruction and led to a widening breach in the Radical Party. In the *Missouri Democrat* Grosvenor proclaimed that most Radicals would support the removal of all political restrictions in the state if Democrats would endorse impartial suffrage. Though in Washington at the time, Drake quickly rebuked Grosvenor in a public letter, insisting that political restrictions would be removed only *after* African Americans gained the right to vote. While Grosvenor and Drake sparred in public, disaffected Radical leaders held another meeting at Planters House in St. Louis. This was unlike the meeting in 1866, when B. Gratz Brown had invited all prominent Radicals, insofar as Schurz invited only twelve of his close allies, including Brown, Grosvenor, and Preetorius. The group formed the "Twentieth Century Club" to discuss political ideas and started meeting every Saturday night for dinner. The name of the club itself indicated the members' desire to leave the Civil War behind them and look to the future. According to a member, the club was one "of the small group of active agencies among many others created near the outset of the liberal republican movement which contributed in no small measure to its success."[20]

Far from merely discussing ideas, the Twentieth Century Club tried to do what the first Planters House meeting had failed to do—take control of the Radical Party. The clash came over the vacant Senate seat. The club wanted Schurz, not Drake's candidate, Benjamin F. Loan, to fill the seat, and Grosvenor began managing Schurz's campaign. Schurz knew the contest over his candidacy represented a larger struggle within the party, explaining to his wife that "the battle in which I am engaged does not turn solely on the senatorship. It involves the leadership of one or the other element, the narrowly despotic or the liberal people in Missouri." Drake also recognized the significance of the contest and spent more time debating Schurz in public than did Loan, but unfortunately for his cause Loan still spoke too much. Schurz later wrote in his memoirs that Loan denounced him "as a foreign intruder, as a professional revolutionist, as a 'German infidel', as an habitual drunk." The performance of Loan, and Drake's reputation as a ex–Know Nothing, united the German community behind Schurz. Grosvenor's deft management, Schurz's skill in debate, and the German support combined to give Schurz the senatorship on the first ballot at the Radical caucus in January 1869.[21]

Schurz's election to the U.S. Senate, however, did little to further the goals of his wing of the Radical Union Party in Missouri. Despite constant cajoling from Grosvenor in the *Missouri Democrat*, the majority of Radicals in the legislature ignored both the question of African American suffrage and easing the voting restrictions against former rebels. Many seemed content to await the outcome of two events in Washington that could settle both parts of the suffrage question in Missouri: Congress was in the process of drafting the Fifteenth Amendment to secure black suffrage nationwide, and the Supreme Court was considering the validity of Missouri's loyalty oath for voters. Grosvenor chafed under the legislature's inactivity, declaring that "sooner or later that policy must prevail which seeks to remove distinctions created by a state of war and justified by the necessities of war." In early June he tried to force the legislature to act, calling for submission of an amendment to the constitution granting suffrage both to blacks and to disfranchised whites. Schurz quickly supported Grosvenor's proposal, contending that "it must be clear to every unprejudiced observer that the enfranchisement of the negro must mean the end of rebel disfranchisement." Drake, however, maintained his old position. He condemned Grosvenor's proposal as "the old and exploded Planters House scheme, dressed up a little differently but still easily recognizable," and insisted upon "justice for the loyal Negro, without any complications about the rebel." The debate over suffrage raged within the Radical Union Party for the rest of the year.[22]

The increasing importance of two issues unconnected to the suffrage questions—free trade and civil service reform—exacerbated the tensions within the Radical Party. During the Civil War the Republican Party had passed high protective tariffs to help Northern industries and raise money for the war effort. According to Marc Egnal, "the Liberal Republican revolt of 1872 revealed the fault lines in the party," and "the bolters were individuals who had never been comfortable with the economic program of high tariffs and national banks, or who had reluctantly and temporarily supported these measures." With Appomattox ending the military necessity for federal economic legislation, a minority of Republicans feared that protective tariffs and other government intrusions into the economy threatened liberty just as slavery had done. Both slavery and protective tariffs, argued free traders, used the power of the state to benefit a special class at the expense of workers. Imposing a tax on workers through a tariff to promote the interests of industrialists was the same, they insisted, as a plantation owner living on the sweat of his slaves. Grosvenor opposed protective tariffs, and upon becoming editor of the *Missouri Democrat* filled its editorial pages with attacks on them, changing the paper into a vocal advocate of free trade. After Congress voted to table a free-trade bill in early 1869, Grosvenor declared that "the monopolists prevailed over the people"; over a year later he was still complaining about "the monopolists who control committees in Congress." Grosvenor publicly debated the tariff issue in St. Louis and even wrote a book, *Does Protection Protect?* promoting free trade. Schurz encouraged Grosvenor's free-trade activity, writing, "Let us have your book as soon as possible. If I can aid you in procuring a publisher I shall be very happy."[23]

While helping Grosvenor campaign for free trade Schurz also began a crusade to reform the country's civil service, which operated on a spoils system in which civil service jobs were political rewards. Besieged by office-seekers upon becoming a senator, Schurz had quickly soured on the existing patronage system—something more experienced Republican politicians like Charles Sumner had experienced in the wake of their party's victory in 1860. Within months of arriving at Washington Schurz wrote to a friend that "the utter absurdity of our system of appointment to office has this time so glaringly demonstrated itself that even the dullest patriots begin to open their eyes to the necessity of reform. I have taken a solemn vow to pitch in for it next winter." That December, while Grosvenor worked on his free-trade book, Schurz introduced a bill in the Senate to reform the civil service and end "the fearful demoralization which the spoils system entails upon our whole political life." Schurz's civil service reform bill echoed Brown's earlier attempt just before he had left the Senate. A majority of Republicans in Missouri, however, continued to support both protective tariffs and the spoils system. Grosvenor and Schurz's championing of free trade and civil service reform became a further wedge between the two factions of Missouri's Radical Party.[24]

News from Washington appeared to solve the disagreement among the Radicals on suffrage and briefly brought the party together in early 1870. The Supreme Court split evenly over Missouri's test oaths for voters and thus did not overturn them. Just a week later the twenty-eighth state ratified the Fifteenth Amendment, making black suffrage the law of the land. Many Radicals, including even Drake, now agreed to consider amendments to modify the loyalty-oath provisions in the constitution, and Grosvenor successfully pushed such measures through the Radical caucus and then the state legislature. The two factions, however, could not agree whether the Radical Party should officially endorse the amendments. The border sections of Missouri, which formed Drake's base of support, opposed the amendments and demanded the opportunity to vote against them while remaining loyal to the party. Grosvenor, meanwhile, insisted the party must take responsibility for fixing the problem it had created. In a long editorial entitled "Shall We Break Faith?" Grosvenor cited the plank in the 1868 Republican platform that had called for the removal of political restrictions on rebels as soon as safety permitted, and asked "whether these pledges do not bind us to do something." Disagreement over party policy on the suffrage amendments maintained the antagonism between the two Radical factions throughout the summer.[25]

The two wings of the Radical Party began sparring over gubernatorial candidates in April 1870, five months before the party convention. The liberals objected to the renomination of Joseph McClurg for governor mostly because of his hostility to the suffrage amendments, but his position on other issues also upset them. The Germans disliked him because McClurg refused to serve alcohol at receptions in the Governor's Mansion, and they feared prohibition. McClurg's support of protective tariffs was enough to earn the enmity of Grosvenor, who summed up his opinion to readers in early April, declaring that McClurg's renomination for governor "would be absurd, because he is not competent to advocate the liberal policy." Grosvenor soon endorsed B. Gratz Brown as a candidate for governor in the *Missouri Democrat*, much to the displeasure of many regular Radicals who considered Brown a renegade. The other Radical editors in the state retaliated against Grosvenor later that summer, excluding him from a party policy meeting and attacking Brown in their papers. The squabbles between the regular and liberal factions soon extended to the apportionment of delegates, a controversy that continued into the convention.[26]

The preconvention fighting became particularly dangerous to the unity of the Radical Party when the Democrats announced, just three weeks before the Radical convention, that they were adopting a "possum policy" of playing dead in the statewide contests and concentrating only on local contests. Disappointed with their performance in the last several elections and still struggling against the test-oath restrictions, leading Democrats in Missouri began considering in early 1870 the possibility of ignoring the statewide offices. A Democratic paper insisted that the "election is something worse than a disgraceful farce. Why then should we engage in it, so long as the farce is played at our expense . . . and humiliation?" In late July the Democratic state central committee officially endorsed the possum policy. The Democrats' abdication of state offices increased the stakes of the Radical convention, for whoever was nominated to run for governor would certainly win the election. The possum policy also made the possibility of a split in the Radical Party a viable option, since without Democratic opposition both the regular and liberal factions of the party could run a candidate with the assurance that a Radical would win. Though a majority of Radicals appeared to favor McClurg, the liberals knew that most Democrats, deprived of their own candidate, would support Brown if he were nominated. The absence of the Democrats left no external threat to unite the Radical Party.[27]

During the first two days of the convention at the state capital in Jefferson City, the Regulars and Liberals fought over the apportionment of delegates. Despite long, heated debates, the Liberals consistently failed in their attempts to redetermine representation. Sensing the growing intractability of both sides, moderates in the party tried brokering a compromise the night before the third, and final, day of the convention. Both the Regulars and the Liberals, however, rejected the moderates' compromise candidate and platform. The Regulars would accept a compromise platform, but insisted on McClurg's nomination, while the Liberals would leave Brown for a compromise candidate, but refused to alter their platform. The showdown came the next morning when the platform committee reported to the convention. Unanimous on all but the plank regarding the amendments on test oaths, the committee submitted two reports. As committee chairman, Schurz reported the Liberal, majority resolution, stating "that the Republican Party stands pledged to remove all disqualifications imposed upon the late rebels." The Regular, minority resolution questioned the safety "of re-enfranchising those justly disfranchised for participating in the late rebellion" and recognized "the right of any member of the party to vote his honest convictions." After a half-hour of debating that only rehashed old arguments, the convention adopted the minority resolution by a nearly 100-vote margin. Defeated once again, the Liberals walked out of the Hall of Representatives and down the hall to the Senate Chamber to start their own convention.[28]

Participants in the new convention quickly made Schurz chairman and produced a platform advocating re-enfranchisement, free trade, and civil service reform. Some of the reforms, argued the platform, were necessary for the survival of a republican form of government. While one plank insisted that "the safety of Republican institutions demands a thorough reform of the civil service of the government," another argued that "the removal of political disabilities, as well as the extension of equal political rights and privileges to all classes of citizens without distinction is . . . essential to the integrity of Republican institutions." Appeals to Republicanism, however, not republicanism, dominated the platform. The first plank listed "the vital principles of the Republican party," and the following planks linked Republican Party principles and history to Liberal positions. The re-enfranchisement plank cited Republican support for black suffrage in 1868 and declared "that it is a violation of vital Republican principles to deprive any man, be he white or black, of a share in the government." The free-trade plank contended "that the Republican party, as it fought against slavery, which deprived a man of the whole of his earnings for the benefit of another, so it now opposes every form of taxation which deprives a man of any share of his earnings for the benefit of another." The emphasis on the Republican Party in the platform was not accidental, for despite leaving the Radical convention, Liberals considered themselves the true Republicans. They needed to stress their Republican roots because of the expected Democratic support. After Brown received the Liberals' nomination for governor, for example, the prominent Democrat James Rollins addressed the convention, pledging to support Brown and predicting the assistance of fellow Democrats. In the days that followed Grosvenor repeatedly insisted that the Liberals represented the Republican Party. "The Radical party of Missouri has tried a little too long to be Radical instead of Republican," he explained, and "the result is the organization of a distinctively Republican or liberal party." A few days later Grosvenor again argued that the Liberals "were the men who saved true Republican principles from overthrow and betrayal," and thus the Liberal bolt "is not a case of separation from a party." The split at the Radical convention, though an escalation made possible only by the Democrats' possum policy, was still a continuation of the struggle between Missouri Liberals and Regulars for control of the Republican Party's organization and direction.[29]

The Radicals did not accept the Liberals' version of events at the convention in Jefferson City. They soon began accusing them of abandoning the Republican Party and scheming with the Democrats. Notwithstanding the endorsement of the Liberals by some prominent Democrats, however, historians agree that there is no evidence of direct collusion between the Democrats and either Republican faction. In most counties the Democrats ran their own tickets against both the Radicals and the Liberals. Schurz, who Hans L. Trefousse insists "honestly sought to stay within the Republican party," tried to make it clear that Liberals were Republicans. At a meeting in early September he spoke highly of Grant, exhorting the crowd to recognize "the many, very many good things he has done while he was President of the United States." Later, when David Wells, former special commissioner of the Treasury, volunteered to travel from Connecticut to campaign for the Liberals, Schurz thanked him, but said "that this contest in our state should be carried through by Missourians exclusively without the appearance of any combination reaching beyond the actual battlefield." Schurz wanted to prevent the Missouri Liberals from appearing as a threat to the national Republican Party or to Grant. The "Address to the People of Missouri," signed by Schurz and other prominent Liberals, asked voters to "look at our candidates. Is there a single one whose past conduct is not identified with the great achievements of which the Republican party is so justly proud?" Responding to charges of political inconsistency, Brown pointed out that while he was advocating emancipation in 1861, McClurg was supporting the rights of Missouri slaveowners. The day after the publication of the "Address," Schurz wrote to Grant's secretary of state: "As to our bolt in Missouri," he explained, "I send you our manifesto. It was a necessary thing."[30]

While most Republicans across the country did not view the Missouri Liberal bolt as necessary, Schurz found support from the New York–based American Free Trade League. Founded in 1865 to lead the Republican Party toward free-trade policies, the League had established an extensive network of agents and contacts across the country, especially in Missouri. League president David Dudley Field, who had one of the largest law practices in New York City and had spent decades reforming New York State's legal code, had helped present the case against Missouri's loyalty oaths before the Supreme Court in 1868. In the following two years Carl Schurz and William Grosvenor both corresponded with League members about tariffs and politics. Grosvenor's connection with the League became so extensive that it published his book on free trade. Dissatisfied with the meager results of their five-year campaign against tariffs, the League held a secret policy meeting in Washington during April 1870 to develop new strategies for promoting free trade within the Republican Party. Representatives of the nation's major free-trade journals attended, including Grosvenor of the *Missouri Democrat*, Horace White of the *Chicago Tribune*, Charles Nordhoff of the *New York Evening Post*, Don Piatt of the *Cincinnati Commercial*, Henry Adams of the *North American Review*, and Edwin Godkin of *The Nation*. The meeting resolved to push for free trade, specie resumption, and civil service reform within the Republican Party, reserving the option of working outside the party only if efforts to influence it failed. When the Liberals in Missouri bolted, the like-minded Republicans in the East saw their move as an experiment in the feasibility of taking control of the Republican Party and anxiously watched the campaign unfold. Nordhoff advised Grosvenor of political events in the East, while both David Wells and Henry Adams offered Schurz help in the campaign.[31]

The connections between the Missouri liberal republicans and the eastern liberal republicans became readily apparent as Republican newspapers across the country began debating the necessity and importance of the Missouri bolt. Most Republican papers condemned Schurz and Brown for splitting the Republican Party. An ardent protectionist, Horace Greeley vehemently denounced the Missouri Liberals in the *New York Tribune*, repeatedly accusing them of forming a "conspiracy to destroy the Republican party." He blamed White's *Chicago Tribune* and William Cullen Bryant's *New York Evening Post* for encouraging the conspiracy, for both were part of a small group of Republican newspapers favoring civil service reform, free trade, and amnesty and supporting the Liberals in Missouri. Nordhoff, managing editor of the *Evening*

Post, took the opposite point of view from Greeley and wrote to Grosvenor during the election that Greeley was trying to disorganize the Republican Party to promote protective tariffs. The *Chicago Tribune* criticized the policy of proscription in Missouri before the convention and warned that the Republican Party could be divided between "those in favor of Universal amnesty and those who oppose it." Following the convention the *Tribune* praised the Liberals' support of amnesty, declaring disfranchisement "a political blunder as well as a moral wrong," and approved of their "flat denial of the monopolist doctrine of 'protection.'" Papers such as Murat Halstead's *Cincinnati Commercial* and Edwin Godkin's *The Nation* also quickly endorsed the Missouri Liberals' stand for amnesty, civil service reform, and free trade. Both papers saw the conflict in Missouri as the beginning of a larger struggle for control of the Republican Party. The *Commercial* predicted, "The Republicans of Missouri have encountered the crisis which must very soon overtake the party throughout the country," and *The Nation* insisted that "there can be no doubt this tendency will spread." Drake soon persuaded Grant that the Liberal bolt was indeed the beginning of a general rebellion against the administration and the Republican Party. Grant gave Drake unlimited control of federal patronage in Missouri to stop the Liberal onslaught, and Liberals were soon purged from government positions.[32]

The resort to patronage as a weapon hurt the Radicals more than it helped, for the Liberals made it an important campaign issue. Even before Drake began using patronage against the Liberals, the "Address to the People of Missouri" had warned that "the integrity of republican institutions is menaced by great abuses . . . in this instance the demoralizing influence of the spoils system." The use of patronage for political purposes, its authors insisted, proved that the spoils system undermined republican liberty, just as they had cautioned in their platform. Liberals condemned Drake's use of federal and state patronage, but reserved special censure for Grant's active participation in the campaign as the unwarranted interference of the national government in local elections. In a series of editorials in the *Missouri Democrat*, Grosvenor argued that Grant's interference in Missouri's election was part of a larger trend threatening liberty in the republic. "During the war, when the very life of the nation was in danger," explained Grosvenor, "we tolerated a concentration of power in the federal government which in earlier times would have been resented and resisted." According to him the federal government continued to concentrate power after the war "until the just limit of national interference has almost been obliterated."[33]

In republican ideology, centralization of power was the greatest threat to liberty, and according to Grosvenor Grant was not the man to reverse this trend because he was "incapable, as a soldier, of comprehending the relations of the States to the nation in our complex system of government." Grosvenor's specification of Grant's military background highlights the distinction between civilian and military power, an important theme in American history. In tracing the coming of the American Revolution, Bernard Bailyn has underscored concerns about the British using and abusing military power. Apprehension about the use, let alone misuse, of military power after the Revolution explains some of the provisions of the Articles of Confederation and the Constitution that sought to ensure that the military remained subordinate to civilian control. During the Civil War many Republicans expressed distrust of the professional military officers from West Point, arguing that talented civilians could do just as well without all the Napoleonic trappings. John M. Palmer, a Republican politician who became a Civil War general and eventually joined the national Liberal Republican Party, developed the dislike of West Point generals common to civilian soldiers who viewed professional soldiers as a danger to republican government. During the war he told his wife, "I would resign tomorrow, but that would only be to increase their perfect control of the military aristocracy." Several members of the liberal republican movement, including Carl Schurz, Charles Francis Adams Jr., and Grosvenor, served in the Union Army and were certainly exposed to similar sentiments against the professional military.[34]

Ultimately, warned Grosvenor, "if this tendency is not checked we shall soon have a centralization of power as absolute as that which existed under Napoleon." A month later Grosvenor was still writing that "good men who see the evils which have grown from abuse of patronage believe that the existence of free institutions is imperiled more from that cause than from any other, . . . that local self-government is being undermined and destroyed by the tendency to centralize all power at Washington." Grant's interference in Missouri politics gave Democrats, already inclined to support the Liberals, another reason to vote for Brown. The *Missouri Democrat* happily reprinted a section from the leading Democratic paper, the incongruously named *Missouri Republican*, declaring "suffrage, tariff, *everything*—save civil service reform—shrinks into small proportions compared with this issue of the preservation of the autonomy and independence of the States, untrammeled by centralized power, and unawed by the presence of the military."[35]

The classical republican warnings about centralized power threatening liberty dominated the campaign. In addition to protesting the spoils system, Liberals continued to argue that free trade and amnesty were essential to maintaining republican liberty. Grosvenor contended that "the McClurg movement is an attempt to capture the Republican Party, and transform it into a tool of monopolists, with political disfranchisement as a means of over coming a hostile public sentiment." The accusation of disenfranchising citizens to benefit oneself materially is an archetypal republican charge. The Liberals more explicitly used republicanism while discussing disfranchisement. Their "Address to the People of Missouri" asked, "Is it not the imperative duty of all friends of Republican institutions to do away with proscriptive laws which must be condemned as unrepublican when unnecessary for the salvation of the republic?" The republican appeals worked, and the Radicals found themselves losing support as the campaign proceeded, particularly for their stand on the constitutional amendments. In an attempt to counter the Liberal charges and court Democratic voters, McClurg and other leading Radicals announced toward the end of the campaign that they personally favored re-enfranchisement. McClurg also ordered election supervisors to enforce the registration acts leniently, which accomplished little other than allowing more Democrats to vote the Liberal ticket.[36]

The Radical effort to attract Liberal and Democratic voters failed miserably. Brown crushed McClurg, defeating the sitting Radical governor 104,374 to 63,336. Though a Liberal candidate, Brown owed his victory to the Democrats, who, according to Thomas S. Barclay's analysis, provided approximately 60,000 of the 104,000 votes. The emerging power of the Democrats becomes more apparent in examining the rest of the election, where they won 4 of the 9 congressional races, 77 of the 138 seats in the state legislature, and three-quarters of the county offices. William Parrish observes that "whether Schurz and the Liberals realized it or not, the triumph of Brown in 1870 was largely a Democratic victory." Thomas Barclay similarly finds that the Liberals "did not seem fully to comprehend the great Democratic gains, and the changed position of the party." Brown seemed to grasp the true dynamics of the situation when he told a crowd right after the election "that in this election I recognize that my obligations are in the largest measure due to the Democratic party," but he later pledged to Schurz that he thought their victory was "of true Republican principles" and had "elevated the Democracy to our own platform and standpoint." Schurz provided a similar interpretation before the United States Senate a month after the election. After recounting the history of the liberal movement in Missouri, he acknowledged that one of the major questions after the election was where Democrats would go in the future. "Candidly speaking," Schurz responded, "I expect that a great many of those who were disfranchised on account of their connection with the rebellion will abhor a reopening of the questions that sprang from the war, sincerely accept accomplished results, honestly identify themselves with the new order of things, and vote accordingly." He expressed similar sentiments in private, writing to Grosvenor in early January that he "was rather startled by the telegraphic announcement this morning

that a Democratic speaker had been elected in the House" of the Missouri legislature, and asked "How is that?" Back in Missouri a Democratic newspaper
explained that the Liberals expected "the Democratic party will join it and
make a majority . . . but the Democrats feel no such dissatisfaction with their
party." The Liberals misinterpreted the temporary support Democrats gave
Brown in order to oust the Radicals as the permanent transfer of Democratic
votes.[37]

The Liberals even misperceived the effects of the 1870 election within the
Republican Party. They had expected that victory at the polls would give them
leadership of the party, but even in defeat the Radicals refused to turn control
over to the Liberals. Barclay finds that the Radicals took "gloomy satisfaction"
in the Democratic resurgence, for they "found it far easier to yield the position
of supremacy to the Democrats than the Liberals." The Radicals, under the
direction of Drake, continued to use federal patronage against Liberal sympathizers and showed no signs that they were ready to follow the Liberal leaders.
Despite the evidence, however, the Liberals not only thought they had taken
control of the Republican Party in Missouri, but thought they were in the process of taking control of the party nationally. Schurz told the Senate that "the
Republican party does contain the elements of a healthy regeneration. . . . The
question is only whether its *best* can also become its *controlling* impulses. . . . I
firmly hope and trust it can be successfully solved." Liberal supporters outside
of Missouri, such as Edwin Godkin and Murat Halstead, also saw the victory as
the beginning of a change in Republican Party leadership. In early December
Samuel Bowles' *Springfield Republican* explained, "Reformers see now more
clearly than they did even a month ago that it is easier to capture the republican
party than it is to make a new one; and though the battle is by no means over,
nor the victory won, it begins to be seen that, if there is to be any bolting from
the republican ranks or any new party, it will be in the name of extreme protection, and in the interest of abuse and not reform." Just as the Liberals wrongly
counted on the Democratic support to be permanent, they mistakenly thought
they had gained control of the Republican Party in Missouri.[38]

The Liberals' misunderstanding of the 1870 Missouri contest led directly to
the national liberal republican movement. In the wake of the Liberals' Missouri
"victory," the American Free Trade League called for another secret strategy
meeting, this time in New York, on November 22, 1870. Schurz and Brown were
invited, as well as Grosvenor, who had attended the April 1870 meeting in
Washington. Mahlon Sands, the son of a wealthy New York businessman and
secretary of the American Free Trade League, explained in the invitations that
"I am instructed by the officers of this society to convey to you their congratu-
lations on the success of the Liberal movement in Mo. It seems to them there

may be ulterior consequences resulting from it of even greater importance than its immediate advantages." The officers of the League, wrote Sands, "are of the opinion that the time is near at hand when a new political movement in favor of Revenue and Civil Service Reform may be started with success," and proposed the meeting to discuss plans "to give the nucleus needed to start the new movement." The plan included the possibility of forming a national alliance between free-trade Republicans and Democrats similar to that which the Missouri Liberals mistakenly imagined had occurred in their state. Not wishing to antagonize Grant further, Schurz and Brown decided not to attend the meeting. Remembering the lessons of meritorious service as a Union major general during the Civil War, Jacob Cox also determined that discretion was the better part of valor and avoided the meeting, for he had recently resigned as secretary of the Interior in a fight with Grant over the spoils system. The absence of Schurz and Cox meant little, though, as both corresponded with Henry Adams and other participants about the meeting. Among the thirty to forty people who did gather in New York to discuss the formation of a new political movement were those who had attended the meeting in Washington in April—David Dudley Field, Joshua Lawrence Chamberlain, Samuel Bowles, William Cullen Bryant, David Wells, Charles Francis Adams Jr., and Edward Atkinson.[39]

The New York meeting shaped the policy of the emerging liberal republican movement. The first issue debated was the relationship of the movement to the Republican Party. According to Henry Adams, "while the League leaned towards a rupture with the Republican Party and an alliance with the democrats, the members of the press favored a different policy." He explained "that neither White nor Grosvenor nor ourselves intended to use the 'new party' except as a threat, for the present." The members of the press prevailed, and the meeting decided to continue working within the Republican Party. The League also lost the debate on the platform. Though the League preferred to concentrate on free trade, the western representatives convinced the meeting "that the issue of Civil Service Reform was a stronger one before the people" and "that the two measures should be advocated together and that for the present our agitation should be restricted, so far as we acted as a body, to these two issues." The League even surrendered the third and final issue of the meeting, agreeing to postpone the creation of a central committee with the eventual goal of calling a convention. Godkin, a member of the press, considered the meeting "very successful." Schurz and Cox also agreed with the decisions reached in New York. Cox insisted to Nordhoff, "The great strength of the support we must have either for the civil service reform or for the revenue reform, must come from and be found in the Republican party." A few weeks later he told Schurz, "Both you and I can do our duty to the country much more efficiently *within* our present party connections than *without.*" Schurz responded that, while he would speak against the administration if necessary, he and Cox shared an understanding of the situation. The new political movement would press for civil service reform and free trade within the Republican Party, for as Nordhoff declared, "It belongs to us to be recognized as the true leaders of the Republican party. If we are not that we are nothing."[40]

The political movement organized in New York on November 22, 1870, was the liberal republican movement. The participants self-consciously created the movement to advance civil service reform and free trade by taking control of the Republican Party, and over the next year they held more policy meetings. Schurz and Cox became regular participants, and Lyman Trumbull also joined. Trumbull was an elder statesman of the Republican Party, having been a senator from Illinois since 1855, an early Lincoln supporter, and a longtime chairman of the powerful Senate Judiciary Committee. Attendance at these policy meetings provides definitive criteria for membership in the liberal republican movement. It was at one of the meetings in December 1871 that participants decided to call a national convention, to be held in Cincinnati, that would transform the small political movement into a national party. In the process of transformation many newcomers with diverse agendas became associated with liberal republicanism, such as the ardent protectionist Horace Greeley, the Southern racist Hinton R. Helper, and the Democratic-leaning David Davis. In conflating the liberal republican movement with the Liberal Republican Party that was born at the 1872 Cincinnati Convention, historians have mistakenly included the newcomers in their analysis of the movement, which has distorted their conclusions.[41]

In the aftermath of Horace Greeley's nomination as the Liberal Republican Party's candidate at the Cincinnati Convention, liberal republicans were at pains to explain the origins and membership of their movement. Days after the convention, Schurz wrote to Greeley:

The proceedings of the Cincinnati Convention have, in some very important respects, disappointed the expectations of many earnest friends of the National reform movement. This movement, as you know, originated in its organized form with a number of courageous men in the West, who had no other object in view than the reunion of the whole people and a genuine reform of existing abuses. It comprised mainly two elements, the revenue reformers, so-called, and the Germans who joined it *en masse.* They both had in view something more than the defeat of Grant. Then the movement expanded and was first joined by the revenue reformers in the East and finally by a considerable number of men with whom opposition to the

administration was the main impulse, among the latter a good many politicians in the traditional acceptation of the term.

Schurz reiterated these points to Greeley and Whitelaw Reid in numerous
private letters throughout May. Though Reconstruction had been one of the
goals in Missouri, as the liberal republican movement expanded nationally, revenue and civil service reform quickly became the movement's central issues.
Schurz chastised Reid for attacking the free traders in the *New York Tribune*,
insisting that "your article attacked in a rather pointed manner the identical
class of persons who started the Liberal Republican Movement." Even when the
Springfield Republican tried to discredit the free traders later in the campaign, it
still recognized them as "the gentlemen who were earliest and most zealous in
the liberal movement." During a campaign speech in 1872, Charles Francis
Adams Jr. described the liberal republican movement that emerged out of Missouri in 1870: "Certain men met together at Washington, and subsequently in
New York—editors, economists, politicians and men of business—few in number, being not more than fifteen or twenty in all, but wielding an enormous
power through the press." According to themselves, the small group of men
who gathered in New York on November 22, 1870, were the liberal republicans,
and they consciously tried to recreate the seeming success of the Missouri Liberal Republicans to take over the national Republican Party and save the
republic.[42]

The circumstances of its birth in Missouri continued to define and shape the
liberal republican movement after it shifted onto a national stage. Because the
movement began in Missouri in 1870, it was formed first around issues peculiar
to that state, and could not possibly have been at heart an anti-Grant movement. Nationally, politicians misread the electoral success of the movement in
Missouri as heralding the restructuring of the Republican Party rather than the
capturing of Democratic votes. This expectation of a fundamental shift in the
Republican Party led many politicians to see the movement's Cincinnati Convention in 1872 as a means of displacing Grant; thus they joined the movement
at the last moment and changed the original nature of liberal republicanism.
Missouri's lack of a two-party system in 1870 created the peculiar environment
in which liberal republicanism originated and made it difficult for both the liberal republicans and politicians throughout the country to understand the true
effect of the state's election. Politicians analyzed the political environment
based on recent election results, but often they miscalculated. Nineteenth-
century politicians, unlike twenty-first-century politicians (and twenty-first-
century historians, I hope), were quite unsophisticated in terms of statistics and
frequently made gross miscalculations—as in Missouri. Such misreading was
endemic to the history of the liberal republican movement.

2

The Liberal Republican Conception of Party, 1848–1872

Y ears before the national phase of the liberal republican movement began, the *Springfield Republican* analyzed the future of the Republican Party. The paper considered political parties to be temporary coalitions organized for reform, but always vulnerable to corruption. "There are times and circumstances in which a thorough break-up of the old organizations is almost a condition-precedent of advance or reform. Parties become incurably corrupt, like cisterns which have accumulated so much filth that you might put in clean water, and take it out dirty, forever." Because political parties naturally became corrupt, "It is often necessary of reform, that old parties shall be given up, and all the political atoms become free to arrange themselves around new centers and obey new attractions." The *Republican* explained, though, that "there is almost always one condition of an advantageous redistribution of political forces, which is not found in the present situation. Generally speaking, change of parties requires the existence of at least a third party, however small it may be, which shall serve as the nucleus of the new organization. . . . It was in this way that the northern whig passed into the republican through the free soil party." In April 1868, the *Springfield Republican* advanced the modest hope that the Republican National Convention in three months would nominate Ulysses Grant, for "perhaps it will be found that Ulysses S. Grant as president, is all the reconstruction that the South, the country at large, or the republican Party need." Four years later, however, the same paper argued that the Republican Party needed reconstruction, because "the war imposed new duties upon it, and also materially changed its character and composition." The *Springfield Republican* and the liberal republicans had decided that Grant could not reconstruct the Republican Party and, drawing on their understanding of the nature of politics, had begun a small political movement to break up the old political parties.[1]

The allusion to the Free Soil Party and the formation of the Republican Party in the *Republican* was not accidental. The liberal republican movement contained a disproportionate number of former Free Soilers compared to the rest of the nation. While the Free Soil presidential ticket had garnered only 10 percent of the vote in 1848, nine of the twelve liberal republicans old enough then to participate in politics had supported it. Many of those too young to experience the Free Soil Party had been influenced by prominent Free Soilers, to whom some of them were also related. All of the liberal republicans active in politics during the mid-1850s helped organize the Republican Party from the grass roots and supported its first presidential candidate in 1856. As leaders of the Republican Party during the Civil War, they faced the challenges of trying to save the Union while maintaining the party's reform impulse. For liberal republicans, political parties were transient reform coalitions that naturally became corrupt and needed constant renewal. Experience in the Free Soil Party, the formation of the Republican Party, and leadership of the party through the Civil War had shaped their understanding of political parties. The liberal republicans' decades of political experience before the 1870s help demonstrate the political flexibility of the Civil War era and help explain the formation of the liberal republican movement.[2]

Two political forces gained strength in the early 1840s: party ties and the issue of slavery. After generations of distrust, Americans were gradually accepting the legitimacy of political parties, and two of them, the Whigs and the Democrats, dominated the political landscape. At the same time, the expansion of slavery into the western territories became a contentious political issue. As the election of 1844 neared, the debate focused on the possible annexation of Texas with its thousands of slaves. Southern Democrats blocked the nomination of their party's expected candidate, Martin Van Buren, because of his anti-annexation position. After a bitter conflict the Democrats nominated James K. Polk, an avid expansionist. Polk won the 1844 election, and outgoing President John Tyler interpreted the victory as a mandate for annexation. Before leaving office Tyler pushed a joint resolution through Congress annexing Texas.[3]

The annexation of Texas angered Mexicans, Whigs, and abolitionists, but it failed to satisfy the expansionistic goals of Polk. Three months after the outbreak of the Mexican War, Polk asked the House of Representatives for $2 million to facilitate the purchase of territory from Mexico when negotiating a peace treaty. David Wilmot, a Democrat in the Van Buren wing of his party, moved an amendment making it "an express and fundamental condition to the acquisition of any territory" that "neither slavery nor involuntary servitude shall ever exist in any part of said territory." While abolitionists naturally supported the Wilmot Proviso, many Northern Democrats also endorsed it to show their displeasure with Polk's victory over Van Buren at the convention and what they considered undue Southern influence in the party. Eric Foner warns that "it would be a serious mistake to dismiss the bitterness of the Van Burenites as merely the normal complaints of political losers," for "the Van Burenites were convinced that Polk's nomination was not the result of open deliberations by party leaders, but of 'the most stupendous intrigue that has ever been successful in this country.'" Despite popular support in the North and passing the House twice, the Wilmot Proviso failed to pass the Southern-dominated Senate.[4]

The failure of the Wilmot Proviso in Congress did not prevent it from raising the divisive issue of slavery expansion in both the Democratic and Whig parties. In New York the Van Buren wing of the Democratic Party, called the Barnburners, was still opposed to the expansion of slavery and bitter about the defeat of Van Buren at the 1844 convention. William Cullen Bryant, editor of the Democratic *New York Evening Post* and a future liberal republican, publicly denounced Daniel S. Dickinson, the Democratic senator from New York who had voted against the Wilmot Proviso, and ridiculed General Lewis Cass, a prospective presidential candidate of the Democratic Party. Bryant was the classic aristocratic Yankee, able to trace his ancestors on both sides back to the Mayflower, educated at the exclusive Williams College in the Berkshires, and published in the prestigious *North American Review* at age seventeen. In Bryant's native state, Massachusetts, the Wilmot Proviso divided the Whig Party. A group of young abolitionist Whigs, known as the Conscience Whigs, decided that "the Wilmot proviso should be the policy—and the test—of a true Whig." Charles Francis Adams, scion of the famous Adams family and editor of the Conscience Whigs' newspaper the *Boston Daily Whig*, attacked the Massachusetts Whig senator who filibustered the proviso, charging that he had tried to shield Southern Whigs from having to vote either way.

In Ohio the strong presence of the Liberty Party and the fiery abolitionism of the Western Reserve caused problems in both the Democratic and Whig parties. Ohio Whigs soon adopted the Democratic-sponsored proviso as their own. Jacob Brinkerhoff, Democratic congressman, coauthor of the Wilmot Proviso, and mentor of future liberal republican Roeliff Brinkerhoff, insisted that "the adoption of the principle of the 'Wilmot proviso' is the only way to save the Democratic party of the free states." Brinkerhoff was an archetype, having attended Williams College a decade after Bryant and coming of age in the Burned-Over District—a section of upstate New York where so many religious revivals took place under Charles Grandison Finney that it looked as if a forest fire had swept the area. Within two years of Finney's moving to Ohio to become president of Oberlin College, a hotbed of abolitionism, Brinkerhoff also moved to Ohio and became involved in antislavery politics. Many Whig and Democratic Party leaders shared President Polk's concern that the controversy surrounding the Wilmot Proviso could destroy the national parties. Salmon P. Chase, leader of the Liberty Party in Ohio, counted on the slavery issue disrupting the national parties and began contacting disaffected Whigs and Democrats across the country to try forming a new antislavery third party.[5]

The early attempts to lure antislavery Whigs and Democrats away from their parties in the aftermath of the Wilmot Proviso failed. Longtime Democrat Jacob Brinkerhoff told Chase at the end of 1847 that while "you have thought best, in order to forward the Great Cause, to disconnect yourself from both the great parties of the country;—I, who love liberty and hate slavery with an intensity few men can emulate, have thought I could best advance the same great Cause by remaining within the pale of the powerful party in which I may [be] said to have been born." Charles Francis Adams came to a similar conclusion in Massachusetts, and few could doubt his political independence or antislavery credentials. Adams had continued his famous family's reputation, established by his grandfather and father, for being political mavericks. John Adams had fought with his own political party while president, and John Quincy Adams had returned to the House of Representatives after his own term as president to fight against slavery. The Liberty Party's poor showing in 1844 made Charles Francis Adams wary of third parties, and he wished to regenerate the Whigs into an antislavery party. The paper he edited insisted in January 1848, "There is more courage in remaining with a party to contend for the establishment of an unpopular principle against a reluctant majority, than in leaving it." Likewise William Cullen Bryant, one of New York's leading antislavery advocates, saw little benefit to leaving the Democratic Party. He explained to his brother in February 1848, "All parties formed for a single measure are necessarily short-lived. . . . I never mean to belong to any of them, unless I see some strong and compelling reason for it."[6]

The continued commitment of Bryant, Brinkerhoff, and Adams to their parties depended on the presidential nominations in 1848. Convinced that the Democrats could not win the presidential election without New York's thirty-six electoral votes, Bryant repeatedly insisted in the *Evening Post* that "New York must be conciliated and given a candidate the people can vote for." He expected the Democratic Party to adopt the free soil view popular among New York Democrats, that slavery should not expand into the West. The Democratic Convention, however, sat both the anti-expansionist Barnburner delegation and the rival pro-expansion, Democratic faction from New York, thus reducing the Barnburners' influence and causing them to bolt. Bryant declared the Democratic nomination of the expansionist Cass for president a "nullity," arguing that the convention merited as much consideration as "an accidental meeting of persons on a steam boat." Unlike Bryant, Adams had little hope that his party would nominate even a nominally antislavery candidate for president, for the slaveowning General Zachary Taylor had long been the favorite for the Whig nomination and had consistently refused to support the Wilmot Proviso. Adams called a meeting of the Conscience Whigs even before the Whig Convention met on June 8, and they agreed that if Taylor were nominated they would hold their own convention to repudiate the Whig nominees and select candidates committed to the Wilmot Proviso. When Adams heard the guns fired on Boston Common to celebrate Taylor's nomination he realized that his days as a Whig were over, writing in his diary, "We are fairly embarked."[7]

Salmon Chase anticipated the results of the Democratic and Whig political conventions, and with the help of fellow Ohioans Stanley Matthews and George Hoadly Jr.—two future liberal republicans—organized a "People's Convention" for antislavery men of all parties, to be held at Columbus on June 22. The Columbus Convention called for all "opposed to the election of Lewis Cass and Zachary Taylor to meet at Buffalo on the 9th of August." Like many of the liberal republicans, Hoadly had been a New Englander before moving to Ohio. After college and law school he became a junior partner in Chase's law firm and a political protégé of the antislavery leader. Matthews grew up in Ohio and became a lawyer in Cincinnati, later a hot spot of liberal republicanism. In the two weeks after the Ohioans held the Columbus Convention, the Barnburners and the Conscience Whigs agreed at their own conventions to send delegates to Buffalo. With the actual organization of a third party—the Free Soilers—in sight, Brinkerhoff finally left the Democrats and journeyed toward Buffalo.[8]

The Free Soil Convention at Buffalo publicly dealt with the conflict between principle and party. After being selected president of the convention, Adams assured his fellow Free Soilers that "you have all assembled here today out of pure devotion to a principle," one that he described as "a contest between truth and falsehood, between the principles of Liberty and the rule of Slavery." The first ten planks of the platform dealt with slavery, opposing the extension of slavery in the West and "the reckless hostility of the Slave power to the establishment of Free Government for Free Territories." The Free Soilers argued that slaveowners had taken control of the federal government and were using it to protect and expand slavery against the will of the majority. Adams and the Free Soilers blamed the national parties for the Slave Power's control of the federal government and threat to national liberty. The platform explained that the Whigs and Democrats "have dissolved the National party organization heretofore existing by nominating for Chief Magistracy of the United States, under slave-holding dictation, candidates neither of whom can be supported by the opponents of slavery extension." The major principle for Free Soilers was thus not only the moral issue of slavery, but the political parties' abandonment of their republican mission, the protection of liberty and democracy.[9]

The theme of party corruption rang throughout the Free Soil Convention. On its first day Adams insisted, "We are obliged, under a necessity which we cannot resist, to denounce the organizations of the old parties as no longer worthy of the confidences of a free people. They have met, and they have shown by their action that they have no system of policy, excepting that which consists in fighting with each other in the endeavor to get place as the prize of their struggles." He repeatedly contended that the parties "do not understand that they are fighting only for expediency, and are expecting nothing but place." On the last day of the convention Brinkerhoff expressed similar sentiments, advising people, "Don't trust politicians. You have trusted them too long already. Trust only yourselves . . . uninfluenced by the hope of office." He declared that unlike politicians, "You do not expect to be appointed on a foreign mission, or to a seat in the cabinet, or to a clerkship in the post office." Getting to the heart of the principle-versus-party conflict, the longtime Democrat explained, "I have always been under the impression—the silly impression it may be thought—that democracy consisted, not in men—not in organizations—but in principles." The Free Soilers attacked the corruption of the national parties by proposing to limit their source of power: patronage. The Buffalo Convention platform called for "a retrenchment of the expenses and patronage of the Federal Government; the abolition of all unnecessary offices and salaries; and the election by the people of all civil officers in the service of the Government, so far as the same may be practicable." Many Free Soilers also worried that the federal government's large holdings of western land could lead to political corruption, and thus they included a plank calling for free grants of public land to settlers. Adams confided to a friend before the convention that he wanted to get rid of the public lands as fast as possible, since they were "nothing but a source of political corruption."[10]

The antiparty, republican rhetoric of the Free Soilers was common to new and third parties in the nineteenth century. Though parties had become an established element of the political scene by mid-century, antiparty rhetoric, harkening back to earlier generations' virulent distrust of anything resembling a political party, still resonated with many Americans. The antiparty tropes of "special interests" and "corrupt politicians" were central themes in almost every nineteenth-century third party. While it would be easy to dismiss the antipartyism of new parties as a calculated attack on the established parties, much of it was sincere. Michael F. Holt contends that a sincere antipartyism was vital in the formation of the Whigs, as "only a passionate devotion to the Revolutionary experiment in republican government and a conviction that Jackson threatened it explain how men with such diverse views on other matters formed such a united front against him." Similarly, Mark Voss-Hubbard thinks that "to cast the antiparty tradition as merely a political idiom indiscriminately deployed by insurgents and party elites alike is to miss its genuine oppositional meaning in movements of popular rage." The perceived corruption in government truly upset the Free Soilers, and for good reason. Mark W. Summers observes that not only were many of the antebellum denunciations of party corruption sincere, but that "corruption *did* endanger the Republic" because "Republican institutions are based on the trust of the people in their fairness. Corrupt use of those institutions makes them less worthy of faith."[11]

The Free Soilers shared another similarity with most third parties: the difficulty of bringing people from different parties together on a common platform. Frequently described as having "all manner of men" and cited for its "heterogeneity," the Buffalo Convention resembled the national Liberal Republican Convention held twenty-four years later. Like the Liberal Republican Convention, the Buffalo Convention had little trouble creating planks for civil service reform and preserving western land for settlers. Ironically, Adams predicted that for the coalition forming at Buffalo, "the most serious difficulty will lie in the protecting system," the same issue—protective tariffs—that would vex the Liberal Republican Convention. The tariff resolution for the Free Soil platform did cause more discussion than any other issue, as former Whigs and Democrats continued their traditional battle over economic policy. Unlike the delegates at the Liberal Republican Convention, the Free Soilers harmoniously agreed to a plank advocating a revenue tariff—a tariff adequate to raise the money necessary to run the government. The two parties also shared a similar experience in nominating their presidential candidates. The idealistic Free Soilers handed the nomination to Martin Van Buren, who had truckled to slavery for years. Likewise, the ideologically motivated Liberal Republicans would nominate Horace Greeley, a lifetime opponent of free trade and supporter of the spoils system. The relative harmony of the Free Soil Convention, though, could not prevent the party from experiencing the fate common to most new parties—failure at the polls. The Free Soil ticket of Van Buren and Adams garnered just over 10 percent of the vote.[12]

The outcome at the polls did not upset the majority of Free Soilers, who had never expected to win the presidency. Many shared the view of Adams that the election of 1848 was the first battle in a great crusade and the beginning of party realignment. Shortly after the election Bryant explained to readers of the *New York Evening Post* that one of the campaign's major results was that "it has so disturbed the composition of the democratic party of the north, that it will compel it to reorganize with the principle of free soil in its creed as a settled doctrine." While the Whigs and Democrats maintained their national dominance over the next four years, and the Free Soil Party lost strength nationally, the Free Soilers in New York, Massachusetts, and Ohio did significantly disrupt the political parties in their states.[13]

Though the Barnburners in New York reluctantly returned to the Democratic Party, few could completely forgive or forget the wounds of the campaign, and the old scars maintained the breach. Bryant editorialized about the division in the New York Democratic Party in 1850, complaining that "even now it [the *New York Evening Post*] is under the ban of the same organization for its uncompromising resistance to the extension of slavery, though we continually hope that the time is not far distant when this heresy, like those which have proceeded it in the history of this journal, may be transfigured into the accepted policy of our party." More upheaval occurred in Massachusetts, where the Free Soilers and Democrats formed a coalition to replace the long-dominant Whigs. Even with the decline of the national Free Soil Party in 1852, Adams still saw the major parties as "effete" (an ironic choice of words, since this was the exact term many party regulars applied to liberal reformers in the 1870s), and thought it inevitable that a new organization must arise. Perhaps the greatest political change occurred in Ohio, where the Free Soilers elected Salmon P. Chase to the United States Senate and threw the state's two-party system into complete disarray. Controlling the balance of power in the Ohio legislature, Free Soilers prevented either of the other parties from organizing the state government and caused unprecedented chaos in the 1849–50 legislative session. The Free Soilers, particularly in Massachusetts and Ohio, learned how easily a third party could disrupt the political system. The impact of the Free Soil Party became even greater in retrospect, as many became convinced that the Free Soilers had started the party realignment of the 1850s.[14]

The Free Soil experience not only emphasized the plasticity of the party system for its members, but also reinforced their understanding of the nature of political parties. Adams, Bryant, and the other Free Soilers demonstrated that their loyalty to political parties was conditional on the parties' principles. While their actions can be seen as pragmatic politics in some instances, in many cases Free Soilers left established parties for one that promised little immediate success. Certainly most Free Soilers were on the fringes of their parties by 1848, but that was mainly because they had unceasingly advocated opposition to the extension of slavery, an issue most Whigs and Democrats preferred to ignore. The Free Soilers viewed parties primarily as a means to reform society, and if parties ceased to reform then they ceased to have a reason to exist. Though historians like Michael F. Holt have shown that issues other than slavery helped destroy America's second-party system, the relatively stable competition between the Whigs and Democrats in the antebellum era that constitutes one of historians' five distinct party periods, the Free Soilers perceived slavery as the salient issue and concluded that principle could drive politics.

Many future liberal republicans shared the lessons and experience of the Free Soil Party with Adams and Bryant. New York City lawyer David Dudley Field joined Cincinnati lawyers Donn Piatt, Stanley Matthews, and George Hoadly in attending the Buffalo Convention and worked actively in the 1848 campaign. In Wisconsin, Horace White marched in a Free Soil parade at age fourteen, and in Massachusetts Edward Atkinson cast his first presidential vote for the Free Soil Party. Younger liberal republicans were often the relatives or assistants of Free Soilers. Henry Adams and Charles Francis Adams Jr. served as aides and secretaries to their father; Roeliff Brinkerhoff studied law under his uncle, the leading Free Soiler Jacob Brinkerhoff; and Charles Nordhoff was the protégé of Bryant. Many Free Soilers did not become liberal republicans, but enough attended the Liberal Republican Convention that abolitionist George Julian recalled, "I attended the Liberal Republican Convention at Cincinnati on the first of May, where I was delighted to meet troops of the old Free Soilers of 1848 and 1852."[15]

*   *   *

The demise of America's second-party system in the mid-1850s created a political vacuum that numerous political parties tried to fill. The Democrats, Free Democrats, Whigs, Free Soilers, North Americans, Know-Nothings, Know-Somethings, and Republicans all competed to maintain or establish themselves as a major party. While the Democrats and Republicans became the two dominant parties by 1860, the question of which parties would survive was in doubt throughout most of the 1850s. For instance, the Know-Nothings were the major second party in the Northeast as late as 1855, and the North American Party polled 22 percent of the vote in the presidential contest of 1856. Some politicians and voters changed party several times during the decade, such as the opportunistic Nathaniel Banks of Massachusetts, who went from the Democrats to the Know-Nothings to the North Americans to the Republicans in the space of five years. Though most were not as nimble as Banks, the increasingly proslavery stance of the Democrats combined with the collapse of the Whig and Free Soil parties forced a majority of the voters and politicians to change their party at least once between 1852 and 1856. Despite the numerous choices available in the 1850s, the vast majority of liberal republicans followed one of two paths to the Republican Party by 1856, coming from either the Democratic Party or the radical antislavery parties. The liberal republicans' political experiences in the chaos of the 1850s demonstrate their concern with certain issues and help explain their expectation that new political parties could succeed in displacing existing organizations.[16]

It is telling that most liberal republicans did not travel some of the more common paths to the Republican Party. A majority of Republicans were former

Whigs, yet only two liberal republicans remained Whigs after 1848 and went directly from that party to the Republicans. Jacob Dolson Cox's short tenure as a Whig hardly counts; he became a Whig in 1852 after graduating from Oberlin College and began working with the Free Soilers within a year. Two years later he was helping to organize the Ohio Republican Party. In contrast to Cox, Samuel Bowles had been a Whig since the mid-1840s and remained one until 1855. Bowles, born and raised in Springfield, Massachusetts, took over operation of his family's newspaper at age eighteen and often silenced the *Springfield Republican*'s usual antislavery position during campaigns to support Whig candidates. According to his biographer, "the paper was governed by loyalty to an individual and a party, rather than an idea," and "in comparison with Mr. Bowles's course in later years, it is noticeable how thoroughly during this period he was swayed by the allegiance and enthusiasm of a party, when that party had no longer any distinctive principles." The party loyalty of Bowles was symbolic of the change in Whig political philosophy since its original antipartyism in the 1830s, for starting in 1840 the Whigs had begun stressing that members had a duty to party. Influential Whigs argued in 1848 that since Zachary Taylor's nomination had followed regular procedures, delegates and constituents had an obligation to support him, since "the integrity and success of a party depend on its rigid adherence to this code." Eric Foner explains that Whigs leaving their crumbling party in the mid-1850s became the conservative and moderate core of the Republican Party, often stressing the importance of party loyalty. Bowles, for example, backed Nathaniel Banks for governor of Massachusetts in 1857, when many leading Radicals refused to support him because of his ties with the nativist Know-Nothings.[17]

While several liberal republicans had been Whigs in the 1850s, none joined the nativist parties in the North, such as the Know-Nothings and the North Americans, that seemed poised for dominance in the mid-1850s. In 1854 the Know-Nothings in Massachusetts captured 63 percent of the vote and elected every state office and almost every member of the legislature. One historian has estimated that 78 percent of the Free Soilers, including most of the leaders, voted the Know-Nothing ticket. Charles Francis Adams was one of the few Free Soilers in Massachusetts not to join the Know-Nothings, and he complained that "four fifths of the organization has left the standard of freedom to enlist itself against a shadow." A few weeks after the election, however, Adams decided that the loss of the "office seekers" had purified the Free Soil Party, which encouraged him to become more active in politics. Adams' experience appears common, since the Know-Nothings also showed strength in New York and Ohio, but no future liberal republicans joined them in those states. Their rejection of the Know-Nothings indicates a differentiation between leaving par-

ties for principle, as they did in creating the Free Soil Party, and political opportunism, for in several instances it would have been in the liberal republicans'
best interest to join the Know-Nothings. Their overwhelming rejection of
nativism in the 1850s also contrasts sharply with historians' depiction of them
as antiforeigner elitists during Reconstruction.[18]

Many liberal republicans refused to compromise their antislavery and anti-
nativist principles in the early 1850s and therefore avoided all of the major parties. Adams and Edward Atkinson condemned the Free Soilers' coalition with
the Democrats in Massachusetts. Atkinson wrote to a friend in 1850, "I don't
like the coalition and can't brag about the state. We may gain a U.S. Senator
but I think we shall lose in the end." Adams suspected that Charles Sumner
bargained away Free Soil principles to secure his Senate seat in 1851, and publicly attacked him a few years later for supporting the Free Soil–Democratic
coalition's new state constitution. In a speech at Quincy, Massachusetts, Adams
charged that Sumner had "listened to the siren song of expediency" and had
"bowed his neck to the iron rod of party." With the collapse of the Free Soil
Party, a few liberal republicans decided to operate outside of party structures.
As treasurer of the organization Citizens of Brookline in Aid of the Free-State
Cause in Kansas, Atkinson helped raise over a thousand dollars to equip John
Brown with rifles and ammunition. At the same time Horace White served as
assistant secretary for the Chicago branch of the National Kansas Committee,
which armed three hundred men sent to defend the Topeka government in
1856. The liberal republicans who remained outside of the major parties before
joining the Republicans, including Carl Schurz and Charles Francis Adams'
sons, became Radical Republicans before the Civil War. According to Foner,
the radicals "had a very expedient attitude toward political parties—they
viewed them as means, not as ends, and they were ready to abandon a party if
it would help further the antislavery cause." He finds that "the radicals repudiated the principle of party loyalty if it meant that party members were bound
to support the policies and nominees of their party even when they disagreed
with them." Even among the Republican radicals the liberal republicans held a
particularly strong disdain for party orthodoxy. While radicals such as Sumner
and Henry Wilson cared more for principle than party harmony, Adams still
thought both had abandoned some of their principles in the early 1850s to form
the Free Soil–Democratic coalition in Massachusetts.[19]

Although Adams did not want to form a coalition with the Democrats in
Massachusetts, many future liberal republicans became Republicans straight
from the Democratic Party. After supporting the Free Soil Party in 1848, Bryant,
David Dudley Field, and Don Piatt returned to the Democratic Party, remaining there until becoming Republicans in 1856. Ohio lawyer Roeliff Brinkerhoff

and *Cincinnati Commercial* editor Murat Halstead also remained active Democrats through 1856, as did Lyman Trumbull, who assured the Senate in July that "I had always been a Democrat. I am so still, and expect to continue so." By the end of 1856, however, the Democratic Party's proslavery principles and subservience to the South drove them into the Republican Party. David Dudley Field revived charges of a Slave Power conspiracy, charging that the Democratic Party had "fallen into the hands of office-holders and political adventurers, serving as the tools of a slaveholding oligarchy." Bryant shared Field's view, but was also cautious of the new Republican Party, telling his brother in a private letter that "I am not a very firm believer in the honesty of parties. All parties include all sorts of men, and the moment a party becomes strong the rogues are attracted to it, and immediately try to manage it." Halstead feared that both Democrats and Republicans, more concerned with offices than principle, would avoid the slavery question in 1856, and he titled his published notes on the conventions *Trimmers, Trucklers, and Temporizers.* The Democratic-Republicans distrusted political parties because they felt that theirs had been corrupted by the Slave Power. Unlike many Whigs, who were forced to leave their crumbling party, the Democrats had to deal with the pain of leaving an established party that was still strong. They did have to make the choice between party and principle.[20]

Many Democratic-Republicans also differed from the Whig-Republicans on several matters of principle. The Whig-Republicans generally favored a national bank, protective tariffs, internal improvements, and a strong federal government. In constrast, as Eric Foner explains, "Most Democratic-Republicans came from a tradition of strict construction of the Constitution, rigid governmental economy, and hostility to tariffs, corporations, banks, and monopolies." In addition, since the former Democrats "viewed the states as the locus of governmental action," Foner finds that "they were extremely fearful of centralized power in Washington." All of the liberal republicans originally from the Democratic Party exhibited these traits, from Bryant with his advocacy of free trade to Trumbull with his respect for the Constitution. Many of the Republican radicals, such as Adams, Schurz, White, and Atkinson, shared the Democratic-Republicans' opposition to traditional Whig economic policies. Adams, for instance, compared the "stupendous oligarchy" of the Slave Power to the national bank and tariffs. Schurz also linked the threat of the Slave Power to other dangers to liberty, arguing, "Let the slave power or any other political or economic interest tell us that we must think and say and invent and discover nothing which is against its demands, and we must interrupt and give up the harmony of our development, or fight the tyrannical pretension, whatever shape it may assume." The Democratic-Republicans and Radical Republicans in the 1850s differed from the Whig-Republicans in expectations both for political parties and for the federal government.[21]

The liberal republicans continued to articulate their vision of political parties even as the Republican Party became established in the late 1850s. Schurz told a crowd in 1858, "Another danger for the safety of our institutions, and perhaps the most formidable one, arises from the general propensity of political parties and public men to act on a policy of mere expediency, and to sacrifice principle to local and temporary success." He lectured the Bostonians that "you hate kingcraft, and you would sacrifice your fortunes and your lives in order to prevent its establishment on the soil of this Republic. But let me tell you that the rule of political parties which sacrifice principle to expediency, is no less dangerous, no less disastrous, no less aggressive, of no less a despotic a nature, than the rule of monarchs." Unprincipled political parties, Schurz warned, "will help to introduce a system of action into our politics which will gradually undermine the very foundations upon which our republican edifice rests." Charles Francis Adams struck a similar note about the nature of political parties in a May 1860 speech before Congress entitled "The Republican Party a Necessity." Adams defended the right of citizens to create political parties, but with the understanding that parties should exist only for certain reasons. He asked, "Is it to be pretended, then, that we, whose rights are liable to be deeply affected by the preponderance in the public councils of such a [slave] power, have no right to associate and organize with the intent to guard against its bad effects?" Adams insisted that "the party thus associated has no purpose which it seeks to conceal. . . . Its leading idea is REFORM, total and fundamental." Before the Civil War many Southerners and Democrats did attack the Republicans as a sectional party dangerous to the survival of the Union, but dedicating an entire speech to defending the mere existence of the party shows Adams' attitude toward parties. Adams thought political parties should be organizations created to advocate reform.[22]

Liberal republicans reinforced their public rhetoric about political parties in their actions and in private letters. Concerned with the relationship between the Know-Nothings and Republicans in Massachusetts, Schurz asked a friend whether the Republicans in Massachusetts will "at last learn that our principles cannot be victorious unless they are clear, pure and consistent?—that by trades and bargains we are bound to lose our honor and the victory at the same time?" In New York Bryant and Fields struck out against corruption in both their old party, the Democrats, and their new party, the Republicans. Field led one of the earliest movements for civil service reform in 1857, when he tried to limit the ability of New York City's Democratic mayor to appoint city officials. In the spring of 1860 Bryant ran repeated editorials in the *Evening Post* criticizing the Republican-controlled state legislature for corruption. The old animosity between Whigs and Democrats certainly played a part in the intraparty squabbles, as former Whigs controlled the legislature. Former Whig Thurlow Weed, a powerful Republican boss and longtime enemy of Bryant, had obtained the promise of large contributions to the Republican Party campaign fund from promoters of New York City street railways in return for guiding the franchises through the state legislature. In a private letter to the Republican governor, Bryant asked that he veto the city railroad bills passed by the legislature, warning, "It is not easy to conceive how intense is the disgust and vehement is the indignation which these corrupt measures have awakened." Bryant doubted "if we have ever had so corrupt a legislature as we have at present," and insisted, "party considerations are not the proper ones for deciding this question. The bills are unrighteous." Regardless of their dubious virtue, the governor did not veto the bills.[23]

Bryant's analysis of the political situation in early 1860 encapsulates both the liberal republican attitude toward parties and the flexibility of Civil War–era politics. Writing to his business partner about William H. Seward's prospects for the Republican presidential nomination, Bryant explained that "the great difficulty which I have in regard to him is this, that by the election of a Republican President the slavery question is settled, and that with Seward for President, it will be the greatest good-luck, a special and undeserved favor of Providence, if every honest democrat of the Republican Party be not driven into the opposition within a twelve month after he enters the White House." Bryant saw the Republican Party as an organization dedicated to solving the slavery question and to reforming society. Once the Republican Party achieved its goals, however, Bryant foresaw the possibility of another political realignment. To Bryant and many liberal republicans, the Republican Party was another temporary organization.[24]

*   *   *

The election of 1860 did little to change liberal republicans' attitudes toward political parties, and they consistently refused to operate according to party discipline during the Civil War, demonstrating their continued perception of the Republican Party as a temporary reform organization. The secession crisis showed that the liberal republicans, like many in the country, considered the party a fragile alliance. South Carolina quickly reacted to Abraham Lincoln's election as president in 1860, passing a bill on November 10 for a convention to consider secession. While other Southern states followed South Carolina's lead, President-elect Lincoln and most other prominent Republicans remained silent, hoping time and Union sentiment in the South would calm the situation. Meanwhile the House of Representatives selected a congressman from each state to create the Committee of Thirty-Three to consider the sectional crisis. The congressman from Arkansas introduced a resolution to the committee on December 13, stating that "the existing discontents among the southern people" were not without cause and that such additional guarantees of "their particular rights and interests . . . as or will or should allay them" were "indispensable to the perpetuation of the Union." Henry Adams, serving as his father's secretary, wrote to his brother Charles that night of their father's distress at the passage of the resolution, which they thought yielded too much ground. He warned, "There's no immediate danger, though it embroils things badly and will inevitably break the Republican line." At the end of the letter Henry Adams reiterated his concerns, explaining, "I'm afraid however I only speak exact truth when I tell you to prepare yourself for a complete disorganization of our party. If the South show any liberal spirit, the reaction will sweep us out dreadfully and thin our ranks to a skeleton."[25]

The response of liberal republicans confirmed Henry Adams's concern for the Republican Party's weakness. Carl Schurz wrote to Lincoln just a few days after the resolution passed, threatening to leave the party if it compromised. He told his wife that the letter declared that "I should never submit to a compromise, and should leave the party the moment it abandoned its principles." He insisted, "I have been reflecting on the question for two days, and I shall not yield." Other liberal republicans began to fear the Republican Party would yield, however, when the Senate committee on the sectional crisis began considering a number of measures, collectively called the Crittenden Compromise, that included reconfirming the Missouri Compromise line allowing slavery in all territory south of lattitude 36"30'. William Cullen Bryant wrote to Lincoln on Christmas Day, explaining that "the restoration of the Missouri Compromise would disband the Republican Party. Any other concession recognizing the right of slavery to protection or even existence in the territories would disgust and discourage the large majority of Republicans in this state and cool their interest in the incoming administration down to the freezing point." He warned Lincoln, "Whatever else be done [about] the slavery question, so far as it is a federal question [it] must remain as it is or the Republican party is annihilated." The Republicans did not yield, but two months later Congress was still considering the Crittenden Compromise as Lincoln made his way East for his inauguration. By late February Samuel Bowles had become so frustrated that he confided to a friend, "I have a great faith in everything but the Republican party, and that, if it chooses, 'may go hang.' . . . I mean to be as loyal as possible, and that isn't very loyal." Before Lincoln could even take office as the first Republican president, numerous liberal republicans threatened to leave and expected "a complete disorganization" of the party.[26]

Bowles' disgust with normal mid-nineteenth-century maneuvering for patronage reflected the attitude of many liberal republicans during the Civil War, an attitude that was also common throughout the country. Most Americans expected that political parties would cease their partisanship during wartime, and that the rhetoric of both parties during the war would generally condemn normal party politics. Professor Francis Lieber, one of the antebellum advocates of political parties in a republic, published a pamphlet entitled *No Party Now But All for Our Country,* in which he insisted, "We do not pursue truth, or cultivate science, by party dogmas; and we do not, we must not, love and defend our country and our liberty according to party rules." Lieber deeply influenced Henry Demarest Lloyd, a student of his at the time who later wrote the invitations to the first national meeting of the liberal republicans, but Mark E. Neely Jr. finds that generally "nineteenth-century politicians did not trifle with the patronage, for it provided the basis of their party organization," and he observes that this continued into the Civil War. Despite the no-party rhetoric, the Republican Party eventually continued the spoils system. The liberal republicans started criticizing the Republicans' use of the spoils system, a vital piece of party machinery, before Lincoln took office, and continued their criticisms throughout the war.[27]

Much of the liberal republicans' early condemnation of the spoils system and corruption focused on Lincoln's consideration of Simon Cameron of Pennsylvania for his cabinet. To the liberal republicans, Cameron's reputation for corruption symbolized all that was wrong with political parties' use of the spoils system. Bryant told Lincoln that "in the late election, the Republican Party, throughout the Union, struggled not only to overthrow the party that sought the extension of slavery, but also to secure a pure and virtuous administration," and warned that "if such men as Mr. Cameron are to compose the Cabinet . . . we shall not have succeeded in the second." Trumbull counseled Lincoln that Cameron was a "trading, unreliable politician" who would endanger the administration. Horace White became so upset at the thought of the corrupt Cameron in the administration that he proclaimed to a friend that "if Cameron goes into the Cabinet I go out of the party. I can stand a good deal of 'pizen' in a political way but I can't stand that." A few days later White reiterated to Trumbull that he could not belong to a party "which places thieves in charge of the most important public interests." Just a few months after Cameron became secretary of War, Murat Halstead publicly assailed him in the *Cincinnati Commercial.* While Halstead admitted that "no one ever suspected Cameron of honesty," he insisted that Cameron had proven himself so incompetent and corrupt "it would be of greater advantage to the country than to gain a battle, to have Cameron kicked out of the Cabinet."[28]

As the Civil War progressed, the liberal republicans continued to assault their party's own use of the spoils system. Collector of the New York Custom House Hiram Barney was one of the few Republicans to take the no-party rhetoric seriously and not use the spoils system to reward faithful Republicans. His reward for such idealism was a flood of complaints from fellow Republicans wanting positions for their people and appeals to Lincoln that Barney be removed for ineffectual political judgment, which the Seward-Weed faction of the Republican Party in New York finally accomplished in 1864. Bryant's long-standing hatred of Seward, partly because of the corruption associated with him, increased his outrage over Barney's dismissal. Encouraged to write a letter to Lincoln on another matter, Bryant told his wife, "After I learned that he had appointed Simeon Draper, the old pipe-layer, Collector at New York, instead of Barney—and appointed him for the reason that he was an active electioneerer, I would not write the letter." Bryant explained to a friend, "I am so utterly disgusted with Lincoln's behavior that I cannot muster respectful terms in which to write to him." Lincoln's actions, though, were perfectly valid in the context of nineteenth-century party politics. Bryant's vehement denunciation of Barney's dismissal for political reasons, even considering that Bryant had recommended Barney's appointment in 1861, indicates a true refusal to accept the patronage system. Several months before Barney's dismissal Bryant had publicly supported a civil service reform bill in Congress. "This bill," proclaimed Bryant in the New York Evening Post, "would do away with what has become one of the most serious vices in our political life, the 'Spoils System.'" He warned that the civil service had become "through the circumstances of the present war, so vast as to be dangerous to the nation, if it should chance to fall into the hands of unscrupulous and wicked men."[29]

The liberal republicans also attacked directly the corruption often associated with the patronage system. Halstead privately complained that Lincoln "is opposed to stealing, but can't see the stealing that is done. I use the mildest phrase when I say he is a weak, miserably weak man." Edwin Godkin confessed to Frederick Law Olmsted, "I am sorry to say I [am] perfectly satisfied the leading republican politicians are worse than the democrats, inasmuch as they are fully as corrupt while making far more pretensions to honesty." Some liberal republicans even publicly charged their party with corruption. During a trial, David Dudley Field—an ex-Democrat—characterized fellow Republican Thurlow Weed—an ex-Whig—as "a leader of that band of profligate men who surround and disgrace Congress, the Legislature and the Common Council, seeking grants of franchise, lands, offices and jobs; corrupting, bribing, soliciting, misleading; living upon the country; public plunderers." Soon after the Republicans took control of the federal government White contended in the

Chicago Tribune that the "tone of morality" was "considerably lower" than it
had been before and that "the frauds and attempted frauds in the treasury . . .
came so fast and from such unexpected quarters, that one is bewildered in con-
templating them." The Republicans regularly attacked corruption and the
spoils system, but usually only noticed the sleaze of Democrats or dissident
Republicans. Most politicians recognized that the spoils system and some corruption were necessary to maintain organized political parties in mid-
nineteenth-century America, so Republican leaders whitewashed their own party's corruption for the sake of unity. Some of the liberal republicans, though,
refused to remain silent for the sake of party unity and assailed their own party
for corruption and use of the spoils system, an indication they took these issues
seriously and possessed different expectations for political parties.[30]

The *Springfield Republican* consistently demonstrated its independent attitude toward political parties throughout the Civil War. With the Union war
effort stagnant in late 1861, the newspaper wondered why people were criticizing it for printing editorials disapproving of how the Lincoln administration
was prosecuting the war: "Nor can we comprehend the notion that the active
and devoted support of the government in its war upon the rebels requires a
man to endorse and praise every act of the administration, or to keep silence
where he cannot approve." Almost two years later the *Republican* was still
defending its outspokenness during the middle of the war, insisting, "A party
is not an end, but a means. It is not something to be served, but it is something
to serve with." On the day before Lee surrendered to Grant at Appomattox, the
newspaper published a long editorial on what loyalty to party and country
meant. According to the *Republican*, "Frauds are endured, thefts are covered
up, all sorts of public criminals are systematically whitewashed—and all
because of this absurd idea that the true way to support a party is to maintain
the infallibility of all its leaders and office holders." The newspaper explained,
"The true idea of loyalty to party, on the contrary, requires the more relentless
exposure and condemnation of the faults and crimes of its representatives."
With friends like the *Republican*, the party's leaders hardly needed the Democrats to criticize them.[31]

*   *   *

The liberal republicans' resistance to Republican Party orthodoxy included
opposition to many of the party's economic policies. In an attempt to broaden
their base of support, former Whigs expanded the Republican platform in
1860 to include planks advocating "immediate and efficient aid" in the construction of a Pacific railroad, and protective tariffs. Secession left the Republicans in control of Congress and able to implement their economic agenda. In
addition, the demands of the Civil War soon forced the Republicans to confront

the nation's inadequate tax system and the shortage of specie by expanding the government's role in the economy. During the first Civil War Congress the Republicans passed such economic legislation as the Union Pacific Railroad Act and the Legal Tender Act. Many Republicans with a Whig background supported the economic legislation for ideological reasons, as they sought a more activist state involved with the economy. Other Republicans, principally those of Democratic origins, disliked the legislation, but supported it as a war or party measure. The liberal republicans, however, appeared more concerned with their antebellum economic and constitutional principles. Even during the middle of a civil war they often opposed their own party's economic legislation.[32]

At the same time the United States was fighting a rebel army in the border state of Missouri in March 1862, Bryant's *New York Evening Post* disparaged the necessity of Congress sponsoring railroad construction. The *Post* cautioned readers that "the pressure brought to bear upon Congress to give aid to several railroads in the country is very great. In some cases a powerful lobby has been organized. Ten or fifteen millions are asked for by all the railroad petitioners before Congress, and every one asks aid upon the ground of 'military necessity.'" The paper insisted, "All of this peculiar kind of legislation will have to be postponed to a season of greater prosperity." Bryant was still concerned with the corruption associated with lobbyists and with maintaining fiscal discipline. A few months later Trumbull objected to parts of the Union Pacific Railroad Bill that he thought infringed on the rights of states. While in favor of using public land in the territories to build a transcontinental railroad, Trumbull argued that the federal government had no right to make internal improvements, inside of states. He told the Senate that the Democratic Party "was right, in my judgment, upon a great many questions. The old Democratic Party was very much averse to going into states to make improvements." A week later, Trumbull warned the Senate that he could not support the bill if it continued to undermine states' rights. Trumbull eventually voted for the Pacific Railroad Bill, but only after further attempts to protect the rights of states.[33]

The liberal republican opposition to the Union Pacific Railroad Bill was mild compared to their vehement and sustained denunciation of the Legal Tender Bill. With the Union running out of specie, Congress began to consider a Legal Tender Bill making the federally issued United States paper notes lawful money for all debts, public and private, throughout the nation. Leonard P. Curry's analysis shows that it would have been difficult, if not impossible, for the Union economy to continue functioning without passage of the Legal Tender Bill. While Congress considered the bill, liberal republicans declared it unnecessary, unconstitutional, immoral, and dangerous to the economy. Horace White, a longtime abolitionist, compared making paper money legal tender to slavery in

the *Chicago Tribune*. William Cullen Bryant repeatedly attacked making treasury notes legal tender in the *New York Evening Post*, asserting that "the arguments of those who insist that the measure is required by the necessity of the
times are utterly without foundation" and "that its constitutionality is so
doubtful that it has been denied by some of our ablest jurists." The *Post* predicted that passage of the Legal Tender Bill would lead to "the evil of debasing
the whole currency of the country, the impoverishment of persons of small
means, the responsibility of a measure that oppresses the poor, and the dreadful
collapse of credit and the wide-spread ruin which will be the closing act of the
drama." The *Post*'s editorials were not public posturing, as Bryant privately lobbied Senator Charles Sumner to vote against the bill, explaining that "the idea
of a necessity for the measure is the shallowest of delusions."[34]

Despite liberal republican pressure, the Republican-controlled Senate passed
the Legal Tender Bill. The continued failure of the liberal republicans to effect
policy indicates how little influence they had; this led to a growing sense of
frustration that, added to their principled party independence, made them even
more outspoken. Within days the liberal republicans again blasted the bill in
newspaper editorials. Samuel Bowles's *Springfield Republican* was the mildest,
contending that "the legal tender clause is injudicious, unconstitutional and
unnecessary, but it can be submitted to if such other measures are linked with
it as will preserve the notes from depreciation." White charged in the *Chicago
Tribune* that "it is facetiously called a 'war measure.' Rag-tag and bobtail are
now coming in as fast as possible." Once more the *Post* was the fiercest critic,
insisting, "That the constitution has been violated we have no manner of
doubt. That the necessity of making the notes of the Treasury a legal tender did
not exist, is to us quite clear. That the consequences of the bill will, in various
ways, be mischievous, is a corollary from these premises." Though Republican
senators overwhelmingly supported the bill—only three voted against it—the
Post promised "that we have given the names of those who voted for the legal-
tender clause, and of those who voted against it, for future reference." Bryant
wrote to Lincoln asking him to veto the legal-tender legislation, but the president signed it into law.[35]

The liberal republicans continued their fight against the legal-tender clause
and Greenbacks throughout the war. With the Union war effort bogging down
and Lincoln's reelection in doubt in early July 1864, Edward Atkinson went to
Washington and lobbied against the use of paper currency to finance the war.
A week after Lincoln's reelection in 1864 and with the Civil War still raging,
Charles Francis Adams Jr. wrote to his father that "the management of our
finances now seems to me not only the greatest but the most inviting field for
usefulness which this country affords." In a series of letters he explained, "The

time has come for at least the enunciation of correct principles. A return to a specie basis for our expenditures is of course the end sought for." Even in an era of ideological politics and political flexibility, the liberal republicans' dogged commitment to principle and lack of party discipline during a civil war was extreme.[36]

The liberal republicans publicly opposed some of their own party's economic policies in newspapers such as the *New York Evening Post* and the *Springfield Republican*. Their development of an independent press during the Civil War era challenged the very nature of the political system. Before the war political parties had directly funded and operated the vast majority of newspapers. Independent newspapers were also affiliated with parties, and they engaged in public issues and were highly partisan, but they relied on circulation and advertising for revenue, giving them editorial independence. Independence did not mean political neutrality, but rather the lack of adamant party allegiance that other newspapers displayed, often for financial reasons. The *Post* and the *Republican* were among the few antebellum independent newspapers. Bowles declared the *Republican's* independence on February 3, 1855, proclaiming, "Whatever it has been in the past, no more shall its distinction be that of a partisan organ, blindly following the will of party and stupidly obeying its behests. It has its principles and purposes. But these are above mere party success." He predicted, "Whenever men and parties are stumbling blocks to the triumph of those principles, they will be as boldly opposed and denounced." Bryant, meanwhile, had shown a willingness to criticize his own party since the 1840s when he was an avowed Democrat, and that did not change during the war. When Lincoln complained to Bryant in the summer of 1864 that the *Post* was assailing him, Bryant responded that "it was not intended to proceed beyond the bounds of respectful criticism, such as the Evening Post, ever since I have had anything to do with it, has always permitted itself to use tow[ard] every successive administration of the government."[37]

Toward the end of the Civil War several liberal republicans in addition to Bowles and Bryant took control of formerly Republican newspapers and made them independent. Starting as reporters in the mid-1850s, Murat Halstead and Horace White earned reputations during the war for muckraking and for controversial stands. White regularly attacked the Republican cabinet, and Mark W. Summers has noted that Halstead's reports made "it clear that news mattered to him more than political apologia." By the end of the war Halstead and White owned and edited two of the most important papers in the country, the *Cincinnati Commercial* and the *Chicago Tribune,* respectively. Summers writes that for men like Halstead and White, "professional journalism backgrounds made them think differently of news than party shills might," and "the personal

pride of self-made men inclined them to go their own way in any case." The
Commercial had always been somewhat independent—once comparing fasci-
nation with party to original sin—but Halstead made the paper still more independent. He tried to insure that paying advertisers, let alone political parties,
could not influence its editorial policy. The masthead of the *Commercial* blazed,
"An Independent, but not a Non-partisan Newspaper." In contrast, the *Chicago
Tribune* had been one of the most reliable Republican papers until Horace
White took control in 1865 and made it the most powerful independent newspaper in the West. In the East, Edwin L. Godkin became editor of the new
weekly newspaper *The Nation* in early 1865 with the stipulation that he would
enjoy absolute editorial freedom. Born and raised in Ireland by English parents,
the thirty-four-year-old Godkin had enjoyed a successful career as a reporter,
working for the *London Daily Times* before emigrating to the United States in
1856 and writing for the *New York Times. The Nation* was his first opportunity
to run his own paper, and its prospectus announced, "The Nation will not be
the organ of any party, sect or body. It will, on the contrary, make an earnest
effort to bring to the discussion of political and social questions a really critical
spirit, and to wage war upon the vices of violence, exaggeration, and misrepresentation by which so much of the political writing of the day is marred."[38]

While it would be easy to dismiss the proclamations of Bowles or Godkin as
mere rhetoric, it was more than a pose. "Independence meant a readiness to
criticize one's own party," according to Mark W. Summers, and "by 1870 many
of the leading Republican 'independents' were going further still. They had
begun to question the very basis of politics, and . . . the right of politicians
to define the issues at all." The political independence liberal republicans had
demonstrated throughout the Civil War, from threatening to leave the Republican Party during the secession crisis to opposing their own party's legislation,
became explicit with the emergence of the independent press. Newspapers such
as the *Springfield Republican* and the *Chicago Tribune* were intended to provide
a check on political parties, making sure they conformed to liberal republican
expectations formed by decades of experience.[39]

*   *   *

This long record of dissent against Republican practices and policies provides
the necessary context for evaluating the liberal republicans' critique of parties
when they sought to seize control of the Republican Party in the late 1860s and
early 1870s, for without that context their statements can seem more self-
serving than they were. Some of their dissent reflected years of accumulated
frustration from not being able to enact their policies, but a significant portion
also came from longstanding principles and independence. Weeks after Schurz
led the Liberal Republican bolt in Missouri he insisted that "I have never been

one to look upon a party as a deity that has supernatural claims upon my vener-
ation," and he questioned the value of party discipline. As Schurz became more
estranged from the Republican hierarchy he argued that party discipline "is
enforced by continual appeals to mercenary motives, and by practices in their
very nature corrupting," and he criticized the Republicans for "that blind and
reckless party spirit which will complacently wink at and be ready to defend
any wrong when perpetrated by a friend, which it would most violently
denounce when merely attempted by a political opponent." By the spring of
1872 he declared that "if there be a party spirit abroad which so subjugates the
hearts of men that they welcome error and deception when the truth stands in
the way of party interest . . . then, sir, it is time for the despotism of party to
be broken." The tendency of historians has been to dismiss the liberal republican attitude toward political parties as a cynical means to rationalize their
movement, and some of their rhetoric certainly was situational. Their attacks
on party discipline did come at the same time that they were trying to undermine the leaders of the Republican Party, but their concept of party also culmi-
nated two decades of words and actions. The liberal republicans consciously
drew on their experiences since the founding of the Free Soil Party in 1848 to
articulate a long-held vision of political parties.[40]

The liberal republicans had lived in an atmosphere of constant party turmoil
and saw little reason for it to stop. Less than a year after the Civil War ended,
the *Cincinnati Commercial* ran a series of editorials discussing the possibility of
party rearrangement. According to the newspaper, "It would be strange indeed,
if such convulsions as this country has experienced within the last five years,
should not break in pieces the old political parties; and he must be of dull perception who does not see it going on." A month later the *Commercial* reiterated
its position: "We have stated that there will be a reorganization of Political parties, and that the NEW PARTIES that will come to pass will be formed according
to the vital issues before the country." The *Commercial* soon cited other newspapers to support its contention that the old party organizations were breaking
up. "Much is said in the public journals of a new political party, the fact being
generally recognized that out of the period of war giving rise to confusion and
singular complications of the present, will grow political organizations materially different from those of the past." Predicating new parties was not guessing,
insisted the *Commercial:* "There is more than the mere appreciation of the
probability of this result. There is a popular consciousness that something of
the kind is going on."[41]

References to their shared political past filled liberal republican speeches and
newspapers. As early as 1866 *The Nation* discussed the prospects of a third party
by analyzing the nation's political history. "The organization of a third party is

not an impossible task," explained the newspaper, for "the Anti-Masons, the Whigs, the Liberty party, the Free Soilers, the Know-Nothings, the Republicans, and the Unionists, were all third parties, some of which rose to great power." The *Chicago Tribune* insisted in 1870 that "the same necessity which in 1848 induced William C. Bryant and his journal, the New York Evening Post, to abandon the democratic party . . . now induces such leaders . . . to effect such a reconstruction and reorganization of the political parties." Analyzing events in 1871, the *Cincinnati Commercial* remarked, "We had incidents somewhat analogous to this at the time of the breaking up of the Whig party." Schurz would remark at the Liberal Republican Cincinnati Convention in 1872, "I recognize here the faces of some of the old guard who, in 1856 and 1860, rallied around the Republican flag." The liberal republicans' allusions to the Free Soil Party and the origins of the Republican Party were in part an effort to portray themselves as the true Republicans, compared to people like Grant who had been Democrats in the 1850s. They also referred to past party experiences, however, to explain their vision of political parties.[42]

The liberal republicans considered reform the central mission of political parties. *The Nation* contended, "The business of a party is not to exist simply and divide the offices, but to take positive and incessant action on a great variety of subjects." According to the *Cincinnati Commercial*, "Our doctrine is that under a Republican form of government there are two legitimate political parties—the party of the Administration and the party of the Opposition—that parties should have no other attachments than those naturally belonging to the friends and opponents of certain measures." Schurz declared, "Party! What more should it be than a mere engine to accomplish objects of public good?" He argued, "The best materials for progressive reforms, the true unselfish reformatory spirit; as well as the healthiest impulses of individual independence, are still to be found among the elements out of which the Republican party is formed." The *Springfield Republican* explained that reform was the basis of the Republican Party, that it "was founded to be a party of progress; to advocate and exemplify a higher political morality than it found in vogue among existing organizations: to be a wholesome and quickening leaven in the republic."[43]

Power, according to the liberal republicans, eventually corrupted all political parties. The call for the 1872 Cincinnati Convention proclaimed, "All parties become corrupt; all parties sacrifice public welfare to retain power." Cox wrote to Schurz, "Ambiguities and avoidance of issues of principle are the life of decaying parties." The Republican Party was no exception. Schurz lamented, "The Republican party has not escaped the fate of all other parties who grow very strong, and are very long in the almost unlimited enjoyment of authority.

The opportunities of the war developed a spirit of jobbery and corruption, which to a dangerous degree, has pervaded our political organism." The *Springfield Republican* agreed that the Civil War had changed the Republican Party: "The war imposed new duties upon it, and also materially changed its character and composition. . . . It has been a fiery ordeal for the republican party,—one that has left deep scars if not fatal wounds. The real or supposed necessities of the war accustomed it to doubtful exertions of power, and to something very like a contempt for constitutional checks and written laws." The newspaper warned that "the republican party, under its present leadership and control, is submitting to the same influences that gained possession of the democratic party, and brought it through corruption to ruin." Trumbull told the Senate that "the Republican Party can only maintain its ascendancy and ought only maintain its ascendancy by being a party of purity, of honesty, of fidelity to the Constitution; and when it becomes a mere spoils party, and is used to cover up frauds and dishonesty, it will soon receive the condemnation of an indignant people."[44]

The liberal republicans expected Republican voters to leave the party if it deviated from its reform origins. Schurz contended, "It is not only desirable but indispensable that a healthy spirit of individual independence and self-criticism inside of political parties be encouraged and developed, even at the expense of party discipline." He predicted back in 1868, "the masses of the Republican Party are now, as they always were, governed by strong moral impulses. They honestly want to do right. They will abandon the party than by a blind support encourage it to go wrong." The liberal republicans based their assumptions of voter behavior on past experience. The *Cincinnati Commercial* warned, "The American people have shown themselves too independent of party or organization and machinery to justify the belief that they will be true to any party which has proved false to itself." Another time the paper cautioned that "the party whip was a very useful instrument of discipline a quarter of a century ago when it was considered almost as serious to lose caste with one's party as to lose it in the church," but now "the party is no longer the prime consideration." The political upheaval of the last two decades gave credence to the liberal republicans' expectations for voter independence, yet *The Nation* was not as sanguine in 1866: "No one can be more averse to the common subservience of Americans to party leaders and party spirit than we are," declared the newspaper, and "it is to be desired that the American people may grow more and more independent of party." A few years later the *The Nation* reminded it readers, "Treachery to party is the very life and soul of political improvement—all new and progressive parties being made up of traitors and 'deserters' from older camps; as, for instance, the Republican organization itself, which is nothing else than a collection of unfaithful Whigs, Democrats, and Free Soilers." Voter movement was not just a part of the political process; liberal republicans considered "treachery to party" beneficial to politics.[45]

The liberal republicans still perceived a flexible political environment in the early 1870s that would lend itself to voter movement. They thought that one of the few things holding the Republican Party together was the Democratic Party. According to the *Springfield Republican*, "The very existence of the democratic organization is an occasion of offense and menace to the Republican party," and "so long as this offense and menace continue, so long, practically, the republican party is likely to maintain itself in unity." The Democratic Party's New Departure in the 1860s—their reaching out to moderates and trying to recover from association with the secessionist South—seemed to indicate its weakness. When prominent Democrats began speculating about not running a national ticket in 1872, the liberal republicans rejoiced. "The democratic party has been an unconscionable while in dying," exclaimed the *Republican*, "but the final hour seems to have come." The *Cincinnati Commercial* insisted, "The restoration of the Democratic party to power is utterly impossible." Even in private, liberal republicans such as Cox discussed "the new crystallization of parties."[46]

For decades those who became liberal republicans had conceived of political parties as temporary reform organizations and had acted on these convictions during an era of political flexibility. In the 1840s antislavery principles led them to leave established parties and create the Free Soil Party. In the 1850s they clung to their reform principles in a political maelstrom that saw the destruction of the Free Soil and Whig parties, the flash of nativist parties, and the emergence of a Republican Party dedicated to containing slavery. During the Civil War, the liberal republicans practiced the nonpartisanship many preached, maintaining their independence and fighting over principle with their own party in the midst of a national crisis. During the late 1860s and early 1870s they continued to see political parties as temporary reform organizations in a politically flexible system. The liberal republican movement's attempt to reorganize the political parties to advance reform fit with their experiences since 1848. Analyzing the situation in 1871, David Wells concluded, "It is essentially the same as the old free soil movement."[47]

3   Preserving the Republic
     while Defeating the Slave
     Power, 1848–1865

For two decades, the men who would create the liberal republican movement were in the vanguard of the antislavery fight. As noted in chapter
2, many of them had belonged to the short-lived Free Soil Party, including Free Soil vice-presidential candidate Charles Francis Adams, and they had
been instrumental in forming the subsequent antislavery party, the Republicans, in the mid-1850s. Some of the liberal republicans had found political parties too slow in attacking slavery and took more radical steps. In 1856 twenty-
nine-year-old Edward Atkinson helped raise over a thousand dollars to equip
John Brown with rifles and ammunition; that same year, twenty-two-year-old
Horace White served as assistant secretary for the Chicago branch of the
National Kansas Committee, which armed three hundred men sent to defend
the free-state Topeka government. Their struggle against slavery put the liberal
republicans in the minority during much of the Civil War era, and they often
faced political and personal repercussions. Adams, the son and grandson of
presidents, lost much of his influence in Massachusetts politics during the early
1850s because of his unwillingness to compromise Free Soil principles. William
Cullen Bryant's antislavery activities hurt his literary career, as Southern editors
refused to print favorable notices about his work.[1]

While many of the liberal republicans opposed slavery for the ethical and
religious reasons common to abolitionists, the majority saw slavery primarily as
a threat to the survival of republican government in the United States. During a
campaign speech for Ulysses S. Grant in 1868, Carl Schurz would explain that
the Civil War came about because "in the South there existed a peculiar interest
and institution—namely, slavery and the aristocratic class government inseparable from involuntary labor, which in its very nature was antagonistic to the
fundamental principles upon which our democratic system of government
rests." Once the Civil War began, the liberal republicans continued to agitate
against slavery. During the war Atkinson became secretary of the New England
Freedmen's Aid Society, which assisted recently freed slaves in South Carolina.
Both Charles Francis Adams Jr. and William M. Grosvenor commanded African American regiments. Lyman Trumbull wrote the Thirteenth Amendment
abolishing slavery. Despite the liberal republicans' commitment to ending slavery, however, and their even stronger dedication to preserving the Union, they

demonstrated reluctance to support the Republican Party's war measures, many of which entailed enlarging the federal government and centralizing power in Washington. Traditional republicanism was a primary force in shaping the liberal republicans' thoughts and actions throughout their two-decades-long struggle to end slavery.[2]

Charles Francis Adams addressed the crowd on the first day of the 1848 Free Soil Convention. He described the coming presidential election "as a contest between truth and falsehood, between the principle of Liberty and the rule of slavery," and insisted that "the question now before us is one, which involves the proposition whether we shall adhere to the solemn principles of the Declaration of Independence; whether we shall deduce government from the consent of the governed." The crowd, which included several future liberal republicans, responded "Yes, yes, that's the question." The issue on which Adams and his fellow Free Soilers agreed was that slaveowners, while only a minority of the population, essentially controlled the federal government. By means of the three-fifths clause in the Constitution—the stipulation that every slave counted as three-fifths of a person in determining representation in Congress—and other intricacies of the antebellum political system, slaveowners held disproportionate power in the United States government, and they used this power to protect slavery. Adams and other Free Soilers considered this "Slave Power" aggressive and tyrannical, willing to destroy republican government in order to preserve the institution of slavery. Though the Free Soil Party was crushed at the polls in 1848, Edward Atkinson wrote to a friend weeks after the election, "I hope and believe that southern domination is at an end. The North is discovered!!"[3]

The North, or more precisely the Republican Party, did eventually discover the idea of the Slave Power in fighting against the South and slavery. Michael F. Holt explains that the "identification of the enemy as the 'Slave Power' had profound ideological ramifications with the electorate because Americans had believed since the era of the American Revolution that power in any form was the mortal enemy of republicanism." The Slave Power argument became so central to the Republican Party that, according to Holt, "often Republicans spoke of saving the nation and its republican principles," and "endless variations on this theme of the Slave Power's threat to Northerners' own liberties and self-government could be quoted from both the public statements and private correspondence of Republicans between 1856 and 1860." The span of years during which Holt finds numerous references to the Slave Power is important; William E. Gienapp observes that "in 1856 this [Slave Power] idea was inchoate and not accepted by all—or even most—Republicans, but in the next few years it would become a major Republican theme." The liberal republicans, however, had been stressing the danger of the Slave Power to republicanism since the 1840s and had brought the theme with them as they helped form the Republican Party in the mid-1850s. They were among the earliest and most fervent believers that the Slave Power represented a clear and present danger to republican institutions.[4]

In 1850, the controversy over admitting California to the Union as a free state produced new outcries about the Slave Power. Even though a majority of Californians and Northerners wanted the state in the Union, Southern congressmen opposed its admittance, as this would disrupt the balance between free and slave states. John C. Calhoun, the senior senator from South Carolina, complained that trying to force California's admittance as a free state was an example of the predominance of Northern influence in the government and its aggression toward the South. William Cullen Bryant, one of the founders of the Free Soil Party, responded to these charges with a detailed explication of the Slave Power in the *New York Evening Post* over the next eighteen months. Directly addressing Calhoun, the *Post* insisted, "It seems to us, on the contrary, that . . . the slaveholders of the south, have everything in their own way. They rule in the great national election of President. . . . They rule in the United States Senate. . . . They rule in the House of Representatives." Several months later the paper ran another editorial entitled "Comparative Political Power of the Slave and Free States." According to the *Post*, "The slave states, notwithstanding the smallness of their population, have an equal representation with the free states in the Senate, and in the House of Representatives, the slaves, though they have otherwise no political existence, are represented as well as their masters." The argument that the South, and particularly slaveholders, held a disproportionate amount of power in the national government was central to the Slave Power thesis. A year later the *Post* argued that the Slave Power's "policy of supporting its interests by strange process of law, imitated from the practice of the arbitrary governments of Europe" was a direct threat to republican government.[5]

Bryant also perceived perils to republican institutions other than slavery. In the spring of 1850 he reviewed the editorial positions of the *Post* since he had taken charge of the paper in 1826. While insisting with pride that "it is not long since we were nearly alone in protesting the acquisition of territory for the purpose of extending the area of slavery," Bryant also asserted his paper's long opposition to a strong central government. The *New York Evening Post*, he noted, "was one of the earliest champions of states rights against the encroachments of federal power," which included such intrusions as internal improvements and the national bank. In an editorial a year later the *Post* discussed the effects of centralization on republican institutions in greater detail. "Our only dangers, heretofore, have arisen from the assumption of federalism," the paper explained, "and if these can be corrected and restrained, there is no reason why the principle of our institutions could not be made to embrace the whole world. Indeed, it is not enthusiastic to look forward to the time when, in the development of civilization, the nations of the earth will form one grand republic." The *Post* warned, though, of the threat to republican government if the urges toward a centralized government were not checked. Remove all local government to Washington, asked the newspaper, and "What indescribable corruption is inevitable to such extensive patronage? What force but that of a standing army could execute such a complicated series of laws?" The answer was that "a system that leads to these results is nothing less than a despotism."[6]

The idea that corruption could lead to tyranny in a republic was common in mid-nineteenth-century America. "When most literate Americans considered the nature of power or republics' fragility," according to Mark W. Summers, "they turned to the views of their forefathers. For Adams and Jefferson . . . knew well that corruption was the inseparable kin of arbitrary power." He explains that "to them, corruption seemed to menace free institutions, as would-be tyrants used public depravity to achieve their ends." The liberal republicans, many of whom had classical educations and several of whom were direct descendants of John Adams, knew well the threat corruption historically posed to republican institutions. Four of the six newspapers that Summers identifies as particularly concerned with corruption in the 1850s—the *New York Evening Post,* the *Cincinnati Commercial,* the *Springfield Republican,* and the *Chicago Tribune*—became liberal republican organs. The *Post,* for instance, regularly ran editorials about politics in Washington with headlines such as "Robbery and Corruption" and "Official Corruption Getting Common Place." On one occasion the paper connected corruption to the risk of tyranny in an editorial about the U S. Navy's transporting of merchandise across the Atlantic for private individuals: "We have condemned it as an illegal assumption of power . . . and have shown that by this unauthorized act of an Executive officer, or of the administration, the public treasury has incurred and paid heavy charges." Around the same time the *Post* announced a more direct military threat to republican government. "It will perhaps be news to our readers," suggested the paper, "to hear that the constitution of California has been framed and adopted under military coercion."[7]

Corruption in the antebellum period was not just a specter the liberal republicans conjured up for political purposes. Summers has discovered that "there *was* corruption, a good deal of it, and though it was more present in cities than in the countryside and in the North far more than in the South, it could be found virtually everywhere." Of course, the vast majority of the liberal republi-

cans lived in Northern cities, and thus witnessed the greatest amount of antebellum corruption. One source of the problem was the government civil
service, controlled by what was known at the time as the patronage or spoils
system. Civil service jobs were considered the spoils of political victory; after
each election the current job holders were regularly fired and the newly elected
politicians' friends and family found employment on the government payroll.
During political campaigns government workers were expected to contribute
money and time to secure the reelection of their patrons. Most reformers of the
time, including the liberal republicans, found the system odious, and the Free
Soil platform in 1848 had called for civil service reform. In the antebellum
period, however, the federal government was small, employing only about
20,000 people. While it was corrupt, the patronage system was not yet a major
source of corruption.[8]

Most of the corruption the liberal republicans perceived before the war centered on politicians allowing others to inappropriately influence their votes.
Some of this took the form of Northern politicians voting for proslavery positions in the hope of currying Southern favor and thus advancing their careers.
This danger was part of what liberal republicans referred to when they discussed the Slave Power. Economic legislation proved another major opportunity for corruption, though opportunities at the federal level had decreased by
the 1850s, for little remained by then of Henry Clay's American System,
designed after the War of 1812 to stimulate the national economy. The federal
government had closed the national bank and ceased major internal improvements, and it had not directly taxed the American people for decades. The only
major economic legislation regularly considered by the antebellum federal government was tariff policy. Tariff legislation habitually led to the corruption the
liberal republicans feared; Robert H. Wiebe describes how the "process in each
case resembled a free-for-all with countless interests grabbing what they could
until the money had disappeared or the gamut of tariff schedules had been
run." Protective tariffs—designed to protect domestic industries from foreign
competition, with rates higher than those designed merely to raise revenue—
were placed only on specific goods, and thus raised the stakes both for lobbying
and for the ensuing corruption.[9]

Bryant had worried for years about the effect of protective tariffs and had
advocated free trade since the early 1830s. He considered protective tariffs a
form of special legislation that enriched a few at the expense of the many and
corrupted the entire government. An 1851 *New York Evening Post* editorial
explained, "There is, on the one side, the general interest of the masses, the
natural right of a free citizen, against a narrow sectional interest of a monopoly
on the other. But that monopoly has a direct and tangible sympathy with the

law makers." Bryant worried that the legislative process creating tariff bills would become mere bargaining sessions, with lobbyists paying off politicians. In another editorial he contended that protective tariffs created "a system of venality and corruption scarcely less odious, and scarcely less widely extended, than that of which the Bank of the United States was the parent." Part of the problem was that the enforcement of protective tariffs required more customs officers, which increased the scope of the corrupting spoils system. Another *Post* editorial stated, "We may hope soon to see the beginning of a reform in the revenue laws, which will not stop until it shall have abolished the whole patronage which the government derives from the Custom House." Even if protective tariffs could be created and enforced without corruption, Bryant still saw them as a threat to republican government. Yet another editorial proclaimed, "Whatever laws grant particular privileges to individuals from which the rest of the community are excluded . . . are of the very nature absolutism. The very method in which we collect our revenue encourages a tendency to absolutism . . . and our representatives parcel it out and squander it almost without responsibility." Protective tariffs embodied one of the primary concerns of the founders of the republic—that factions would fight over the spoils of government and corrupt its republican institutions.[10]

At the end of an editorial against protective tariffs Bryant warned, "Absolutism is a distemper which is constantly breaking out in the body politic, and is scarce ever healed in one part before it makes its appearance in another." From the mid-1840s, slavery was the form of absolutism that appeared to break out most often. After the Compromise of 1850—which included a strong fugitive slave law in exchange for California being admitted to the Union as a free state—the next major controversy concerning slavery occurred in 1854, when Democratic Senator Stephen A. Douglas of Illinois proposed a bill to organize territorial governments for Kansas and Nebraska. To secure support for the bill—and a future presidential bid—Douglas acquiesced to Southern demands that the territories be opened to slavery, proposing that the settlers be allowed to decide whether these areas would become free or slave states. The Kansas-Nebraska Bill outraged many Northerners, as it overturned the Missouri Compromise of 1820 that had prohibited slavery in those territories. Antislavery advocates charged that this was another example of the Slave Power subverting the nation's republican institutions, for how could a republican form of government work if a minority could alter for their own selfish ends compromises that had been agreed upon by the majority?[11]

The liberal republicans led the chorus of Northern outrage against the Kansas-Nebraska Bill. Samuel Bowles's *Springfield Republican* contended, "It makes the government of the great Republic of the World an engine for the strengthening and advancement of the worst sort of human slavery. It is legislation against the spirit of the age, against the spirit of republicanism." The *New York Evening Post* argued, "The admission of slavery into Nebraska is the preparation for yet other measures having in view the aggrandizement of the slave power." In Illinois Horace White called a supporter of the bill a "Doughface," an epitaph used for weak-willed Northerners who helped the Southern Slave Power. Despite the fierce opposition of liberal republicans and many other Northerners, Douglas convinced enough Northern Democrats to vote with the South to pass the Kansas-Nebraska Bill. Just a few months after the bill passed, Carl Schurz wrote to a former professor of his in Germany that he had decided there could now be no compromise with slavery. "It is not the philanthropic side of the question which has brought me to this conclusion, but the direct and indirect effect of the system upon the whole Government of the United States, the aristocratic character of Southern society, the demoralising influence of the slave-power upon politicians of the North."[12]

While stirring up protests throughout the North, the Kansas-Nebraska Act also affected the political parties of the time. The Northern wing of the Democratic Party split evenly over the bill in the House of Representatives, with many protesting Douglas's leadership and some beginning to leave the party. The Whig Party, already weakened because of ethnic issues and the controversy over slavery, finally disintegrated in 1854, maintaining its organization in only a few states. Several new parties vied to fill the vacuum left by the Whigs in the North, including the anti-immigrant Know-Nothing Party. The Know-Nothings attracted widespread support, including that of many prominent future Republicans. Remarkably, the liberal republicans, though condemned by historians for being anti-immigrant, universally avoided the Know-Nothings. As a recent immigrant himself Carl Schurz predictably condemned the new party, but others also lashed out at it, including Samuel Bowles, who attacked the methods of the secretive organization, arguing in the *Springfield Republican* that "secret political organizations, in a Republican government, are in the last degree reprehensible." The liberal republicans helped organize the Republican Party, a coalition of ex-Whigs, anti–Nebraska Democrats, and Free Soilers united to oppose the expansion of slavery. Escalating violence in Kansas between pro- and antislavery forces increased the importance of the slavery issue and helped to establish the Republicans as the chief opponent of the Democrats by 1856.[13]

To broaden their base and avoid charges of being the "Black Republicans," members of the new party concentrated their arguments against slavery on the Slave Power. In a letter to an antislavery meeting in early 1856, William Cullen Bryant used the threat of the Slave Power to justify helping free-staters in Kansas, declaring, "I fully agree with you as to the importance of a combined effort to assert the rights of the great body of American citizens against the encroach-ments of an oligarchy—a class of proprietors who seek to subject other inter-ests, even the most sacred and dear[,] to their own." Referring to the fact that many of the Kansas antislavery advocates had come from the Northeast, he reminded people that "with the republics of old it was a matter of course to answer the calls of their colonies with instant sympathy and aid," and suggested organizing the entire region of the free states "into a great association for breaking up the conspiracy against the rights of our countrymen."[14]

Events during the next year seemed to confirm Republican concerns about the Slave Power. The caning of Charles Sumner by a South Carolina congress-man, the proslavery Lecompton Constitution proposed for Kansas, and the Dred Scott decision all became examples of how Southern slaveowners were undermining the liberties of white Northerners. To stir up the North, Republi-cans, including the liberal republicans, increasingly developed more in-depth explanations of how the Slave Power threatened republican institutions. In Bos-ton, the cradle of the American Revolution, Carl Schurz detailed the aggressions of the Southern slaveowners, insisting that "they speak of a republican form of government—they speak of democracy, but the despotic spirit of slavery and mastership pervades their whole life like a liquid poison." Interestingly, although during Reconstruction the liberal republicans would at times display impatience with uneducated Irish and African American voters, Schurz now argued that "it is an old dodge of the advocates of despotism throughout the world, that the people who are not experienced in self-government are not fit for the exercise of self-government, and must first be educated under the rule of a superior authority." To objections that the slaves were ignorant, Schurz replied, "There is no better schoolmaster in the world than self-government, independently exercised." He returned to the theme of the Slave Power in a later speech at Samuel Bowles' hometown of Springfield, Massachusetts, to demonstrate that Democratic leader Stephen Douglas did not understand the issue of slavery. "Dealing with slavery only as a matter of fact, and treating the natural rights of man and the relation between slavery and republican institu-tions as a matter of complete indifference," Schurz explained, "he is bound to demonstrate, that slavery never was seriously deemed inconsistent with liberty."[15]

The attacks on the Slave Power upset many white Southerners, of course, who started arguing that it was actually the Republicans who threatened the nation's republican institutions with their constant assault on the right of peo-ple to own and transport slave property. The cries of white Southerners led Charles Francis Adams to give a speech before Congress in 1860 to defend the necessity of the Republican Party, in which he provided one of the most thorough expositions of Republicans' perception of the Slave Power as a threat to liberty. He began with the standard charge that twenty of the ninety-eight Southern congressmen held so-called "slave seats" because, through the clause of the Constitution that allotted congressional representation for three-fifths the number of "persons not free," that was the portion of the Southern delegation that represented slaves. He portrayed the slaveowning interests as wielding even more power by arguing that every Southern congressman "derives a sufficient proportion of his political vigor" from slavery. With the constantly increasing number of slaves, Adams predicted that the Slave Power would only grow stronger, and concluded, "The imagination recoils from the idea of a Government, professing to be founded on human freedom, and yet containing within itself all the ramifications of a power capable of being as absolute as any oriental despotism." He proclaimed that the Southerners, though a minority of the population, already controlled a disproportionate share of the federal government.[16]

The next part of Adams' argument against the Slave Power was less common among Republicans. Unlike the liberal republicans, the majority of Republicans were former Whigs who had brought to the new party their economic agenda of internal improvements, a national bank, and a protective tariff. Discussing slavery as a commercial corporation worth an estimated $3.5 billion, Adams asked, "In comparison to this, what was the Bank of the United States? What is the Bank of England?" In the same vein—which must have been impressive coming from John Adams' grandson—he inquired, "Nay, what about the East India Company? The Complaint was made of the latter, that its members controlled a few venal boroughs in Parliament. But here the stockholders sit constantly 'by virtue' of their stock, in both Houses of Congress, in the Cabinet of the Executive, and on the bench of the highest judicial court." Compared to earlier commercial corporations, Adams declared, "I have observed nothing in the pages of history so skillfully adapted to the establishment of a stupendous oligarchy." He asked how it could be that those whose rights were affected by such a concentrated power as the institution of slavery did not have the right to organize. "Such a notion was not entertained when the case of a comparatively trifling moneyed corporation was in question, nor when the supposed ascendancy of insignificant manufacturing interests was thought to be alarming. How, then, can it be advanced in the face of a combination of wealth and political power in comparison with which the bank and the tariff were but as atoms in the creation?" Just months before Adams's speech, William Cullen Bryant had written in a private letter that manufacturers "are wealthy active and powerful—powerful through concert of action, and they have influenced even the politics of the federal government. . . . They have tyrannized over the majority with a protective tariff."[17]

The comparison of the Slave Power to banks or tariffs is significant for several reasons. First, it highlights how the liberal republicans differed in their origins from the majority of Republicans, who had come from the Whig Party with a nationalistic, probusiness economic agenda that embraced national banks and protective tariffs. In contrast, many of the liberal republicans had come to the Republican Party from the ranks of the Democrats and Free Soilers, parties that opposed many of the Whig economic ideas. While few Republicans at this time focused solely on economic issues, the liberal republican's willingness to use tariffs and banks as negative examples demonstrates fundamental differences between them and the majority of Republicans over economic policy and the role of the national government, issues that would later help spark the liberal republican movement. Second, the bank and tariff analogies demonstrate that even before the Civil War, the liberal republicans thought of slavery and economic issues as comparable and conceived of them in the same republican terms. This does not mean that they were less interested in slavery than other Republicans—far from it. Most of them had opposed slavery long before the vast majority of those who became Republicans, and many leaned toward the Radical wing of the party. Though national banks and protective tariffs could threaten republican institutions, the liberal republicans agreed that in 1860 the primary threat to the United States' republican form of government came from slavery.[18]

The *Springfield Republican* concentrated on the Slave Power during the 1860 presidential campaign, emphasizing its effect on the freedom of white Northerners in order to rally voters. Slaveowners, the paper argued, "claim the privilege of conducting the government in all the future, as they have in all the past, for their own benefit and in their own way." Responding to Southern threats that a Republican victory would lead to secession, the newspaper challenged its readers: "This sway, the most disgraceful and shameless of anything in the history of the government, must now be thrown off or else the Union will be dissolved. Let's try it! Are we forever to be governed by a slave-holding minority?" The test of throwing off the Southern domination would be useful no matter the result, according to the *Republican*, for "if the country can only exist under the rule of an oligarchy, let the fact be demonstrated at once, and let us change our institutions." Allusions to the threat posed by the Slave Power did not abate with Abraham Lincoln's victory in the fall of 1860, for Republicans used it to stiffen the resolve of Northerners during the secession crisis. Two days after South Carolina seceded from the Union, Horace White showed no inclination to compromise in the pages of the *Chicago Tribune*, insisting that "the present troubles have their origin in the arrogant assumptions of the Slavery Oligarchy." Directly appealing to the heritage of the American Revolution, he lectured readers that "we would be unworthy descendants of the founders of our government were we to suffer ourselves to be either bullied or coaxed into a violation of its spirit."[19]

Edward Atkinson likewise argued during the secession crisis that the North could not give in to the South without sacrificing the nation's republican institutions. In an elaborate article he explained how slavery had already made republican government in the South a farce. Working his way from Genesis through the Roman Republic to the American Revolution, Atkinson argued that republics depended upon educated and intelligent citizens. Upon reviewing social conditions in the South, he insisted, "Here, then, we come at once to the foundation of a policy and the cause of this struggle. Whether it will or no, it is the inevitable tendency of the Cotton dynasty to be opposed to general intelligence. It is opposed to that, then, without which a republic cannot hope to exist; it is opposed to and denies the whole results of two thousand years of experience." He then directly compared the pretensions of republican government in the South to the fall of the Roman Republic, writing that "on the intelligence of the mass of whites the South must rely for its republican permanence, as on their arms it must rely for its force; and here again, the words of Sismondi, written of falling Rome, seems applicable to the South." After quoting Sismondi on the disappearance of small farmers in the waning days of the Roman Republic, Atkinson declared that "the destruction of the republican form of government is, then, almost the necessary catastrophe." Threats to republicanism were not confined to the South, according to Atkinson, because slavery had infected the national government since its founding. He insisted, "What two thousand years ago was said of Rome applies to us:—'those abuses and corruptions which in time destroy a government are sown along with the very seeds and both grow together.'"[20]

The linkage of corruption to the Slave Power's tyrannical threats to republican government was common. Many liberal republicans argued that as a minority trying to preserve its power, slaveholders used corrupt means to control the federal government. Adams told Congress, "It is not to be concealed, that all over the country there is a well-defined impression that, for the sake of retaining power, corruption has been tolerated, if not actively encouraged." The *Springfield Republican* desired the Republicans to win in 1860 "so that the whole horde of corrupt officials at Washington may be swept by the board, and something of decency and purity introduced there." While some of the charges of corruption may have been mere political rhetoric, the liberal republicans expressed enough private concerns about corruption, often with regard to their own party, to suggest that some of it was a genuine concern. Carl Schurz wrote several letters to his wife in 1860 outlining how he planned to make "Relentless War on Corruption" his platform. He assured her, "I am going to convince the Republicans that my war on corruption was meant seriously and that, in this fight, no quarter will be given." William Cullen Bryant even wrote to President-elect Lincoln, reminding him that "in the late election, the Republican Party, throughout the Union, struggled not only to overthrow the party that sought the extension of slavery, but also to secure a pure and virtuous administration of the government." The challenge for Lincoln and the liberal republicans became how to fight a civil war against the tyrannical and corrupt Slave Power while maintaining the integrity of their republican institutions.[21]

*   *   *

The liberal republicans viewed the Civil War primarily as a contest to preserve the Union and republican government. "The primary object of the war is the restoration of the Union," declared the *Cincinnati Commercial* in 1862, and "involved inextricably with the restoration of the Union . . . is the preservation of our Republican form of Government." During the first year of the Civil War such was a common refrain for the *Commercial*, which on several other occasions argued that the war was for "the preservation of a Republican form of government" and that losing "would be fatal to our republican institutions." The *Springfield Republican* expressed similar sentiments in 1864, insisting that "we are fighting not only to save the Union, but to rescue the democratic idea, almost lost and subverted, and to make our governments and institutions henceforth and forever just, free, and republican, in fact and in spirit." The liberal republicans regularly discussed the Civil War as a continuation of their conflict with the aristocratic Slave Power and a test of republican institutions.[22]

The Confederate Army did not pose the only challenge to republican government. The liberal republicans universally advocated a vigorous war effort, but they often had qualms about what that entailed. They had traditionally opposed such extensions of federal power as the subsidizing of railroad construction, the creation of a banking system and national currency, and the protection of industry through tariffs. Though constantly concerned about centralization and corruption as threats to republican government, the liberal republicans reluctantly supported the expansion of presidential powers, a new tariff, a national currency, and military rule in the South as temporary war measures to preserve republican government from the immediate threat of secession. "Next to the overshadowing question whether or not the unity of the republic is to be maintained," warned the *Republican* in 1863, "there is nothing of greater interest or importance at present than the determination of the effect to be wrought by these commotions upon our constitution of government, and the ascertaining what changes or adaptations to our system, if any, are to be made in meeting the new exigencies that are upon us." The liberal republicans' discussion of the war in republican terms and their weariness of war measures foreshadowed their concerns for republican government after the Civil War.[23]

The liberal republicans continued their antebellum attacks on the Slave Power during the Civil War, arguing that it had caused the conflict, and that as long as it existed it would threaten republican government. In early 1862 the *Cincinnati Commercial* assumed that none would "deny that the institution of slavery has a marked effect upon the character of the people among whom it exists. Beyond a doubt its influence in the Southern States has been to degrade labor, and to establish castes among white men. It is therefore unfavorable to the growth of the principles by which a Republican form of Government must be sustained." Though in the midst of war, the paper rehashed the history of the Slave Power in great detail, explaining how Southerners had controlled the Democratic Party and the national government while only a minority. The *Commercial* described how "thus the few leading men of one section of the country and that the smallest, using slavery to keep the people subservient at home, and holding under two-thirds caucus rule and with the force given by discipline and directness of purpose, the machinery of the most powerful political party known in our history, became the rulers over the nation."[24]

Two years later the *Springfield Republican* offered a comparable indictment: "The people of the South . . . have taken pains to demonstrate to us that we cannot live in peace with slavery; that it is an element of discord so powerful as to be irreconcilable with the national safety. They have shown us by all possible means that its entire spirit is hostile to republican institutions." Like the *Commercial*, the *Republican* renewed the classic antebellum attacks on the Slave Power, charging that "they have brow-beaten our representatives in Congress, have corrupted our legislation, have fought free labor in our virgin territories, have destroyed the rights of free speech wherever they have had the power . . . all on the behalf of slavery." In an 1863 editorial the *Republican* also discussed the relationship between slavery and republican government as a theoretical issue, the newspaper insisting, "The question has often arisen whether a slave-holding community can properly be said to have a government republican in form." Unsurprisingly, it concluded that "experience has already been furnished of its hostility in spirit to our republicanism." In an editorial in May 1864, the paper argued that the long war has "been necessary for the utter exhaustion and the irremediable destruction of the slave power of the south" and that "it was absolutely necessary that the entire power of this oligarchy should be summoned into the field, and there forever defeated." By July 1864, with Grant besieging Richmond and Sherman a few miles away from Atlanta, the *Republican* rejoiced that with "the institution of slavery destroyed, its essentially despotic and aristocratic spirit will soon die out of society."[25]

While seeking to destroy the Slave Power, the liberal republicans did not want to diminish the concept of states' rights. Most Republicans agreed that the South had corrupted the notion of states' rights, but the liberal republicans were among the most aggressive in rhetoric and action to defend what they considered the proper boundaries of federal and state relations during the course of the Civil War. The *Springfield Republican* lectured that just because "a false notion of state rights has produced secession and the civil war, it does not follow that there is not a true doctrine of state rights. Much less does it follow that the true antidote for secession is centralization and the substantial annihilation of state sovereignties." The newspaper worried that "the natural tendency now is to vibrate to this extreme, and to make the federal government so strong as to absorb the power of the states," because "the distribution of power between the general and the local authorities is the peculiar characteristic of our republic." More than once during the course of the war, the *Republican* advocated the antebellum relationship between the states and federal government as the postbellum goal. In 1863 the newspaper argued, "The reestablishment of the old doctrine and fact of state rights and not the annihilation of all state rights, is the end to be sought," and again in 1864 it insisted that "the general government necessarily has much power in its hands in a time of war, but it does not follow that it will permanently arrogate to itself any of the rights belonging to the states." Lyman Trumbull put these states' rights sentiments into action. While willing to grant public lands for the building of the Pacific Railroad through federal territories, Trumbull repeatedly fought against federal intrusions in the states. The Republican senator explained that the Democratic Party "was right, in my opinion, upon a great many questions. The old Democratic Party was very much averse to going into States to make improvements." A weak central government reduced the danger of a tyrant threatening republican institutions. The liberal republicans' support of states' rights in the midst of the Civil War should make unsurprising their insistence on returning power to the Southern states during Reconstruction.[26]

Many liberal republicans saw the struggle to preserve the Union and destroy the Slave Power as a test of American republican institutions before the entire world. Less than a month after the Confederates fired on Fort Sumter, Samuel Bowles's *Springfield Republican* began an editorial explaining that "there was a time, and that not many months ago, when to the people of the United States and the world, a republic seemed the weakest of all forms of government." The paper lamented that during the secession crisis "it is not to be wondered at that Americans felt ashamed of their country, and learned to look upon republican institutions as a stupendous failure." The response to Fort Sumter, though, proved "the Strength of the Republic." According to the *Republican*, "No other form of government could have done what the American people have accomplished in twenty days." Two years later the *Republican* told its readers that "now the hour of trial has come, and the world is watching to see whether a republican is a strong or weak form of government." According to the paper foreign nations were "sneering at our republican institutions" and "have always said . . . there is not force enough in a republic to carry on a war; the people will rebel against authority and the republic will crumble into ruins." Samuel Bowles's paper emphatically replied, "A republic *will* stand the test."[27]

The struggle for republican government in America symbolized for the liberal republicans a larger, worldwide struggle to replace despotic forms of government with republican institutions. "The true test of prosperity in a republic is the elevation of the masses," began a long *Springfield Republican* editorial comparing labor in the South to the condition of the English working class. The newspaper found little difference between the masses of the South and of England, concluding that "such, then, is the benignant working of an aristocracy, whether among whites or mixed races, whether sheltered by a limited monarchy or tolerated beneath republican forms." Many in the Union felt little love for England during the Civil War, with the constant threat that the preeminent power in the world would recognize the Confederacy. While cotton and geopolitics contributed to England's interest in supporting the South, the *Cincinnati Commercial* thought antirepublicanism was the unifying force. "The existing harmony between the British Tories and the Copperheads and Traitors of America, regarding the questions arising out of the American rebellion and war has often been remarked. The common feeling which they indulge is that of a hostility to democratic institutions—to a republican form of government."[28]

The Slave Power, the Confederacy, and foreign nations, however, did not represent the only threats to republican government during the Civil War. The war effort required unprecedented levels of government power to organize a huge army, manage the economy, and maintain control during a civil war, and for many liberal republicans the means of war often conflicted with its ends. In 1863 the *Springfield Republican* discussed the tension inherent in giving the central government a great deal of power to fight a war to preserve republican institutions. "Are we thus tending towards centralization and the gathering of powers in the hands of the general government? No doubt we are. Shall we then soon be under a despotism? That is a matter not to be so quickly pronounced upon." The answer, according to the newspaper, was to win the war before the war measures themselves undermined republican government. The *Republican* concluded that with peace "will cease alike the occasion and the possibility of power so vested in the hands of any administration for the subversion of our liberties. *We must make the government strong quickly that it may not be strong too long.*" Throughout the Civil War liberal republicans demonstrated this ambivalence toward war measures, seeing them simultaneously as saviors and threats to the republic.[29]

Abraham Lincoln's actions in the first months of the war, most notably his suspension of the writ of habeas corpus, foreshadowed the extraordinary powers he would assume as commander in chief. Lincoln understood the extent of the power he was assuming in suspending the writ, but regarded this as an exception appropriate for a temporary state of emergency. The liberal republicans realized that the crisis of the Civil War required strong measures, but still felt conflicted about the president's possession of so much power. Lyman Trumbull walked this tightrope in the middle of 1861. While he introduced a bill giving generals the right to suspend the writ of habeas corpus, Trumbull expressed weariness with Lincoln's assumption of that power while Congress was out of session, telling the Senate, "I am disposed to give the necessary power to the Administration to suppress this rebellion; but I am not disposed to say that the Administration has unlimited power and can do what it pleases." He returned to the issue a year later, proclaiming, "I repudiate this whole doctrine of uncontrollable power in the president as dangerous to republican institutions."[30]

The attitude of the liberal republican press toward Lincoln's imposition of martial law and suspension of habeas corpus bordered on the schizophrenic. When Democrats complained in early 1863 that Lincoln was taking away their liberties, the *Cincinnati Commercial* responded that "those who are alarmists on the subject of the enormous powers vested by Congress in the Executive, are those who would view with complacency the utter overthrow of the Federal authority." The *Springfield Republican* similarly attacked the opposition, contending that "all the rigor that the government shows against it [the rebellion] is displayed against despotism and arbitrary power and in favor of freedom," and "it need not take long to conclude that our rights are not in danger at present." The newspaper demonstrated the partisan nature of its defense by arguing that "the perpetuity and soundness of our institutions are in far greater danger from popular passion and the violence of party conflict than from any direct ascendancy or usurpation on the part of our rulers." Despite aggressively defending Lincoln's actions, the *Republican* still acknowledged, "But may there still be danger if a military power is left long in the hands of a president? No doubt there might be."[31]

This fickleness toward Lincoln's expansion of presidential power continued throughout the Civil War. In October 1862 the *Springfield Republican* announced, "The last proclamation of the president, making martial law general over the country and suspending *habeas corpus* in regard to a certain class of offenses is very much misconceived, and in some cases maliciously misrepresented," and "We stand by him now." The "now" lasted little more than a month. While rejoicing in late November that finally "the government acts as if it meant to put down the rebellion," the newspaper insisted that "this matter of arbitrary arrest and confinement of accused and suspected persons has been overdone." It argued that "the cases must be few indeed where there is a necessity for arresting without explanation, imprisoning for a month, and then releasing without explanation. The process looks too despotic for a free government." The *Cincinnati Commercial* displayed a similar ambivalence, both defending and attacking Lincoln's actions in a November 1862 editorial. At first the newspaper insisted that only those "tainted with treason and sympathizing with traitors" had denounced "the action of the Administration, and construed what was a necessary act in defense of the national existence into a design to centralize power and restrict the liberties of the individual." It explained that "the peril, however, was extreme and a resort to extreme measures was conceded to be a vital necessity." By the middle of the editorial, though, the newspaper asked, "In what is this different from the Star Chamber?" and by the end concluded that there is "an assumption of powers not clearly delegated by the people, and exercised so blindly and so extraordinarily as to give the appearance of despotism." Even within the space of a single editorial, the liberal republican press could demonstrate both its understanding of the need for vigorous war measures and the fear that such measures could undermine republican government.[32]

All of the liberal republicans consistently agreed, at least, that too much power temporarily in the hands of the president was far preferable to the military gaining power. Trumbull approved of an 1861 bill to confiscate rebel property, but refused to endorse it "on the ground which has been advanced in some quarters, that in times of war or rebellion the military is superior to the civil power." He continued, "I warn my countrymen, who stand ready to tolerate almost any act done in good faith for the suppression of the rebellion, not to sanction usurpations of power which may hereafter become precedents for the destruction of constitutional liberty." The *New York Evening Post* likewise cautioned that "in times of war the greatest danger lurks in the tendency to military encroachments." Lincoln and Secretary of War Edwin M. Stanton deserved the "utmost credit" and "the gratitude of the whole nation," according to the newspaper, because of "their sedulous determination to keep the military power subordinate to the civil power." The *Springfield Republican* dealt with the issue in an editorial titled "The Army and Liberty." Acknowledging that some are "concerned lest the great military force now in the employ of the government should be used for purposes of despotism," the newspaper replied "undoubtedly there is a possibility of danger in this direction; but it is rather in the future than in the immediate present." The *Republican* argued that the best way to avoid the danger of military usurpation *"must be found in carrying the war vigorously and quickly through to a necessary termination,"* for if not, "We shall have to keep great armies on our frontiers, and be always ready for war. *That is precisely our danger,* so far as an army is concerned." Significantly, considering how the army would change after the Civil War, the *Republican* also stressed that the current army of citizen-soldiers was relatively safe compared to the professional armies of other nations. The conditional acceptance of military power to suppress the rebellion foreshadowed how quickly the liberal republicans' tolerance for the use of military power during Reconstruction would become strained.[33]

The war measure the liberal republicans had the least problem with was the emancipation of slaves in states that had seceded from the Union. According to Mark E. Neely Jr., Lincoln himself had to adjust his views of the Constitution to contemplate such an assumption of power as emancipation represented. Liberal republicans, though, had little trouble with emancipation, and most actually complained that the president was moving too slowly. The *Cincinnati Commercial*, it is true, constantly emphasized that the war was primarily about preserving the Union; it embraced emancipation only as a war measure. It must be remembered, however, that the newspaper was located on the border with Kentucky and its editor, Murat Halstead, lived further south than any other liberal republican editor. Henry Adams, while serving as his father's secretary in London and away from the rapidly shifting attitudes toward emancipation in the United States, also disapproved of those he considered "extreme Abolitionists"; what he wished to see was gradual emancipation. But the strong emancipationist positions of Carl Schurz, Edward Atkinson, and William Cullen Bryant were more typical of the liberal republicans. Schurz declared to Charles Sumner in the first year of the war that "we must proclaim the emancipation of the slaves." In 1862 Edward Atkinson wrote repeatedly about emancipation to a friend. One letter described his disappointment with Lincoln for not sustaining Union General David Hunter's action of freeing slaves in his military district. Another letter complained about General McClellan's incompetence, but astutely consoled that "as abolitionists, however, we gain by delay in the war." After Lincoln issued the Emancipation Proclamation in 1863, Bryant wanted more, asking a New York crowd, "Have we not suffered mischief enough from slavery without keeping it any longer?" In this one instance, at least, most of the liberal republicans embraced the expansion of Lincoln's presidential powers.[34]

Some of the war measures that most troubled the liberal republicans actually had little to do with Lincoln. The Civil War quickly strained the country's limited financial infrastructure, and this was primarily the responsibility of Congress to fix. At the beginning of the Civil War the federal government had few means to raise revenue or manage the economy, for the only national tax was a small tariff, and no federal reserve, national bank, or national currency existed. Resorting to the easiest option, the government started borrowing money through issuing bonds, but by early 1862 it had already borrowed millions of dollars, causing Union credit to waver and thus endangering the war effort. To preserve the Union's economic ability to continue the war, Republicans in Congress pushed through a series of bills creating the first national currency and making it legal tender. The bills' sponsors repeatedly referred to these as "war measures," though many former Whigs had advocated such legislation for years. According to Michael F. Holt, "Only the exigencies of the Civil War would force Republicans with Democratic antecedents to acquiesce in essentially Whiggish Republican banking and monetary policies." With few liberal republicans coming from the Whig ranks, most opposed the currency legislation on principle, and many refused to acquiesce to it even as a war measure.[35]

Horace White compared the Legal Tender Bill to slavery, proclaiming, "If the present war shall but teach the American people the double lesson that they cannot make chattels of human beings, and they cannot make money out of paper, it shall be cheap at any price." William Cullen Bryant, a longtime hard-money advocate, argued that through such legislation the federal government was usurping powers it was never meant to possess. "It is clear to me," he wrote in a confidential letter to Senator Charles Sumner, "that the framers of the constitution never meant to confer upon the federal government the right of issuing Treasury notes at all, and the reason was that they meant to tie its hands from making them a legal tender." Bryant's insistence that the Constitution did not give the federal government any right whatsoever to issue treasury notes was extreme even for a former Democrat, as before the war Democratic administrations had a long history of issuing non-legal-tender treasury notes. Despite regular protests in the *New York Evening Post* that the Legal Tender Bill was an "evil," Congress passed the monetary legislation. Bryant was so worried about the monetary situation that just after the Army of the Potomac suffered a bloody repulse at Cold Harbor that severely depressed Northern morale, he confided to a close friend that "my greatest fears arise from the state of the currency."[36]

Even those liberal republicans who supported the monetary legislation emphasized that it was merely a temporary war measure. Samuel Bowles, one of the few former Whigs in the liberal republican movement, wrote in the *Springfield Republican* that "our financial system, if it can be called a system, is a series of temporary expedients, calculated and adapted to a short war." Early in the war Murat Halstead expressed concern in the *Cincinnati Commercial* that allowing the federal government to issue currency might plant "the seed of a power in the government that may be easily debased to the worst uses and become a fearful oppressor of the political rights of the people." A longtime ally of Ohio's favorite son, Treasury Secretary Salmon P. Chase, Halstead accepted what he considered a dangerous increase in the power of the central government when the failure of Union credit forced Chase to support the Legal Tender Bill. Still, Halstead always referred to the bill as a temporary war measure. In a far from ringing endorsement, the *Commercial* argued "It is plain that the bill must be passed. It is clearly the best thing that can be done. There is no help for it." On other occasions the paper assured readers that "it is a financial necessity" and a "financial policy which the government has been compelled to adopt."[37]

Financial necessity also helped lead the Union to adopt higher tariffs. Whigs had long advocated high tariffs as a means to protect home industries, and many historians consider the tariffs enacted by the Republicans during the war as an implementation of Whig polices. The liberal republicans, though, reacted to higher tariffs just as they had to the Legal Tender Bill. The *Cincinnati Commercial* made specific reference to "the War Tariff," suggesting that this also was a temporary war measure. The newspaper even deemed the advocates of protective tariffs to be enemies just slightly better than the Confederates in 1861, declaring that "as soon as we are through with the Southern rebels we must conquer the thick-headed Tariffites." Few in Congress listened to the *Commercial*, for by 1865 the nation was committed to high tariffs and federal promotion of industry.[38]

Unlike the majority of Republicans, the liberal republicans did not agree that the federal government should use tariffs, even during wartime, to protect industry. The *Springfield Republican* complained in late 1864 that "the high tariff is gradually killing the goose that lays the golden egg," as protective tariffs became so high that they started to reduce both imports and revenue. The newspaper predicted, "It will probably be found necessary to make important changes in the present system," but lamented, "A radical change is hardly possible now." A few months later the paper suggested that in the present crisis Congress should "adjust the tariff to the highest revenue figures"—code for eliminating the protective elements of the tariffs and designing them to maximizing revenue. The *New York Evening Post*, a longtime advocate of free trade under William Cullen Bryant, suggested in early 1865 that a means of encouraging the South to surrender would be making free-trade principles the permanent policy of the nation. Many liberal republicans had long objected to protective tariffs on economic grounds, but they also considered it an abuse of power for Congress to decide which industries the government would protect and which would be allowed to struggle on their own.[39]

Creating a central government with too much power was just one threat to republican institutions inherent in the war measures, according to the liberal republicans. While declarations of martial law or protective tariffs clearly increased the federal government's power, they also worried that such measures could destroy republican institutions through rampant corruption. The protective tariff and the 1862 Legal Tender Act, for instance, were pieces of legislation that favored some citizens over others and encouraged businessmen to lobby politicians. The *Cincinnati Commercial* described how the new taxes had led to a situation in which "every class of person, capable of working out special legislation for their relief and aggrandizement, at the expense of the whole people, are encouraged to become representatives in the lobby." The *New York Evening Post* likewise portrayed unsympathetically those favoring the Legal Tender Bill, explaining, "These are the speculating gentry—men whose brains are teeming with projects to make their own fortunes at the public expense." The growth of the federal government also exponentially increased the number of civil service jobs available in the spoils system, making patronage a major source both of party power and corruption. Just months after Lincoln was elected to his first term as president, as Republicans besieged the new administration for jobs, the *Springfield Republican* complained that "it is, therefore, doubly humiliating and sad that hardly ever before in the history of the country has there been such a strife for office as now; for it shows how strongly the love of office has found its way into the American mind, and how many men there are who are ready to sacrifice their business, their independence, and themselves, for a share in the spoils of political victory." Throughout the nineteenth century newspapers regularly criticized political parties for corruption, but these are instances of Republican newspapers attacking their own party.[40]

In liberal republican newspapers the discussion of corruption continued throughout the entire Civil War. The *Cincinnati Commercial* and the *Springfield Republican* regularly recounted "the enormity of the corruption and profligacy which is patent in the conduct of the war," with editorials telling tales of the "Public Robberies" and "frauds upon the government." The *Commercial* did not consider corruption a trivial matter, at one time suggesting the "relentless pursuit and deadly punishment of the public robbers." Liberal republicans worried about corruption because it destroyed the virtue necessary for republican government to function. "The time has come for Congress to come up to the stern work of vigilantly, rigidly and constantly scrutinizing appropriations," according to the *Commercial,* so as to put "a check upon the tendency to individual extravagance which is so closely associated with a profuse expenditure of public money." The *Republican* hoped that perhaps the virtue of the citizens would stiffen the resolve of those in government. "When presidents and cabinets, camp and Congress fail us," proclaimed the newspaper, in a classic republican trope, "we must go back of them to the private citizens of the Republic—to the men and women at home, where virtue dwells and is fostered, and to whom and whose virtue lies the last and only appeal." By the end of the war, however, the *Republican* had begun doubting that virtue existed anywhere in the nation. After discussing the rise of drunkenness, gambling, and debauchery during the war, the newspaper insisted, "It is time to make a stand against the evils that threaten our destruction. . . . Social corruption will do us more injury than the war."[41]

After more than a decade of fencing with the South over slavery, the beginning of the Civil War finally allowed the liberal republicans to directly fight the threat slavery posed to republican government. The Civil War posed countless challenges to the Union, ranging from finding enough soldiers and equipping the army, to developing a strategy to beat the Confederacy, to energizing the economy. In retrospect, *The Nation* asserted, "Under the pressure of a terrible danger and of a supposed necessity, one half of the nation cheerfully acquiesced in usurpations of power by Mr. Lincoln, which is now settled were justified by no law." To the liberal republicans, however, the war measures were a double-edged sword, one that allowed them to strike at slavery and the rebellion that endangered republican government, but that also, by creating a powerful central government and increasing opportunities for corruption, threatened the republican institutions they were meant to preserve.[42]

4

The Liberal Republican Dilemma over Reconstruction, 1865–1868

After enduring four years of war the liberal republicans, like most Northerners, were ready for peace and had no plans for a lengthy reconstruction of the South. Their objective during the Civil War had been to maintain republican government, and this remained their paramount goal during Reconstruction. Immediately after Appomattox most of the liberal republicans foresaw little difficulty in finally destroying the slave aristocracy of the South and reforming the Union. Carl Schurz wrote a friend in June 1865, "To restore the Union in political form is a trifling matter." He insisted, however, that "our aim is not fulfilled by that means. The Union must be reconstructed upon the basis of the results of the great social revolution brought about during the war in the South. A free labor society must be established and built up on the ruins of the slave labor society. Now, the difficulty lies here: The Southern people have not abandoned their proslavery sentiments." For many of the liberal republicans, incorporating freedmen into Southern society was part of creating republican institutions there. Horace White urged a United States senator in late 1865 "to hold out to the Southern States a constant inducement + invitation to enlarge their suffrage, in other words to make their States republican in fact as well as in name."[1]

During the presidency of Andrew Johnson the liberal republicans tried to shape a Reconstruction policy that would quickly restore republican government throughout the nation, change the basis of Southern society, and provide the freed slaves with basic protections, but events conspired against them. The intransigence of white Southerners and Andrew Johnson complicated the liberal republicans' plans, leading them to advocate a more thorough reconstruction of the South, one that often required the use of seemingly tyrannical power. Over a year before Appomattox the *Springfield Republican* had predicted, "There are great and many objections to keeping the whole South under military or provisional governments until the strength of the rebellion is everywhere exhausted. It would open a wide door to official corruption and oppression, and would create temptations almost irresistible." The ideal of republican institutions and the chaotic circumstances drove the liberal republicans in different and often seemingly contradictory directions during the first years of Reconstruction.[2]

Throughout 1865 the liberal republicans reflected on the past and present challenges to the idea of republican government. General Jacob Cox summed up the causes of the Civil War in a speech during the gubernatorial campaign for Ohio, explaining, "We saw, in short, that slavery was an irreconcilable antagonism to free institutions; that its tendency was toward barbarism, and that the Republican Government our fathers had founded could only be preserved by its overthrow." The victory of the Union not only preserved such government for the United States, according to the liberal republicans, but would also serve as an example for the rest of the world. Under the headline "The Strength of the Republic," the *Springfield Republican* in April 1865 proclaimed that "we have demonstrated to the world what has never been proved—the superior strength of popular government." Less than a month later the newspaper complained, "It is melancholy to see how little faith in the people and in our republican institutions exists among many who aspire to be political managers." The liberal republicans saw the Union's triumph as a victory for republican government, but they still saw dangers during the period of Reconstruction. While the *Cincinnati Commercial* argued that "the conquest of the American Rebellion will stand on record for ages as one of the most memorable examples afforded by history of the capacity of a Republic to sustain itself in war," it also warned, "We must proceed to show an example equally illustrative of the rapidity and thoroughness of the applications of the healing principles of Republicanism in the work of reconstruction."[3]

The military occupation of the South was crucial to any attempts for meaningful reconstruction. In numerous editorials during the summer of 1865 the *Cincinnati Commercial* acknowledged, "We understand very well that we must, for a time, keep a strong army, and hold our military grip upon the Southern States." At this time the newspaper was often unapologetic about what it termed "Military Domination in the South," lecturing that "if the Southern people are so anxious to rid themselves of military domination, all they have to do is go about their business quietly and orderly, show by their acts a determination to yield obedience to the Government and the laws." The *Springfield Republican* likewise opined, "We have said, and repeat it, that the whole question of military domination in the South is measurably in the hand of the people themselves. It will be continued until there is ample assurance that the withdrawal of soldiers will not be followed by civil disturbance and convulsion, and the oppression of those, white and black, who have been our steadfast friends." The difficulty lay in determining how long military force would be necessary to secure the fruits of victory and protect the freedmen.[4]

The actions of President Andrew Johnson and white Southerners in the latter half of 1865 radically changed the prospects for Reconstruction. Though claiming to follow Abraham Lincoln's so-called 10 percent plan for Reconstruction, which was supposed to quickly readmit Southern States by only requiring 10 percent of the population to pledge allegiance to the United States in order to establish a new state government, Johnson was more lenient than the former president had apparently planned to be. While Lincoln had explicitly stated that his plan would not be the final act of Reconstruction, Johnson saw these measures as the end of the process. The new president also pardoned most of the high-ranking Confederate military and civilian officials, allowing them to take an active part in forming the new Southern governments. White Southerners responded to Johnson's leniency by essentially refusing to accept any of the results of the war. Most Southern states enacted what came to be known as Black Codes, sets of laws that tried to recreate slavery in everything but name by putting numerous restrictions on the rights of African Americans. Mississippi and Texas refused to ratify the Thirteenth Amendment abolishing slavery. The new Southern governments also looked a lot like the old ones, as the states elected a host of former Confederates to state office and sent others to Congress, including former vice president of the Confederacy Alexander H. Stephens, who was elected to the United States Senate. Edward Atkinson advised an administration official that he had previously defended President Johnson, "but this was before the State Govts were passed over to elected State officers. That move has created most profound distrust."[5]

The *Springfield Republican* still expressed some optimism about the prospects for a quick Reconstruction in the mid-fall of 1865. The newspaper praised the *Army and Navy Journal* for asserting "the necessity of keeping a considerable force in the reclaimed states until civil law and social order are fully restored, which will not probably be for some months to come, or until the new relations of labor have been adjusted." Other liberal republicans, particularly those few with close contacts in the South, saw mounting problems with Reconstruction. Atkinson, who corresponded with many in the South due to his cotton business and his role in the New England Freedmen's Aid Society, predicted to an administration official that "the slightest spark would start an insurrection among the Southern Negroes which would be utterly disastrous." Interestingly, Atkinson concluded, "I also feel that while such an insurrection would have to be quelled by force, yet that the Negroes would be perfectly justified in their resistance to the abuses now tolerated." While touring the South in the summer of 1865 to assess the progress of Reconstruction, Carl Schurz came to the opposite conclusion about the freedmen starting an insurrection, but not about the abuses they faced or the likelihood of violence. Schurz advised Senator Charles Sumner that "the military rule cannot be withdrawn for sometime. The great rock we have to steer clear of, is a general collision between the whites and blacks, which, in my opinion, would be brought on at once by the withdrawal of our forces." Less than a month later, he wrote his wife from Mississippi that "if we were to remove our troops today, the Southern States would swim in blood to-morrow." The blood would not come from an insurrection of blacks, however; Schurz stressed that "the only high light in this dark picture is the conduct of the negro," for they had "passed from slavery to freedom without making a single attempt to take vengeance for past sufferings."[6]

While recognizing the need for the army in the South, the liberal republicans clearly saw an inherent contradiction in the use of military force in trying to create republican institutions. By the fall of 1865 William Cullen Bryant recognized the increasing difficulties with Reconstruction. He wrote to a friend in England that "here in America we are earnestly occupied with the problem of restoring the revolted states to their place in the Union. There is more perplexity in settling the new questions to which this gives birth, than there was in dealing with these states while in rebellion." Bryant concluded, "I hope the thing will be done with as little exercise of arbitrary power by the federal government as possible." The liberal republican newspapers expressed similar sentiments in the closing months of 1865. The *Springfield Republican* insisted, "Clearly we must have reconstruction as rapidly as we can have it with safety to the Union and justice and protection to all classes at the South. Permanent military government is out of the question. It is inevitably attendant with great evils, and is inconsistent with our entire political system." The *Cincinnati Commercial* similarly contended, "It is not in accordance either with our national interest or the principles of our government, to keep up a heavy standing army in time of peace." It elaborated, using classical republican rhetoric, that "as the standing armies of the Old World despotism are virtually a standing menace to other powers, as well as their own discontented subjects, so the absence of a great army in the Republic of the United States, is a token of our independence."[7]

Carl Schurz fully recognized the contradictions of using despotic means to a republican end in his *Report on the Condition of the South,* submitted to Congress in December 1865. He mentioned the resistance of white Southerners and the danger they posed to the freedmen throughout his report, repeatedly arguing that the atmosphere in the South necessitated the federal government maintaining military forces in the South. At the end of the report Schurz offered an opinion on the constitutional aspects of Reconstruction. As a refugee from the crushed Revolution of 1848 in Europe he acknowledged, "Nothing is more foreign to my ways of thinking in political matters than a fondness for centralization or military government." With prophetic foresight Schurz wrote that "if the social revolution in the south be now abandoned in an unfinished state, and at some future period produce events provoking new and repeated acts of direct practical interference—and the contingency would by no means be unlikely to arise—such new and repeated acts would not pass over without most seriously affecting the political organism of the republic." The proper republican method for completing the great social revolution, according to Schurz and other liberal republicans, was to give the freedmen political power so that they could protect themselves, without recourse to the central government or the army Schurz succinctly—for him—explained his rationale to a friend in the middle of 1865: "So long as the states are not restored to their constitutional relations with the central government, that government has the power in its hands and can find the means through which the results of the revolution can be fixed that thereafter the southern population can no longer alter them."[8]

The Republican Congress faced several potential problems in crafting legislation that would accomplish the goals of Schurz and the other liberal republicans. Afraid that the congressmen elected under the Southern state governments would thwart new Reconstruction measures, Republicans considered not allowing them to join the Thirty-ninth Congress. Edward Atkinson approved, and he told Johnson's secretary of the Treasury that the Northern electorate had convinced their congressmen to use every parliamentary device possible to avoid seating the Southern congressmen. In actuality, almost all of the Republicans in Congress united to prevent the men from the new state governments from taking their seats in Congress, thus giving the Republicans a large majority and the ability to control Reconstruction legislation. The absence of the Southerners from Congress, however, highlighted the internal divisions within the Republican Party. A group known as the Radicals, led by Thaddeus Stevens and Charles Sumner, advocated such measures as permanently expanding the power of the federal government to protect the freedmen, redistributing land, and extending suffrage to all African Americans. Conservative Republicans tended to be satisfied with the measures President Johnson had taken, while moderates fell somewhere in between, considering the Radical positions too extreme, yet thinking that the federal government needed to do more than Johnson had done to protect former slaves. At this time a majority of Republicans in Congress still supported President Johnson, but agreed that his Reconstruction policy needed revision.[9]

Lyman Trumbull presented a new plan for Reconstruction at the beginning of the Thirty-ninth Congress in January 1866. Trumbull's leadership made sense, as he was a moderate Republican, chairman of the Senate Judiciary Committee, and had previously written the Thirteenth Amendment. He introduced two pieces of legislation, the Freedmen's Bureau Bill and the Civil Rights Bill. The first bill extended the existence of the Freedmen's Bureau, which had been organized during the war to care for freed slaves and gave the federal government the power to intercede in the relations between black and white Southerners by voiding the Black Codes and providing for military and judicial protection of the freedmen. While Radical Republicans contended that the bill did not go far enough, conservatives in Congress objected that it extended the power of the central government and the military into areas traditionally controlled by individual states. Trumbull defended his bill, explaining that the Freedmen's Bureau was not intended as a permanent institution and arguing that "the war powers of the Government do not cease with the dispersion of the rebel armies. They are to be continued and exercised until the civil authority of the Government can be firmly established." The Civil Rights Bill went further than the Freedmen's Bureau Bill, defining all persons born in the United States, except Native Americans, as citizens and detailing the rights to which they were entitled, regardless of race. This bill had the potential to change the nature of federal-state relations, as traditionally states had determined citizenship and were responsible for protecting citizens' rights. Conservatives attacked this bill as well and Trumbull defended it, asserting that "the bill draws to the Federal Government no power whatever if the States will perform their constitutional obligations."[10]

Though a majority of liberal republicans supported Trumbull's legislation, they expressed sentiments that placed them at various points along the spectrum from moderate to Radical. The *New York Evening Post* echoed Trumbull in emphasizing the conservative aspect of the bills, insisting that "they are, of course, only temporary in their nature, intended to meet an exceptional condition of things, and as soon as the late insurgent states shall have returned to order, and are prepared to resume the great duty of enforcing universal justice, which is the supreme duty of government in general and of a republican government in particular, they will of necessity cease to operate." *The Nation*, traditionally considered a conservative journal because of its positions later in the nineteenth century, declared that "whatever military force may be necessary to afford to every freeman, of whatever color, the protection which the Constitution guarantees him, in person and property, we must maintain. . . . The absolute domination of a few men over any spot of our soil is the vilest kind of oligarchy—no very great improvement on feudalism." Other liberal republicans agreed with Schurz that Congress needed to go further and provide freedmen with political rights. Edward Atkinson told Secretary of the Treasury Hugh McCulloch "there is but one course, and that is to establish and enforce justice and equal rights (not of necessity universal suffrage but equal suffrage) in the south." Horace White went further than Atkinson, proclaiming in the *Chicago Tribune* on February 10, 1866, "We are Radicals and we don't quarrel with the name." A few days later the newspaper called for "universal suffrage for the Negro race, perpetual disenfranchisement of all inveterately disloyal citizens, and the immediate trial of [Jefferson] Davis." While few regular Republicans or liberal republicans went as far as White, by February 1866 most had embraced Trumbull's Freedmen's Bureau and Civil Rights Bills as necessary amendments to Presidential Reconstruction.[11]

Andrew Johnson changed the dynamics of Reconstruction on February 19, when he surprisingly vetoed the Freedmen's Bureau Bill. The veto shocked Republicans, both because Johnson had previously expressed little opposition to its measures and because at that time it was unusual for presidents to use their veto power. Johnson argued that the bill would undermine the development of the freedmen by implying that they did not have to work for a living and would create an immense permanent bureaucracy that endangered the rights of citizens. Ultimately, he found the bill unconstitutional, stating, "I cannot reconcile a system of military jurisdiction of this kind with the words of the Constitution." Trumbull responded the next day with a lengthy speech in the Senate, at several points directly challenging Johnson, pointing out that the president had been exercising such military jurisdiction in the South for almost a year and reminding him that the bill explicitly stated that the Freedmen's Bureau was a temporary agency. Trumbull acknowledged that "the bill contained powers which could be abused in reckless hands," but explained that they were under the control of a president he trusted and that "the moment that any State does justice and abolishes all discrimination between whites and blacks in civil rights, the judicial functions of the Freedmen's Bureau cease." While many Republicans considered Johnson's veto a declaration of war on Congressional Reconstruction, Trumbull tried to maintain friendly relations with the White House even as he resubmitted the bill for congressional override. "I thought, in advocating it, that I was acting in harmony with the views of the President," Trumbull declared, and ended the speech insisting that his remarks were "made without any unkind feeling toward the Executive."[12]

Horace White blasted Johnson in the *Chicago Tribune* for the veto, urging that "the forces of freedom be so marshaled that the first move of the enemy shall be the last." While White and some others of the more radical liberal republicans assailed Johnson, the majority seemed to follow Trumbull's lead, trying to give the president a second chance while maintaining their position that Presidential Reconstruction would not suffice. Trying to spread the blame, the *Springfield Republican* argued, "Distrust, suspicion, the conceit of power, the obstinacy of theory, the infirmities of temper on both sides have brought

affairs to the very verge of discord." Still, the newspaper did not lessen its support for the bill, insisting that "for the present the Freedmen's Bureau, military
occupancy, and the United States Courts must be our reliance." The *Republican*
even advocated the more radical step of black suffrage. "The great point," it
stated, "is to secure protection and justice to the freedmen. The ballot would
have best done this."[13]

A few of the most conservative liberal republicans actually approved of
Johnson's veto and his position on Reconstruction. Murat Halstead, a thirty-
seven-year-old Ohio native and career journalist, had supported Johnson's
Reconstruction policy in the *Cincinnati Commercial* throughout 1865 and continued his support into early 1866. Significantly, the only other liberal republicans to vocally support Johnson also came from Ohio, a state with close
connections to the South. Jacob Cox, one of the most conservative and racist
of the liberal republicans, met with the president just days after the veto and
offered a sympathetic ear. Though according to Eugene Schmiel, one of his
biographers, the Oberlin-educated Cox entered the Civil War as a radical on
the question of slavery, he soon displayed a great deal of racism and uneasiness
about the place of blacks in the postwar United States. Just weeks after Lee's
surrender at Appomattox, Cox wrote that it required "a hardier faith in pure
democracy than I have to believe it safe to transfer millions of uneducated
slaves to full responsibility as electors and law makers in one bound." Education and time would help little, he felt; his biographer correctly describes him
as "a strong believer in Anglo-Saxon superiority." Cox wondered "if a republic
can exist without homogeneity of race in its citizens." During his inauguration
as governor of Ohio on January 8, 1866, Cox endorsed Johnson's policies and
indicated that he thought Reconstruction had run its course.[14]

In the weeks after Johnson's veto, however, Cox became worried that while
a split remained between the president and the majority of Republicans, Democrats were increasingly uniting behind Johnson. Ironically, Cox found himself
in a position similar to that which he would occupy in May of 1872. While he
held some opinions in common with the Democrats, Cox hated them and
refused to work with them. He agreed with the president that the military
aspects of the Freedmen's Bureau Bill went too far, but personally pleaded with
Johnson to sign the Civil Rights Bill, arguing, "The provisions for enforcing
this civil rights bill are many of them objectionable, but they are *civil* provisions, under the checks of civil law and legal responsibility, and are not the
unrestrained despotism of military power which was embodied in the freedmen's bureau bill." He explained, "My own view of the negro problem has been
and still is that *ultimately* it will be found that the separation of the races will
become a necessity; but as no one can tell how long it will take the natural

causes which are at work to bring about that result, I recognize the necessity and propriety in the meantime of giving to the freedmen a large measure of kindness and protection." By signing the Civil Rights Bill, Cox insisted, Johnson could recapture control of the Republican Party and Reconstruction.[15]

Johnson did not follow Cox's advice. Contending that the Civil Rights Bill constituted a "stride towards centralization, and the concentration of all legislative powers in the national Government," Johnson vetoed it on March 27, 1866. Though the liberal republicans had worried throughout the Civil War that the federal government was growing too powerful, Johnson's second veto stunned them. William Cullen Bryant wrote to his daughter that "the President probably did not know what he was doing when he returned the bill to Congress." Trumbull railed against Johnson in the Senate, insisting that in private conversations Johnson had never expressed "the least objections to any of the provisions of the bill" and attacking the veto message point by point. After reviewing a number of Johnson's decisions as president, Trumbull asked, "In view of these facts, who is it that is breaking down the barriers of the States, and making strides toward centralization? Is it Congress, by passage of this bill, or the President, who without law, is arrogating to himself far greater powers?" *The Nation* praised Trumbull's speech for its "exceptional cogency and power," and castigated Johnson's veto message, claiming that in comparison, "Chief-Justice Taney's celebrated opinion becomes almost respectable." The *Springfield Republican* declared that Republicans "cannot give up national protection to the weak and minority classes in the South" and that Johnson, with his veto of the Civil Rights Bill, had abandoned the party. "It is as clear a principle of the Republican party, as a palpable duty of the national authority," insisted the newspaper; "The party is nothing if it does not do this—the nation is dishonored if it hesitates in doing it."[16]

While the majority of Republicans, including the liberal republicans, saw Johnson's second veto as a virtual declaration of war between himself and Congress, Ohioans Cox and Halstead initially continued to back the president. Cox's support wavered, however, as Johnson moved closer to the Democrats, and by midsummer the governor of Ohio had broken with the president. Halstead likewise maintained his earlier support of Johnson immediately after the second veto, blasting the Freedmen's Bureau and Civil Rights bills in the *Cincinnati Commercial*. He argued that "the class of legislation attempted by Congress, and which the President combats in his veto messages, is revolutionary, because it is subversive of our system of Government." The Civil Rights Bill, according to the *Commercial* the next day, "proposes a meddlesome espionage, backed by arbitrary power, and to fix in our form of government a system of impertinent and rasping despotism of the most intolerable character." But

Johnson's increasing alliance with the Democrats drove Halstead, as it had Cox, to a drastic change in opinion by the summer. Echoing Trumbull's earlier complaints that Johnson was the one seeking to centralize government with his vetoes, the *Commercial* declared, "The President will not be allowed to assume dictatorial powers," and it compared him to Oliver Cromwell. By December the newspaper was explaining that there may have been too much centralization of power "under the exacting conditions of a vast war, in which the capacity of Republican government to sustain itself was sorely tried," but that "the limitation, by Congress, of the overgrown power of the President . . . may be taken together as favorable tokens of the substantial return of peace." The *Commercial* displayed a great deal of flexibility in using republican rhetoric to support radically different positions within a short span of time, showing why historians often refuse to take such statements at face value.[17]

The *Commercial's* break with Johnson quickly led the newspaper to reevaluate its position on protecting the freedmen. "We have millions of freed people," declared the newspaper in May 1866, "and we are under obligations that we should be dishonored forever if we neglected, to afford them protection." The *Commercial* also took a different tone with the white Southerners, asking, "How shall we accommodate our republican form of government to the management of a numerous and warlike people, who are scattered over a vast territory, and have attempted to destroy the Republic?" These were issues the Republican majority in Congress had already considered. While they had quickly overridden Johnson's vetoes of the Freedmen's Bureau and Civil Rights bills, the Republicans realized that to permanently change the South, Reconstruction measures would have to be placed beyond the reach of the president or future Congresses. The answer was the Fourteenth Amendment to the Constitution, which replicated the Civil Rights Bill and also included measures to disenfranchise the majority of former Confederates until 1870 and link the representation of a state in Congress to the number of men allowed to vote. Depending on the individual motives of congressmen, the last measure was designed either to induce Southern states to allow African Americans to vote or to drastically reduce the South's political power. Since Congress had already passed the Civil Rights Bill twice, the civil-rights provisions of the Fourteenth Amendment caused little debate compared to the two new sections, which would have major effects on the composition of the voting populations and the political power of Southern states. Like the Republican Party as a whole, the liberal republicans disagreed among themselves on these aspects of the Fourteenth Amendment.[18]

The proposal to tie a state's congressional representation directly to its number of male voters caused the most heated debate. Conservative Republicans tended to think that the amendment went too far in trying to force the South to give African Americans political rights, while Radical Republicans like Charles Sumner considered it a lack of principle to induce, and not demand, suffrage for African Americans. William Cullen Bryant thought the section of the Fourteenth Amendment on black suffrage was a good compromise and supported it in the *New York Evening Post.* "I am strongly in favor of negro suffrage," he wrote in a private letter in March, "and I wish to see our government take measures which will ultimately secure it to them, without danger to the public peace, or violence to the structure of the government." Bryant objected to Sumner's plan of forcing black suffrage on the South because he "apprehended the worst consequences from this—a bitter hatred of the North, a fiercer and more brutal contempt of the rights of the Negro, the necessity of a large standing army, disturbances, tumults, and perhaps bloodshed, a vast and corrupting executive patronage, twelve millions of people under the direct rule of the central government without a voice in legislation, and the republic converted into an empire." Some of Bryant's fears about forcing black suffrage on the South were expressed through classic tropes of republicanism, such as fear of citizens being without a voice, the dangers of a strong central government, and the risk of the republic eventually becoming an empire. Murat Halstead struck similar chords when endorsing the suffrage section of the Fourteenth Amendment in the *Cincinnati Commercial.* Explicitly recalling the republican arguments against the Slave Power conspiracy, the *Commercial* insisted, "This is a good proposition that commends itself to the good sense of the people who are not for the unconditional reinstatement of rebels; and who are not agreed that one voter in South Carolina shall have as much power in the National House of Representatives as two votes in Ohio; and who do not believe that the rebels should come out of the rebellion with their political power increased by counting the whole number instead of three-fifths of the Negroes." While perhaps sounding conservative to modern ears, the positions of Bryant and Halstead placed them with the moderate Republicans.[19]

The majority of liberal republicans sided with the Radical Republicans, arguing that the Fourteenth Amendment did not go far enough to secure political rights for African Americans. Horace White had advocated universal suffrage in the *Chicago Tribune* for months, insisting that "a freedman without a vote, is not a freedman," and other liberal republicans joined him. "We do not understand the hesitation which Congress shows in asking the country to agree to anything which looks toward securing the freedmen the means to protect themselves which are offered in universal suffrage," opined *The Nation,* for "all the arguments against it are based on things temporary, fleeting, and evanescent," while "the national pride in its republicanism, in its equality are all fighting in favor of the very thing which Congress is so afraid to touch." Carl Schurz discussed some of the dangers in advocating African American suffrage during a campaign speech in the fall of 1866. "As a general plan of reconstruction, as a foundation for the future political development of this great Republic, this Constitutional amendment never appeared to me broad enough," Schurz told the audience, for "you must enfranchise all the loyal men, black as well as white, thus effecting a safe reconstruction of the whole Republic by enlarging the democratic basis of our political system." He explained, "I am vilified as an advocate of Negro suffrage, I am willing to take the abuse and stand by my convictions. That the Constitutional amendment falls short of this, I heartily deplore. Still, I fondly hope that we shall reach the great consummation." The *Springfield Republican* expressed similar sentiments, arguing that "the suffrage question is not to be got rid of. It must be a leading question in our politics until it is settled, spite of all the efforts of the politicians to shove it aside or dodge it. The congressional reconstruction scheme ignores it, and for this reason, if for no other, that scheme cannot bring final settlement."[20]

While advocating suffrage for African Americans was considered radical in 1866, the arguments the liberal republicans used in its favor demonstrated that they foresaw few more such radical measures, and a quick end to Reconstruction once suffrage had been accomplished. Responding to Radical Republican Thaddeus Stevens's call to give the freedmen land, Horace White's *Chicago Tribune* countered, "Give him his rights, Mr. Stevens, and he will ask no land." The *Republican* and Schurz emphasized that suffrage would "bring final settlement" and "reach the great consummation." Most liberal republicans thought that once African Americans had the power to vote, the federal government would no longer need to provide economic help or protection, for they would have the ability to provide for and defend themselves.[21]

The theory that suffrage alone would make African Americans self-sufficient and successfully end Reconstruction was consistent with republican ideology, for it emphasized the idea of the independent citizen and a weak central government. Aside from their commitment to white supremacy, many Democrats would have supported the liberal republican goal of an independent citizenry and a weak central government, as it matched their own beliefs about government. The liberal republican's faith in the efficacy of suffrage, however, underestimated the resolve of white Southerners to control the social, political, and economic life of the South and made the liberal republicans appear naive, if not indifferent, about the plight of Southern African Americans. While thoroughly committed to creating a free-labor system of small landowners in the South, Edward Atkinson disliked the idea of forced land redistribution. He explained to Henry Ward Beecher, "I have utterly opposed confiscation of large estates and the gratuitous division among the freedmen. The large estates will soon be broken up by sale, device, or by the burden of taxation and in order to know how to use the land the freedman must attain his title by working for it." The *Republican* expressed such opinions as early as April 1865, declaring "the war has accomplished more than its original object as declared by Congress. Not only is the rebellion thoroughly subdued; but slavery also has perished out of the land, and four millions of recent slaves have entered upon a career of free labor, education, and improvement, which will ultimately qualify them for all the prerogatives of American citizenship. So much is secure, in spite of remaining prejudice in the South and affected skepticism in the North." "Instead of pausing to conjure up possible evils," advised the newspaper, "the friends of liberty will rejoice in what is already achieved and steadily press on."[22]

Citing former Massachusetts Governor John Andrews's statement that "the former rebels must be reinstated in their political rights or they must be exterminated," the *Springfield Republican* also argued that it was best to restore full political rights to all white Southerners. Most of the liberal republicans agreed with the newspaper and criticized the provision of the Fourteenth Amendment disenfranchising the majority of former Confederates until 1870. *The Nation* considered disenfranchisement of white Southerners much more radical than the enfranchisement of African Americans, contending that plans for taking away political rights were "expedients that fifty generations of tyrants and conquerors have tried and found worthless." Such repressive measures, predicted the newspaper, "are certain to fail here, because our polity, our religion, our manners, our theory of government, of morals, and of human nature are but a series of protests against them. We have repudiated them as solemnly as men can do. If there be any principle at the base of our government and society, it is that the great remedy for disaffection is equality, protection, freedom of speech and that there is no worse way of making men orderly and submissive to law than putting them under a ban or disability." Horace White and William Grosvenor separately came to the same conclusions in 1866, calling for universal suffrage throughout the South for both blacks and whites. Carl Schurz, who had won his U.S. Senate seat in 1869 largely because of his opposition to disenfranchisement, ironically was one of the few liberal republicans to defend the provisions in the Fourteenth Amendment suspending the political rights of former Confederates, though even he considered this a temporary expedient.[23]

Understanding the liberal republicans' positions on the Fourteenth Amendment helps to place into perspective their eventual opposition to Reconstruction. Generations of historians have argued that racism led them to change their minds about Reconstruction during the late 1860s and advocate the return of elite whites to political office in the South. John Sproat has insisted that the liberal republicans acquiesced to the compromise of 1877 that ended Reconstruction "because they became almost preposterously impatient with the Southern Negro." Eric Foner cites Edward Atkinson, Jacob Cox, and *The Nation* to contend that by 1870 "a remarkable reversal of sympathies had taken place, with Southern whites increasingly portrayed as the victims of injustice, while blacks were deemed unfit to exercise suffrage." Nancy Cohen describes how "liberal reformers proceeded to reverse their assessments of the classes in the South," citing "a new, insidious racism," and "talk of ineradicable racial traits" as reasons.[24]

The liberal republicans, though, remained remarkably consistent during Reconstruction on issues of suffrage, making it difficult to argue that they had a reversal of sympathies or that some newfound racism shaped their politics. From 1866 onward they had consistently opposed disenfranchising white Southerners, and Carl Schurz had authored the general amnesty plank in the 1868 Republican platform. In addition, many of the liberal republicans had supported black suffrage for conservative reasons. Even while urging political rights for African Americans in 1866, *The Nation* conceded, "Negro suffrage may be a bad thing, an inexpedient thing, a thing that, if established, will prove the ruin of the country." Arguing that the liberal republicans were racist is easy, as almost all of them expressed racist sentiments. Don Fehrenbacher, however, has shown that modern scholars often overestimate the importance of racism in the mid-nineteenth century. In his seminal article on Lincoln and the question of racism, he explains that "race itself was not then the critical public issue that it had become for us," and notes that "our own preoccupation with race probably leads us to overestimate the importance of racial feeling in the antislavery movement." He argues that "terminological difficulties may also arise in the study of history, and such is the case with the word 'racist,' which serves us badly as a concept because of its denunciatory tone and indiscriminate use." Branding the liberal republicans racists is prejudicial and does not explain their actions. Most of them did not have a "reversal of sympathies" between 1866 and 1870, for their positions stayed the same. The liberal republicans had never considered African Americans equals and had always disapproved of political proscriptions against white Southerners, often for classical republican reasons that had little or nothing to do with race.[25]

The election of 1866 became a referendum on the Fourteenth Amendment and Reconstruction. Horace White still considered the Fourteenth Amendment "a politician's dodge rather than a work of statesmanship," and almost all of the liberal republicans agreed, arguing that it did not go far enough toward universal suffrage for African Americans and went too far in disenfranchising white Southerners. Ultimately, though, the liberal republicans endorsed the amendment as a necessary part of reconstructing the South. White saw the election of 1866 as "the grandest popular decision in history," and an overwhelming Republican victory convinced many Republicans that they could finally reconstruct the South without interference. Thaddeus Stevens and the Radical Republicans introduced a Reconstruction bill in the House at the beginning of the next congressional session. The bill would abolish the Southern state governments created under Johnson, divide the South into military districts, and, like the Fourteenth Amendment, would disenfranchise white Southerners who had supported the Confederacy. Despite the Republican ascendancy at the polls and in Congress, much debate arose surrounding the House's Reconstruction Bill.[26]

The liberal republicans agreed that the South needed further reconstruction, but considered Stevens's bill too harsh, particularly in its disenfranchisement of white Southerners. Acknowledging that "the present state of governments in the southern states neglect justice," the *New York Evening Post* argued that "this state of things must be remedied, of course, but the remedy is not contained in Mr. Stevens' bill," for "it would substitute one evil for another." Henry Adams certainly considered Stevens's bill evil, for he predicted to his brother that under the bill, "the whole South must be soon like Greece and Asia Minor; a society dissolved, and brigandage universal." Clearly expressing racism, Adams argued that "though it is now law that the Negro is better than the white man, I doubt whether even the Negro can restore order to the South," and that "these bills are monstrous." The *Springfield Republican* likewise demonstrated a good deal of racism and elitism—along with classical republicanism—in its criticisms of the Reconstruction Bill. In language similar to that of Adams, it contended, "The proposition to disenfranchise the entire white population of the South . . . and to give the just emancipated blacks the entire political control of ten states of the Union is simply monstrous." The newspaper declared, "It is better that the South be governed by ex-rebels than by fools. The true republican idea and the only safe practice is to let all vote upon equal terms, and to exclude leading rebels from national offices." The distinction between disenfranchisement of most white Southerners and the exclusion of former Confederate leaders from office may seem arbitrary to modern Americans, but made a great deal of sense in the historical context of Reconstruction. Until the democratic reforms in the 1830s, officeholders throughout the United States commonly had to meet higher property qualifications than mere voters. In addition, the election of former Confederate leaders to national office during Andrew Johnson's Presidential Reconstruction had outraged Republicans and helped lead to Congress's taking control of Reconstruction. According to the *Republican*, Congress should concentrate on three things to reconstruct the South:

equal suffrage under the Constitution, the exclusion of former Confederate
leaders from political office, and enough troops in the South to enforce the
laws.[27]

The *Republican*'s call for enough troops in the South reflected the liberal
republicans' surprising support of the military aspects of the Reconstruction
Bill as a temporary measure. Referring to the implementation of military rule
in the South, the *Republican* insisted that "the system is not approved; it is only
tolerated as a temporary thing, and there is not a thinking man in the North
who would not shrink with horror from the idea of a permanent military government over any portion of the American people." *The Nation* used semantics
to justify military governments in the South, arguing that "the state of war lasts
until society is restored to its natural and normal condition"; and, "If the war
is a civil one, it lasts until civil government is fully restored by legitimate
authority. This has not been done in the Southern States." The newspaper
opined that "Mr. Stevens' bill is the first step in this direction, and it is a necessary step," for "no election ordered by Congress could be fairly conducted
unless the Federal troops were authorized to protect voters and maintain
order." Lyman Trumbull, a longtime opponent of military incursion into civilian affairs, reluctantly supported the military provisions of the bill, explaining
to a family member that "it is the last thing to put the rebel states under military rule but the People there behave so badly, there seems to be no way of
protecting loyal men."[28]

Trumbull and other liberal republicans helped to alter Stevens's bill so that
the Reconstruction Act of 1867 would be more palatable to them. Their major
concerns, besides disenfranchisement, were the lack of provisions for readmit-
ting the Southern states back into the Union, and equal suffrage. Trumbull
managed to amend Stevens's bill in the Senate to include a series of steps the
Southern states would have to take to regain home rule. The *Springfield Republican* repeatedly urged that ratification of the Fourteenth Amendment be
included as one of the prerequisites of readmission, though the paper acknowledged that "there is no denying that we are compelling the South to agree to
amendments that it would not voluntarily accept, but if anything can justify
such compulsory changes under a republican government, surely a rebellion
that has cost us so much has given the fullest justification." After much debate
in Congress, ratification of the Fourteenth Amendment was included as a condition of the Southern states' readmission.[29]

The revised version of the bill that became the Reconstruction Act of 1867
satisfied most of the liberal republicans and they reluctantly supported it, helping to give it a veto-proof margin of victory in Congress. Significantly, however,
the liberal republicans considered the legislation the end of Reconstruction. "It

is a law that will put an end to anarchy and restore constitutional Union and freedom to the people of the rebel states," argued the *Chicago Tribune;* it would mean that Reconstruction was "an accomplished fact." The *Springfield Republican* similarly thought that with the Reconstruction Act of 1867, "the speedy and right reconstruction of the South is assured." In the Senate debate over the bill, Trumbull had said, "What more do you ask? What else would you have? Can anybody think of anything else to require of these people except to put their governments in loyal hands, adopt the constitutional amendment, adopt universal suffrage, and keep rebels out of power? What more I ask can be required of them?"[30]

The end of the Civil War thus drove the liberal republicans in seemingly contradictory directions. The long-perceived threats to republican government posed by the Southern slave system and its vestiges led them to try reconstructing the South. Reconstruction, however, required the use of federal power that the liberal republicans had to admit could be seen as tyrannical. "I would be the last man on earth to sound the praise of military rule," Schurz explained in an 1868 campaign speech for Grant. "I would denounce it even in this case, had it not been the necessary means of transition from the reign of wrong to the reign of right." The difficulty for the liberal republicans was how long the Union could maintain the strong central government needed to accomplish the work of Reconstruction without destroying republican institutions in the process. They knew they wanted to replace the antebellum Slave Power aristocracy in the South with an environment friendly toward republicanism. In the first years of Reconstruction they planned and actively sought to protect the freedmen, to provide African Americans with some civil and political rights, and to create a free-labor system. White Southern intransigence, however, meant they could not carry out their plans for Reconstruction without using and enlarging the authority of the federal government, which would lead to centralized power and increased corruption. Essentially, the liberal republicans were caught between the proverbial rock and a hard place, for they could not establish republican governments in the South without damaging the nation's republican institutions. In the end, they would decide that as much had been done in reconstructing the South as could be done without destroying republican government throughout the nation, and they reached a compromise that satisfied no one.[31]

5

Legacies of the Civil War
Threaten the Republic,
1865–1872

Five days after Robert E. Lee surrendered the Army of Northern Virginia to Ulysses S. Grant at Appomattox, with other Confederate armies still in the field, the *Cincinnati Commercial*'s lead editorials were headlined "Reducing the War Establishment" and "Hints Toward Economy." The newspaper declared that "it would, of course, be disastrous to put the sword in its scabbard before the time when it can safely be done, but may we not reasonably indulge a confidence that the heat of the war is over, and that its burdens ou[gh]t to be taken from our backs as fast as possible?" The *Commercial* was reacting to the huge increase in the size and power of the federal government during the course of the Civil War. The army had swelled from sixteen thousand to over two million soldiers, the civil service had expanded exponentially, the first national income tax was instituted, protective tariffs were enacted to help industry, and massive internal improvements such as the Pacific Railroad had been started. History books about the federal government during the Civil War have such titles as *Blueprint for Modern America, The Greatest Nation of the Earth*, and *Yankee Leviathan: The Origins of Central State Authority in America*. As Jean Harvey Baker has observed, "The fighting of a civil war had ineffably centralized powers in the national government unheard of two decades before."[1]

The liberal republicans wished to rein in the growth of federal power and dismantle the economic legislation that they had viewed dubiously, as war measures, from the start. After years of struggling to ensure that Union success on the battlefield would destroy the Slave Power that had threatened the safety of republican institutions, they worried that maintaining the war measures could endanger the same institutions. *The Nation* argued that it was "a mistake for anybody to keep on preaching after the war was over, and its necessities and anxieties had ceased, that the issue of the legal tenders . . . was a good, legitimate, and normal exercise of the powers of government." The *Cincinnati Commercial* declared, "We are at peace, and commerce should once more be left to resume, in some degree, its natural channels, and there is no excuse for piling on a probationary tariff." The war had also encouraged the growth of the federal civil service and of huge corporations, both of which the liberal republicans perceived as potentially dangerous sources of corruption and tyranny. Lyman

Trumbull insisted that "the monstrous Tammany frauds never could have existed in such proportions before the war." From 1865 through early 1872 the liberal republicans increasingly expressed fears that the expanded civil service, the federal economic legislation, and the growth of huge monopolies during the Civil War all posed dangers to the United States' republican form of government.[2]

Andrew Johnson's use of patronage as a weapon in the conflicts over Reconstruction made the spoils system a major political issue. The Civil War had led to a massive increase in the size of the federal government, and even with post-war retrenchment, the civil service still numbered over 50,000 workers by 1868. The president of the United States, as both the head of his party and of the executive branch of the government, controlled the majority of the patronage dispensed via civil service jobs. Abraham Lincoln had masterfully used patronage to hold the new Republican Party together during the turmoil of the Civil War, as different factions and people within it vied for power. Granting such positions as postmaster as a reward for loyalty was common in the antebellum period, but Lincoln also took advantage of the new patronage opportunities the war created, such as strategically selecting some of his generals for their political strength among key constituencies. While many of the liberal republicans who were newspaper editors complained of the spoils system during the Civil War, those few such as Lyman Trumbull who were active politicians used the system pragmatically to build loyal political organizations. Johnson emulated Lincoln's use of the spoils system at first, but as the congressional Republicans increasingly fought him over Reconstruction he started to use patronage as a weapon to attack his enemies. Republicans, including the liberal republicans, saw Johnson's use of the patronage system during the battles over Reconstruction as a threat both to their political fortunes and to the republican form of government.[3]

When the Republicans refused to seat Southern congressmen in late 1865, rumors began circulating that Johnson planned to use the spoils system against his congressional opponents. Federal appointees in Illinois who formed the backbone of Trumbull's political organization warned their patron that Johnson would dismiss the supporters of all who opposed his Reconstruction policy. Despite the threat, most liberal republicans remained silent about the spoils system during the first quarter of 1866, perhaps concentrating on Reconstruction or hoping not to antagonize the president. *The Nation* proved an exception, though significantly it did not attack the president in its general plea for reform of the civil service. The newspaper argued along classical republican lines that the spoils system was "intensely oligarchical," but feared it would be "a long time before any party acquires enough conscience and public spirit to

use its power to deprive itself as well as its adversaries of the means of reward-
ing its underlings out of the public purse."[4]

Johnson started to purge the civil service of those loyal to his opponents in
April 1866, when the conflict between him and Congress over Reconstruction
flared into open warfare. Trumbull, as author of the Freedmen's Bureau and
Civil Rights bills, faced the brunt of Johnson's wrath. For months the senator
received a constant stream of letters from civil servants in Illinois who had lost
their jobs. Horace White, intimately connected with Illinois politics as editor of
the Chicago Tribune, wrote frantically and repeatedly to Trumbull in Washington warning of how the president's actions could undermine their political
position. Johnson's power to dismiss Trumbull's appointees threatened to
destroy the political organization Trumbull had built over the last decade, and
it came at a particularly vulnerable time, as the Illinois senator was due for
reelection in 1867. For liberal republicans like Trumbull and White, the spoils
system now represented a real threat to their personal and political fortunes,
making their calls for civil service reform at least somewhat self-interested and
pragmatic.[5]

The liberal republican crusade against the spoils system, however, also contained real ideological components. Fundamental differences over the course of
Reconstruction had caused the split between Johnson and Congress and the
ensuing patronage fight. In the effort to secure the passage and enforcement of
new Reconstruction legislation, the Radical Republicans presented partisan civil
service reform measures that would strip Johnson of the power to appoint and
dismiss officeholders and to control his cabinet. The liberal republicans, like the
Radicals, supported civil service reform efforts during Johnson's administration
partly because such reforms were directly linked with reconstructing the South
and protecting African Americans. In addition, Johnson's use of patronage
power to thwart the will of Congress raised the specter of one-man rule, long
considered one of the gravest dangers to republican government. Unlike the
Radical Republicans, though, many of the liberal republicans also considered
dangerous the concentration of patronage power in the Senate. Calling the civil
service reform efforts of Radical Thaddeus Stevens too limited because they
concentrated only on Johnson, the Cincinnati Commercial argued that the
spoils system "in the conduct of the public business, is safe in the hands of no
man, and of no party. Whether wielded by a renegade Republican President, or
by an orthodox Republican Senate, it is an evil menacing to the public welfare."
The newspaper insisted, "If we are to exchange the sweeping and despotic
power of the President over the official lives of men for a power equally sweeping and despotic in the hands of the Senate, it may be made a question whether
the country will have gained or lost by the operation." After Grant replaced

Johnson as president, Lyman Trumbull still worried about congressional influence over patronage, and he introduced a bill prohibiting congressmen from recommending the employment of any person in any of the executive departments. The penalty for improperly interfering in the civil service, which would apply to congressmen such as Trumbull himself, was a fine of up to $1,000. He argued that such restrictions on patronage were necessary because "ours is emphatically a Government of checks and balances, upon the proper maintenance of which the perpetuation of our republican system essentially depends."[6]

The liberal republicans also differed from many other Republicans calling for civil service reform during Johnson's administration by emphasizing how it corrupted republican institutions. During a campaign speech in 1866, Carl Schurz charged that "the President openly uses the whole patronage of the government as a machinery of corruption." After the election the *Cincinnati Commercial* pleaded for civil service reform as offering "the least facilities for extravagance, nepotism and corruption." *The Nation* predicted that passage of Rhode Island Congressman Thomas Jenckes's civil service reform bill would do "more to save the people from corruption, more to preserve the Government from mischief, more to renew and restore and sustain the virtues of the Republic, than all the legislation of the last decade." While clearly hyperbolic, the argument demonstrates that the liberal republicans saw corruption as endangering the virtue necessary for the survival of republican institutions. "Between corruption and the rise of tyrants lay indissoluble links of cause and effect," explains Mark W. Summers, for those who still trusted in the ideas of republicanism; the liberal republicans still clung to their ideology and believed that "if corruption ran politics, then despotism would replace a republic swiftly, as people bartered their liberties for a share of the plunder." Edwin Godkin asserted that "it may be said, without exaggeration or misrepresentation, that the civil service of the United States is so arranged as to afford strong encouragement to dishonesty of nearly every degree. The loss of money to the government is but a small part of the evil which flows from the system"; for instead of encouraging virtue in the population, "the chief influence it exerts is exerted on the side of vice and immorality."[7]

While many Republicans lost interest in civil service reform after Grant replaced Johnson, the liberal republicans saw his election as an opportunity to intensify their reform efforts. They hoped that Grant would end the corruption associated with the spoils system, and Carl Schurz planned to make civil service reform his signature issue. In the first month of Grant's administration, with the liberal republicans still hopeful about the new president, Schurz wrote to his wife, "I shall make civil service reform, one of the weightiest questions coming before us, my specialty." In subsequent letters to Margarethe he asserted, "Never have I been more strongly convinced that an end must be put to the present system of appointments," and "The civil service reform is closest to my heart." After writing civil service reform legislation, Schurz explained that "the main point I want to establish by my bill is to avoid the quadrennial scandal of universal office hunting . . . and thus provide for the republic an honest and economical administration and cleanse our political life of the corrupting element of office seeking."[8]

Schurz's maiden speech in the Senate demonstrated his commitment to civil service reform, which had only been buttressed when the head of the Republican Party in Missouri used patronage against him. Insisting that "by far the worst and most dangerous effect of the spoils system is the demoralization of the public sentiment," Schurz explicitly and repeatedly referred to the dangers of the system. "I maintain that republican government will rather gain than lose, and gain immensely, by a reform which takes from the machinery of the public service its partisan character, and which will remove from our political life that most dangerous agency of corruption and demoralization which consists in partisan patronage." If the country could not control the spoils system, Schurz wondered, "Has republicanism really arrived at its wit's end?" The strident rhetoric may appear calculated, but Schurz had written the letters to his wife claiming that civil service reform was "closest to my heart" almost a year before his political fight with Grant. Circumstances made Schurz's heartfelt and long-awaited speech against the spoils system appear to be merely partisan bickering.[9]

Jacob Cox was another liberal republican whose arguments against the spoils system may appear tainted by his problems with Grant. Three months after essentially being forced to resign as Grant's secretary of the Interior, Cox blasted the use of the civil service for political patronage in a thirty-two-page article in the North American Review. Cox littered his article with references to republicanism, explicitly arguing a number of times that the spoils system constituted a mortal danger to republican institutions. "The climax of the abuse of patronage has been capped. It becomes simply a machine for free representation of the people," he argued; and the civil service "must be thoroughly reformed, unless we are to admit that republican government is a failure." He wanted to "declare patronage in all its forms to be anti-republican and dangerous to the state," and he predicted that "until an entirely satisfactory system is reached, no other question in political economics should be regarded as superior to it, because no other affects more vitally the pecuniary interests of the people, or the success and stability of real republicanism in our government." One might question Cox's motivation, but not that his opposition to the spoils system was expressed in republican terms. In addition, Cox had long been considered a reformer and had in fact come into conflict with Grant over what he considered the abuse of patronage in the Department of the Interior. It is difficult to dismiss his concerns about the affect of the spoils system as entirely self-interested, when he and other liberal republicans had considered such issues in terms of republican ideology for decades.[10]

Edward Atkinson likewise feared that corruption endangered republican government, but as an industrialist he did not see the spoils system as the greatest danger. "My experience," wrote Atkinson to Edwin Godwin, "leads me to believe that there is very little absolute corruption among the members of Congress"; rather, "the corruption is in lobby influence—which can always be bought." He worried that lobbying and corruption could lead to Congress's passing "protective or special legislation." The *New York Evening Post* defined such legislation, explaining "by special legislation we mean that kind of law making—and it is the kind most common in our statute books—which consists of taking a sum of money out of the public treasury and presenting it to a private individual." The pieces of special legislation that concerned the liberal republicans in the first years of Reconstruction were the tariff and currency measures passed during the Civil War to help secure Union victory. Even as the liberal republicans concentrated on fighting Johnson over Reconstruction, they saw economic legislation looming on the horizon as the next great issue for the nation. In January 1866, just before the controversy with Johnson began in earnest, the *Cincinnati Commercial* announced that "the financial questions are becoming the great questions. Let them be attended to." As for Reconstruction, the newspaper expressed hope "that the whole winter will not be spent in talking about various aspects of the Negro question, and the really important measures crowded into a few of the last weeks of the session." The fight over Reconstruction following Johnson's vetoes of the Freedmen's Bureau and Civil Rights bills refocused the liberal republicans on Reconstruction. The *Springfield Republican* spent the majority of a mid-1866 editorial blasting Congress for "weak and vacillating" actions on Reconstruction, but it ended by declaring, "It is in matters of business that this Congress has failed most signally," citing the failure to reduce the currency, bring about specie payments, and reduce the tariff. By the time Congress had established its dominance over Johnson in 1867, *The Nation* was predicting that "as soon as the Reconstruction question is disposed of, the question of tariff and revenue will become the great political issues." The liberal republicans saw protective tariffs and paper money as measures that might have been necessary to win the war, but were certainly uncalled for and potentially dangerous during a time of peace.[11]

During the Civil War, to secure the credit of the nation the Union started printing paper money and passed laws making it legal tender. In the aftermath of the war the liberal republicans argued that allowing the government to manipulate the monetary system centralized too much power in the Treasury and created too many opportunities for both public and private corruption. Picking up on the normal republican fears of tyranny and corruption, Godkin's weekly newspaper contended that maintaining legal tender "was like arguing for the perpetuation of martial law" and led to a "disturbing influence on trade and on private and public morals." William Cullen Bryant, a longtime advocate of hard money, also raised concerns that the Legal Tender Act had concentrated too much power in the central government. "The possession of a large surplus of coin, with liberty to sell it at discretion, makes the [Treasury] Secretary now the most powerful operator in the gold market," declared Bryant's *New York Evening Post*, and "in behalf of the people we protest against the lodging of so much power over their public interest and private fortune in the hands of any one man."[12]

While some of the liberal republican newspapers discussed how the Legal Tender Act gave the government too much power, most of the liberal republicans focused on how the currency laws created corruption that could corrode the virtue of the citizenry that was necessary for republican government. The lobbying surrounding such legislation would account for some of the corruption, insisted the *Chicago Tribune*, which reported that eastern banks already had agents in Washington lobbying Congress. The very existence of government-printed paper money also contradicted the moral philosophy and political economics most liberal republicans had learned in school, which considered attempts to make paper money legal tender a dangerous lie that would lead to speculation and corruption. Charles Francis Adams wrote to Elbridge G. Spaulding, the author of the Legal Tender Act, that "so long as a legal tender note remains in circulation at less than its professed value, it is a solemn lie." Acknowledging the difficulties of the Civil War, Adams did not fault Spaulding for his monetary policy during the conflict, but questioned the continued necessity of greenbacks. "The worst of it," complained Adams, "is that the moral sense of a people is permanently blunted by the resort to such an expedient." A fellow Bostonian, Atkinson, expressed similar concerns, privately writing that "the great *moral* question of today is the currency question," for "capitalists, speculators and middlemen are *stealing* this share of annual product which under natural law belongs to labor, by use of false money." Not only did the failure to return to the gold standard mean theft to the liberal republicans press, but they also feared it would diminish the virtue necessary for the maintenance of republican institutions by encouraging luxury throughout society. The *Cincinnati Commercial* predicted that unless the country returned to the gold standard, "Extravagance will be the rule both in public and private life"; the *Springfield Republican* warned that among the evils of greenbacks "is the promotion of extravagance beyond all bounds." *The Nation* contended that "a better device for loosening the bonds of social morality than the Legal Tender Act could hardly have been hit upon."[13]

The liberal republican opposition to allowing paper money to remain legal tender had little to do with partisan politics or personal financial interest. While Henry Adams considered the government's policies so dangerous that he sold all of his U.S. securities, most liberal republicans had advocated hard-money policies for decades and considered Andrew Johnson's Treasury secretary, Hugh McCulloch, a friend. In one of their many exchanges, Atkinson told McCulloch, "I am as you are aware urgently desirous to see a contraction of the currency, an end to the speculation and even to the extravagant profits of my own branch of business. It is unwholesome." David M. Tucker has examined the business dealings of the liberal republicans and concludes that on the issue of currency, they "thought and wrote from the perspective of moral philosophy and political economy rather than from economic self-interest."[14]

The liberal republicans attacked protective tariffs as another source of tyranny and corruption. William Cullen Bryant and the *New York Evening Post*, opponents of protective tariffs for decades, contended about the Republican Party that "there are leaders in it whose tendencies are towards the most dangerous concentration of power, who are not emancipated even from the antiquated twaddle of protectionism and patronage." The word "emancipated" would have conjured thoughts of slavery for nineteenth-century Americans. Other liberal republicans also compared protective tariffs to slavery, the ultimate form of tyranny. "What is protection but slavery," William Grosvenor asked, for "you may earn as much as you can but somebody shall have laws to take your earnings as much as he pleases." The American Free Trade League often described the tariff as an issue of "commercial freedom" versus "commercial slavery" and considered itself a new abolition party. The *Cincinnati Commercial* explicitly explained how protective tariffs threatened liberty, insisting that "any legislation which fails to recognize the exact equality of all men, and to respect and protect their individual rights so far as the same may be done with due regard to the general welfare, is unrepublican."[15]

In discussing the problems of corruption associated with protectionism, the liberal republicans explicitly dismissed as unimportant the liberal economic arguments against it and concentrated on the classical republican concern that protectionism destroyed public virtue. While he thought protective tariffs prevented the economy from functioning at peak efficiency, Henry Adams contended in the *North American Review* that "the nation is young and overflowing with animal strength, and the mere pecuniary loss could be borne. But unfortunately this is not all." Adams wrote, "There is a political result of far greater moment, in the debauching effects of the system upon parties, public men, and the morals of the State." It is unlikely that Adams's words in the *Review* were mere political rhetoric, for at the time he was writing the article he was making the same arguments to Edward Atkinson in private correspondence. Advising Atkinson to ignore protectionists in England, Adams wrote that "if I am right, it follows that our time and labor will be most usefully spent in a regular hand-to-hand fight with corruption here under our eyes," for "the whole root of the evil is *political* corruption; theory has really not much to do with it." Both in public and private Adams argued that his concern over the effects of corruption on republican institutions—not liberal economic theory—drove his opposition to protective tariffs. *The Nation* agreed, explaining that "we consider the strongest objection to protection, in a country as rich as this is the constant temptation it holds out to legislative corruption."[16]

The liberal republicans considered legislation that favored a special interest both unfair, because it favored one group at the expense of others, and dangerous, because it encouraged corruption. The liberal republican press argued that protective tariffs were designed "for the calculated advantage of special interests" and that "such a system is a tax upon the people for the benefit of the manufacturers chiefly." The *New York Evening Post* reported, "There are dozens of instances of such bargain and sale in the Tariff bill," and contended that "within the last few years the final step has been taken. The various protected interests having discovered by experience that the politician is not a trustworthy laborer unless he is bought very early, have determined on securing him body and soul on a permanent contract." Liberal republicans in Ohio also argued that protectionism "promotes corruption in legislation and plunder in high places." The *Cincinnati Commercial* used Radical Republican Thaddeus Stevens as an example, discussing how as a congressman from Pennsylvania Stevens regularly defended the high tariffs protecting his state's iron industry. The newspaper also alleged that Stevens, who owned a few small iron mills, favored protective tariffs for personal profit, claiming that "he is interested in iron mills, and therefore wishes to force the people to buy his iron at his price." Grosvenor insisted, "No republic will tolerate such exclusive favoritism." The *North American Review* agreed, contending that the protective system "is complicated, irritating, wasteful of money, and corrupting of morals. No other legacy of the war is fraught with such danger to the independence of our people and the integrity of our political system."[17]

The relationship between protective tariffs and the growth of monopolies was another aspect of protectionism that worried the liberal republicans. The *Cincinnati Commercial* wrote accusingly that "the Prohibitory Tariff men are exceedingly active to secure monopolies for their several interests," and the *Chicago Tribune* proclaimed, "The high tariff ring live upon monopoly." Carl Schurz railed against "the so-called industrial monopolies fostered by a protective tariff." Concerns about monopolies extended beyond their connection to tariffs, as liberal republicans expressed fear that corporations had become so big and powerful after the Civil War that they could subvert the political process and destroy republican government. "The accumulation of capital in the hands of comparatively few individuals and corporations," explained Godkin in 1867, "has already begun to influence political contests, and, if we are not greatly mistaken, its worse results are yet to be seen. To enumerate at length the dangers to republican government which may spring from this state of things would need an article itself." Over the next several years the liberal republicans expanded upon Godkin's argument and wrote dozens of articles exploring the danger monopolies and huge corporations posed to republican institutions.[18]

Godkin considered the link between corruption and monopolies obvious, dismissively stating that "the connection of commercial immorality, that is haste and unscrupulousness in money-getting, with political corruption, hardly needs explanation or illustration." Charles Francis Adams Jr., however, discussed in a number of articles over the span of a few years the specific ways in which monopolies caused corruption. Like most of the liberal republicans, Adams acknowledged that "combinations of capital and labor which amount to monopolies can alone satisfy the present enormous requirements of modern society," but warned that "giant corporations are far more likely to combine to rob the community" through their ability to manipulate legislation. Three years later he returned to the same topic. In examining the nature of business Adams contended that "corporations are necessarily selfish," and thus "public questions and political and moral questions mean nothing." According to him, "One consequence of this has been the growth of a most corrupt system of legislative manipulation and log-rolling," as "the great corporations openly ally themselves with political parties." [19]

The corruption associated with huge corporations concerned liberal republicans for two reasons. First, like any type of corruption, it undermined the virtue necessary for republican government to function. Second, corporations' ability to corrupt legislatures also gave them such enormous power that they could overwhelm republican institutions and take control of the government. "We need some controlling check in the Constitution," contended the *Cincinnati*

Commercial, "to the fearfully growing power of railway and other corporate monopolies, which by successively buying and controlling State Legislatures and judiciaries, are marching with steady strides to a point of vantage where it is no hyperbole to say, that a single corporation of say twenty men may claim, with little power of successful contradiction, to own the United States." In the Senate Carl Schurz repeatedly warned of "the great dangers threatening from the growing power of great moneyed corporations; how that power is already felt in State and national politics, and bids fair to exercise a controlling influence, dangerous even to our free institutions." In classical republican thought the specter of unrestrained power was the greatest threat to liberty. Usually the power emanated from the government, but in this instance liberal republicans found dangerous concentrations of power growing in the private sector.[20]

The Adams brothers explicitly explained how the growing power of monopolies and huge corporations threatened republican government. "Here are two systems growing and expanding side by side," wrote Charles Francis Adams Jr., "the representative republican system of government, adapted to a simple and somewhat undeveloped phase of society; and the corporate industrial system, the result of a complex and artificial civilization. How long can they develop together?" He deliberately compared postbellum corporations to the Slave Power that his father and other older liberal republicans had fought against for decades, and found the corporations the greater threat. While acknowledging that "the slave power was welded together by nine hundred millions of property" and "the destruction of slavery was accomplished after twenty-five years of agitation and four years of civil war," Adams argued that compared to huge and omnipresent corporations, the Slave Power "controlled only one section of the country and could be combated in another." He predicted, "Our political system cannot much longer sustain the conflict with corporations. Modern civilization has created a class of powers which are too strong for the control of our governments." Henry Adams agreed with his brother's conclusions. He expounded, "The belief is common in America that the day is at hand when corporations far greater than Erie—swaying power such as has never in the world's history been trusted in the hands of private citizens, controlled by single men like Vanderbilt, or by combinations of men like Fisk, Gould, and Lane, after having created a system of quiet but irresistible corruption—will ultimately succeed in directing government itself." Adams feared that "unless some satisfactory solution of the problem can be reached, popular institutions may yet find their existence endangered."[21]

The liberal republicans singled out railroads, the largest corporations in the United States at the time, as the monopolies most dangerous to republican government. While admiring "the growth of the wonderful railroad system of the country," Charles Francis Adams Jr. and other liberal republicans also wanted to discuss "a few of the more obvious dangers with which the portentous development seemed to threaten our political institutions." Some of the dangers were similar to those they saw arising from corporations in general, such as the corruption of legislatures and unchecked power. They also expressed fears singular to the railroad industry, such as concern that the railroad monopolies were gobbling up western land the nation needed to support small farmers. Perhaps most significantly, liberal republicans agreed with Adams that "it is easy to portray dangers: it is very difficult to suggest remedies," and they actually started to discuss how the government might cope with huge monopolies. Their intense analysis of the relationship between railroad monopolies and republican institutions provides great insight into their thinking.[22]

The liberal republicans repeatedly argued that railroad monopolies' lobbying for bills in legislatures, like the lobbying of other corporations, led directly to corruption that endangered republican government. According to the *Springfield Republican*, "It is here, in the lack of discriminating justice and independence in legislative action, that we shall fail, if we shall fail at all, in meeting the responsibilities, and protecting ourselves from the dangers, to which the creation of these great railroad corporations expose us. In the independence, in the virtue, in the impartiality of our legislators rests the whole problem." Against the "capitalized corruption" of the railroads, the newspaper acknowledged, "The contest is formidable, we know; to many it seems the most fearful the republic has ever encountered." The last statement is remarkable, considering that just four years earlier the nation had barely survived the bloody Civil War. After the Massachusetts state legislature defeated a railroad bill in 1870, the *Republican* rejoiced that "the old commonwealth had been in great peril; the purity and independence of her legislation . . . all have been endangered, but all, we dare to feel and say, have been saved." *The Nation* expressed less optimism for defeating the corruption associated with railroads. In an article titled "Railroads Again," the newspaper told its readers, "Log-rolling is going on; wire-pulling is going on; and very soon open bribery will come into fashion." A month earlier, under the title "Railroads in the Legislatures," the newspaper fondly recalled "when a great party made the corrupt influence of corporations the text of some of their best political homilies." *The Nation* recounted that "pictures were drawn of consequences which may be recognized as the actual condition of to-day. There were to be agents—and we have lobbies; there was to be bribery—and we have log-rolling; there was to be unlimited speculation—and we have little else."[23]

The aspect of railroad speculation that particularly concerned the liberal republicans was the government land grants. "Not even the tariff has led to so much lobbying, so many corrupt influences, and such neglect of other public business, as the incessant applications of railroad and other corporations for more grants of public lands," complained *The Nation*. Besides the corruption, which they found inherently dangerous, many liberal republicans worried that the concentration of land in the hands of a few corporations would endanger the continued existence of large numbers of small landholders, whom they considered the foundation of a republican society. "The future welfare of our country, and the cause of republican liberty in America, depends upon the class of independent freeholders," argued the *Cincinnati Commercial* in an editorial attacking "Another Land Grab" by the railroads. The newspaper insisted, "Free land is absolutely necessary to our people . . . to create and sustain an intelligent yeomanry as the back-bone of the Republic." Such rhetoric was common; a month later the *Commercial* reiterated that "our free institutions rest, and must continue to rest, upon the elements of virtue, knowledge, and patriotism, which are to be found in their greatest perfection in an independent class of freeholders." There is a long history of connecting the survival of republican government to the existence of small landholders. According to James L. Huston, since colonial times "Americans believed that if property were concentrated in the hands of a few in a republic, those few would use their wealth to control other citizens, seize political power, and warp the republic into an oligarchy." Henry Adams harped on exactly this point when discussing the huge amount of land the Erie Railway controlled, explaining that "this property was in effect, like all great railway corporations, an empire within a republic." For liberal republicans the concentration of land in railroad corporations, aided by the government, both limited the growth of the small-landowner base necessary for a republic and created a huge concentration of power.[24]

The liberal republicans showed little reticence in warning of the railroads' growing power and trend toward despotism. In an editorial titled "The Consolidation Era," the *Springfield Republican* discussed the creation of railroad monopolies and asserted that "there is danger, of course, in the great power of the gigantic corporations so built up." The *Cincinnati Commercial* declared, "It should never be placed in the power of a moneyed corporation to dictate the price of flour, meat, grain and other commodities." It warned that railroad corporations were grasping at the power "which lays a whole continent under tribute." Other liberal republicans explicitly compared the railroad corporations to institutions historically considered threats to republican government in the United States. Both the *Republican* and Charles Francis Adams Jr. called the railroad corporations the "railroad power," a phrase reminiscent of the Slave Power that many had considered a menace to republican government before the Civil War. Adams, who ironically would serve as president of the Union

Pacific Railroad in the 1880s, also likened railroad monopolies to some of the traditional boogiemen of early America, such as the Catholic Church since colonial times, and the United States Bank during the Jacksonian era. Some of the liberal republicans were working at cross-purposes at this time, however. David Dudley Field, brother of conservative Supreme Court Justice Stephen J. Field, who opposed government regulation of business activities, served as counsel for tycoons Jay Gould and James Fisk in the Erie Railway litigation in 1869.[25]

The intellectually gifted Adams brothers debated in prominent journals whether the New York or the Pennsylvania railroads posed the greatest danger to republican government. Henry Adams wrote about the property, money, and power of the Erie Railway Company in New York. "Over this wealth and influence,—greater than that directly swayed by any private citizen, greater than is absolutely and personally controlled by most kings, and far too great for public safety," he argued, "the vicissitudes of a troubled time placed two men in irresponsible authority." For Henry, the concentration of power in the hands of two individuals, Jay Gould and James Fisk Jr., represented the danger of tyranny. Charles Francis Adams Jr., however, considered the Pennsylvania Railroad "probably to-day the most powerful corporation in the world" and intertwined politics with business in comparing it to other railroads. The Pennsylvania Railroad's "organization, as compared with that of its great rival, the New York Central, bears the relation of a republic to an empire. Caesarism is the principle of the Vanderbilt group; the corporation is the essence of the Pennsylvania system." He explained that this was natural, as New York had always exalted the individual leader while in Pennsylvania the party and corporation were always supreme. Charles worried more about the well-oiled corporation in Pennsylvania than the individuals in New York, for he predicted that "with this perfect machinery and subordination there is no reason why to-day the corporation should not assume absolute control of all the railroads of Pennsylvania. Indeed, it could take possession of the State government, if it really desired to do so." Despite the burst of sibling rivalry, both the Adams brothers and other liberal republicans agreed that railroad monopolies in the hands of individuals or corporations represented too great a concentration of power within a republic.[26]

Under the headline "The Revolt of the Merchants Against the Tyranny of the Railroads," *The Nation* praised New York merchants for defending everyone's liberty against the railroad monopolies. "Next to the right of personal liberty, the most sacred, most essential right, most pervading right of the citizen of a free country is the right of locomotion and transportation. Personal liberty itself is of no avail, is indeed a mockery, if not accompanied with the unrestricted right of moving person and property from place to place." Railroads,

according to the newspaper and the New York merchants, regularly used kickbacks, extortion, and other forms of corruption to hinder trade and limit people's freedom to travel. Amazingly for a newspaper considered by many
historians to have been inflexibly committed to classical liberal economics, *The
Nation* argued that the protest of the merchants "annihilates by a simple appeal
to the inalienable right of free locomotion all the bulwarks which shallow theo-
rists and designing advocates have built up around the railroad monopoly on
the basis of non-interference, competition, and corporate rights." Classical liberalism idealized the concept of unrestrained free markets, yet here was a liberal
republican newspaper insisting that the appeal to freedom of movement "annihilates" such arguments. *The Nation* went even further, contending that the
public had finally realized "that the attempt to place the control of essential
popular rights in the hands of individuals and corporations has resulted in
unbearable abuses, and that the very existence of popular liberty absolutely
requires that this control, surrendered in ignorance, and wantonly perverted,
shall be entirely resumed by the people, or else so thoroughly limited as to correct existing abuses and prevent the perpetration of new ones."[27]

While *The Nation* concluded that "it is neither necessary nor desirable to
enter now upon a discussion of remedies," other liberal republicans had surprisingly been looking toward the government to solve the threat of the railroad
monopolies for years. In an early 1867 issue of the *North American Review*
edited by Henry Adams, Charles Francis Adams Jr. insisted, "There can be little
doubt that the existing railroad franchises are easily within the reach of the
community, either for the purpose of readjustment of interests or annihilation." Another article in the same issue of the *Review* argued that "the monopo-
lizing tendency of the carrying trade, whether it relate to the transmissions of
telegraphic messages, of freight, or of human passengers" required "the proper
adjustment of which all of the skill and foresight that modern legislation is master." Suggesting that the government could annihilate the railroad monopoly
or legislate economic matters directly contradicts the principles of classical liberalism and appears at odds with republicanism. Charles Francis Adams Jr.
contended, however, "The railroad corporations, necessarily monopolists, constitute a privileged class, living under a form of government intended to inhibit
all class legislation. We must, then, see our government fail in this unexpected
crisis, or we must strengthen it in such a manner as to enable it to vindicate its
authority." The thought of strengthening the government seemed unrepublican, but much as with the threat of the Slave Power and trying efforts to win
the Civil War, the liberal republicans looked for ways to address the danger of
railroad monopolies without overacting and making the government too strong
in the process. Their discussion of how to use the government to check the

power of railroad monopolies demonstrates their continued republican concern with tyranny and corruption.[28]

One option implemented after the Civil War was for individual states to try regulating some of the worst abuses of the railroad monopolies. State governments started to create railroad commissions, often including on them those associated with the liberal republican movement or party, such as Charles Francis Adams Jr. in Massachusetts and the German American leader Gustave Koener in Illinois. The railroad commissions tried to prevent corruption, particularly by regulating fare structures that often made little sense and included kickbacks from companies that were the railroads' most important customers. The *Springfield Republican* agreed in 1870 that the railroads in Massachusetts posed a problem but worried about some of the proposals coming from the Adams-led commission, explaining, "To throw open the whole question of regulating the fares and freights of all the railroads in the state to every Legislature would be such an invitation to corruption and demoralization as no friend of a pure government ought to be willing to extend or even to harbor for a moment. It would be asking the railroad monster to take permanent possession of the state house." While the *Republican* and other liberal republican voices had used cries of corruption and domination by the railroads to warn of danger, now the paper feared that involving the government too much could exacerbate the problems, demonstrating the liberal republicans' conflicted thoughts on government power for any purpose. A year later, however, the *Republican* praised the Massachusetts legislature for passing some of the railroad bills suggested by Commissioner Adams, arguing, "Perhaps the most important act of the Legislature on this subject, however, is that which forbids higher charges for freight for a short distance than for a long distance upon the same road." The Springfield newspaper quickly revealed its local interest in such measures, pointing out for its example of such "anomalies" that it was often cheaper to ship goods from the West to Boston than to Springfield, even though Springfield was on the way to Boston.[29]

By 1871 Adams had decided that state regulation of railroads did not go far enough. "Regulation through State authority has proved the saddest failure of all, for the energetic whole can hardly be controlled by the incompetent government of a part," argued the Massachusetts railroad commissioner. Though a longtime opponent of expanding the power of the federal government, he contended, "It may be very unfortunate that our great lines of railroad should become national routes, but such considerations cannot control the fact; national routes they are, and as such they cannot much longer be controlled under State laws. The Federal government must assume a certain degree of active jurisdiction as regards them, and that very shortly." Adams left little doubt where he stood, reiterating "that the national government must then, soon or late, and in greater or less degree, assume a railroad jurisdiction, is accepted as an obvious conclusion." While Adams thought the need for the federal government to regulate the railroad industry was obvious, it was actually quite progressive, since it would be almost another two decades before the Populists—who would include some former liberal republicans—would make national regulation of the railroads a major issue in the late Gilded Age. The appeal to federal-government intervention also indicates the flexibility of some liberal republicans in trying to balance private and public power to maintain an environment suitable to republican institutions.[30]

Adams also proposed another solution to the railroad monopolies more radical than government regulation: the idea of government ownership of the railroads. "The tendency of popular thought is now undoubtedly towards the ownership of railroads by the community," asserted Adams. Acknowledging "that the government should engage in business, whether as producers, as carriers, as bankers, or as manufacturers, is opposed to the whole theory of limited governmental functions," he still thought the success of government-run railroads in Belgium and the agitation for them in England "make it eminently desirable that the experiment should be tried, if only with a view of testing a theory and giving a new direction to inquiry." Remarkably for someone usually suspicious of government power, Adams wanted some states to experiment with government-owned railroads as a trial for possible federal control of all the railroads in the nation. The *Springfield Republican* wasted little time in blasting Adams's idea as anti-republican. "The whole theory of our republican government is the strictest possible limitations of its offices," insisted the newspaper, and "all the teachings of reason are against a republican state managing a public work." While commending another of Adams's suggestions on the railroads six months later, the *Republican* returned to the topic of government ownership, maintaining that "this notion, we are sure, must soon give way to other experiments, much more congenial to our republican system." Adams himself doubted whether successful government ownership of the railroads at the state level would indicate that the federal government could manage the nation's railroads. He argued, "It is impossible, in view of past experience, not to entertain grave doubts as to the result of any experiment of this sort, made through the political machinery which exists in America." Directly attacking the spoils system, he asserted that "the Federal government is peculiarly and obviously unfitted for any work of the sort,—certainly until a thorough and sweeping reform of the civil service is effected." Ironically, the federal government did a great deal during the Civil War to create the huge railroad monopolies in the first place.[31]

*   *   *

The liberal republicans thus saw protective tariffs, railroad monopolies, and the spoils system all working together to foster the tyranny and corruption that could threaten republican government in the United States. They believed that the government's economic legislation during the Civil War, particularly protective tariffs, had helped create monopolies. The huge new monopolies posed a danger to republican institutions, but the federal government could not act because the spoils system and growing corruption undermined its virtue. In the minds of the liberal republicans the new emphasis on civil service and tariff reform did not constitute an abandonment of African Americans, for they felt they had accomplished their mission of destroying slavery. Back in 1859, during the heat of the sectional crisis, Carl Schurz had prophesized, "Our present issues will pass away. The slavery question will be settled, liberty will be triumphant and other matters of difference will divide the political parties of this country." For the liberal republicans the measures used to win the Civil War had both saved and endangered the republic. While eliminating the Slave Power and thus protecting the experiment of republican government, the war measures had also created new forms of concentrated power and a corrupt government unable to protect its citizens' liberty. These were the "other matters of difference." Carl Schurz described liberal republicanism in early 1872 as "the reaction against the easy political morals and the spirit of jobbery which have grown and been developed in times of war." Liberal republicans thought that instead of the Slave Power, the legacy of the Civil War now endangered republican government.[32]

6

Grant and the Republic, 1868–1872

I
n their long struggle to preserve republican government, the liberal republicans initially embraced Ulysses S. Grant as a savior. From the late 1840s onward their classical republican ideology had led them to fight against various perceived forms of corruption and tyranny threatening the nation's republican institutions. During the antebellum period, most of their focus had been on the dangerous effects of slavery. While battling the Slave Power during the Civil War, the liberal republicans increasingly expressed concerns about the measures being taken to ensure victory, such as protective tariffs and the growth of federal power. By 1868, they wanted to finish the reconstruction of the South and turn their attention to the corruption and centralization of power that had taken root in government during the war. They thought Grant would renew republican government in the United States and eagerly embraced his presidency. Grant soon disappointed the liberal republicans, however, as he seemed to exacerbate the existing threats to republican institutions, creating more corruption and acting tyrannically. Their hesitant opposition to Grant in 1872 represented the continuation of a long struggle to preserve republican government.

The liberal republicans were among the earliest and most enthusiastic Grant supporters. In late 1867 the *Springfield Republican*, *The Nation*, and the *New York Evening Post* began a long campaign to make Grant the Republican Party's presidential candidate. The newspapers repeatedly expressed faith in his ability and judgment, with the *Republican* declaring, "The real republican platform for 1868 will be Ulysses S. Grant, as embodying honesty, executive ability, justice and generosity to the South, and an earnest purpose to restore the Union." Such sentiments were not mere political rhetoric, for the liberal republicans privately expressed similar confidence in Grant. Edward Atkinson wrote to his friend David Wells in early 1868 that in the political intrigue between Grant and Andrew Johnson, "Grant is too honest and too self-sacrificing and only by his integrity has carried the day." While also reflecting his growing frustration with Johnson, Atkinson's letter still confounds the traditional assessments of liberal republican attitudes toward Grant and demonstrates impossibly high expectations for Grant's ability to reform the government.[1]

After Grant's nomination at the Republican Convention held in Chicago in May 1868, the liberal republicans quickly joined the presidential campaign. As usual in Civil War–era politics, the liberal republican newspapers ran constant assaults on potential challengers while lavishing praise on their chosen candidate. *The Nation,* for instance, attacked longtime Republican Salmon P. Chase when the opportunistic Chief Justice of the Supreme Court began flirting with the Democrats after losing the Republican nomination to Grant. "A man's fitness for the presidency is rather a question of character than of acquirements," argued *The Nation,* and "there is little in our humble opinion to be said for the Chief-Justice, and a great deal to be said for Grant." The liberal republicans' partisan support of Grant in some instances included their assuming formal roles in his campaign. Carl Schurz stumped across the country proclaiming that "no fitter man than General Grant could be found" to reconstruct the nation, and Horace White served as an insider in the Grant campaign machine.[2]

The liberal republicans' enthusiasm for Grant reflected their belief that his election would signal the end of Reconstruction and the beginning of a comprehensive reform of the government. Upon Grant's nomination, the *Springfield Republican* insisted that the reason he had been chosen "was because of a general sentiment that precisely this man was needed to secure the full and final reconstruction of the South, to inaugurate a thorough and searching retrenchment in the expenses of the government, to introduce into the civil service the same high standard with which his military selections have ever been made." Atkinson informed a Republican congressman in July that corruption in Congress would destroy the Republican Party, as "no honest or decent man can be content in a party of which a majority declare themselves to be thieves and swindlers. I trust Genl Grant will disown such a connection as every honest man must."[3]

Reconstruction, however, was the key campaign issue. Carl Schurz focused on it in his major campaign speech and cast it in typical republican terms. Reviving the antebellum Slave Power arguments, he contended that the Civil War had been about the struggle "to break the power of aristocratic class government in the South," and that "we liberated only four millions of blacks, but we delivered thirty millions of whites from the odious yoke of grasping aristocracy." He also placed the Civil War in the context of the worldwide struggle for republican government, insisting that if the North had failed to preserve the Union, "For centuries the advocates of despotism would have triumphantly pointed to this most ridiculous failure as often as a friend of liberty dared to pronounce the word Republic." Schurz maintained that "to prevent the return of aristocratic class rule, you must not confine the right of suffrage to one class, but you must extend it over the masses of people without arbitrary distinction." For Schurz, the extension of suffrage included both African Americans and former Confederates; he strenuously argued for black voting rights in his speech and had proposed a resolution at the recent Republican National Convention to give amnesty to all white Southerners.[4]

Schurz's speeches were not mere campaign rhetoric. Busy on the campaign trail for Grant, he privately pleaded with his wife, "Do not be angry with me for assuming so much work. I have already for twelve years fought for the good cause according to my strength. I must not and cannot let anything stand in the way of a last great effort which will bring the work to completion and guarantee us against a reaction. If we are victorious now, it will be the final act of the great drama." Phrases such as the *Republican*'s "full and final reconstruction of the South" and Schurz's "final act of the great drama" indicate the liberal republican state of mind. After decades of struggling for republican government and against slavery, they believed Grant's election would permanently secure the fruits of victory from the Civil War and end the need for continued reconstruction of the South. The idea that Grant's election marked the end of Reconstruction did not place the liberal republicans outside the mainstream, for it was a conviction shared by many in the nation, including other Republicans.[5]

After Grant's victory in November, in the period between the election and Grant's taking office, many of the liberal republicans both privately and publicly discussed their expectations for the new administration. Removed from the partisan atmosphere of both the presidential campaign and the first few months of a new administration, they had less reason than usual to shape their words for political purposes. While they certainly hoped to influence Grant— Horace White had sent him a book on free trade in 1866, convinced that he would be the next president—most assumed they had won a victory with Grant's election and fully expected to influence the new administration. In January *The Nation* ran a long editorial on the remaining work of the Republican Party, listing Reconstruction, fiscal policy, and corruption as major issues. According to the newspaper, "Under these circumstances it is safe to say that the ability of the party to discharge its obligations to the colored population depends on its success in dealing with the other problems of the day. People will not much longer accept devotion to 'human equality' or 'equal rights of man' as an excuse for the condition of the finances and the civil service." It concluded that "in other words, people are more concerned about the kind of government in which the black man is to share than about the precise mode or time in which he is to share in it." Though direct, *The Nation* reflected the attitude of many of the liberal republicans. In the months before Grant took office, they emphasized that they expected him to clean up the spoils system, the general corruption, and the financial legislation associated with the Civil War.[6]

In the months before Grant's inauguration many liberal republicans declared civil service reform the primary issue for the new administration, and they anticipated the president's cooperation. Carl Schurz gave a speech in Congress attacking the spoils system. Privately, he told his wife that it was the issue closest to his heart and would become his specialty. Though disappointed in Grant's early appointments, particularly his selection of relative unknowns for many cabinet positions, Schurz wrote to his wife that "as regards the greater political questions, he shows a tendency to hold with great loyalty to the program of the Republican party, and that of course is the main thing. Everything indicates a determination at all costs to avoid a conflict with Congress, and so we shall doubtless get along well with him." The *Springfield Republican* praised Schurz's Senate speech as the best ever given on the spoils system, for "he sees clearly the present evil," and the paper agreed that Grant would help reform the civil service. The *New York Evening Post* likewise proclaimed, "The first and especial work which Gen. Grant undertakes is to clear the government of those who take its money without giving an equivalent," for "they have grown to be a great power; if united, perhaps they would be the greatest political power in the land. It is a work scarcely second to that of destroying Lee's army itself, to destroy the system of plunder which now threatens our institutions." William Cullen Bryant expressed hope that Grant could and would destroy the corruption in government just as he had vanquished the Army of Northern Virginia. One day after his editorial appeared in the *Post*, Bryant wrote to his youngest brother, "I have been told that Grant makes no secret of his resolution to stop the plunder of the public that is carried on, partly by fraud, and partly by legislation, for personal objects. Of course, he will encounter a terrific opposition, but it is said that he has made up his mind to meet it."[7]

Other liberal republicans focused on economic legislation as the issue that Grant should tackle. During the presidential campaign Horace White had complained in the *Chicago Tribune* that "so potent are the issues growing out of the existence of slavery that it is futile to attempt to fix the public attention upon any others, however momentous." After the election he identified the tariff as the momentous issue that bothered him, warning that the tariff bill "now being rushed through Congress by the representatives of special interests, aided by the bulk of Southern carpetbaggers, is a diabolical outrage." The passage reflects White's intense feelings about tariff legislation and shows how economic legislation was interacting with Reconstruction policies to sour some liberal republicans on Reconstruction. The *Tribune* increasingly attacked the Republican governments in the South as the congressmen from those states started to support the Whiggish economic policies of the Republican Party, such as protective tariffs. White was not alone in seeking to end Reconstruction and emphasize economic issues. In January Atkinson explained to a friend what he thought the country needed. Prefacing his remarks with the caveat that "before the war I was an abolitionist of the Radical stripe," Atkinson wrote, "There are in my mind three points to be aimed at: 1. Complete reconstruction on the basis of impartial suffrage. 2. The re-establishment of the specie standard as speedily as possible. 3. As near an approach to free trade as the necessity of revenue will allow." The order of Atkinson's goals clearly indicates that he wanted to finish Reconstruction with a moderate solution so that the country could move on to other issues. Bryant echoed this attitude a few months later, writing to a friend that "the great question of the day with us is commercial reform, or revenue reform."[8]

The election of Grant and imminent passage of the Fifteenth Amendment, which would prohibit states from denying citizens the right to vote because of their race, color, or having been enslaved, signaled to most liberal republicans that the gains of the Civil War had finally been secured and that it was time to concentrate on new hazards to republican institutions. In May *The Nation* explained, "We have always maintained that the quarrel could not be over until one side or the other had gained the victory, and lately it has been apparent enough that the victory could only be assured by the election of Grant and the passage of the Fifteenth Amendment. One of these is accomplished and the other not quite yet." Within a few months the newspaper would remark as an aside, "ever since the Reconstruction question was fairly disposed of." Horace White, who had helped run guns to John Brown in the 1850s, declared by the middle of 1869, "Old issues are fading from sight. Slavery is abolished and impartial suffrage established, or so nearly so that there is scarcely enough difference of opinion to make a campaign upon. The right of every man to exchange the products of his labor freely is as sacred as any right that God had given him." The *Cincinnati Commercial* agreed, arguing that it was about time "to recognize the fact that the political issues in this country are undergoing a complete change. The Negro in politics is a dead issue. . . . The most important and vital issue remaining above the political horizon is the question of tariff and taxation." Atkinson, a self-described abolitionist since 1848, succinctly explained, "The election of Grant settles the Southern question." For the liberal republicans, Reconstruction had served its purpose of eliminating the Slave Power's threat to republican institutions. Now they expected Grant to end Reconstruction and focus on the new threats that had emerged during the course of the Civil War.[9]

The liberal republican's high expectations for Grant to renew republican government slowly eroded during his first administration. The continued intransigence of white Southerners, exemplified by the rise of the Ku Klux Klan in the late 1860s, forced the federal government to become temporarily more active in asserting its authority in the South. While sympathetic toward Southern blacks, the liberal republicans saw such legislation as the Force Bills of 1870 and 1871 as the continuation of a dangerous trend toward centralized power. For many of them, however, the most troubling aspects of Grant's presidency had little to do with Reconstruction. Not only did Grant fail to push for tariff and civil service reform as many had expected, but his administration became involved in a scheme to annex Santo Domingo, the dubious sale of weapons to France during the Franco-Prussian War, conflicts over appointments, and numerous other scandals. The very real corruption and abuse of power associated with the imbroglios of the administration led many liberal republicans to conclude that, far from restoring the nation's institutions, Grant's presidency posed a direct threat to republican government.

Expectations for peace were similarly dashed, as Grant's election set off another wave of white resistance in the South. Democrats gained control of the Georgia legislature in late 1869 and proceeded to expel its black senators and representatives. Republicans in Congress responded by recommending that Georgia's U.S. senators not be seated in Congress until the expulsion was rescinded. The normally mild-mannered Lyman Trumbull, who had authored and supported earlier Reconstruction legislation, decided that the federal government had interfered enough in state affairs. He repudiated the recommendation of his own committee to not admit the Georgia senators and gave several impassioned speeches denouncing the continued accumulation of power in Washington. Responding to fellow senators' arguments that Congress had the right to intervene in Georgia to fulfill the Constitutional guarantee of a republican form of government, Trumbull insisted, "This is what republican government means—a representative government; and the further that power is taken from the people the greater the danger is that their liberties will be encroached upon." He warned, "It would be a surrender of human rights to imperial, centralized government if the people of this country should ever consent to surrender up all their rights of liberty to the central government here at Washington." The constant refrain of centralized government and endangered liberties lies at the heart of republican thought, and Trumbull may have reached its zenith when at one point he simply declared, "All government is an evil."[10]

A more prolonged debate about continued federal activity in the Southern states occurred with the rise in Ku Klux Klan violence after Grant's election. Just as Southern intransigence had radicalized Congress in 1866, the Ku Klux

Klan's campaign of terror overcame Republicans' increasing reluctance to intervene in the South. Republicans pushed the outer limits of constitutional change during Reconstruction with a series of Force Bills in Congress. While they wanted to stop the Klan violence, the Force Bills proved too radical for many of the liberal republicans, who feared the further expansion of federal power. During debate on one of the early, more limited Force Bills in 1870, Trumbull stated, "I agree that the wicked organizations should be put down," but he refused to support giving the president the power to suspend the writ of habeas corpus, because "the people of this country prize their liberties too highly to trust anybody with this power of military despotism, except when pressed by invasion or rebellion."[11]

The liberal republicans reacted more strenuously against the Ku Klux Klan Bill of 1871, the last of the Force legislation. The bill, for the first time in United States history, designated certain crimes committed by individuals as offenses punishable under federal law. For many of the liberal republicans, it went too far in destroying the traditional barriers between the federal and state government that they thought helped to protect citizens' liberty. "Show me that it is necessary to exercise any power belonging to the Government of the United States in order to maintain its authority and I am ready to put it forth," Trumbull contended in Congress, "but sir, I am not willing to undertake to enter the States for the purpose of punishing individual offenses against their authority committed by one citizen against another." He argued in republican terms, insisting, "I believe that the rights of the people, the liberties of the people, the rights of the individual are safest among the people themselves, and not in a central Government extending over a vast region of country." While acknowledging that the Ku Klux Klan existed, Carl Schurz joined Trumbull in expressing fear that the anti-Klan legislation threatened republican institutions by concentrating too much power in the hands of the federal government. "Although I willingly admit that the evils to be combated at the South seem to require strong remedies," Schurz maintained, "here a remedy is proposed, placing power in the hands of the President of the United States which I would confide to no living man." He apocalyptically warned that maybe a "time will come when a part of the Republic will be so deeply sunk in anarchy and rule of violence that nothing but a strong, consolidated central Government, invested with arbitrary powers, can remedy the evil." If such a time should come, Schurz hoped that "we should have manliness enough to declare that this great experiment of local self-government has failed."[12]

The liberal republican press also worried about the reach of the Ku Klux Klan Act of 1871. Like Trumbull and Schurz, *The Nation* expressed fears that the legislation concentrated too much power in the federal government. While declaring that the United States should enforce the Constitution "at whatever the cost," *The Nation* opposed the act because "it consists simply in attempts to substitute for the state machinery, which is the only means of protecting life and property known to the Constitution of the United States, the machinery in use under the arbitrary and centralized governments of Europe—that is, the withdrawal of criminal cases from the jury, and their committal to single judges appointed by the central authority and armed with extraordinary powers." The *Springfield Republican* surprisingly argued that "the oppressive violence" meant that "the emergency is so threatening that it could hardly be considered safe for Congress to adjourn without enlarging the federal authority in some such way as it now seems certain to do." Significantly, though, the *Republican* and the *Cincinnati Commercial,* which referred to the Klan as "murderers and assassins," considered the Klan violence a result of the failure of Republicans to embrace their plan to end Reconstruction through universal suffrage and universal amnesty. Both newspapers bitterly lamented that "this violence has delayed reconstruction, and defeated, or rather delayed a declaration of universal amnesty," a policy they believed would eliminate the Klan by taking away "all real or even fancied occasion of complaint on the part of the southern people." When Grant finally used the Klan Acts to declare martial law in several South Carolina counties in late 1871, the *Commercial* thought it as favorable a time as any to test the legislation, but editorialized, "We have our doubts whether even the enforcement of the law will effectually break up the Ku-Klux association."[13]

While certainly the liberal republicans, like many of their contemporaries, had long considered blacks inferior to whites, they continued to think of blacks as citizens. It would be simplistic to think racism was the driving force behind the liberal republicans' ebbing support for Reconstruction. The *Springfield Republican* praised Grant's nomination of two blacks as ambassadors to Haiti and Liberia in April 1869, prophesizing that "the time will come when color will cease to be a test of fitness or a reason for distinction, either for or against the children of Africa." The newspaper declared that until such time "when the races will be so blended that it will cease to be a distinction . . . this people have still a long credit against us which we must spend years, if not centuries, in paying. School houses, homestead grants, postoffices, senatorships and a good many other valuables must be turned in to clear off the score, and it is a satisfaction to see Grant acknowledging the debt."[14]

Well into Grant's first term the liberal republicans carried on an explicit discussion of how different races could coexist in a nation with a republican form of government. Under the headline "The Question of Race," the *Cincinnati Commercial* noted, "No assertion has been more constant among the unbelievers of American Republicanism than that our experiment or government, will sooner or later, turn out a failure," and elaborated:

Perhaps the most frequently reiterated argument of the prophets of our political downfall, is that the presence of so many and such diverse races in our experiment of government must produce discord and disintegration. Here we are, it is said, a vast conglomerate of all nations and races—the wild Irishman, the stolid German, the idle Spaniard, the obstinate Englishman, the frivolous Frenchman, the barbarous African, and a multitude of other nationalities that no man can number, mingled piggledy-piggledy together on the broad level of absolute equality, and trying the hopeless experiment of republican government with these materials.

Immediately after referring to so many blatant stereotypes, though, the *Commercial* optimistically contended that "as the case stands, are not the diverse races that make up our concrete nationality on the whole pretty well fused?" *The Nation* likewise mixed racism with optimism in an editorial of mid-1870 entitled "The Race Question." After going through the standard mid-nineteenth-century concepts of evolution and racist stereotypes of blacks, it concluded, "It will require a much longer time than it is worth while for us to talk about to bring him into the condition of our own race." Still, while *The Nation* predicted that "there can be no question that a most difficult problem for the coming legislators of this country arises from the mingling of the diverse races under its government," it insisted that "we are far from asserting that it is impossible to combine several races in one society."[15]

A short editorial in the *Cincinnati Commercial* about the Ku Klux Klan in late 1871 illustrates the complex nature of the liberal republicans' attitude toward blacks during Reconstruction. When Grant sent troops to North and South Carolina, the *Commercial* hoped that "if the proof of guilt can be brought home to them, and a few examples made, it will be very likely to improve the condition of society, especially if the colored men, imitating the example of the Negroes in Kentucky, make good use of their guns when assailed by the masked marauders." On the one hand, the newspaper was suggesting that blacks shoot white men who attacked them, an empowering notion which would have been considered extremely radical a decade earlier. On the other hand, the *Commercial* wanted blacks to act so that the government would not have to become involved, a stance it would probably not have taken if white citizens had been assaulted.[16]

For decades the liberal republicans had fought to end slavery and maintain republican government. After the Civil War they cared about the plight of blacks and helped support Reconstruction, but their primary goal remained preserving republican government, and they tried crafting legislation that would not permanently create a strong central government. In the end, they cared more about the preservation of republican institutions than the protection of blacks, and by 1871 they began to see these as mutually incompatible.

Questions of race and republican institutions arose again in the debate over Grant's attempted annexation of Santo Domingo in early 1871. The circumstances surrounding the attempt made it a scandal, for a combination of the Navy's desire for a Caribbean base and Americans' interest in business opportunities led Grant to have his private secretary, Orville Babcock, negotiate the agreement—without the knowledge of the secretary of state. Babcock's involvement appeared fishy, as he personally owned land on the island that would appreciate significantly with annexation. Before the disreputable nature of the plan came to light and became the center of attention, however, much of the debate focused on the effects of annexing a Caribbean island populated with blacks. The racial aspects of annexing Santo Domingo made for strange bedfellows in Washington. Grant argued that annexation might encourage Southern blacks to emigrate there, which could be seen as a form of the colonization Lincoln had advocated during the Civil War, while Frederick Douglass, one of the fiercest critics of Lincoln's colonization ideas, wanted the United States to annex Santo Domingo to uplift the island and its people. Democrats who had supported Caribbean expansion before the Civil War when slavery was legal now opposed annexation, and they found an unlikely champion in Charles Sumner, chairman of the Senate Foreign Relations Committee and a longtime abolitionist, who fought annexation because he feared it would threaten the independence of neighboring Haiti, the hemisphere's only black republic.[17]

The liberal republicans opposed the annexation of Santo Domingo on the ground that tropical climates were unsuited to republican governments. Carl Schurz gave one of the early speeches against the annexation, asking his fellow senators to "read that history . . . of all other tropical countries, and then show me a single instance of the successful establishment and peaceable maintenance for a respectable period of republican institutions." He repeatedly stressed that race was not the issue, insisting, "Say not that this is the failing of the races living there alone, for I will prove to you that the Anglo-Saxons have been tried under the tropical sun, and have, in the main points failed." The reason republican government did not work in the tropics, according to Schurz, was that "while the temperate climate stimulates the exercise of reason and the sense of order, the tropical sun inflames the imagination to inordinate activity and develops the government of the passions." Such ideas that the environment shaped peoples and societies, particularly that colder climates forced advancement while warm climates induced idleness, were widely held in the nineteenth century and even well into the twentieth. Schurz used such theories to their utmost to try to distance his arguments from any taint of racism: "You see, indeed, here a blending of races going on which, as its result leaves one united American people; and I may say that here, upon our soil, I am not afraid of any foreign element that may come to share our fortunes with us, not even the Chinese"; for Schurz insisted that "assimilation here . . . is assimilation upward." Since Schurz was convinced that republican government would not take root in the tropics, he contended that "the very acquisition of that territory would put us on the high road to military rule." Schurz warned the Senate that "the satrapies you erect will be so many nurseries of rapacity, extortion, plunder, oppression, and tyranny, which will, with the certainty of fate, demoralize and corrupt our political life beyond any degree yet conceived of, and impart to our Government a military character most destructive of republican attributes." Again and again in the speech he worried "how we may maintain the integrity of our republican institutions" while expanding into the tropics. In a conclusion filled with classical allusions, Schurz argued, "The Republic stands at the present moment like Hercules at the parting of the ways; one running southward, pointing to a repetition of the Roman empire . . . the other pointing northward to the great republican power of the future."[18]

Many liberal republicans praised Schurz for his January 1871 speech against annexation, indicating that he had represented their views. Jacob Cox wrote to Schurz, "Your speeches on Civil Service and on St. Domingo I have read carefully and with great interest, and most heartily endorse everything you have said in *both*." Cox specifically mentioned Schurz's discussion of republican government in the tropics, proclaiming, "I was glad of your boldness in putting squarely before the country the fact extension into tropical regions is proven by all experience to be dangerous to republican institution." In a page-long article about annexing Santo Domingo, *The Nation* concluded that "the late speech of Senator Schurz is, however, so exhaustive as to the impolicy of annexation that but little could be added." Though the increasingly racist Cox explicitly stated that part of his opposition to annexation was because of Santo Domingo's black population—he told Schurz, "I advocate the separation of the races as the logical consequence of the most radical abolition"—Schurz before Congress and Godkin in *The Nation* carefully stressed that the environment, not the inhabitants' race, made the tropics unsuitable to republican government.[19]

The liberal republicans soon perceived a more direct threat to republican institutions from the annexation of Santo Domingo than just the absorption of areas they considered inhospitable to republican government. While negotiating the treaty, Grant ordered U.S. naval vessels to support the government of Santo Domingo, without congressional approval. Carl Schurz and other liberal republicans quickly condemned Grant's use of force without congressional approval as a violation of the Constitution and a danger to the integrity of republican government. "We have heard Senators speak of extending the blessings of republican government to San Domingo. I would respectfully suggest to those Senators that it is time to see to it that the integrity of republican government be preserved at home," Schurz declared to the Senate. He ignored the issue of annexation during two days of debate in the Senate, concentrating on Grant's usurpation of war powers from Congress. Analyzing the nature of the United States government, Schurz explained that the power to declare war must reside in the legislature, and "it cannot be otherwise in a truly republican Government. This is a condition sine qua non of republican institutions." Schurz raised the traditional bogeyman for republicanism, the specter of one-man rule. He proclaimed it time that "such practices, so strongly smelling of personal government, should be held up to the contemplation of a republican people, and that a republican Senate, who have sworn to maintain the fundamental laws of this Republic, should openly and emphatically pronounce their disapproval of them." If Grant's actions went unchecked, argued Schurz, "then the integrity, nay, the very existence of republican government in this country hangs on a slender thread." While Schurz's dire warnings may seem exaggerated in retrospect, the *Springfield Republican* wholeheartedly agreed, contending that the Grant administration's "zeal to secure the coveted annexation led them beyond the proprieties of the executive" and judging Schurz's speech "very able and convincing."[20]

For liberal republicans the annexation of Santo Domingo posed many different types of threats to the preservation of republican institutions in the United States. Both the means of annexation—Grant's apparent usurpation of war-making powers from Congress—and the end—trying to extend republican government to the tropics—appeared fraught with the traditional dangers to republican institutions: autocratic one-man rule and a dependent citizenry. The third traditional threat to republicanism, corruption, also became associated with the annexation. Both the thought of expanding the responsibilities of a federal civil service they already considered wracked with corruption and their increasing disappointment in the virtue of members of Grant's administration led the liberal republicans to believe that annexation would exacerbate an already dangerous problem. "Anybody who, with the condition of the civil service of the Government in every department," contended *The Nation*, "still desires the speedy annexation of Cuba and St. Domingo, with their semi-barbarous populations, to the United States, is a person with whom there is perhaps not much use in arguing." When the involvement of Grant's personal secretary in negotiating the treaty came to light, liberal republicans began correctly inferring that members of Grant's administration had used the government for their own personal advantage. Schurz declared, "It is time, at last, in the face of these glaring facts that we should do our utmost to dispel that most dangerous confusion of ideas which represents to us the United States, the Government, and the person of the President as one and the same thing."[21]

As the Radical Republicans had had their expectations with regard to Andrew Johnson and Reconstruction dashed, many of the liberal republicans soon had their expectations that Grant would reform the civil service similarly crushed. During the campaign and in office Grant advocated civil service reform in principle, but in practical terms the most he did was create a special commission to study the problem, a tactic long used to placate people without really doing anything. "We are afraid it is true, in spite of Gen Grant's excellent generalizations for civil service reform," commented the *Springfield Republican*, "that there is no very hearty and practical sympathy with the needed reform among the executive rulers at Washington." The liberal republicans appeared to understand the difficulty Grant had in fighting a system so entrenched that even the Lincoln administration had had difficulty taming its partisanship to help the war effort. According to Henry Adams, "The experience of the present government has shown that even a President so determined in character and so strong in popular support as General Grant shrank from the attempt to reform the civil service as one beyond his powers." The problem of the spoils system, Adams argued, would only be solved by an appeal "to the people, to return to the first principles of the government, and to shut off forever this source of corruption in the state." Even as relations between Grant and the liberal republicans became strained, Lyman Trumbull still found Congress more complicit in the corruption of the spoils system than Grant, explaining in Congress that "it is the great source of evil in our civil service system that Congressmen have usurped functions belonging to the executive branch of the Government." While they wished that the president would take a more active role in reforming the civil service and combating the corruption associated with it, the liberal republicans also understood that Grant had not created the spoils system and was in some ways a captive of it.[22]

While the liberal republicans had disliked the spoils system for years, their distrust of Grant and his administration grew gradually. Grant dashed their high expectations for his presidency with his initial cabinet choices, which astonished members of both parties. Unlike Lincoln, who had adroitly chosen the most powerful and well-known leaders of the Republican Party for his cabinet, Grant selected his secretaries as though he were choosing staff officers in whom the main qualification he sought was loyalty. Some of his cabinet appointees, such as the new secretary of the Navy, were relatively unknown even in their home states, and others posed significant conflicts of interest. Alexander T. Stewart, Grant's nominee for secretary of the treasury, was one of the nation's largest importers and did more business with the treasury Department than any other U.S. citizen. Despite the questionable cabinet selections, however, the liberal republican press continued to support Grant publicly. The *Chicago Tribune* backhandedly complimented him, explaining that "two months have passed away, and it cannot be affirmed that we have a strong administration. Its moral power has been frittered away by small absurdities, which, fortunately, have no bearing upon the sincerity, the truthfulness, or the high purpose of the President or his advisers. We doubt if there ever was an administration with more good intentions at heart, or less aptitude for carrying them into effect." Later the same month the *Tribune* gave a more optimistic assessment of the administration, exclaiming that Grant's first few months in office had given America "a more perfect peace and a more certain and enlarged prosperity than the country has known for many years." *The Nation* was kinder still, stating, "We are inclined to think the Administration, on the whole, a rather strong one," asking that "as regards the Cabinet and the general policy of the Government, for heaven's sake let us for once give the President at least six months' trial."[23]

Grant did not get a six-month honeymoon. By June of 1869 the *Springfield Republican* was referring to "the general disgust which followed many of the appointments made by Gen Grant." *The Nation* waited until September, but then declared, "Grant's Administration has not only made bad appointments, but probably some of the worst ever made by a civilized Christian government. On this point none of his friends and admirers, and we count ourselves amongst the number, can deny feeling deep and bitter disappointment." Significantly, the liberal republican angst about presidential appointments came well before Grant started dismissing liberal republican appointees in late 1870, such as Secretary of the Interior Jacob D. Cox. Having supported Grant in the hopes of reinvigorating the nation's virtue, liberal republicans became dismayed at his failure to reform the spoils system and at his questionable appointments. In addition, after 1870 a series of scandals involving the Grant administration came to light. Vice President Schuler Colfax was part of Credit Mobilier, a fraudulent construction company designed to skim funds off the Union Pacific Railroad. It was also revealed during Grant's first term that in 1868 Colfax had accepted a $4,000 campaign contribution from a contractor who had supplied the government with envelopes while Colfax was chairman of the Committee on Post Offices in Congress. The president's family became involved in the 1871 Gold Scandal, when Grant's brother tried to help Jay Gould corner the gold market. And Grant's private secretary, who had earlier inappropriately negotiated the Santo Domingo treaty, became linked with the infamous Whiskey Ring in 1871 by taking money from a group of distillers who bribed federal agents to avoid paying whiskey taxes. The liberal republicans began to see the Grant administration not just as apathetic toward civil service reform and bumbling in its appointments, but as active participants in the increasing corruption that endangered republican institutions.[24]

The liberal republicans became even more concerned with the perceived corruption of the Grant administration after the fight in Congress over Santo Domingo. When opposed by congressional Republicans, including the liberal republicans, Grant decided to use the spoils system and his appointive power to maintain party discipline. Charles Sumner, one of the longest-serving Republican senators and the party's abolitionist conscience in the Senate, was ousted as chairman of the Senate Foreign Relations Committee for his opposition to the annexation of Santo Domingo. Secretary of the Interior Jacob D. Cox and Special Commissioner of the Revenue David Wells were forced out of office. It was in mid-1870 that a schism within the Missouri Republican Party led to the so-called Liberal Republican Bolt led by Carl Schurz. Grant sided with the other wing of the Republican Party in Missouri and used his patronage power to punish Schurz's faction. Many historians have considered the liberal republicans' advocacy of civil service reform and opposition to Grant merely chagrin at losing power and positions. Grant's use of corrupt means to gain personal ends, however, such as his use of the spoils system in Missouri and his manipulation of the Senate over Santo Domingo, demonstrated exactly why liberal republicans considered corruption a threat to republican government. The *New York Evening Post* compared Grant to past presidents the liberal republicans thought had arrogated power to themselves at the expense of the nation's republican institutions. According to the newspaper, "Not even Buchanan's interference in Kansas was more gross and unblushing than President Grant's attempt to coerce the Missouri Republicans to do his will and not their own. No President except Andrew Johnson has ever tried, by wholesale removals from office and by the appointments of his favorites, to impose his 'policy' upon the party." Ironically, the newspaper neglected mentioning another Andrew—Andrew Jackson—whose successful removal of people from office to put his stamp on the Democratic Party in the 1830s helped create the spoils system. While the *Springfield Republican* thought the blunders of the Grant administration did not yet warrant a new party, it warned, "The dominant party cannot afford to lose a great many of its members, or endure a great deal more of the discipline it has been undergoing the last year." Schurz and other liberal republicans complained that Grant was using the Republican Party as his personal tool for self-aggrandizement and labeled his insistence on party discipline a form of tyranny dangerous to republican institutions.[25]

The cries of corruption and party despotism continued with the politically charged issue of the United States government's sale of guns to France, starting in 1870, during the Franco-Prussian War. Through a series of intermediaries, the government reportedly sold seven hundred thousand guns and one hundred million cartridges to the agents of the French government, a seeming violation of U.S. neutrality. At first the liberal republican press demonstrated little concern about the issue, explaining "business is business." Carl Schurz brought the matter to the attention of the State Department, which ended the practice, but some of his fellow German Americans criticized what they considered a tepid response. When Grant began using his patronage power against liberal republicans after the Missouri bolt, Schurz decided to raise the issue of the arms sales again. In addition to the dubious legality of selling arms to one belligerent while proclaiming neutrality, questions arose over large discrepancies—around $10 million—between the money the Treasury Department paid out and what it received. The possibility that here was another example of corruption, according to Schurz, made the arms sale "a symptom of a morbid tendency of our political life, and as such its importance goes far beyond the question involving the mere sales of arms. I said, and I repeat, the moral and intellectual atmosphere which renders such productions possible is so unhealthy that republican government cannot long live in it." Schurz called for a Senate investigation, a measure the liberal republican press now enthusiastically supported.[26]

With open warfare now existing within the Republican Party, senators loyal to the administration perceived Schurz's call for an investigation as a political attack upon the president. Senators Roscoe Conkling and Oliver Morton blasted Schurz in the Senate, calling into question his loyalty to the Republican Party and the United States. Schurz engaged the pro-administration senators in debate for days, contending that "you may try to throw suspicion upon the motives of those who attack corruption, but it will be in vain. The people understand that when motives are called into question, the motives of those who are serving as the henchmen of power are no less open to doubt than the motives of men who spurn to seek its favors at the expense of an honorable independence and their convictions of duty." He later lectured his opponents that "while you call our action the offspring of a factious spirit, you call yours patriotism. Patriotism, sir! If this becomes the standard of patriotism in this country, then good night free institutions and republican liberty." The fight over the French arms sale was politically sensitive, as it came just months before the Republican National Convention and held the possibility of alienating German Americans, a significant constituency within the Republican Party. As Schurz argued, the motives on both sides were complex. The liberal republicans had been concerned with corruption for a long time, but had shown little interest in investigating the arms sales until their break with Grant. Members of the administration, meanwhile, had been involved in an enterprise of dubious legality and almost certain corruption, and seemed intent on covering up another scandal.[27]

The reaction of the Grant administration and its allies in the Senate seemed to be the aspect of the French arms sale that most upset the liberal republicans, for Schurz described it as "despotism of the party." At the direction of the administration, Republican senators such as Conkling and Morton attacked those raising the issue of the arms sale, tried to prevent an investigation, and finally agreed to create a Senate committee to look into the affair only if Schurz was excluded from it. Such high-handed measures against a U.S. senator trying to investigate corruption in the executive branch struck liberal republicans as party despotism, a perfect example of corruption and tyranny working together to subvert the most republican of institutions, the Senate. Alluding to the image of a slave master, Schurz lectured Conkling on the floor of the Senate that "the crack of the party whip has lost its power in these days of ours." Lyman Trumbull came to Schurz's defense, asking, "Has it come to this, that Republicans, faithful to all the principles of the party, but hostile to official corruption and dishonesty, shall not be permitted to meet together to combine and give force to their views without incurring the displeasure of other members of the party? Sir, I recognize no such party allegiance."[28]

Schurz needed little help, though, as he soon returned to castigating the senators insisting on party discipline and loyalty to the administration: "Show me the vilest despotism in the world, show me in that despotism the vilest sycophants, rolling in the dust at the foot of the throne, and those sycophants will justify the vilest acts of despotism upon the identical doctrine." After graphically insinuating that the senators supporting Grant were sycophants serving a tyrant, Schurz explained, "I am very far from comparing any Senator on this floor with any of those sycophants; but let me tell them it is alarming, it is humiliating to find something like this doctrine, which is the very foundation of all irresponsible power, of all arbitrary government, advocated in the American Senate; and as a Senator, as a friend of republican institutions, and as an American, I declare I would rather have this right hand cut off than that it should sign my name to such a doctrine." Not through with the dramatic oratory, he contended, "Let this go on, and you will prepare for absolute power on one side and for absolute and degrading subservience on the other; and indeed we have already gone very far," for "the friends of popular liberty and republican institutions may well say that evil days are coming."[29]

The liberal republicans had helped nominate Grant, had campaigned for him, and had defended him in the first months of his presidency, all in the hope that he could reverse the trends of centralized power and corruption that they feared were undermining the nation's republican institutions. Grant not only failed to reform the civil service, eliminate protective tariffs, or end Reconstruction, but actually seemed to be drastically increasing the levels of corruption and actively centralizing power in the federal government. Henry Adams wrote to Schurz in early 1871 that "between the Force Bill, the Legal Tender case, San Domingo, and Tammany [New York City's government, which had become the byword for corruption in the Civil War era], I see no constitutional government any longer possible." A few months later Schurz gave a speech arguing that "the patronage, that system of selfish and arbitrary favoritism, has made the public offices the mere spoils of the victorious party. The officers of the Government have become a political army, commanded by one man and his satellites. It rests with the President to use his power to appoint and to remove as a machinery of corruption and intimidation." The *Springfield Republican* likewise contended that Grant "has simply allowed himself to manage public affairs as if he was our master and not our servant—our landlord and not our steward." Terms such as "political army," "master," and "corruption and intimidation" struck at the deepest chords of traditional republican fears. While many of the liberal republican warnings of danger to republican government occurred in public and dealt with politically charged issues, other expressions took place in private correspondence. It is telling that perhaps the most alarmist discussion was a private exchange between David Wells and Jacob D. Cox. Wells actually asked Cox about the possibility of Grant using the military to take over the government if he lost the election in 1872, to which the former secretary of the Interior responded that "my acquaintance with Grant prevents my assent to the idea that he could be the man for a political coup d'etat." But the liberal republicans' distrust of Grant had reached the point where they were privately discussing the possibility of Grant literally overthrowing republican government in the United States to create a military despotism.[30]

7

The National Phase of the Liberal Republican Movement, 1870–1872

The proceedings of the Liberal Republican Convention in Cincinnati upset the original liberal republicans. Carl Schurz wrote, "I cannot think of the results of the Cincinnati Convention without a pang," and Edward Atkinson began a letter by simply stating, "I have just returned from Cincinnati where I left my scalp." The reason for the liberal republicans' pain was the unexpected nomination of Horace Greeley as the new party's presidential candidate. In the weeks following the convention, they tried to determine how Greeley, an outsider who had agreed to attend the convention only a month earlier, had been nominated in place of their preferred candidates, Charles Francis Adams and Lyman Trumbull. Much of the discussion centered on a meeting between B. Gratz Brown, Frank Blair, and Greeley's representatives the night before the convention was to nominate a candidate, for the next day Brown withdrew from the presidential contest, threw his support to Greeley, and was then nominated as vice-presidential candidate. Murat Halstead's *Cincinnati Commercial* and Samuel Bowles' *Springfield Republican* both attributed Greeley's victory to a deal struck at the meeting, with Bowles privately insisting, "It was the work of fate and Frank Blair." Analyzing his defeat, Charles Francis Adams concluded in his diary that "my name developed a very formidable strength which was only overcome by some intrigues of managers from New York and Pennsylvania." According to Schurz, the convention had been successful until "at the decisive moment taken possession of by a combination of politicians striking and executing a bargain in the open light of day— and politicians, too, belonging to just the tribe we thought we were fighting against." The liberal republicans' outrage at Greeley's supposed nomination by a "combination of politicians" begs a more important question: Why were Greeley and these politicians at the Liberal Republican Convention in the first place?[1]

The liberal republicans saw the Cincinnati Convention as the ultimate means to gain control of the Republican Party. As detailed in chapter 1, in 1868 Carl Schurz and twelve other Republicans had formed the Twentieth Century Club in Missouri and over the next two years had tried forcing the state's Republican Party to adopt universal amnesty, civil service reform, and free trade. After a two-year battle against the state's most powerful Republicans, the

Twentieth Century Club had used the opportunity of the Democrats' not running a gubernatorial candidate in 1870 to hold their own convention, expanding
their small group into the Liberal Republican Party of Missouri. The transformation of their club into a party necessitated including many new people, often
with different agendas, but Schurz and the others had managed to maintain
control. The Liberal Republicans' victory in the gubernatorial contest directly
led to the organization of a national liberal republican movement, with many
of the same leaders and issues. Like its predecessor in Missouri, the national
movement consisted of a small group of influential men who wanted to control
the direction of the Republican Party, and they faithfully followed the example
set in Missouri. As the liberal republicans tried to turn their movement into a
national party during the winter and spring of 1872, they invited other Republicans dissatisfied with President Grant's administration, such as Horace Greeley,
to join their ranks, even though they disagreed on many issues. Liberal republican Jacob Cox did not like the Grant administration, but had "no faith in a
campaign based on personal antagonism to Grant, and have looked to our convention far more as the promise of a future party of distinct and true principles
of political economy and administration, than as a means of electing a president this year." If the issues of free trade and civil service reform were the central focus of the liberal republican movement and the Cincinnati Convention,
Cox reasoned that "on these questions Greeley and his associates are the natural
leaders of the party in opposition to our views, and we must therefore expect
the new crystallization of parties to put G. and us in these natural and true
relations to each other, viz., of antagonistic leaders." In the months before the
convention Schurz and the more politically ambitious liberal republicans
forced the other members in the movement to accept Greeley, an outsider in
favor of protective tariffs who was associated with political corruption in New
York, as a participant at the Cincinnati Convention. The liberal republicans lost
control of the transformation from movement to party, however, and Horace
Greeley took over, forever changing the course of liberal republicanism.[2]

Sheer lack of political talent, as opposed to political innocence or anti-Grant
calculation, destroyed the liberal republicans' chances at the Cincinnati Convention. Political talent was important throughout the mid-nineteenth century
in determining the fate of political parties. Superior leadership had enabled the
Republicans to succeed, while inept politicians and campaign mistakes had
helped to destroy the Know-Nothings and Whigs in the 1850s. The liberal
republicans likewise made repeated political blunders before and during the
Cincinnati Convention that led to Greeley's nomination, demonstrating the
necessity of skillful leadership for political parties to survive in the fluid political
environment of the Civil War era. In addition to political ineptitude, the liberal

republicans also suffered from a malady that had hurt the Whig Party—selfishness among the leaders. With the Whigs, selfishness took the form of leaders disregarding the party's welfare in order to advance their own careers, as exemplified by the insatiable presidential ambitions of Daniel Webster and Henry Clay. For the liberal republicans the most damaging cases of selfishness were the lack of presidential ambitions among their favorite candidates. Neither Charles Francis Adams nor Lyman Trumbull truly wanted to run for president, and their reluctance hamstrung the liberal republicans at Cincinnati. The blunders of liberal republican managers at the Cincinnati Convention and the lack of ambition among their preferred candidates ultimately cost the liberal republicans control of the Cincinnati Convention and the Liberal Republican Party.[3]

The national phase of the liberal republican movement began on November 22, 1870, in New York City. The American Free Trade League, impressed with the victory of the new Liberal Republican Party in Missouri, invited its leaders, Carl Schurz, William Grosvenor, and B. Gratz Brown, to a meeting to consider future plans. Mahlon Sands, secretary of the American Free Trade League, wrote that the success of the Liberal movement in Missouri seemed to foretell a great opportunity to reform national politics. Sands and the leaders of the League thought the time was ripe to start a new national movement to advocate free trade and civil service reform."[4]

William Grosvenor represented the Missouri liberal republicans at the New York meeting. Thirty to forty men greeted Grosvenor in New York, including Horace White of the *Chicago Tribune,* Charles Nordhoff and William Cullen Bryant of the *New York Evening Post,* Don Piatt of the *Cincinnati Commercial,* Samuel Bowles of the *Springfield Republican,* Edwin Godkin of *The Nation,* Henry Adams of the *North American Review,* and David Dudley Field, Joshua Lawrence Chamberlain, David Wells, Charles Francis Adams Jr., and Edward Atkinson. Though Carl Schurz and former secretary of the interior Jacob Cox did not attend the meeting for fear of alienating President Grant, both received reports of the proceedings. The participants decided that the new liberal republican movement would work within the Republican Party to advocate civil service reform and free trade. Before adjourning, the meeting discussed the propriety of effecting a permanent organization. "We proposed the appointment of a central committee with a view to calling a convention," Henry Adams wrote to Cox, but "I was soon satisfied that there was great danger of our committing a serious blunder by acting without sufficient preparation." The liberal republicans agreed to postpone forming a central committee while they organized the movement. Like their predecessors in Missouri, this group of liberal republicans wanted to forge small, unified organizations that might gain control of the Republican Party, but that also held the potential to form the foundation of a new party if necessary.[5]

At the New York meeting the liberal republicans began planning for direct action, deciding to try influencing the organization of the new House of Representatives while simultaneously setting up permanent lobbying groups in Washington. Their first ambition failed miserably. James G. Blaine convinced the liberal republicans to support him as Speaker of the House in exchange for picking a free trade chairman of the House Ways and Means Committee, and then refused to appoint their choice after he was elected. The effort to establish lobbying activities in Washington was more successful, as it led to the creation of the Tax Payers' Union. The geographically diverse executive committee of Wells, Atkinson, Sands, White, and Cox made the Missourian Grosvenor the salaried director of the Union and assigned New Yorker Henry Demarest Lloyd and Ohioan Roeliff Brinkerhoff as assistants. Only twenty-three years old, Lloyd edited the Union's newspaper, the *People's Pictorial Taxpayer*. (By 1872 Lloyd would join the editorial staff of the *Chicago Tribune*, though he became best known for his 1894 muckraking *Wealth Against Commonwealth*, which analyzed Standard Oil and attacked the power of monopolies.) With many familial and business connections already established in the area, Brinkerhoff toured the Midwest speaking against protective tariffs. Grosvenor, though, wanted to do more than lobby and sought to use the Union to create a secret grassroots organization for the new political movement. After months of work he reported to Wells that he had the "names of reliable workers in every district in the U.S. but 8, in every county of 73 districts, in over one thousand counties, and in every town of 215 counties. By the end of the next month I shall have, for all practical purposes an organization of the friends of reform reaching down to townships, and extending through the greater part of the country." Most importantly, according to Grosvenor, "nobody will call it an organization, and therefore nobody will know that one exists." Despite the extent of the organization, Grosvenor and the liberal republicans still wanted to keep the leadership of their movement restricted to a small number of Republicans, and by March 1871 Schurz characterized the "liberals as the only compact, confident body within the party . . . who will . . . be successful in gaining control."[6]

While Grosvenor secretly developed a grassroots organization from Washington, D.C., liberal republicans in Ohio publicly organized the Central Republican Association of Hamilton County. Over a year earlier the American Free Trade League had sponsored the creation of the Ohio Free Trade League in Cincinnati and had continued to help it financially. Several members of the Ohio League, including president George Hoadly and executive committee member Stanley Matthews, joined with Jacob Cox to form the new association.

Though declaring themselves members of the Republican Party in the first sentence of their published announcement, Cox and the others insisted that the Republican Party must adopt universal amnesty, free trade, and civil service reform. Much as the liberal republicans in Missouri had done in 1870, the Ohio association made classic republican arguments for their positions. They found "the policy of disfranchisement to be incompatible with a proper regard for the fundamental principles of Republican Government," and insisted that "the present system of duties . . . promotes corruption in legislation and plunder in high places," and "that the maxim 'To the victors go the spoils,' is immoral, unwise, and detrimental to the public service, and that its tendency has been to corrupt the life blood of the Nation." Cox, Matthews, and Hoadly viewed their association as an example other liberal republicans could use to capture the Republican Party.[7]

The similarities between the Central Republican Association of Hamilton County and the subsequent Liberal Republican Party were not accidental, for they followed the same plan. Cox asked Schurz to come speak to the new association in Ohio, telling him that "we have begun modestly at home, and hope our example will be followed elsewhere, as we follow yours in Mo." Schurz agreed with this interpretation of events, telling Cox, "The platform you adopted . . . agrees in substance with our liberal Missouri platform" and that "similar associations ought to be organized all over the country." Schurz asked Edwin Godkin to rally the independent press around "such organizations inside of the Republican party as we started in Missouri and as have now been started in Ohio under the leadership of ex-Secretary Cox," for he expected "to see similar things spring up in other states, and when the preliminary movements of the next Presidential election come on, such organizations may be strong enough to represent a formidable balance of power." The ultimate goal, according to Schurz, was that "the liberal and vigorous element of the Republican Party, who alone can save its future usefulness, will have a chance to assume control of the organization and shape its future policy."[8]

The man who controlled the Republican Party in 1871 had created many potential allies for the liberal republicans among both Republicans and Democrats. Republicans in many states resented President Grant's interference in battles within state Republican Parties, while Democrats throughout the South continued to chafe under Reconstruction. Despite the temptation to draw on the widespread discontentment and enlarge their movement, the liberal republicans carefully distanced themselves from Democrats and from other malcontent Republicans. In the beginning of the year Schurz stressed to his fellow liberal republicans that they would establish "organizations inside of the Republican party." Just as in Missouri in 1870, the liberal republicans expected to receive support from Democrats, but their goal was to gain control of the Republican Party, and they wanted to demonstrate that they were not going over to the Democrats, whom many of them simply distrusted. Edward Atkinson, for example, told David Wells, "The animus of the party is bad. The mass dishonest. The few honest men . . . cannot control it." Liberal republicans also wanted only certain Republicans in their movement. Schurz, Godkin, and newcomer Lyman Trumbull privately discussed the type of Republicans who should lead the movement, while liberal republican editors publicly attacked other Republicans at odds with Grant, particularly Horace Greeley. Samuel Bowles' *Springfield Republican* contended that "Mr. Greeley, though professing independence and neutrality, belongs rather to the Fenton, anti-Grant and anti-custom house ring" and feared his "past experience does not justify us in hoping for any great results in the way of practical reform at his hands." For Bowles the fight over patronage between Rueben Fenton and Roscoe Conkling, New York State's two Republican senators, represented all that was wrong with a party founded to reform American society. Murat Halstead's *Cincinnati Commercial*, while occasionally discussing Greeley as a possible presidential candidate, prophetically predicted that his nomination would result in "a campaign of caricature and derision." Though sharing a similar goal, the liberal republicans refused to embrace many Republicans and Democrats also opposed to Grant.[9]

As the plotting for the Republican National Convention increased, in the fall of 1871 Schurz started to flirt with the Democrats in the hopes of strengthening the liberal republicans' hand. He told an audience in Nashville that if neither the Republicans nor Democrats could end the current abuses in government, "then the creation of a third, a new party, would be needed—a party composed of those elements of both the old which according to their tendencies and aims, belong together." Schurz proposed that like-minded Republicans and Democrats form Reunion and Reform organizations throughout the country, while emphatically reassuring friends that his plan was that "in case of Grant's nomination we shall have a third movement to beat both him and the Democrats." Though the liberal republicans wanted Democratic support, they still wanted to maintain the purity of their own movement. Cox and the Ohio liberal republicans refused Schurz's direct request to integrate Democrats into their Central Republican Association of Hamilton County, choosing instead to form a separate Reunion and Reform organization. Aware that a small group had determined the outcome in Missouri the year before, the liberal republicans purposefully kept their movement a compact, unified body.[10]

As Grant's renomination appeared more certain, the worried liberal republicans met in Washington in December 1871. Horace White, Lyman Trumbull,

Carl Schurz, and David Wells "warmly approved" Grosvenor's plan "that each in his respective state should proceed to invite a meeting of Republican reform friends for consultation." The invitations, Grosvenor insisted, should clearly state their commitment to amnesty, revenue reform, hard money, and civil service reform. "Each meeting," he explained, "should resolve to work for these reforms within the Republican lines as long as there should be hope of success, and failing then, as soon as an opportunity should be presented of fighting for them without endangering the settlements of war issues, should be prepared to fight independently." Trumbull, like Grosvenor, preferred to remain within the Republican ranks, writing to a friend, "I do not intend to be driven out of the Republican party." Not surprisingly considering Grosvenor's influence, the national liberal republican plan for 1872 mirrored the issues and tactics of the Missouri Liberal Republicans in 1870 as they attempted to gain control of the Republican Party. Liberal republicans unable to travel to Washington so near Christmas time, such as Atkinson and Jacob Cox, received reports of the meeting and approved of the plan.[11]

Grosvenor put the Washington plan into operation, organizing in Missouri the first Liberal Republican state convention for January 24, 1872. The call for the convention at Jefferson City, Missouri, repeatedly asserted that the Missouri Liberal Republican bolt in 1870 was the model for the larger national movement in 1872, contending that "the time seems ripe for an uprising of the people, in kind not unlike that which swept this state in 1870,"and stating that "Missouri has marked out the way." The issues remained the same, with resolutions passed for amnesty, free trade, and civil service reform. Schurz, unable to attend, sent a letter assuring the participants "that the same principles which the Liberal Republicans of Missouri inscribed upon their banner in 1870 are now in issue on the larger field of national politics." Just as in 1870, the Missouri liberal republicans appealed to classic republican arguments to support their positions, warning against "the growing encroachments of executive power" and "the resort to unconstitutional laws." B. Gratz Brown told the crowd that the current administration "will not be loath to erect a despotism within the nation." The final action of the Missouri Liberal Republican Convention was to call a national convention for Cincinnati on May 1, 1872. The call did not specify whether the convention was to nominate a presidential candidate, as many liberal republicans continued to hope the mere threat of a third party would give them the leverage necessary to exert strong influence on the Republican Party.[12]

Liberal republicans across the nation endorsed the call for the Cincinnati Convention. Cox, Matthews, Hoadly, and Johann B. Stallo quickly sent the Missouri Convention a public letter "heartily sympathizing with the views and purposes which have dictated this call." The liberal republican press characterized the convention as an "army of observation" that would pressure the Republican Party to reform itself. According to the *Springfield Republican*, "whether it takes positive action or not, and presents candidates for the presidency or vice presidency or not, all depends very much upon the conduct of the administration party." In the month following the call many liberal republicans began to hope they were gaining power within the Republican Party and talked about postponing the Cincinnati Convention until after the Republican Convention. The *Republican* explained that "the reform republicans of the West called the Cincinnati convention in May with the conviction of the certainty of Gen Grant's renomination by the republican convention in June. It was a mistake." Both the *Republican* and the *Cincinnati Commercial* advised holding the convention after the Republican Convention in June, "in order that they may accept the nominee of Philadelphia, if it be a man on whom they can unite." The liberal republicans continued to hope they could control the Republican Party, though Trumbull confided to a friend that the convention "will take action to secure the nomination of some Liberal Republican in case the Philadelphia Convention is not satisfactory."[13]

Grant and the other Republicans did not remain idle while the liberal republicans plotted in early 1872 to gain control of the party. The Republican majority in the United States Senate sent liberal republican bills to die in committee and packed new committees with Republicans loyal to Grant, an action that would later enable the Republicans to quickly co-opt the Liberal Republican platform during the campaign. In preparation for the important spring elections in New England, the National Republican Executive Committee organized patronage and money on a massive scale to thwart the liberal republicans' momentum. Money and patronage helped the party to victory in the New England elections and helped secure Republican state organizations throughout the country for Grant's renomination. During the course of March, often even before the state conventions, chairmen of Republican state committees from California to Texas to New Jersey reported to the secretary of the Republican National Committee, William E. Chandler, that their states' delegations would vote for Grant.[14]

By March most liberal republicans realized that Grant had secured his renomination and became determined that the Cincinnati Convention should nominate a presidential candidate. Samuel Bowles complained to Schurz of Republicans' "acquiescence in Grant" and suggested starting a new party at the Cincinnati Convention. Johann B. Stallo told a meeting of German Americans in Cincinnati that the Republican Party had lived out its days and pleaded with them to support the Cincinnati Convention. The *Cincinnati Commercial* warned that although "making nominations was not contemplated when the call was first issued, . . . the certainty of Grant's renomination at Philadelphia, however, may modify the original policy." Soon the *Commercial* was certain, acknowledging that "it is settled that President Grant will be nominated by the National Convention of the Republican party for re-election." The liberal republicans began to discuss nominating a presidential candidate to challenge Grant.[15]

*   *   *

The prospect of the Cincinnati Convention producing a viable presidential candidate aroused the interest of many public figures not associated with the liberal republican movement. Presidential movements began for Salmon P. Chase, Charles Sumner, Andrew Curtin, John M. Palmer, and B. Gratz Brown in the spring of 1872, but none of them developed into serious candidates. Though well connected to many liberal republicans, Chase's undisguised ambition for the presidency during the last two decades and his current poor health scared off many supporters. Lyman Trumbull's power made it difficult for fellow Illinoisan John Palmer to gather enough support, and Palmer's contentious, contrarian nature certainly did not help his prospects. As a general during the Civil War Palmer had resigned his command over a dispute about seniority, and as Illinois' Republican governor during Reconstruction he consistently vetoed his own party's legislation. Andrew Curtin, a Pennsylvanian, was an early victim of the Greeley boom, as they were both ardent protectionists seeking support from a similar geographic area. Charles Sumner, locked in a vendetta with Grant but still committed to Reconstruction, ignored the overtures of the liberal republicans. Sumner also had an almost two-decades-long feud with Charles Francis Adams and was wary of joining anything with which his fellow Bay Stater was associated. Brown, though part of the liberal republican movement in Missouri, had alienated most of the liberal republicans since his election as governor by acting, in their eyes, more as a Democrat than as a reformer. Brown actually became the fulcrum for a split in the Missouri Liberal Republican Party, particularly when his second cousin Francis P. Blair was elected as a Democrat to the United States Senate in 1871. Brown and Blair emphasized ending Reconstruction and working with the Democrats, positions that quickly and significantly estranged them from the liberal republican movement.[16]

While Chase, Curtin, and Brown received votes at the convention, they remained second-tier candidates. In the months preceding the Cincinnati Convention Charles Francis Adams, Lyman Trumbull, Horace Greeley, and David Davis emerged as the four leading candidates for the liberal republican presidential nomination. Most of the liberal republicans preferred either Trumbull, the only one of the four truly associated with the movement, or Adams, who shared similar positions and had two sons active in the movement. They were less fond of Greeley, with his protectionism and connection to corruption in New York, but some hoped to capture the support of his powerful *New York Tribune*, whose weekly edition, distributed across the country, made Greeley one of the most well-known and influential men in the country. The liberal republicans did agree that Davis's flirtation with the Democratic Party made him unacceptable. The preconvention maneuvering of the four candidates helps explain why Horace Greeley won the nomination at the Cincinnati Convention and reveals much about the nature of the liberal republican movement.

Both of the candidates favored by the liberal republicans—Lyman Trumbull and Charles Francis Adams—combined the Republican credentials, political independence, and reputation for honesty the liberal republicans sought. Elected to the United States Senate as an anti-Nebraska Democrat in 1855, Trumbull had quickly become a founder of the Republican Party and had authored many of Congress's most important bills in the last decade and a half, including the Thirteenth Amendment. Though responsible for much of the Republican legislation from 1861 to 1871, Trumbull had also demonstrated his independence from the party during the Andrew Johnson impeachment trial of 1868, breaking ranks to cast one of the decisive votes acquitting the president. He continued to show political independence during Grant's administration, criticizing the president from the Senate floor and joining the liberal republican movement in 1871. Adams likewise was a founder of the Republican Party and had acquired a reputation for statesmanship while minister to Great Britain from 1861 to 1868. Much as James Buchanan's posting as minister to Great Britain in the early 1850s had allowed him to avoid divisive domestic controversies and made him an attractive presidential candidate in 1856, so Adams's distance from the heated political atmosphere of Washington during and immediately after the Civil War increased his appeal.[17]

The liberal republicans also liked the public support for Trumbull and Adams. Since January 1871 Trumbull had received letters from across the country encouraging him to run for president. One Californian wrote, "There is a strong current moving here in favor of Trumbull . . . for our next President." Many who were upset with the corruption surrounding the Grant administration particularly liked Trumbull's reputation for honesty. One correspondent simply explained, "I have something to say in regard to preferences for the president. I want an honest man. I believe you are that man." Another expected a little more, telling Trumbull, "More than a year ago I announced you as my choice for the next President. . . . And now I hope you can save the country from corruption, pillage, high taxes, class legislation, and central despotism." Adams began receiving letters after Trumbull did, but they were just as insistent that he run for president. A Cincinnati resident assured Adams that "our most widely [circulated] and influential Republican paper ... has editorially committed itself to your support for President." A more significant indication of public support than letters written to the prospective candidates themselves were the letters of support written to other people, for self-interest less likely motivated the writers. Prominent Republicans in New England corresponded between themselves over the possibility of an Adams candidacy, with one explaining to another that "I have received letters as earnest as your own, from many men who are strict Republicans and who will, like you, vote for Charles Francis Adams if they can. . . . We have had four years of a soldier, I think we need four years of a statesman." Many people across the country wrote to Carl Schurz, whose foreign birth disqualified him from becoming president, advocating Trumbull or Adams for president.[18]

Schurz and the other liberal republicans weighed the strengths and weaknesses of Trumbull and Adams as candidates. Trumbull's supporters in Illinois were actively promoting his nomination. On April 1, 1872, one David Davis lieutenant warned another that "there is a strong Trumbull feeling at Springfield." Davis detested Trumbull from their days of Whig-Democratic rivalry, and they kept watch on each other's fortunes as the convention neared. Ten days later one of Trumbull's friends wrote him of the Illinois call for the Cincinnati Convention, assuring him that "of those that have signed there is but two or three for Judge Davis. The others are for your nomination." Trumbull also received the endorsements of Illinois' foremost Republicans, including Governor John M. Palmer and German-American leader Gustave Koerner. As an active liberal republican for over a year, Trumbull had many connections within the movement nationally, telling Horace White in one letter of separate meetings or correspondence with Edward Atkinson, David Wells, William Grosvenor, and Samuel Bowles. Trumbull's work in the movement assured fellow liberal republicans that he shared their principles and goals. Charles Nordhoff advised Schurz that "if you nominate Trumbull we shall have a leader great enough to encourage even timid lieutenants." In contrast, Adams' only connection to the movement was through his two sons, and some liberal republicans, particularly those from the West who did not know him well, questioned his commitment to free trade and other issues important to them. Atkinson, a Bostonian and strong Adams supporter, received numerous questions about Adams' positions, including one from Grosvenor. "In your last you ask who can respond for Mr. Adams as to his seeing to the Treasury? Answer," responded Atkinson, "all of us here. He is with us heartily and I know no one whose selection of a cabinet I should be more sure." Still, doubts persisted, and Adams' lack of direct affiliation with the movement remained a major detriment.[19]

Adams's biggest advantage over Trumbull lay in his long absence from the United States while ambassador to England. The *Cincinnati Commercial*, perhaps inauspiciously, argued that Adams "has the advantage that made James Buchanan President—that of being out of the country during a time of trouble." Many liberal republicans thought Adams's absence from the political struggles of the Civil War and early Reconstruction, with which Trumbull was associated, would help bring the Democratic support they needed to win. The *Springfield Republican* explained that "while his [Adams's] republicanism is beyond dispute or taint, he would be more acceptable to the democrats than any other man of the party." A Democrat thought that "the connection of Judge Trumbull with the McCardle case would lose 40 percent of the whole democratic vote, while the South would be left to choose between the author of the reconstruction acts and the President who simply obliged the law in carrying them into execution." The allusion to the McCardle case referred to Trumbull's role in representing the federal government before the Supreme Court in 1868 to argue that the court had no jurisdiction to issue a writ of habeas corpus for W. H. McCardle—a Mississippi editor accused of libeling the commander of the army then occupying his state—on the grounds that McCardle was accused of military offenses. Adding to the Democrats' unhappiness with his role in the case, Trumbull had submitted to the War Department a bill for $10,000. The *Commercial* worried that "Trumbull is the author of a good deal of the legislation of which the Democracy most complain, and there might be a disposition among them to support the fighting man Grant rather than the lawyer Trumbull." With good reason, one of Trumbull's supporters reported that Adams was "the favorite of the liberal and democratic press in Cincinnati" because "he had been withdrawn from the strife of parties for some years and would be, therefore, more acceptable to democrats." Trumbull further hurt his standing with Southerners and Democrats just weeks before the convention by inadvertently referring to them as "traitors" during a speech at Cooper Union in New York. Horace White warned Trumbull that his remark had caused "great harm at the South."[20]

Schurz was particularly interested in gaining Democratic support for a Liberal Republican nominee and began meeting with the Democratic National Chairman, August Belmont, in early April. A native of Germany like Schurz, Belmont had emigrated to the United States in 1837 at the age of twenty-one and had settled in New York City as a banker. By 1860 he had become chairman of the Democratic National Committee, a position he held until the 1872 election debacle. Belmont had favored Adams as a presidential candidate since 1868;

John Wentworth, one of David Davis' lieutenants, observed that once again "Belmont uses his position and money for Adams." Belmont told Schurz that "in regards to candidates I find an overwhelming desire for Charles Francis Adams not only here in the West but also in New York. He is by far the strongest and least vulnerable man and will draw more votes from Grant in your party than any other name you can select, while I am sure that the whole Democratic party will go for him to a man." Belmont's associate Manton Marble likewise advised Schurz that "the nomination of Charles Francis Adams would defeat the re-election of Grant. It has always been obvious that Mr. Adams would be among the best of Presidents." After a month of meeting and correspondence Schurz and Belmont arranged to have the Democratic National Convention meet after the Liberal Republican Convention so that the Democrats could nominate the Cincinnati nominee. They also agreed that Adams would be the strongest candidate. Adams attributed the talk of himself as a presidential candidate "mainly to Mr. Schurz." Other elements of the liberal republican movement also pushed for Adams, however. The American Free Trade League, comprised of fellow Bay Staters such as Atkinson and with Democratic contacts, thought Adams the best choice. Wentworth reported to Davis that "the Free Trade League have united all our opponents upon Adams" and that "David A. Wells was one of the strongest pushers for Adams." Out West, members of the Central Republican Association of Hamilton County became convinced that Adams supported the liberal republican platform, and J. D. Cox decided that "my own tendency has been to favor C. F. Adams." From late March the liberal republican press had also begun regularly advocating Adams. The *Cincinnati Commercial* argued that the best assurance for the nation's honor and integrity "is contained in the name of Charles Francis Adams, and in none other can it be found in equal degree. His name would be the best possible platform." The *Springfield Republican* insisted that "beyond all others, Mr. Adams seems pointed out by his position, his character, his experience, and his record . . . as the strongest man for the leadership of the new movement."[21]

Despite the increasing support for Adams, liberal republicans continued to embrace both Adams and Trumbull as potential candidates. While privately talking about Adams' nomination with Belmont in mid-April, Schurz spoke with Trumbull at Cooper Union Institute in New York, the same place where Abraham Lincoln had gained momentum for his presidential nomination twelve years earlier. Atkinson, who was writing letters vouching for Adams' positions, told Trumbull that he had substantial support in New England and begged him "to give the word publicly." Some of Atkinson's willingness to accept Trumbull stemmed from the urgings of William Grosvenor, never a strong Adams supporter, who constantly warned that the movement might need a western man to head the ticket. Wells, the force behind the Adams movement according to Wentworth, wrote a series of letters in March and April assuming that "Trumbull of course leads for President," and pleading, "can't we get Chas. Francis Adams for V. P?" Even as the Adams movement gained strength Wells seemed satisfied with either Trumbull or Adams, often switching the order of their names when writing about the two as potential candidates. The week before the convention, the *Chicago Tribune*, long a Trumbull ally, urged the liberal republicans to nominate Trumbull for president. The rest of the liberal republican press, already committed to Adams, endorsed Trumbull as the ideal vice-presidential candidate. The *Springfield Republican* touted Trumbull's statesmanship, while the *Cincinnati Commercial*, eyeing the electoral map, argued that if Adams were to become the presidential nominee, "then we want a Vice President who will give us strength in Illinois,—Trumbull first choice." As the Cincinnati Convention neared, the liberal republicans agreed that the nomination of either Adams or Trumbull would represent both the principles of the movement and its best chances for success. While preferring Adams to head the ticket, most liberal republicans seemed content with either combination of the two men. The difficulty lay in convincing either the reserved Adams or Trumbull to seek the nomination.[22]

Trumbull was cautious about becoming a candidate despite the early and widespread support. Back in March 1871 Trumbull had told William Jayne, his brother-in-law, that "some persons are writing me on the subject [of the presidency], but I do not think it best for me to do anything about it." The reason, according to Trumbull, was that "the old impeachment radical element would, I think, be strong enough to defeat me in any national convention." Several months later, while organizing the liberal republican state conventions, he again denied his interest in the presidency. Trumbull complained to a supporter that the talk of him as a candidate limited his ability to influence and push reforms. As the convention neared, Illinois liberal republicans, including John Palmer and Gustave Koerner, began pressing Trumbull to declare his candidacy. They both wanted to see Trumbull elected and were certain that declaring his candidacy would help the liberal republican movement, for as Koerner explained to Trumbull, "a certainty or high probability of your nomination will bring many good republicans to Cincinnati who otherwise will stay away and wait for results." Koerner, a prominent German American leader, assured Trumbull of his popular support and begged, "Could you by telegram inform me that you will be a candidate and accept the nomination?" In response to a similar letter from Palmer, Trumbull stated that he "had no desire for the nomination." Trumbull's responses appear more sincere than coy, for if he had wanted to be president he needed the active support of people like

Koerner and Palmer. Despite considering himself the best candidate, Trumbull apparently lacked the necessary driving ambition. Far from seeking the presidential nomination, Trumbull indicated to David Wells in early April that he would accept the vice-presidential nomination if Adams headed the ticket. And just days before the convention Trumbull instructed Horace White, his representative for Cincinnati, that "I do not think I ought to be nominated unless there is a decided feeling among those assembled and are outside of rings and bargains that I would be the stronger than anyone else. Unless this is the feeling I think it would be best not to present my name at all." The language concerning "rings and bargains," while common in public speeches, was rare in the confidential correspondence between a politician and his manager. Jayne and White would still go to the Cincinnati Convention to work for Trumbull, but the senator's refusal to embrace his candidacy limited the momentum and organization his representatives could use to secure the nomination.[23]

Adams was similarly reticent about a presidential nomination at Cincinnati. Six weeks before the convention, as talk of his nomination increased, Adams wrote in his diary that "if the country called me into its service, it was my rule to obey." He preferred to avoid the nomination, however, as he found that "I am well satisfied with the singular increase I enjoy of the public estimation to desire to impair it by contamination with the dirt of electioneering." A few weeks later he told a correspondent that "my disinclination to public life has grown with my years," and upon receiving a letter suggesting his nomination Adams confided to his diary that "I cannot think of it without a shudder." While nineteenth-century politicians were normally coy and were expected to appear disinterested, Adams' reference to "the dirt of electioneering" in a private diary and his continued reluctance to seek the nomination was unusual. Adams' behavior fits David F. Musto's theory of the "Adams Family myth." Musto contends that the dynamics of John and Abigail Adams' relationship during the American Revolution produced a family myth that the Adamses must serve the nation, but "that merited reward should never be sought by political maneuvers but rather should be awaited patiently." According to Musto, while the myth dominated the Adams family psyche for four generations, "the second and third generations [Charles Francis Adams belonged to the latter] most felt the pressure of the family mind to attain high positions of honor, not by political manipulation but as the just reward of a grateful nation." Ironically, John Adams and John Quincy Adams were political animals who merely tried to *appear* above politicking. Still, many of Charles Francis Adams' uncles and siblings could not stand the pressure of the family myth. While Adams was the most successful of his generation, his biographer Martin Duberman finds that "the thought of the nomination, in fact, genuinely appalled him." Adams rejoiced that with his approaching diplomatic trip to England, "I shall be free from that annoyance by leaving the country and the passing of the convention." Before Adams left for England, however, David Wells sent him a letter reporting the increasing movement to nominate him and asking that someone be given authority to act for him at Cincinnati. The letter and growing talk of his nomination led Adams to share with his diary the fear that "this looks for the first time somewhat serious to me. . . . I still live in the hope that something may occur to give a wholly new truth to the current. I want no better position than that which I now occupy."[24]

Adams tried to end speculation about his nomination with a blunt letter to Wells. "I have received your letter and will answer it frankly. I do not want the nomination." In case of an "unequivocal call" Adams would consider accepting the nomination, but he instructed Wells that "if I am to be negotiated for and have assurances given that I am honest, you will be so kind as to draw me out of that crowd." Adams refused to give anyone authority to speak for him and concluded that "if the good people who meet at Cincinnati really believe that they need such an anomalous being as I am (which I do not) they must express it in a manner to convince me of it, or all their labor will be thrown away." After writing the letter Adams recorded in his diary that "I wrote a reply to Mr. Wells which will I think prove decisive. . . . I think I shall hear no more of negotiating for a nomination." Though published before the convention, the letter apparently had little effect on public opinion. Adams' supporters, such as the *Springfield Republican* and the *Cincinnati Commercial,* proclaimed it an example of his honesty and independence, while those already opposed to Adams, such as the *New York Tribune* and Republican papers, declared it a vague, aristocratic response. The most important repercussion of Adams's letter would come at the convention, for he would have no representatives managing his support or negotiating deals. The prospect of people making pledges for him at the Cincinnati Convention so worried Adams that he decided that since "I will not consent to be a party to such an auction my sons will not go."[25]

In contrast to the reserved Trumbull and Adams, Horace Greeley needed no encouragement to seek the liberal republican nomination. Despite gaining recognition as one of the nation's leading reformers and journalists over the previous three decades as owner and editor of the powerful *New York Tribune,* Greeley had never achieved the political offices he craved. Greeley's passion for office, which according to his biographer was "based in part upon his egotism, in part upon a desire for recognition of his contributions to the nation's welfare, and in part upon a sincere zeal for public service," led him to run for office repeatedly. From late 1840 to 1870 Greeley sought a Congressional seat three times, a U.S. Senate seat twice, the New York governorship, and the office of state comptroller. Though a power in New York State politics, he managed to win only his first race for Congress in 1848, losing every other nomination or election. Part of the difficulty lay in the fact that William Seward and Thurlow Weed, the Whig and later Republican state party bosses, repeatedly used Greeley as a sacrificial lamb for unwinnable races and prevented him from entering the winnable ones. After decades of frustration Greeley finally broke with Seward and Weed, more intent than ever to gain public office. From 1870 onward an increasing number of people began mentioning Greeley as a possible presidential candidate. Greeley embraced this talk, and during the summer and early fall of 1871 went on two speaking tours through the South and Midwest to promote a presidential bid. Following the speaking tour Greeley received letters from across the country assuring him that "your Presidential stock is rising rapidly" and that "you are the Peoples candidate for the next President." Despite his availability and popularity, the question that remained was whether Greeley would be the liberal republicans' choice for president.[26]

Greeley shared little of the liberal republicans' backgrounds or goals, and during the initial stages of the movement Greeley had repeatedly referred to it as "the conspiracy to destroy the Republican party." Though Greeley was an early abolitionist and Republican who had come to dislike Grant and favor an end to Reconstruction, as did most of the liberal republicans, political differences and personal feuds far outweighed these similarities. Unlike most liberal republicans, who had come to the Republican Party from the ranks of the Free Soil or Democratic parties in the 1850s, Greeley came from the Whig Party. This difference estranged him from the liberal republicans in a number of ways. Many remembered Greeley's political opposition in the late 1840s and early 1850s. Wells thought that the situation in 1871 was "essentially the same as the old free soil movement. Greeley and others encouraged that movement, persuaded the democrats that they would go with them until after the Buffalo Convention . . . but a few weeks before the election, the *Tribune* concluded to go for Gen Taylor [the Whig candidate]." Over twenty years later Wells was still bitter about "the bad faith of the Whigs in 1848." Some of the political fights in the 1840s led to personal feuds that continued into the 1870s. As a Whig and protectionist in the 1840s, Greeley was usually at odds with his rival New York editor William Cullen Bryant, who at that time was a Democrat and a free trader. The political and professional animosity became personal when a disagreement over the Wilmot Proviso in 1848 led Greeley to accuse Bryant in the *Tribune*, "You lie villain! willfully, wickedly, basely lie!" Bryant never forgot the insult. Sixteen years later he refused to recognize Greeley at a small breakfast party, insisting, "He's a blackguard—he's a blackguard," and in 1870 he used the *New York Evening Post* to help defeat Greeley's campaign for Congress.[27]

Greeley's Whig ancestry was even more important in separating him from the liberal republicans on economic policy, for he continued to favor the Whig policy of protective tariffs. Greeley became the biggest opponent of the American Free Trade League and dedicated the pages of the *Tribune* to attacking the liberal republicans' calls for free trade. He personally attacked many of the liberal republicans advocating free trade, particularly David Wells. Greeley not only insisted that reappointing Wells as Special Commissioner of the Treasury in 1870 would be "a waste of money, for which Congress would not be justified," but also accused him of taking bribes to advocate free trade. Greeley's *Tribune* laid out "our reason for believing that Wells is bought and paid for by the Foreign interests." In addition to disagreeing bitterly with the liberal republicans on free trade, Greeley had little interest in their main issue, civil service reform. Greeley was so involved with the corruption that passed for New York City politics in the Civil War era that in January 1872 Bowles complained in the *Springfield Republican* that Greeley "consented to be one of a ring of ward politicians, largely made up of office-holders or office-seekers."[28]

Despite some sharp critiques of him in their newspapers, both Murat Halstead and Bowles mentioned Greeley as a possible presidential candidate. Halstead's *Cincinnati Commercial* began discussing Greeley as a presidential hopeful in November 1870, and a year later bragged that it "was among the foremost newspapers of the country to name Horace Greeley for the next president." Though a proponent of free trade, the *Commercial* repeatedly insisted tariff policy was a congressional, not an executive, issue and asked, "Can't we afford to overlook his Tariff tomfoolery?" Bowles' *Springfield Republican*, while consistently critical of Greeley's poor record on civil service, agreed that "no president has ever yet vetoed a tariff bill, no president is ever likely to," and mentioned him at least once as a leading presidential candidate. The talk of a Greeley candidacy in the *Commercial* and *Republican* was probably just speculation, though, as both papers more strenuously backed other candidates, and Greeley remained aloof from the liberal republican movement.[29]

When the liberal republicans decided in January 1872 to hold a national convention that May, some seriously began to consider getting Greeley to support the movement. Many of the politicians and editors in the movement pragmatically recognized the difficulty of fighting the entrenched power of the Republican Party and saw the advantage of having Greeley and the powerful *New York Tribune* on their side. Bowles and Halstead attended Greeley's sixty-first birthday party on February 3, 1872, where much of the conversation focused on Greeley as a presidential candidate. Like Bowles and Halstead, most of the liberal republicans who began courting Greeley wanted his support for the Cincinnati Convention, not his nomination. Two weeks after the birthday party

Senator Carl Schurz met with one of Greeley's lieutenants in Washington and insisted that "if Mr. Greeley will put the *Tribune* in the Republican opposition to Grant and in favor of the Cincinnati Convention at once, success is certain." Most of the politicians and editors realized that the price for Greeley's support at Cincinnati would be a compromise on free trade. Both of the U.S. senators in the movement knew Greeley's condition for cooperation. Trumbull acknowledged to his free trader friend Horace White that "the only trouble with him will be on the tariff, and that I think can be got along with." Trumbull showed his motivation for getting along with Greeley in the same letter, reporting that "the *N.Y. Tribune's* circulation has increased 25,000 since its liberal course. The people are ready and organization is all that is needed for complete success." Bowles likewise argued to free traders like Wells that the liberal republican movement would lose too much by excluding Greeley simply over the tariff issue. Though Greeley had publicly attacked his free trade positions, Wells agreed with Bowles. As long as free traders controlled the convention, Wells asked, "Can we afford to despise his help?" A correspondent to Schurz summarized the attitude of the more pragmatic liberal republicans, insisting that the tariff was primarily a legislative matter and that "under such circumstances I see no harm in the Greeleyites joining under our banner to defeat the Grant party unless they want a man like Greeley himself nominated." Liberal republican politicians and editors did not want Greeley as their candidate, but were willing to compromise on the tariff to gain his support at the Cincinnati Convention.[30]

The possibility of *rapproachment* between the more pragmatic liberal republicans and Greeley upset many of the more idealistic members of the movement. While liberal republican politicians and editors were increasingly concerned with winning in 1872, the more idealistic members of the movement wanted to stay focused on principles and long-term party building. Schurz and Trumbull bore the brunt of liberal republican anger over the possibility of a compromise with Greeley, receiving numerous letters from the likes of Edward Atkinson, Roeliff Brinkerhoff, and J. D. Cox, who were afraid the convention "would waive any declaration of principles" and "admit Greeley." One of Schurz's lieutenants reported "letters from Mr. Godkin and others expressing fear that the influence of Greeley and others will destroy the influence of the L. R. Convention." Cox was the most eloquent advocate for refusing to compromise with Greeley, telling Grosvenor in late March that he feared "the New York opposition to Grant + Conkling (which I cannot help looking upon as a purely personal opposition) was assuming a certain control of the liberal movement without having any other ground of affiliation with us except the current dissatisfaction with the existing condition of things." He explained that he would not participate in such a contest, because "my zeal for the liberal movement is based upon the belief that it may make itself the great party of the future by adopting and occupying the platform of true principles in regard to taxation and finance, as well as the true doctrine of reforms in administration." Another liberal republican who hoped not "to be sold out at Cincinnati merely for the purposes of killing Grant" warned Trumbull that "if we must swallow Greeley for the sakes of carrying a political end I think it will be dearly bought."[31]

Despite the opposition of many liberal republicans, Greeley became convinced by the end of March that the liberal republican movement had agreed to compromise on the tariff. Greeley endorsed the Cincinnati Convention in the *Tribune* with the stipulation that "the issue of free-trade and protection . . . be left for settlement to the people in their Congressional districts." Many of the more idealistic liberal republicans were unhappy. Atkinson insisted that "the Greeley endorsement of the Missouri platform excites distrust because we cannot believe it to be honest." Cox offered a fuller explanation to Schurz, declaring that "most of us in Ohio have not yet been convinced that a gain has been made in the coalition with the Greeley men on the tacit assumption that the Revenue Reform part of our movement shall be held in abeyance." Compromising, even temporarily, on the issues at the core of the liberal republican movement was dangerous, Cox warned, as "ambiguities and avoidance of issues of principle are the life of decaying parties, but the death of new ones."[32]

Greeley's alliance with the liberal republicans started a fierce competition among both sides to gather forces for the Cincinnati Convention. With no formal party structure in existence, the Cincinnati Convention would be an open one, in which the official convention delegates would be chosen by the convention itself after their arrival. Whoever could get the most people to Cincinnati would control the convention. Greeley and his supporters had already courted disaffected Republicans like Governor Henry Warmoth of Louisiana and immediately began organizing delegations to the Cincinnati Convention throughout the country. Trumbull, who had wanted to include Greeley, soon worried that "there will be several delegations present from N. Eastern and Southern States who will be controlled by N. Y. influence through which they have been gotten up." The contest was not limited to controlling delegations. Greeley's chief lieutenant, Whitelaw Reid, collected a dossier on Grosvenor. Coincidentally, throughout April Grosvenor repeatedly called on Atkinson to ensure that the liberal republicans would have enough strength in Cincinnati to counteract Greeley. He warned that "if you, and the men who like you deem it [free trade] the only vital question, and are wholly indisposed to take hold of the fight if it is to be merely a personal one against Grant, remain away, or fail to rally friends in sufficient strength to counteract the efforts made from other quarters, you know, as well as I, what the results of the convention will be." Cox certainly knew what would happen if Greeley gained control of the convention, telling Atkinson that "we must have serious consultations with our Revenue Reform friends if we are to save the Convention from disaster."[33]

The presidential aspirations of Supreme Court Justice David Davis represented another potential disaster for the liberal republicans at Cincinnati. Davis claimed that when a group of Illinois legislators called on him in Washington in January 1871 to suggest he run for president he had never before taken such talk seriously, but admitted that "after they left, I had not walked six blocks before I had my entire cabinet picked out." Old political allies Jesse Fell and Leonard Swett soon became Davis' campaign managers, traveling all over the country to promote his name for president. Many newspapers around the country began discussing Davis as a possible presidential candidate for 1872. His supporters were not certain, however, which party might nominate the Republican Davis, since he appeared more popular with the Democrats than with his own party. The liberal republicans' Missouri Call in January 1872 seemed to offer the perfect solution, and Davis' campaign managers began organizing his forces for the Cincinnati Convention.[34]

Unfortunately, Davis had even less in common with the liberal republicans' backgrounds and goals than Greeley. Like Greeley, Davis had become a Republican from the Whig Party in the early 1850s. While Greeley had been a leading abolitionist, as were most of the liberal republicans, Davis had felt contempt and hatred for abolitionists, and as late as 1854 did not want the Whig Party "abolitionized." Illinois state politics were in flux during 1854, however, as the Democratic-sponsored Kansas-Nebraska Bill in Congress altered political affiliations across the country. In Illinois the Whig Party started to dissolve over the slavery issue, the Democratic Party split into pro-Nebraska and anti-Nebraska factions, and the new Republican Party emerged as a power. After the November elections in 1854 it became apparent that if the Whigs, anti-Nebraska Democrats, and Republicans could unite, that they would have fifty-one votes in the Illinois legislature, compared to the Democrats' forty-seven, and could elect a United States Senator. Davis favored Abraham Lincoln, a Whig, but the five anti-Nebraska Democrats refused to vote for a Whig. To avoid allowing a pro-Nebraska Democrat to win, Lincoln eventually advised the Whigs and Republicans to elect Trumbull, an anti-Nebraska Democrat. Davis was furious with Trumbull's stage-managed victory and also disliked Trumbull's Democratic origins, telling a friend, "I dont feel satisfied with his election. He has been a Democrat all his life—dyed in the wool—as ultra as he could be. His antecedents dont suit me." The senate election started a lifelong feud between Davis and Trumbull, as they became leaders, respectively, of the conservative and Radical wings of the Republican Party in Illinois. Davis gained prestige and power in the Republican Party in 1860 by managing Lincoln's nomination and subsequent campaign. During the Civil War Davis and Trumbull battled for Lincoln's attention, patronage, and direction of the Republican Party. Their hostility reached such a point that Davis once insisted, "Trumbull is the most selfish man that ever lived."[35]

The differences between Davis and the liberal republicans became more pronounced during the period immediately after the Civil War. From 1865 through 1868 many liberal republicans had been active, if ambivalent, about reconstructing the South. Grosvenor wrote in 1865 that "to defeated rebels the Constitution gives no political rights whatever" and that "military control must be maintained, until there is sufficient evidence . . . that the rebel communities can be safely restored to their political powers." Trumbull wrote the Civil Rights and Freedmen's Bureau bills in 1866 that theoretically gave the federal government sweeping powers to protect African Americans in the South, but according to historian Michael Les Benedict, Trumbull maintained his constitutional conservatism and preserved the old federal system. Nevertheless, many in the nation saw Trumbull's Reconstruction legislation as radical, and President Andrew Johnson began vetoing it. Most of the liberal republicans agreed with Horace White and the *Chicago Tribune* that by obstructing Congress's Reconstruction plans, Johnson was plotting to "overthrow and destroy the labor of the nation wrought in the blood of a half million patriots." In this highly charged political environment, Davis wrote the majority opinion in the 1866 Supreme Court case *Ex parte Milligan*, which declared unconstitutional any military trials of civilians where civil courts were still able to function. Although Davis explicitly said in his decision that it had no relevance to what was going on in the postwar South, the case was widely regarded as a blow to Reconstruction, and Radical Republicans likened it to the infamous Dred Scott decision. Davis remained more conservative on Reconstruction than the liberal republicans, even as the movement began to advocate the end of Reconstruction through universal amnesty and suffrage. The *Milligan* case had important political consequences. While most Republicans reviled Davis for the *Milligan* opinion, Democrats embraced him as their champion. Davis was mentioned as a possible Democratic presidential candidate in 1868, and by 1872 Democrats provided most of his political support.[36]

Many of the liberal republicans who had pragmatically decided to accept Greeley became worried that embracing Davis, with his connections with the Democrats, would doom their movement. The liberal republican attitude toward the Democrats in 1872 was the same as it had been during the Missouri bolt in 1870. It paralleled Abraham Lincoln's balancing act in the 1864 presidential campaign, when he courted Democrats by creating the Union Party, while securing his base in the Republican Party from Radical challengers like John C. Fremont. Liberal republicans knew that they needed Democratic votes to succeed—that was one of the primary reasons Schurz favored Adams as a candidate—but feared the Democrats' taking control of the movement or their support alienating the majority of Republicans. While the liberal republicans did not care for the current state of the Republican Party, they still considered it better than the Democratic Party. White advised Trumbull, "We could support Cincinnati as a Republican movement not encumbered by Democratic complications or endorsements. We could not support it if it had a Democratic 'send off.'" Trumbull meanwhile tried to reassure leading Illinois Republicans that Democrats were not controlling the liberal republican movement. In early March he wrote to Gustave Koerner that "the time has come to reform the Republican organization, and I believe it can be done without turning the govt. over to the Democrats." A month later Trumbull told Illinois Governor John M. Palmer that he could still "see no chance to reform and correct existing abuses through the regular republican organization," but insisted, "the democratic party is demoralized, and cannot rally if it would, and I would not trust it with power if it could." Bowles expected the new party to consist of one-third former Democrats, though he confided to a friend that "the 'average republican' is afraid of even the ghost of the Democratic party, and until it can be absolutely allayed, I have no very great hope of seeing the organization of a large, powerful, and effective reform party." Bowles assured Charles Sumner that the Cincinnati Convention would be "purely republican in its character."[37]

The liberal republicans warned Democrats, both publicly and privately, to stay away from the Cincinnati Convention. "The very existence of the democratic organization is an occasion of offense and menace to the Republican party," insisted the *Springfield Republican*, and "so long as this offense and menace continue, so long, practically, the Republican party is likely to maintain itself in unity." The *Chicago Tribune* argued that "the dissolution of the Democratic party must be the condition precedent to any movement of Liberal Republicans." Bowles told Schurz to warn the Democrats against interference in the Republican power struggle, suggesting, "They should remember the fate of the man who broke in upon the quarrel of the husband and wife." Trumbull insisted that "to be successful the Cincinnati meeting must be distinctly Republican," and White thought "the Democracy ought not to go near Cincinnati."[38]

Democrats continued to advocate Davis despite the liberal republicans' obvious hostility toward Democratic involvement in the Cincinnati Convention. One of Davis's lieutenants reported to him that "the feelings of the Democrats towards you is almost marvelous," and a Democratic congressman advised Atkinson that the liberal republicans should nominate Davis if they wanted Democratic votes. Trumbull thought "the democrats are injuring Davis by committing themselves to him in advance." Davis meanwhile remained quiet and refused to distance himself from the Democrats. One of Davis's advisors suggested that a "limited number of representative Democrats ought to be on hand for consultation," while another hoped "democratic friends . . . could spike all [our] opponents . . . from our state at Cincinnati." White wrote to Trumbull that "the impression among Republicans generally is that Judge Davis had been coquetting with the Democratic party. This I fear would be fatal to any attempt to get Republican votes." Just before the convention the *Cincinnati Commercial* reported that "a parcel of Democratic Congressmen have been working up the Judge Davis Scheme, and he will make a serious show of strength. His real weakness is in the appearance of elaborate effort in his behalf."[39]

Davis further alienated liberal republicans in the months before the convention because of his association with the Labor Reform Convention and the manner in which his supporters prepared for Cincinnati. In the aftermath of the Civil War, with the growing size of the permanent working class and growing disillusionment with the free-labor ideal, workers increasingly organized to advocate economic reforms. While some organized national unions, other groups of workers tried using political pressure to force the government to enact laws and policies favorable to laborers. Among the most widely advocated measures were having the federal government flood the economy with cheap paper money to reduce interest rates and help those in debt, and passage of legislation reducing the maximum daily hours of labor to eight. Of course, such monetary policies and government intervention in industry were anathema to the liberal republicans, but the ambitious Davis coyly courted labor's support before the Liberal Republican Convention. The Labor Reform Convention met in February 1872 in Columbus, Ohio and nominated Davis for president on a platform to reform the country's monetary system and establish an eight-hour work day. Not wanting to commit himself either way on the nomination, Davis ambiguously responded that "the Presidency is not an office to be either sought or declined." The attempt at ambiguity failed, though, as Davis became associated with the Labor Reform Convention. The liberal republicans had little interest or respect for the Labor platform. In a letter that somehow ended up in Davis's hands, Grosvenor argued, "I do not think the elements opposing Grant can be united upon Judge Davis, simply because of the platform upon which he has consented to stand." Davis' managers did not agree and began organizing large numbers of his supporters to attend the Cincinnati Convention. The wealthy Davis provided railroad passes and hotel rooms, enabling his managers to gather approximately 500 supporters in Cincinnati, by far the largest delegation for a single candidate. Even worse, about half of his delegation were Democrats, later reported to include "nearly the entire Democratic delegation of the House of Representatives from Illinois and Indiana, and many other states." The liberal republicans were outraged by what they saw as Davis's attempt to buy the nomination, particularly with Democratic help. The *Cincinnati Commercial* insisted that "the Cincinnati Convention will not be composed of a small lot of fellows whose railroad and hotel expenses can be paid by an ambitious candidate or two, as was the case with the squad that nominated DAVIS . . . at Columbus."[40]

*   *   *

The months of political maneuvering by the liberal republicans and potential candidates set the parameters for the Cincinnati Convention. Despite the hopes of people like B. Gratz Brown and Salmon P. Chase, by late April the field of realistic candidates had narrowed to Adams, Trumbull, Greeley, and Davis. The liberal republicans liked Adams and Trumbull, but were divided over what to do about Greeley and the tariff. Those without a professional interest in politics remained committed to free trade and opposed to Greeley, while liberal republicans like Schurz had become convinced they could elect the next president if they could only secure the support of Greeley and the *New York Tribune*. Greeley, meanwhile, wanted the presidential nomination but would not accept a free trade platform. The one thing all of the liberal republicans and Greeley agreed upon was the unacceptability of Davis. As liberal republicans, delegates, and reporters converged on Cincinnati in the days before the convention, the intrigue intensified. Though several thousand traveled to Cincinnati for the convention and over seven hundred served as delegates, the decisions of fewer than a dozen men determined the outcome. A small group of liberal republicans decided they could compromise with Greeley to defeat Davis and gain the support of the *Tribune*, while still maintaining control of the convention.

The liberal republican editors started arriving in Cincinnati several days before the convention and began planning strategy. By April 26 Bowles was in Cincinnati meeting with Halstead of the *Cincinnati Commercial* to promote Adams's candidacy, and the next morning White arrived in Cincinnati to organize Trumbull's forces. On April 28 Bowles and Halstead met Henry Watterson, editor of the *Louisville Courier-Journal*, at the train station and took him to meet White and Schurz at the St. Nicholas Hotel. Though a former Confederate and current Democrat, Watterson enjoyed close connections with many liberal republicans. When Watterson returned to Cincinnati after the Civil War with Confederate money in his pocket that was as worthless as the gray army uniform in his bag, his uncle Stanley Matthews offered him a loan and found him a job at the *Cincinnati Evening Times*. While in Cincinnati Watterson became friends with other liberal republicans, including fellow newspaperman Halstead and his next-door neighbor George Hoadly. By 1869 Watterson was editor of the *Louisville Courier-Journal* and began making contacts with liberal republicans throughout the country. Watterson and Schurz started corresponding in 1870, and during the fall and winter of 1871 Watterson traveled East to meet the likes of Lyman Trumbull and Samuel Bowles. Watterson shared the liberal republicans' dislike of Reconstruction and protective tariffs and increasingly urged the Democratic Party to support the new movement as the Cincinnati Convention approached. Upon arriving at the St. Nicolas Hotel on April 28, Watterson and the liberal republican editors organized a fellowship they called the "Quadrilateral"—in reference to the four great fortified towns used by Austria to dominate northern Italy. Watterson recounted that "we resolved to limit the Presidential nomination of the convention to Charles Francis Adams, Bowles' candidate, and Lyman Trumbull, White's candidate." To increase the prospects for their candidates the Quadrilateral decided to attack what they perceived as the greatest threat, the rising momentum for Davis. The day after the Quadrilateral formed, April 29, the *Springfield Republican, Chicago Tribune, Louisville Courier-Journal,* and *Cincinnati Commercial* all ran editorials describing how "a squad of Democratic Congressmen have been fixing up things for Davis." The *Commercial* concluded "that the nomination of Judge Davis here as a 'liberal' would be no less a weakness than a fraud."[41]

While the Quadrilateral began working against Davis on April 28, Whitelaw Reid arrived in Cincinnati to organize support for Horace Greeley. The thirty-five-year-old Reid was a career journalist who had served as the managing editor of Greeley's *New York Tribune* for the last few years, but he had personal experience in political intrigue. He had spent most of the Civil War as a reporter in Washington and had made enough political connections to supplement his newspaper income with sinecures, such as librarian of the House of Representatives and clerk of the House Committee on Military Affairs. Reid had joined other Radical Republicans in 1864 who thought Abraham Lincoln was too conservative and had unsuccessfully tried to replace him as the Republican Party's presidential nominee. Eight years later Reid was in charge of manipulating a presidential nomination and his two biggest challenges, preventing a free trade platform and securing control of the New York delegation, were intertwined. Since the liberal republicans did not have state organizations, the Cincinnati Convention itself would choose the official delegates once the convention started, and approximately 30 of the 153 New Yorkers in Cincinnati favored free trade. The morning after arriving in Cincinnati Reid attended a meeting of the New York delegation in the St. Nicholas Hotel as they tried to work out their differences on the tariff. After some discussion Reid put forth Greeley's solution to the tariff dilemma. "Finding ourselves not fully agreed with respect to Free Trade, as opposed to Protection," Reid explained, "we respectfully recommend the grave issue involved in that controversy to the careful study and unbiased adjudication of the people, urging them to choose members of Congress who truly embody, and will faithfully reflect, their will on that subject." Greeley and Reid hoped that making the tariff a question for Congress, instead of the president, would eliminate it as an issue at the convention and facilitate Greeley's nomination. As the New York delegation discussed leaving the tariff to Congress Reid heard of the Quadrilateral, which was meeting in the drawing room between the bedrooms of Watterson and Schurz at the St. Nicholas Hotel. Reid asked why he and the powerful *New York Tribune* were being left out of this editorial fellowship. The Quadrilateral debated whether to include Reid, with some of the editors arguing that he should not be included because, unlike themselves Reid was a subordinate, while others objected to any representative of Greeley. Watterson recounted forty years later that he persuaded the others to accept Reid by arguing that "in this movement we shall need the 'New York Tribune.' If we admit Reid we clinch it. You will all agree that Greeley has no chance of the nomination, and so, by taking him in, we both eat our cake and have it." Bowles, Halstead, and White agreed with Watterson's logic and invited Reid to join the Quadrilateral.[42]

The day Reid joined with the editors, the Quadrilateral met for dinner at Halstead's home to discuss the threat of Davis. Reid reported in the *New York Tribune* that "the talk of the Liberal editors is unanimously against Davis," specifically citing Halstead, Watterson, and Bowles. At the April 29 dinner the Quadrilateral agreed to denounce Davis in their papers again the next day, but in a more organized fashion than the scattered attacks of the 29th. Each member agreed to write an editorial for the next day attacking Davis from a different direction, such as accusing him of being in league with the Democrats or trying to buy the nomination. The *Springfield Republican* argued that "Davis is in no true sense a republican," while the *Cincinnati Commercial* insisted that the Davis supporters were trying to "nominate their candidate by force of impudence and lung power." The Quadrilateral gave early copies of their editorials to Halstead, so that on the same day they appeared in each editor's newspaper, Halstead could print them in the *Cincinnati Commercial* as an indication that national public opinion was against Davis, which might influence the delegates already in Cincinnati.[43]

Watterson recounted that the Quadrilateral's editorial assault on April 30 destroyed the Davis movement, insisting, "The Davis boom went down before it. The Davis boomers were paralyzed." Historians have accepted Watterson's interpretation, often quoting him to explain how "Davis' candidacy collapsed under the weight of this unfavorable publicity," and ignoring Davis after April 30. At the time of the convention, however, Davis supporters continued to hope for victory until May 2 and did not attribute defeat to the editorial assault. Most of the telegrams to Davis on April 30 ignored the editorials and concentrated on the division of the Illinois delegation that occurred the same day. Davis supporters at Cincinnati outnumbered the supporters of Trumbull and Governor John M. Palmer of Illinois by at least five to one and should have controlled the Illinois delegation, but for the sake of harmony Jesse Fell, one of Davis's managers, consented to divide the delegation, giving a quarter each to Trumbull and Palmer. While Fell reported to Davis that it was the "best that could be done under the circumstances" and another of Davis's supporters said "we think nomination insured by the arrangement," the judge's most experienced political operative, John Wentworth, feared that "Davis has conceded too much." Despite his initial pessimism, Wentworth still predicted on the first day of the convention, May 1, that the "final contest [is] likely to be between Davis and [J. D.] Cox." By noon of the second day Wentworth realized that Davis could not win, because "all the disposition of the seats in the hall and all the influence about Cincinnati is against Davis." He reported, "Trumbull's friends lead the cohorts of the opposition," which included the Free Trade League, "anti-Grant Senators," and newspapers. A few days after the convention another Davis supporter ignored the actions of the newspapers, noting that "in my judgment if the delegation from Illinois had gone for you with undivided front, you could have been nominated."[44]

Exaggeration of the effectiveness of the Quadrilateral's April 30 editorial attack on Davis in historical accounts marginalizes the more significant role of the Quadrilateral at the Cincinnati Convention. In an examination of how Reid secured Greeley's nomination, James G. Smart insists that one of Reid's "significant accomplishment[s] during the convention . . . was his entrance into the Quadrilateral, which meant a serious acceptance of Greeley." The liberal republican editors initially did not want to include Reid in their fellowship because Greeley was not a liberal republican and did not agree with many of their positions. Watterson eventually convinced them they needed the *New York Tribune*, and at the time the editors considered the greatest threat to the convention to be the possibility of Davis being nominated. Once Reid joined, the first action of the Quadrilateral was to attack Davis. The liberal republican editors thus included Reid on April 29 at least partially to lessen the chances of Davis's nomination. The continuation of the Davis threat until May 2 forced the liberal republicans to compromise with Reid and Greeley throughout the convention. Wentworth accurately predicted on May 2 that the liberal republicans and Greeley "may agree to kill Davis, but then the assassins have got to fight for the man among themselves."[45]

In the months before the convention the tariff had dominated discussions among Greeley and the liberal republicans. While Greeley refused to associate himself with a free trade platform, many of the liberal republican editors and politicians were inclined to compromise on the tariff to secure his support. Just days before the convention started, Trumbull asked a Greeley manager, "How would it do to say nothing about the tariff? Would not that be better than to have an equivocal resolution or than to turn the matter over to congress?" William Grosvenor spoke for most of the liberal republicans from the Free Trade League, however, when he stated he could "not see how anybody can obtain admission who does not approve of the Missouri call," and vowed to make the convention adopt a free trade platform. In the days before the convention the liberal republicans and Greeley's representatives held a number of meetings to try to resolve the tariff issue.[46]

In the first series of meetings, two days before the convention, protectionists and free traders reached a tentative compromise—a general declaration for revenue reform, while proclaiming the tariff a congressional issue. Though the compromise did not commit the nominee to free trade, the declaration written by David Dudley Field stated "that the best form of taxation is that which will yield the necessary revenue with the least expense and interference with the business of the people." The proposed compromise brought little agreement. According to the *Springfield Republican,* "Many free-traders, notably David Dudley Field and Mr. Wells and Horace White, are ready to accept this disposition of the question. Senator Schurz will probably acquiesce also, but such reformers as Atkinson of Boston and Gen Cox and the Cincinnati German leaders are so far implacable." While most of the protectionists at Cincinnati "seemed disposed to accept it," Greeley did not like the compromise. The day before the convention he telegraphed Reid that "any common profession of faith by Free Traders and Protectionists will be a juggle or a capitulation. We can honestly agree to disagree and nothing else. Field's resolve summons us to surrender. Count me out if any such is adopted."[47]

Greeley demanded, both privately and publicly, that the platform simply declare the tariff a congressional issue with no statement of principle. The *Cincinnati Commercial* complained that "for a time there was an impression that the tariff plank of the platform was settled, but it is not so. The differences between the free traders and the protectionists are more apparent and ugly the more they are examined." The intractability, though, was limited to the likes of Atkinson and Cox, who had opposed the first compromise measure. The liberal republicans who were already inclined to compromise readily acceded to Greeley's demands. Wells, a leading free trader, agreed to a plank admitting irreconcilable differences on the tariff and turning the matter over to Congress. Under the headline "Too Much Principle," the *Commercial* explained that while Wells and Greeley were willing to compromise, "we have a few highly esteemed gentlemen in our midst who are bedeviled with immense conceits of the importance of their views." The *Commercial* insisted that fellow liberal republicans refusing to compromise on the tariff "are no doubt animated by excessively pure motives, and perhaps gifted with a superfluity of doctrinal intelligence, but they are incapable of sacrificing a phrase to accomplish a deed. They are a lovable but not comfortable people." It concluded, "The honest and only thing to do here about the tariff is to let it alone." The liberal republican editors and politicians, along with free traders such as Wells, were thus not only willing to give in to Greeley's demands but also to publicly rebuke the liberal republicans still committed to a free trade platform.[48]

The convention began on May 1 with the liberal republicans in control, able to determine the degree to which they would compromise. As chairman of the Liberal Republican State Convention of Missouri that had originally issued the call for the Cincinnati Convention, Grosvenor called the convention to order at noon. He named Judge Stanley Matthews temporary chairman, a motion carried unanimously. Matthews thanked the delegates for the honor and declared that the American people "would no longer be dogs to wear the collar of party." Grosvenor then proposed adjourning until ten the next morning so that the citizens of each state at the convention could determine their delegates, but loud cries of "Schurz" quickly rang from all parts of the hall. After being conducted to the front of the stage Schurz proclaimed "the 1st of May is moving day," refused to give a speech, and encouraged the convention to begin the "practical business" of selecting delegates.[49]

The dominance of the liberal republicans on the first day of the convention, providing the temporary chairman and delivering the only three addresses, did not extend to the selection of delegates. This was another tactical political mistake on the part of the liberal republicans, who seemed to disdain work on the key Credentials Committee. Much like the William Lloyd Garrison abolitionists in the antebellum period and the muckraking journalists of the Progressive Era, the liberal republicans idealistically and optimistically believed they could sway people solely with the power of their intellectual and moral arguments. Many liberal republicans served on the platform committee or, like Schurz, took highly visible honorary positions in the convention. Still others, like the Quadrilateral, preferred to remain aloof from the actual machinery of the convention, intending to control it from outside. These mistakes would haunt the liberal republicans throughout the convention, starting with the selection of New York's 68 delegates, the most from any one state.

The meeting of New Yorkers at Cincinnati led to a "heated and almost bitter" conflict on the afternoon of May 1. The earlier attempts at compromise among the New Yorkers at Cincinnati had failed and the 126 Greeley supporters determined that the state's vote should be cast as a unit for Greeley. Mahlon Sands and Henry D. Lloyd, the officers of the American Free Trade League who had written the invitations to the first national liberal republican meeting eighteen months before, led the protests of the 27 free traders from New York who wanted delegates to be able to vote their individual preference after a couple of complimentary votes for Greeley. Referring to the origins of the liberal republican movement, Lloyd explained "that this is a rebellion instituted because those who control the regular Republican organization have used its machinery to force upon us their policy regardless of the views of the minority." He argued that in forcing all the delegates to vote for Greeley, "the meeting was doing just what the platform denounced in the old organization as its demand for the surrender of political freedom," and insisted he would "resist this as he would any other form of tyranny." The New York caucus finally agreed that the delegation would vote for Greeley as a block until twenty delegates asked to withdraw, in which case the majority of delegates would once again decide to whom the delegation would give its bloc vote. The compromise resolution was practically meaningless since the caucus selected only three free traders to serve as delegates, while proportionally they should have had eleven spots. Lloyd kept his promise to resist the "tyranny," and along with Sands, Fields, and twenty-two others, submitted a complaint to the Credentials Committee the following morning, protesting the New York caucus' selection of delegates and voting instructions. Later that afternoon, just after Schurz was named president of the convention, the Credentials Committee decided against the free traders' protest. The liberal republican editors and politicians in control of the Cincinnati Convention on May 2 placated Greeley by giving him the New York delegation, at the expense of original members of the liberal republican movement.[50]

While Greeley secured control of the New York delegation on the second day of the convention, the platform committee began dealing with the tariff controversy. The composition of the platform committee itself reflected a compromise with Greeley, as it included prominent protectionists. In addition, the liberal republicans placed on the committee, such as Wells and committee chairman White, had already indicated their willingness to compromise. The *Cincinnati Commercial* advised, "The proposition which Mr. Greeley is understood to have submitted, to allow the question of protection and free trade to be determined by the people in their Congressional elections, ought to commend itself to the good sense of the Convention." Despite days of preconvention meetings, the composition of the committee, and the urgings of the liberal republican press, disagreement still existed over the tariff. The most ardent free traders among the liberal republicans, such as Cox, Hoadly, and Atkinson, refused to compromise, threatening to bolt the convention if the other liberal republicans gave in to Greeley. The committee itself could not agree on the exact wording of the plank, and the tariff question came to dominate the convention. According to the *Commercial,* on the first day "almost the whole interest in the discussion among the leading men about the platform still centers in the Tariff plank." The next day a Davis supporter reported, "All confused by a probable distraction on tariff. Penna will not accept platform of committee. This question may seriously affect nomination." The *New York Tribune* agreed, reporting that "in consequence of this [tariff] struggle the talk about nominations has attracted less attention." Neither side wanted to determine the nominee before establishing the convention's tariff policy, as the free traders insisted they could not compromise on both the platform and candidate, while even the liberal republicans realized that "Greeley on a free-trade platform is, of course, an absurdity and impossibility." Greeley himself stood strong as the committee continued to discuss the platform, telegraphing Reid that "we can make no compromises. . . . If the convention wants a Free Trade plank, let it make one, and we will drop out. We are nought to be bought or wheedled."[51]

The lack of a platform made the delegates increasingly impatient, as many wanted to begin the nomination process. Attributing the platform difficulties to the tariff, the delegates decided to take matters into their own hands on the second night of the convention, May 2. The delegates enthusiastically voted to suspend the rules to allow the convention itself to decide the tariff issue without referring it to the platform committee. As the convention began directly debating the tariff, Greeley supporter Cassius Clay of Kentucky "counseled exclusion of the apple of discord," arguing "that the Tariff question was overshadowed in importance by questions of restoring popular rights and sovereignty to the people of the Southern States." Stanley Matthews, a liberal republican, responded that "one of the reasons why I entered into this movement . . . was that I might assist in emancipating the politics and business of this country from the domination of rings. I mean political rings in Washington, I mean railroad rings which are stealing our public land. And I mean pig-iron rings which are robbing this country." In the midst of the great applause following Matthew's speech, Atkinson came to the floor to announce that the committee had agreed to a tariff plank and would submit the platform on May 3. The committee, though, had not resolved the tariff issue and continued to debate it all night.[52]

The next morning before presenting the platform Horace White addressed the convention, giving a good summary of liberal republican principles. He argued that Grant's abuse of power and failure to reform the legacies of the Civil War endangered the existence of republican government. Phrases such as "usurped powers not granted by the Constitution," "tyrannical arrogance," and "base sycophancy . . . unworthy of Republican freemen" peppered the speech. The Grant administration, according to White, "have stood in the way of necessary investigations and indispensable reforms" and "are striving to maintain themselves in authority for selfish ends by unscrupulous use of the power which rightfully belongs to the people." Significantly, White paid Reconstruction little attention. Only one of the address's fifteen sentences referred to Reconstruction, and that was the twelfth sentence. White's remarks accurately reflected the liberal republicans' primary concern with safeguarding republican institutions and their secondary interest in Reconstruction.[53]

The platform White presented differed greatly from his address, for it clearly represented major compromises with Greeley and only the remnants of the liberal republicans' original principles. Where the national liberal republican movement had agreed to concentrate on civil service reform and free trade, the first four planks of the platform dealt with Reconstruction. While recognizing "the equality of all men before the law" and pledging to support the Thirteenth, Fourteenth, and Fifteenth Amendments, the planks also called for amnesty for all former rebels and an end to Reconstruction. The fifth plank finally mentioned one of the liberal republicans' two primary issues, stating, "The Civil Service of this Government has become a mere instrument of partisan tyranny and personal ambition . . . and breeds a demoralization dangerous to the perpetuity of republican government." At last, with the sixth plank, the platform dealt with the controversial issue of tariffs. Schurz had convinced the free traders to accept Greeley's compromise position late the previous night, and the plank read, "Recognizing that there are in our midst honest but irreconcilable differences of opinion with regard to the respective systems of Protection and Free Trade, we remit the discussion of the subject to the people in their Congress Districts." The remaining six planks—three of which averaged fewer than twenty words—unenthusiastically covered the liberal republicans' secondary issues, such as returning to specie payment and opposing grants of land to railroads and other corporations. One called on the government to treat all foreign nations on fair and equal terms, alluding to the Santo Domingo and French arms sales scandals. Placing Reconstruction at the head of the platform, referring the tariff to Congress, and essentially capitulating to all of Greeley's demands demonstrated that the liberal republican editors and politicians were willing to abandon the tariff, some of their colleagues, and the original aims of their movement to gain Greeley's support. The liberal republicans naively thought they could compromise on the platform because they still mistakenly believed that they controlled the convention and could determine the nomination of the presidential candidate.[54]

* * *

With the platform settled, the convention was finally ready to nominate a presidential candidate. Five days of political maneuvering in Cincinnati had caused the fortunes of the four leading candidates to swing wildly. Davis had the greatest momentum just before the convention, but the Quadrilateral's editorial attack, the division of the Illinois delegation, and the united opposition of liberal republicans combined to destroy his candidacy by the morning of May 3. Adams moved ahead of Trumbull as the clear favorite among the liberal republicans during the convention, many favoring Trumbull as Adams's vice-president. Schurz advised the convention in his presidential address that "unless I greatly mistake the spirit of this day, what the people now most earnestly demand is, not that mere good intentions, but rather that a superior intelligence, coupled with superior virtue, should guide our affairs; not that merely an honest and popular man, but that a statesman be put at the head of government." The description of the "statesman" resembled Adams, and many of his supporters later claimed that if the voting had been held immediately after Schurz's speech on May 2, Adams would have easily won the nomination. The controversy over the tariff plank in the platform, of course, delayed the nomination of a candidate and was one of the important areas in which the liberal republicans compromised with Greeley. The repeated compromises—allowing Reid in the Quadrilateral, giving up control of the New York delegation, and abandoning free trade—removed obstacles to Greeley's nomination and gave him momentum heading into the last day of the convention. Under the headline "Shall the ticket be Greeley and Brown or Adams and Trumbull?" the *Cincinnati Commercial* insisted the morning of the balloting that "we regard it entirely certain, therefore, that either Adams or Greeley will be nominee for the first office."[55]

Already excited by unanimously passing the platform, the convention grew more frenzied as state after state cast their first votes to nominate the presidential candidate. Before the results of the first ballot could be announced, B. Gratz Brown asked to address the convention. As president of the convention, the decision was Schurz's, and the Missouri senator had good reasons for not letting Brown speak. While he had been a founder of the liberal republican movement in Missouri, in the last eighteen months Brown had started working closely with the Democrats and had become a rival of Schurz. In addition, Brown was not a member of the convention, and even members were not normally allowed to address the convention during the middle of balloting. Since Brown had received a substantial number of votes, however, Schurz thought it proper to let him speak. Brown thanked the delegates who had voted for him, but urged them to hereafter vote for Greeley. The speech surprised few delegates, as the morning editions of the *Cincinnati Commercial* and other newspapers had predicted the "scheme," but the convention became a sea of confusion as delegations started changing their votes from Brown to Trumbull and Greeley. The scene became so chaotic that the next day the *Commercial,* the *Springfield Republican,* and the *New York Tribune* all reported different vote counts for the first ballot. Schurz eventually suggested just announcing the vote as it stood and proceeding to a second ballot. With some delegations giving complimentary first votes to their favorite sons, none of the delegates came close to winning on the first ballot, though Adams and Greeley established themselves as the primary contenders, respectively finishing first and second.[56]

The second ballot demonstrated the ineffectiveness of the Brown "scheme" and an opportunity for the liberal republicans to elect one of their favorites. While Greeley gained only about two-thirds of Brown's delegates, leaving him still over a hundred votes away from the nomination, Adams and Trumbull combined for more than enough votes for one of them to win. Adams' and Trumbull's earlier refusal to proclaim their candidacies and build organizations seriously hurt the efforts to unite their support. Though some of Adams's actions may have been an attempt to appear as a popular candidate, the liberal republican press repeatedly discussed the lack of organization among Adams's supporters. In the days before the convention the *Springfield Republican* often reported on the "independent, unorganized desire for Charles Francis Adams," and on the eve of the convention it lamented that "Mr. Adams seems not to be so strong, to-day, as before, but this is apparently because there is no organization or gang at work for him." During the convention the *Cincinnati Commercial* commented on enthusiasm for Adams, adding "this is the more remarkable, when we consider that the Adams men are less compactly organized, and more indifferent to the details of what is called 'work' on such occasions, than the friends of any other candidate." Private letters confirm the newspapers' observations. Just hours after the convention ended, Winslow Pierce wrote to Adams that there had been a great deal of strength for him "even though you had no friends, or acquaintances, at the convention to be consulted with by your supporters. Immediate personal friends of others were thickly distributed in every quarter, while the two or three you had there, were scarcely seen—much less consulted with by any of the friends who supported you." Pierce insisted that "could you have had at Cincinnati two or three intelligent and judicious personal friends, whose words of encouragement and organizing power could have been somewhat controlling among the chaotic elements, and who would have made the nomination of Mr. Adams the sole object," then the convention would have nominated Adams. The refusal of Adams to have representatives at the convention, even his own sons, who had been involved in the liberal republican movement since its inception, sabotaged his chance for the nomination.[57]

Despite the lack of a manager, Adams could still have won the nomination on the third, fourth, or fifth ballots with only a portion of Trumbull's votes. The *Cincinnati Commercial* recognized that "it was within the power of Trumbull's friends to have nominated Adams on the fourth or fifth ballots, but they were not prepared for the emergency." Unlike Adams, Trumbull had a manager, but White made a series of decisions that ensured that neither Adams nor Trumbull would win the nomination. A few days after the convention Wells wrote to Trumbull explaining that "if you have heard from White he has doubtless told you that Atkinson and myself were only awaiting his word to carry our New England votes from Adams to yourself, but the opportunity was never afforded us." White had already told Trumbull, however, that "my judgment was, from the beginning of our meeting here that you could not be nominated but I did not tell anybody so." White did not use his power to switch Trumbull votes to Adams, because, as he explained to Trumbull, "if I had taken the responsibility of withdrawing your name as suggested by your letter, I should never have had any standing in Illinois opinion—certainly not among your friends." The liberal republicans were not organized enough to take advantage of the repeated opportunities they had on May 3 to nominate either Adams or Trumbull.[58]

While the liberal republicans squandered chances to nominate Adams on the first five ballots, Reid kept the Greeley forces together, gradually picking up votes and staying within striking range of Adams. Getting control of the New York delegation helped Reid immensely, for with little work he could depend on the largest delegation in the convention voting for Greeley—in the first five ballots New York never cast less than 62 of its 68 votes for Greeley—and be ready to take advantage of a fluid situation. As the roll call began for the sixth ballot, the convention became even more chaotic. "The scene at this point was exciting in the highest degree," recounted the *Cincinnati Commercial;* "Delegates were jumping in their seats, shouting and waving their hats in the wildest enthusiasm." The Illinois delegation, which had been splitting its votes between Trumbull and Davis, withdrew for a consultation during the sixth ballot. It returned to find all the other delegations had already voted and that Greeley was ahead of Adams for the first time. The Illinois delegation announced its votes—27 for Adams, 1 for Trumbull, and 12 for Greeley. With the unexpected support for Greeley from Illinois, numerous delegations started trying to change their votes to Greeley. According to the *Commercial*, "There was a great confusion at this point, and repeated raps of the gavel failed to bring the convention to order," while the *Louisville Courier-Journal* simply reported that "all order ceased." Schurz, as president of the convention, announced "there has been so much confusion in the changes made that it seems to be impossible to get the exact figures." The secretaries of the convention confirmed to Schurz that they had been unable to keep up with the changes of votes and he declared it necessary to call the roll of states again to ascertain the true vote. With a nomination in sight the crowd shouted Schurz down with cries of "No. No." He gave in to the crowd, announcing that "the vote as it was finally cast up, barring the mistakes that may have been made," gave Greeley a majority. Schurz concluded that "the majority of the votes have been cast for Horace Greeley; therefore Horace Greeley is the nominee of this convention for President of the United States."[59]

Though a climax, Greeley's nomination was too neat an ending for the liberal republicans' disorganized and ignominious convention. Upon the announcement of Greeley's nomination, a delegate motioned to proceed immediately to the nomination of a vice-presidential candidate. Despite being president of the convention, all Schurz could manage was a ten-minute break before starting the nominations, not enough to restore any semblance of order. H. L. Burnett from Ohio nominated Lyman Trumbull, only to have one of Trumbull's lieutenants, Gustave Koerner, announce that the Illinois senator "would not accept the candidacy for Vice President under any circumstances." Then an Iowa delegate nominated Jacob Cox, only to have Burnett declare he was authorized to say that Cox's name was not to be put before the convention. Once again, the liberal republican leaders displayed their selfishness, failure to communicate, and lack of political skill to manage the convention. Despite Koerner's announcement, Trumbull finished a strong second to B. Gratz Brown on the first, and indecisive, ballot. Before the second ballot Koener returned to the stage, explaining that he had telegraphed the senator as some doubt had been expressed about his refusal to accept the vice presidency. The answer, according to Koener, was an emphatic no. The liberal republicans had a legitimate chance to claim the second spot on the ticket, yet seemed apathetic. According to the *Cincinnati Commercial*, "There was scarcely any interest manifested in the proceedings at this point. It was understood that the Blair and Brown party, having handed over their goods, were ready to receive pay." The conspiracy theory appears unjustified, since the liberal republicans' taking themselves out of the race was what allowed Brown to easily win the vice-presidential nomination on the second ballot. In the end the *Commercial* could not even be certain of the vice-presidential voting, as "many of the delegates had left the hall, and no full vote could be taken, or, if taken, fully understood in the confusion."[60]

The liberal republicans lost control of their movement at the Cincinnati Convention. For eighteen months they had tried to replicate their apparent success in Missouri on a national scale, gathering Democrats and disaffected Republicans to support their ideologically motivated program of civil service reform, free trade, and the end of Reconstruction. They favored Charles Francis Adams and Lyman Trumbull as the most ideologically compatible and politically available candidates, while courting the support of Horace Greeley and the *New York Tribune*. Though many were experienced politicians, the liberal republicans repeatedly made political miscalculations: counting on candidates hesitant to work for the nomination, continually compromising with Greeley, and mismanaging the balloting. They lost control at the convention not because they were naive reformers or because the delegates rationally chose Greeley, but because the liberal republicans, despite their experience, were poor politicians. Schurz's actions the evening after Greeley's nomination best describe the effect of the liberal republicans' political mistakes. Koerner recounts in his memoirs that while Schurz was detained finishing the official record with the convention secretaries, several of the liberal republicans returned to Stallo's house for dinner. According to Koerner, "Schurz entered the room. He said nothing but at once sat down before the grand piano, which was open, and played Chopin's funeral march."[61]

8

The Experience of a Third Party in the Nineteenth Century

Why did the Liberal Republican Party lose the election of 1872? Most historians have explained the Republican landslide victory as a predictable function of Grant's popularity. Reducing the election to mere personalities, however, misses the significance of the 1872 campaign for nineteenth-century American politics. Contemporary expectations of party realignment in 1872—the Liberal Republicans, other disgruntled reformers, Republicans, and Democrats all expected that at least one of the major parties would disappear that year—demonstrate the fragility of the party system in the early Gilded Age. The Liberal Republicans had a chance to upset the existing parties, but they were wracked by internal divisions. The Republicans and Democrats compounded the internal problems of the Liberal Republicans. The Republicans developed new strategies that both major parties would use to neutralize third-party threats throughout the Gilded Age. The Democratic leaders ordered their rank and file to support the candidacy of Horace Greeley, but they could not deliver the promised votes. An analysis of the 1872 campaign shows the complex reasons why Grant beat Greeley and demonstrates both the opportunities and difficulties for third parties during the mid-nineteenth century.[1]

The Liberal Republicans' experience with the changing party landscape since the late 1840s led them to expect that a reorganization of the political parties was possible, if not likely. Self-interest, of course, also influenced their assertion of party upheaval in 1872, for they realized that the threat of the Democratic Party kept many Republicans loyal to the party of Lincoln. Before the Liberal Republican Convention in Cincinnati on May 1, the *Springfield Republican* explained that "the very existence of the democratic organization is an occasion of offense and menace to the Republican party" and "so long as this offense and menace continue, so long, practically, the republican party is likely to maintain itself in unity." The paper also declared, however, "The democratic party has been an unconscionable while in dying, but the final hour seems to have come." The *Cincinnati Commercial* agreed, insisting that "the restoration of the Democratic party to power is utterly impossible." During the campaign the *Commercial* continued trying to reassure Republicans that "the election of Mr. Greeley can not restore the Democratic party to National power. With that election the Democratic party will cease to exist." Privately, though, one Liberal Republican politician complained in July, "The great difficulty in the way of reforming this present state of things is the persistence of the Democratic party in not dying. If it had the ability of the old Whig party to go in to liquidation and get out of the way decently there would be a much better chance than I can see now for a new organization." The Liberal Republican discussion of party reorganization during 1872 surpassed mere political opportunism, however, for Liberal Republicans publicly analyzed the nature of political parties and privately expressed a desire to break up both the Democrats and the Republicans.[2]

Liberal Republican newspapers and speeches explained how and why the existing political parties were supposedly breaking up in 1872. The *Springfield Republican* ridiculed political writers who possessed "the foolish notion that American politics have somehow undergone a casting process, and received a shape which they are to retain, rigid and inflexible, for all time." According to the *Republican*, "it does not require the study of books to teach any moderately observant and intelligent man that political organisms, like all others, are continually undergoing modifications. The times change, and parties change with them." The reason was that "the old boundary lines which have separated the people, are wholly obliterated in some places, and have become very indistinct in others. We are clearly on the eve of a political reconstruction." The *Republican* did not confine its expectation of disintegration to the Democratic Party, asserting on two days in a row that "both of the great political organizations, as we have known them for the last dozen years, are cracking and tottering." The *Chicago Tribune* proclaimed that the results of the Cincinnati Convention would "dissolve existing parties and enable the best men of both old parties to unite as a new political organization." The *Tribune's* use of "best men" differs from the elitist connotation of the title of John G. Sproat's book, *"The Best Men,"* for the number of men necessary to form a political party exceeded the small elite Sproat and other historians refer to when using the phrase. The *Cincinnati Commercial* agreed that "if either of the great parties of the day should be broken up, the other would go to pieces. Each is the conservator of the other." George Julian reiterated the idea of party mortality on the campaign trail, declaring, "Political parties are not immortal." According to Julian, "Political parties have their time to be born and their appointed time to die. They grow up out of certain political exigencies, and when the exigency passes away, the party itself is compelled to get out of sight." He gave examples from American history—the Federalist, Whig, and Know-Nothing parties—which each "had its work to do, and when it did it, it died and was buried." Julian explained that similarly, "The Republican party was born out of the exigency of slavery in the National Territories . . . has had its day, and its time for final reckoning has come." Ironically, just as the machine politics of the Gilded Age was developing and the major parties were reinventing themselves, Julian predicted that the Republican Party was dead, because "you can't apply an old party, like a piece of machinery, to a new job. It never was done in politics, and never will be done."[3]

Participants in the new party did not confine their discussion of reorganizing the older political parties to newspapers and speeches. They often used the promise of destroying the existing parties to try to entice disgruntled liberal republicans to support Greeley. An early member of the liberal republican movement, Frederick Law Olmsted, could "not think of a worse thing to do, any possible thing, than for us to make the old humbug of a patriarch President." Best known as the author of travel journals of the antebellum South and as the landscape architect responsible for Central Park in New York City, Olmsted was a Yale-educated native New Englander immersed in liberal republican circles. Samuel Bowles, editor of the *Springfield Republican* and one of Olmsted's best friends, repeatedly tried to persuade him that Greeley's nomination could serve a useful purpose. In one letter Bowles argued that "the great expression of the convention was the demand of the popular mind of the South and the West for a revolution in politics, a reconstruction of the parties," and in another that "the first great desideratum in our politics is a very large and a very deep graveyard, and that Greeley seems to be the chosen of the Lord to dig it." On the same day, in separate correspondence, Bowles wrote to both Olmsted and David Wells, another liberal republican unhappy with Greeley, that the nomination "has created a political revolution already." Wells also received private letters from Horace White and Lyman Trumbull insisting that the Democratic and Republican parties were doomed. In a letter marked "Private," White declared to his friend that "what we want to do most is to destroy + pulverize two old rotten political parties + I think we should do it." Trumbull admitted that "Cincinnati disappointed everybody," but contended that Greeley's "nomination will have one good effect, which is to blow up both party organizations. This is a great gain." He asserted that "the Democratic party is already hopelessly divided + . . . the Republican party is rapidly disintegrating." Trumbull used similar language in responding to William Cullen Bryant's plea that he not support Greeley because his administration "cannot be otherwise than shamefully corrupt." Trumbull explained that "I wish I could see something better than to support Mr. Greeley but I do not. . . . Greeley's nomination is a bombshell which seems likely to blow up both parties. This will be an immense gain." The Liberal Republicans' assertions in private letters to close friends of confidence in party reorganization indicate that this was not mere political rhetoric, but the reflection of a sincere belief in the plasticity of the political parties.[4]

Like Olmsted, Wells, and Bryant, many original members of the liberal republican movement had believed before the Cincinnati Convention that a political revolution was possible, but then refused to join the Liberal Republican Party because they feared Greeley's nomination would only strengthen the Democrats. Judge Stanley Matthews, a founder of the early liberal republican organization in Ohio, told a Republican crowd during the campaign that it had been "a movement intended to work the disintegration of both political parties." Though still convinced that the Republican Party "has been guilty of sins, both of omission and commission," he worried more about Greeley and the Democrats. Standing on a stage with the Republican vice-presidential candidate, Matthews proclaimed his "determination to support and vote for General Grant and Henry Wilson as the candidates of the Republican party." Another founder of the liberal republican movement in Ohio, George Hoadly, reached the same conclusion. In an address titled "Grant or Greeley—Which?" he explained that "the condition under which I entered this movement was that it should be a movement from the people, and not party men; that the Democratic party should die. Instead of its being dead, I find it alive." Thus, Hoadly announced, "I propose to vote for Grant." Bryant and the *New York Evening Post* likewise feared that Greeley would disrupt the Republican, not the Democratic, Party and decided to support Grant. The *Post* proposed that the only reason free traders endorsed Greeley was that "they take Greeley's nomination and election as the most convenient means of breaking up the existing régime, and producing a general chaos," but the paper expressed dread that "the deplorable part of this mischance is that it endangers the Republican party." Matthews, Hoadly, and Bryant's rejection of Greeley did not likewise imply rejection of a potential political revolution. All three clearly had expected a disintegration of political parties before the Cincinnati Convention, and while they may have thought that Greeley's nomination had delayed the break-up, one of the reasons they decided to support Grant was fear that the Democratic Party might survive while the Republican Party dissolved.[5]

Other liberal republicans opposed to Greeley remained convinced that his nomination could still disrupt both the Democratic and Republican parties. While Edwin Godkin's *Nation* acknowledged early in May that "the Cincinnati Convention must, as far as the general aims and objects of those who called it are concerned, be pronounced a failure," the same article insisted that "on one result of the Convention the friends of reform may heartily congratulate themselves, for it is certain and substantial. The existing party organizations are broken up." *The Nation* repeatedly analyzed how Greeley could destroy the

Democratic Party in particular. Before the Democratic National Convention in July the paper contended that "it must be admitted that the nomination of Greeley by the Democrats will be, on the whole, the most ludicrous end which ever overtook a great organization. . . . It surpasses in absurdity, if that be possible, the nomination of Greeley by the Cincinnati Convention, because the party in electing Greeley *ipso facto* perishes, and perishes in the most ignoble way." Godkin explained that "if they fail to elect him, then disheartening defeat coming upon demoralizing disgrace destroys all that remains of them. If they succeed . . . the attempt of a weak man to conduct an administration which carries an opposition within itself, must plunge the country into discord and confusion from which it will be glad to escape through the crystallization of new party forms out of the ferment and dissolution of the old." Godkin refused to support Greeley despite his conviction that a Greeley presidency could break up the existing party structure. During the middle of the campaign Godkin told Carl Schurz that he was "going off yachting for three weeks, heartsick of politics." The reason was that "what I seek is not a sham break-up of parties, such as the Greeley movement promises, but a real break-up, involving something more than the construction of a new party machine out of the pieces of the old ones."[6]

Jacob Cox shared with Godkin both the hope of reorganizing the existing political parties and a dislike of Greeley. Immediately after the Cincinnati Convention Cox met with Wells, Atkinson, Godkin, and a few other liberal republicans who all agreed that the manner of Greeley's nomination absolved them of any responsibility to support him. Nevertheless, Cox thought that some good could come if the Democrats also nominated Greeley. He contended to Wells in May, "The attempt to make the party support Greeley is manifestly destruction to the party organization, for which we have cause to be glad." Cox reiterated a common liberal republican belief that "if we divide the Democracy, we have in that very act rendered the disruption of the Republicans inevitable, for we all agreed that nothing kept the Republican party together the past four years but the fear of the return of *secession* Democrats to power." As the summer wore on, however, Cox became more disillusioned. "If the Democratic party had had the good sense and patriotism to dissolve itself in 1865, or the Republican party had had the wisdom to make the Democrats dissolve then, we should already have found the elements crystallizing about new centers. But," complained Cox, "wisdom, patriotism + good sense were lacking then, and now we seem doomed to a tedious interregnum in which parties are held together only by habit of cohesion and the desire for spoils." Cox still expected a reorganization of the political parties, but decided to remain aloof from politics "until the parties of the future" were defined. Godkin and Cox's conviction that the existing party structure was breaking up is significant because, having rejected the entire campaign of 1872, neither had political motivations for contending that the nation was in the midst of a party revolution.[7]

Republicans and Democrats had a vested interest in preventing the break-up of the current party structure, and they discussed this frequently. Immediately after Greeley's nomination by the Liberal Republican Party, the Republican *New York Times* charged that "Mr. Greeley has chosen to exhibit a reckless disregard for the continued existence of the Republican Party" and his nomination was "an attack upon the existence of the Republican Party." A few days later the paper ran an editorial entitled "Does the Country Need the Republican Party?" While stipulating that "no party can survive, or ought to survive, the time when its members become convinced either that the objects on which they originally combined are accomplished, or that other objects have become of greater importance," the *Times* insisted that the Republican Party had not reached such a point. By the time the Republican National Convention was held in June, the *Times* was declaring, "There is not even the prospect of success to induce Republicans to join the effort of the Greeley faction to break up the party." Though the *Times* increasingly argued that the Republican Party would not dissolve, the mere discussion of the issue reveals that the paper at least considered it a possibility. In addition, it articulated the same assumptions as the liberal republicans, that political parties were temporary organizations with limited life spans. Private letters to the chairman of the National Republican Committee, Edwin D. Morgan, from its secretary William E. Chandler and from committee member Grenville M. Dodge corroborate the *Time's* public assessment. While Chandler and Dodge became increasingly confident as the campaign progressed, they expressed fear as late as August. When the Democrats held their convention in early July, Morgan felt compelled to reassure Chandler, "Don't be scared about the Democratic Presidential nominee. He will be badly + disastrously defeated, and his party also."[8]

While worried about the survival of their own party, Republicans were certain the coming election would destroy the Democrats. A week before the Democratic Convention in Baltimore nominated Greeley, the *New York Times* predicted that "the regular candidates of the Republican Party are sure of numerous supporters among the Democrats, in case the Baltimore Convention destroys party allegiance by nominating a Republican." During the convention the *Times* ran headlines like "THE DEMOCRATIC WAKE." The paper rejoiced that "the Democrats will today take the first steps to insure their final extinction as a political party" and commented sardonically that "it is a little melancholy to see them voluntarily inviting the most ignominious end which ever befell a great organization." The *Times* had little political motivation for discussing the demise of the Democrats, since it was too late to stop them from nominating Greeley, and the destruction of the Democratic Party could only encourage Republican defections. In addition, the newspaper accounts are similar to the correspondence among Republican leaders at the time. Just after Greeley's nomination at the Baltimore Convention James Edmunds, national head of the Union League, received a report from Georgia exclaiming that "the Democratic party has ceased to exist." The letter explained that "the action of the Baltimore Convention has caused utmost chaos in politics of this state," but asserted that "the indications are strong, however, that many old Whigs will repudiate the bidding of the late Democratic party." Secretary of the Interior Columbus Delano likewise wrote to the secretary of the Republican National Committee after the Democrats nominated Greeley. He observed that "as the D. Party is virtually dissolved, its old members will probably feel a little likely to re-arrange their party relations. The Republican party in my opinion should at once realize this fact." Delano suggested creating organizations "so that those who desire to come can do so at once and with as little embarrassment as possible." Both publicly and privately, Republicans viewed the Democrats as a "*defunct party*" in 1872.[9]

The Democrats had been trying to revive their political fortunes ever since secession in 1860 had temporarily removed their Southern base and tainted all Democrats with treason. Their defeat in the 1868 election demonstrated their continued vulnerability and made the reorganization of parties once again seem possible; many had already predicted the demise of the party during the 1864 campaign. In 1870 the Democrats initiated the "New Departure," publicly accepting such results of the Civil War as the Thirteenth, Fourteenth, and Fifteenth Amendments, in an attempt to restore their image and capture the political center. While in retrospect the Democrats' adoption of the New Departure in 1870 made the reorganization of parties less likely because the party was thus reducing its vulnerability, at the time many Democrats saw the alliance with Greeley and the Liberal Republicans as a death omen. The Democratic *Savannah Morning News* declared that the acceptance of Greeley meant "political suicide." Democratic Congressman Michael C. Kerr of Indiana expressed similar sentiments in a letter to Edward Atkinson, predicting that the Democrats' endorsement of Greeley would mean "dishonor and political ruin" for his party.[10]

Not all Democrats feared their endorsement of Greeley would destroy the Democratic Party. Cyrus McCormick, chairman of the Democratic State Committee in Illinois, saw the possibility of a complete reorganization of both political parties that could help the Democrats. In a private letter during the campaign he exclaimed, "Nothing has equaled in politics the present overwhelming revolution." The Democratic *New York Herald* was even more explicit in a series of editorials throughout the summer of 1872. Immediately after Greeley's nomination at Cincinnati, the *Herald* cautioned, "A political revolution has just been inaugurated" that "places both the administration and democratic parties in a quandary." A month later, after the Republicans renominated Grant, the paper warned that Democrats "are at a crisis of their history . . . in the present breaking up of the old party organizations." The *Herald* advocated that the Democratic Convention endorse Greeley, though the paper acknowledged, "It will mark the most extraordinary party transformation in our political history. In fusing the democratic with the Cincinnati party, the former, as it were, disappears." The *Herald* cited the rise and fall of the Federalist and the Whig parties to demonstrate that the dissolution of parties was normal in United States politics.[11]

Just before the Democratic Convention in July, the *Herald* printed a long discussion on the nature of political parties in an editorial titled "The Ups and Downs of Our Political Parties." The paper argued that "the most important conclusions suggested from the rise and fall of each of our political parties of the past are these: that no political party in this country, unless founded upon great principles or ideas, can stand, and that when a party has fulfilled its mission it breaks up, dissolves and disappears." The passage bears a striking resemblance to remarks made in Republican and Liberal Republican newspapers and campaign speeches. Recall that the *New York Times* had earlier contended, "No party can survive, or ought to survive, the time when its members become convinced either that the objects on which they originally combined are accomplished, or that other objects have become of greater importance." And a few weeks after the *Herald*'s editorial, George Julian told a crowd that "political parties have their time to be born and their appointed time to die. They grow up out of certain political exigencies, and when the exigency passes away, the party itself is compelled to get out of sight." The amazing similarities between the Democratic, Republican, and Liberal Republican attitudes toward the nature of political parties make it difficult to believe that this was simply political opportunism, for it would have been difficult for all three to find political advantage in the same arguments. Their common view of political parties as temporary associations founded on great principles shows the dominant myth and theory of party in the mid-nineteenth century.[12]

Liberal Republicans, regular Republicans, Democrats, and disgruntled reformers all viewed political parties as temporary organizations and believed that a reorganization was occurring in 1872. The assertions are found in newspapers, campaign speeches, and private letters. The agreement between public and private sources, and between people with different political agendas, indicates a sincere and general assumption in 1872 that political reorganization was likely. This expectation does not mesh with the division of United States political history into five relatively static party periods, the third of which stretches from 1860 to 1896, as argued by the New Political History. Ironically, the *New York Herald* declared in 1872 that "as we have shown in our Presidential recapitulation, our political history may be divided into five periods. Each of these historical divisions is distinctly marked, but none so broadly or by so great a political revolution as this fifth period."[13]

*   *   *

Contemporary expectations of a political reorganization in 1872, of course, failed to materialize. Traditionally, historians have analyzed all aspects of the 1872 campaign simultaneously, which can sometimes help to show interparty conflicts, but this approach limits our understanding of the Liberal Republicans' intraparty conflicts. Concentrating on the Liberal Republicans alone in the first months after the Cincinnati Convention can highlight the preexisting fissures that became more apparent immediately after the convention, the distinction between the movement and the party, and how these internal divisions contributed to the Liberal Republican loss in 1872.[14]

The combination of antiparty appeals and lack of party discipline made internal divisions common in third parties throughout the nineteenth century and often led to their defeat. For instance, the Free Soil Party's nomination of a former Democrat for president in 1848 annoyed former Whigs in the party, contributing to poor results on election day. Controversy over paper money versus silver split the academic-reform community of the Greenback Party in the late 1870s. The Liberal Republicans, however, took third-party internal division to an extreme. The surprise nomination of Horace Greeley at the Cincinnati Convention caused chaos among the original liberal republicans, who considered his politics, principles, and personality anathema to their movement. For two months after the convention, members of the movement publicly squabbled among themselves and with Greeley over the course of the Liberal Republican Party, doing irreparable harm to the chance of political reorganization.[15]

Amazingly, the newspapers that had been supportive of the liberal republicans were among the first to discuss the divisions in the movement following the Cincinnati Convention. In the same edition of the *Springfield Republican* that announced Greeley's nomination, Samuel Bowles reported that "the Ohio delegation had an indignation meeting this afternoon. Many of its leading men called Greeley and Brown all the hard names they could think of, and said they would not vote for them. Brinkerhoff said he would vote for neither Greeley nor Grant, but Judge Hoadly would both vote and stump for Grant." Bowles also recounted dissatisfaction among eastern liberal republicans, explaining that "Mr. Atkinson and Mr. Wells went East sadly and sorrily doubtful what they should do." The *Cincinnati Commercial* and the *Chicago Tribune* likewise discussed disunity among the liberal republicans in their May 4 editions. A few days later the *New York Tribune* reported that Brinkerhoff had announced his resignation as a member of the Liberal Republican State Central Committee and that Stanley Matthews "had left the Convention in disgust."[16]

The published accounts of many liberal republicans' dissatisfaction with Greeley's nomination pale in comparison with their private correspondence. Upon learning the results of the Cincinnati Convention, Charles Francis Adams Jr. confided to his diary, "Greeley nominated!!! Words fail to do justice to my disgust + surprise." George Hoadly found the words to express his feelings, declaring, "I left the Convention when Greeley was nominated. My sense of self respect would not allow me to remain longer. The fraud was patent, consummated under my eyes, and stank into my nostrils." David Wells urged Edward Atkinson "not to submit to Mr. Greeley's nomination," and a group of liberal republicans committed to free trade, including Atkinson, Wells, Edwin Godkin, Mahlon Sands, and Henry Demarest Lloyd, met at Steinway Hall in New York City on May 30 to consider "the best mode of retrieving the mistakes of the Cincinnati Convention." Those who gathered at Steinway Hall agreed to invite 150 people—embracing liberal republicans, Democrats, and Greeley supporters—to a private conference at New York's Fifth Avenue Hotel on June 20 to discuss how to resolve their differences and defeat Grant.[17]

Many of the liberal republicans responsible for calling the Fifth Avenue meeting, however, were more interested in defeating Greeley than Grant. The invitations, signed by Schurz, Cox, Bryant, Wells, and Brinkerhoff, explained that the meeting was "for the purpose of consultation and to take such action as the situation of things may require," implying that Greeley could still be replaced. The day after the Steinway Hall meeting an attendee explained to Schurz that "the original friends of the Cincinnati movement in this city cannot and will not support Greeley under any circumstances" and that "we know that you were in favor of Adams and feel it is not too late to procure the nomination." The next day Atkinson rejoiced to Schurz that "I think we have destroyed what little chance there was for Greeley and my hope now is that a third party organized can throw the election into the House. I am aware that Grant would then be elected, but I prefer Grant to Greeley." In the first edition of *The Nation* after the Steinway Hall meeting, Godkin argued that "to accept Mr. Greeley as the champion of revenue reform would be, to our mind, destructive of what morality there is left in party politics." In perhaps the most unequivocal stand against Greeley, Charles Francis Adams Jr. wrote to his father in mid-June that "the utter defeat of Greeley,—his defeat in such a way to show that the movement broke down under its own grotesque dishonesty,—is the great desire of my heart just now."[18]

The circumstances of Greeley's nomination and disagreement over whether or not to support him fractured the ranks of the liberal republican movement. Many liberal republicans in the Free Trade League suspected that William Grosvenor, an employee of the league and founder of the liberal republican movement in Missouri, had helped fellow Missourian B. Gratz Brown secure the nomination for Greeley in exchange for Brown's nomination as vice-presidential candidate. After returning from Cincinnati Mahlon Sands and Henry Demarest Lloyd ransacked Grosvernor's New York office, confiscating his personal papers, lists of free traders across the country that had been prepared for the Free Trade League, and the official books of the Missouri State Liberal Republican Committee. According to Grosvenor, "They had become convinced that I had 'sold out' the cause of Free Trade." When Grosvenor complained to Schurz and Atkinson about his treatment, Sands explained that "after what we considered this disastrous result of the Cincinnati Convention, and the evident trade effected between Greeley, the ultra Protectionist, and Brown, the ultra Free Trader, our belief in the good faith of men in general was shaken, and Col. Grosvenor did not escape suspicion." Sands thought it natural that they "entertained suspicions concerning Grosvenor's good faith after what happened at Cincinnati." Atkinson himself confided that "I do not yet distrust Grosvenor, although I told him that when Gratz Brown sold out I feared for a little time that he was also a party in the trade." Atkinson and Schurz eventually brokered a peace between Grosvenor and the Free Trade League, but hard feelings lingered. Cox tried to justify Sands and Lloyd's actions to Grosvenor a few weeks later, concluding with regrets "that you are not with us."[19]

Members of the Free Trade League also blamed Quadrilateral members Samuel Bowles and Murat Halstead for allowing Greeley to win the nomination at Cincinnati. A week before the Steinway Hall meeting, Atkinson told Charles Sumner that "of one thing I am satisfied. The only men who can be relied on to stick are the free-traders. We should have carried the day at Cincinnati had not we been emasculated by the actions of Bowles, Halstead, and others who looked to the alliance of Greeley as essential." Atkinson and the free traders would have been even more convinced that Samuel Bowles had sold them out had they known of the editor's Machiavellian maneuvers after the convention. In the month following the convention Bowles corresponded with both Whitelaw Reid, Greeley's campaign manager, and representatives from the Free Trade League, often sharing the private thoughts of one group with the other without permission. For example, at the end of May Bowles wrote to Wells that "I send you both Mr. Reid's letters, one intended to be shown you, and the other not." Two weeks later Lloyd sent Bowles an invitation to the private Fifth Avenue conference, and the editor responded that "I heartily approve of the proposed conference and wish it may result in substituting Adams for Greeley." That same day, however, Bowles also sent Reid a description of the proposed conference and a copy of his "note of response to the invitation." Bowles told Reid that he did not know whether he would attend the conference, but that "if it is to be made up of simply stolid opponents of Greeley, I certainly shall not." Bowles probably did not feel guilty about the duplicitous behavior since he blamed the free traders for the convention fiasco, privately telling Wells that "Atkinson et al showed their capacity to 'butcher things' at Cincinnati." He explained in the *Springfield Republican* that "had Mr. Atkinson of Boston and his friends given up the contest earlier and more gracefully on the [tariff] resolution, the convention would have come to a nomination a day earlier and obtained Mr. Adams."[20]

The time and energy that had gone into the liberal republican movement made recriminations among its members fierce. Bowles and the other editors in the movement, particularly Murat Halstead and Horace White, had also staked their businesses and professional reputations on the Cincinnati Convention, and thus had more to lose than Atkinson and the members of the Free Trade League. None of the editors liked Greeley's nomination; the *Cincinnati Commercial* publicly admitted right after the convention that "we shall make no attempt to disguise our opinion that the nomination of Greeley and Brown was not the most fortunate possible issue of the labors of the Convention," and Bowles privately acknowledged to Wells that "I don't like the issue of Greeley or Grant. I wish it could be Adams." The pragmatic concerns of running major newspapers inexorably linked to the convention led them to try salvaging something, however, from the disaster at Cincinnati. Immediately after the convention Bowles publicly discussed his reservations about Greeley's candidacy and explained in the *Springfield Republican* that "the Cincinnati Commercial and the Chicago Tribune for these reasons may stand, for the present at least, in a critical and independent, and perhaps hesitating position toward the ticket." The *Commercial* acknowledged that "we are looking upon this nomination as an experiment, and awaiting events." In early June the *Republican* admitted, "It is quite true that the Republican would welcome the substitution of Mr. Adams for Mr. Greeley." After discussing some of the problems with Greeley's candidacy, the *Republican* declared that "if it is 'lukewarmness' towards Mr. Greeley to recognize these facts, then the Republican is certainly guilty of it, and likely to continue permanently guilty of such conduct."[21]

Editors of the smaller newspapers in the liberal republican movement, possessed of more financial freedom and not part of the Quadrilateral that tried to control the Cincinnati Convention, mocked the larger newspapers for their halfhearted support of Greeley. Edwin Godkin argued in *The Nation* that "the Springfield *Republican* and the Chicago *Tribune* are the only two influential papers which were instrumental in getting up the Cincinnati movement which make even a pretense of warmth in supporting him, and we suspect in both cases it is done with much heaviness of heart and bitterness of spirit." William Cullen Bryant was more pointed in criticizing his fellow editors. He maintained in the *New York Evening Post* that the involvement of Bowles, Halstead, and White in the convention as editors compromised their integrity as both politicians and journalists. "If the delegate is simply a private citizen, he pledges himself to vote the ticket put forth by the party," explained Bryant, "but if he is a journalist he finds himself in an altogether different position. The code of political morality commands him to make his journal a party organ; his duty as an impartial critic of men and measures quite as sternly orders him to do nothing of the kind. The result is a compromise of some sort which affords a great deal of amusement to the godless public, and at the same time seriously damages the reputation of the journal."[22]

Schurz was the central figure in the shattering of the liberal republican movement. Like almost all members of the movement, Schurz was disappointed with Greeley's nomination. In a private letter to Bowles he complained that "to see a movement which had apparently been so successful, beyond all reasonable anticipations, at the decisive moment taken possession of by a combination of politicians striking and executing a bargain in the open light of day—and politicians, too, belonging to just that tribe we thought we were fighting against—and the whole movement stripped of its higher moral character and dragged down to the level of an ordinary political operation; this, let me confess it, was a hard blow." Schurz's complaint resembled the typical expressions of antipartyism in third-party movements, but he also may have found the results of the Cincinnati Convention so painful because he had more at stake than any other member of the liberal republican movement. As the undisputed leader of the movement since the late 1860s, Schurz realized that his political fortunes were tied to its success or failure. He wrote to Greeley that "although I abstained in the Convention from exerting any influence in favor of this or that candidate, I feel some personal responsibility in the matter," and told Reid that "I have so much of personal responsibility in the Liberal Republican movement that its failure, one way or the other, cannot be a matter of indifference to me." After a long interview with Schurz, White wrote to Grosvenor that "He thinks his political career is ended." In the weeks following the convention Schurz refused either to endorse or to reject Greeley.[23]

Schurz feared that Greeley's nomination had destroyed the principles of the liberal republican movement while providing little chance of beating Grant. He explained to Greeley that the movement had begun with free traders and Germans in the West, expanded to free traders in the East, and was then joined "finally by a considerable number of men with whom opposition to the Administration was the main impulse." The problem, according to Schurz, was that "of the three elements which met for cooperation at Cincinnati, the one which had the least to do with originating the movement and which came in after it had grown to be formidable and promising, seemed to have shaped, by the usual appliances of the political trade, all the practical results so far obtained." Schurz argued "that the appearance of political trickery could not fail to shake the whole moral basis of the movement" and that this had already seriously weakened the liberal republican movement, limiting Greeley's chances of victory. Schurz expressed particular concern about the reaction of the German community, his base of support, to Greeley's nomination. Germans were suspicious of Greeley's past as a protectionist and prohibitionist. Schurz declared that at the time of the convention, "we had nearly the whole German vote with us," and "when we came out of the convention, that force was almost entirely lost to us." Schurz had reason to worry, for in the first week after the convention his was the only German newspaper to endorse Greeley. He told Grosvenor in a confidential letter that "I do not think that as things now run, success is certain or even very probable." He observed that "the opposition in the Democratic ranks is becoming more determined every day" and predicted that "we can scarcely hope to make up by gains from the Rep. ranks what is thus lost on the Dem. side." Schurz also knew that "the Free Trade people are going to do something, and you cannot prevent them." He concluded that "the difficulty really consists in there being no harmony between our candidates and the true spirit of the movement; and the worst of it is that this cannot be denied."[24]

The Greeleyites and the different factions of the liberal republican movement all pressured Schurz to support them in the weeks following the convention. Greeley and Reid repeatedly wrote to Schurz, asking him to endorse Greeley and start campaigning for him. The editors of the major newspapers and Grosvenor, having decided Greeley was now the only viable chance for the movement, also urged Schurz to announce immediately for Greeley. White wrote Schurz that "a dreadful rumor comes to me from Washington which runs something on this wise: That Carl Schurz, having led his young friends up to the cannon's mouth, is about to leave them in the ditch." Grosvenor lectured

Schurz that "you are in danger, I fear, of making a fatal mistake—fatal not because it won't lead to success but because it would destroy confidence throughout the country in your good sense + political good faith. You have led thousands of men into a hazardous movement. . . . Now if you draw back, Schurz, a very large number will feel that you are not acting in good faith with them." Other liberal republicans wanted the opposite, pleading with Schurz to repudiate Greeley and return the movement to its original direction. Hiram Barney reported to Schurz that "Mr. Bryant + Mr. Godwin have such strong personal objections to Mr. Greeley that they will on no account support him for the presidency," and Godkin asked, "Is there no way out of the wretched mess into which the Cincinnati nominations have plunged us?" Schurz agreed that "the situation is perplexing and humiliating in the extreme, and I would do anything to escape from the necessity of supporting Greeley against Grant." More than a week before the Steinway Hall meeting, Schurz instructed Godkin that "the best thing to be done is that proposed by the *Evening Post:* To make another nomination, and to resort to that end not to the dangerous machinery of a convention, but to get up a meeting of 'notables.' "[25]

The Steinway Hall meeting followed Schurz's advice, calling the Fifth Avenue Hotel conference for June 20 in an effort to find a more acceptable candidate than Greeley. One of the participants wrote Schurz that "we know that what you do will be done with a single eye to your convictions. We never will think otherwise, but oh how heartily we wish those convictions will soon determine you to oppose Greeley in time to have your influence used for the procuring of the nomination of another at Baltimore [the Democratic Convention]." Schurz was telling the liberal republicans who supported Greeley a different story, though. A few days after the Steinway Hall meeting, Schurz told Grosvenor that "a good many of the opponents of Greeley think that something can still be done to restore to the movement its original character. I, myself, think there is one chance in ten." The next day White reported to Grosvenor that Schurz's "present concern is to get Wells, Godkin, Cox, + the Steinway Hallers back into line" and that his "present plot is to hold a meeting of all the Adullomites [people favoring Charles Francis Adams's candidacy], together with a number of pronounced Greeley men, such as Trumbull, Palmer, yourself + myself in New York on the 20th of June to canvass the possibility of substituting somebody else for Greeley at Baltimore. Of this S. thinks there is one chance in a hundred. I think there is no chance in a thousand." Schurz went to the Fifth Avenue conference with a complex agenda, attempting to return the liberal republican movement to its original path, preserve his and the movement's political reputation, and conciliate the various liberal republican factions.[26]

The Fifth Avenue conference changed the nature of the liberal republican movement, for liberal republicans had to follow either political expediency or principle. For those whose careers and fortunes were tied to politics, the pressure to salvage something from the Cincinnati Convention was too much, and most decided to support Greeley. A week before the conference White advised Trumbull that "of course there is nothing to be done now but to go for Greeley and go strongly," and he began making deals with Greeley's representatives. White still hoped to get liberal republicans unhappy with Greeley "back into line." The conflict between principle and political expediency was clear in White's and Trumbull's speeches on June 20, in which they switched from their earlier declarations that the movement was not simply anti-Grant to accepting anyone who might beat Grant. Trumbull provides a good example of the transition to supporting Greeley. Months before the Cincinnati Convention he had told a friend, "I suppose Grant will be renominated & I think much better of him than of his surroundings. Can we correct the abuses & reform the finances with him?" Just after the Cincinnati Convention, though, Trumbull explained to Bryant that "having favored the Cincinnati Movement + Greeley having received the nomination, I see no course left but to elect him + endeavor to surround him as far as possible with honest men."[27]

Trumbull was one of the first to speak at the Fifth Avenue conference, and he set the tone by insisting that "to the question that comes uppermost among us there is only one answer which occurs to me reasonable or possible. How are we to defeat Grant? By supporting Greeley." Wells, in what one free trader called a "defection," reiterated Trumbull's position, declaring that "there is only the question of beating the man who scandalizes the country in the White House, and on that question I see no other recourse than Horace Greeley." Horace White and other liberal republicans spoke in a similar vein. Atkinson, Stallo, and Parke Godwin of the *New York Evening Post* were the only ones to speak in opposition to Greeley, proclaiming that they would not sacrifice their principles to beat Grant. At one in the morning, after a long day of debate, Schurz finally rose and endorsed Greeley. According to the *New York Herald,* "the effect of this speech, delivered with great vim and earnestness, was most demoralizing to the free traders, and settled the question as to what they would do." The Fifth Avenue conference adjourned immediately after Schurz's speech, with the majority of the participants in the liberal republican movement having accepted the political necessity of supporting Greeley.[28]

The liberal republican newspapers that still refused to support Greeley after the conference explained the significance for the movement of supporting the Liberal Republican Party's candidate. The *New York Evening Post* lambasted the conference: "On the whole, we may say that the meeting furnished a rather disheartening illustration of the partisan condition of politics, and of the profound want of respect even among those calling themselves reformers for the animating spirit of reform, in other words, of principle." *The Nation* expressed a similar opinion, finding that "Senator Schurz, in explaining his position, in the evening acknowledged that he expected no reforms from Mr. Greeley," and that "in short, the only benefits that were mentioned as likely to result from Mr. Greeley's election were the reunion of the North and South and the defeat of General Grant, and of course this is equivalent to an admission that the whole movement has degenerated into 'something to beat Grant.' "[29]

Many individual liberal republicans also refused to support Greeley even after the Fifth Avenue conference. Atkinson, Stallo, Hoadly, Bryant and about twenty others met at the Fifth Avenue Hotel again on June 21 and drew up a platform advocating free trade, civil service reform, and the end of Reconstruction. The platform proclaimed that "Horace Greeley does not represent these principles, but has been a lifelong opponent to the most essential of them." They nominated William Groesbeck, an Ohio Democrat, and Frederick Law Olmsted as an opposition presidential ticket, describing them as "men fully in accord with our principles, and of such character and ability to be worthy of the confidence of the American people." Neither Groesbeck nor Olmsted cared for the dubious honor of being nominated by twenty-five men—both refused the nomination, and Olmsted actually hid when reporters tried to notify him of it. (Olmsted did happily accept another presidency in 1872, when he was appointed president of the Department of Public Parks in New York City.) The *Springfield Republican* mocked the "irreconcilables" for not realizing "that the revolutionary movement had grown too large and acquired too great velocity to be easily forced back into its original channel."[30]

Many leading liberal republicans either returned to the Republican Party or abandoned politics altogether when the two days of conferences in New York made it clear that Greeley was the only alternative to Grant. Upon returning from New York Atkinson decided that "I have played my last card in politics and shall not be bothered any more." Though Atkinson later determined to vote the Republican ticket, he never again took such an active role in politics. Cox and Henry Adams likewise refused to participate in the campaign of 1872. Godkin, meanwhile, wrote to Schurz that "the more I think about him [Greeley], the more satisfied I am that I can have nothing to do with him. The conference at New York confirmed me in this opinion." Godkin's *Nation* and Bryant's *New York Evening Post* supported Grant through the rest of the campaign. As one liberal republican remarked, "That Grant is an ass, no one can deny, but better an ass than a mischievous idiot." Other liberal republicans shared this sentiment and took an active part in the campaign for Grant and against Greeley. Charles Francis Adams Jr., Stanley Matthews, and Hoadly all gave public speeches supporting Grant. Adams concluded his by declaring, "I shall this year again cast my vote for President Grant—not alas! This time with the glad confidence in which, four years ago, I cast it for General Grant; but as the most direct, and indeed, only way left open of rebuking that species of political cant and chicanery of which the history of the Cincinnati movement was, in its last stage, an unequaled example." Anticipating Greeley's loss a week before the election, Godkin typified most liberal republicans by rejoicing to Atkinson that "we shall have our revenge for Cincinnati on Tuesday."[31]

The liberal republicans who did join the Liberal Republican Party and support Greeley quickly discovered that they were no longer in control. Schurz and Trumbull stumped the nation making speeches, Grosvenor worked for the campaign in New York, and Bowles, Halstead, and White all used their newspapers to promote Greeley. Those who had helped create the party, however, were kept on its fringes. While Greeley and Reid wanted speeches and publicity from the liberal republicans, they refused to include them in the inner circle of the campaign. For instance, none of the original members of the liberal republican movement, including Schurz, was placed on the Liberal Republican National Committee, and the chairman of the committee was Ethan Allen, a longtime crony of Greeley's. Similarly, the chairman of the Liberal Republican Congressional Campaign Committee was Senator Reuben Fenton of New York, a man renowned for his corruption and detested by most liberal republicans. Schurz, Grosvenor, Bowles, and the others found themselves on the outside of the campaign, working for the type of politician they had started the movement to defeat.[32]

The relationship between Greeley and the liberal republicans supporting him became more strained as the campaign progressed. Bowles had earlier advised Reid that it was "very important that Mr. Greeley should be dealing with such men as Schurz, Trumbull, and Sumner," insisting that "the gang that are running the machine now is not inviting, and only helps to deepen the distrust of Greeley's surroundings." Before the Fifth Avenue conference, Greeley and his friends had made some concessions to win the support of liberal republicans like Schurz and White, agreeing that Greeley, known for his indiscretion, would not write any public letters and would give Schurz and Trumbull veto power over cabinet appointments. After the Fifth Avenue conference, however, friction increased between Greeley and the liberal republicans supporting him. For example, White complained to Reid in late June that "Mr. Greeley has written one letter at least since the tacit agreement which he made," and threatened that "my wife sails for Europe next month. If I supposed that this business . . . was to continue I would certainly sail with her + remain until after the election." A few days later White reiterated his point to Reid, arguing that "what troubles me more than any one particular letter is the fact that we have a candidate who does not know better than to write any letters, especially after he has had the danger fully explained to him. One thing is certain, I am not going to stand in the range of his fire much longer."[33]

Schurz also had trouble with Greeley, the latter responding defensively to a missive on civil service reform. Greeley began the correspondence by announcing, "I pass over the allusion to my political associates, barely remarking that an imputation so vague can never be specifically repelled." Soon after the letter Greeley asserted his independence in choosing a cabinet, writing to Reid, "I have given *no* assurance to the *personnel* of the cabinet, should it ever be my duty to construct one. Neither Hutchinson, nor Fenton has ever spoken to me on the subject. As to Grosvenor, I am not likely to paddle out assurances or promises of any kind through *him*." Greeley also clearly indicated his relationship with the liberal republicans. Bowles had earlier told Reid that "I don't wish or expect him to 'supplicate' any man's support. But certain men being his friends and supporters he has a right, and it seems to me a duty, to invite them to confer with him and to give them his confidence." Responding to this suggestion, Greeley wrote to Reid that "as to Sam. Bowles, and the rest, I am always glad to see and to confer with them, but I do not *solicit* interviews nor support. I shall be glad to meet the Senators you name, or any of them, but not as a supplicant for their support." Far from not just working well with the few liberal republicans supporting him, Greeley was not even directly corresponding with most of them.[34]

Back in early May, right after the Cincinnati Convention, Trumbull had predicted to Bryant that "Greeley's nomination is a bomb shell which seems likely to blow up both parties." Just the opposite occurred. After the Cincinnati Convention the liberal republicans repeatedly divided into warring factions, attacking each other's integrity, principles, and common sense. The few liberal republicans who supported Greeley and joined the Liberal Republican Party were kept on the fringes of the party their movement had created. Greeley's nomination was a bombshell that blew up the liberal republican movement, helping to ensure that the Liberal Republican Party would also fail.[35]

*   *   *

The regular Republicans compounded the internal problems of the new party. Their adoption of the Liberal Republicans' most popular positions and their use of patronage led to the resounding defeat of the Liberal Republican Party, a fate similar to that of most third parties in the nineteenth century. While it may seem that the Republicans reacted as American political parties usually do when confronted with such a challenge, the major parties' methods of dealing with third-party threats were not constant throughout the nineteenth century, but gradually evolved. In the antebellum period third parties such as the Free Soilers and the Know-Nothings had advocated the issues of antislavery and nativism, and neither the Democrats nor the Whigs had tried to any significant extent to appropriate these issues with piecemeal reforms. In addition, the small size of the civil service before the Civil War had limited the power the major parties gained from patronage. The Republicans' actions during the summer of 1872, which contributed significantly to the reelection of Grant, represented rapidly developing strategies that the major parties would use to eliminate third-party threats throughout the Gilded Age.[36]

The Republican Party began using its legislative and patronage power to weaken the impact of the liberal republicans even before the Cincinnati Convention. In an effort to deflect criticism about abuse of the patronage system, in December 1871 the Republican-controlled Senate created a Committee of Investigation and Retrenchment to examine the New York City Customs House. Senator Aaron Cragin of New Hampshire, a Republican politician since the mid-1850s, rejoiced that having the party publicly investigate corruption in the New York Customs House "saved us from being destroyed." Several months later the Senate also created a committee to investigate the allegedly illegal arms sales to France during the Franco-Prussian War. Despite Schurz and Trumbull's prominence in raising the issues of both civil service reform and the French arms sales, neither was invited to join the committees. Grant did invite renowned reformer George William Curtis to become chairman of the newly created Civil Service Commission in June 1871, co-opting at least some of the reformers. Though Grant privately thought the rules impractical, he adopted the commission's report in January 1872, which *The Nation* hailed as "a great triumph of reform." Grant also approved by executive order the commission's supplementary recommendation of March 1872, declaring that henceforth "honesty and efficiency, not political activity, will determine the tenure of office." During the Cincinnati Convention in May, Republicans in Congress authorized $25,000 to continue funding the Civil Service Commission.[37]

After Greeley's nomination at the Cincinnati Convention, the Republicans redoubled their efforts to deflect the momentum of the Liberal Republican Party. The Republicans in Congress passed a bill reducing tariff rates by 10 percent, to woo away some of the free traders upset with the nomination of the protectionist Greeley. "The new Tariff and Tax bill bothers the 'Liberals' badly," taunted the *New York Times*. "They declared it would never pass and it passed. They pronounced it was a hollow pretense of reduction, and it is undeniably a solid reality, lifting fifty-four millions off the tax-payers' shoulders." The Republicans, however, spent more time dealing with the major issue emerging out of the Cincinnati Convention: Greeley's focus on ending Reconstruction and promoting sectional reconciliation. The Republican Congress passed an amnesty bill on May 22, similar to legislation that had failed in Republican-controlled Congresses in 1870 and 1871. Bowles predicted to Wells the day before the bill passed that "Washington is just waking up to the new ideas and trying to take advantage of them for its own benefit." Sure enough, the Republican *New York Times* started giving Republicans credit for the bill even before it was passed, writing that "it was to be hoped that before adjournment, the Senate will grant to the country the general amnesty which the House of Representatives has several times approved, which President Grant has emphatically urged." A few days after the amnesty bill passed on May 22, the Democratic *New York Herald* sarcastically observed that "it is curious to observe the effect the political movements of the day are having upon the republican senators and Congressmen." *The Nation,* while still opposed to Greeley, likewise reasoned that "the Cincinnati movement has done something for the South. There can be little doubt that the strong expressions of opinion made at the Convention, both in the platform and in the speeches, did frighten Congress at the last hour into passing the Amnesty Act." Through the amnesty bill, which allowed all but a few hundred former Confederates to hold office again, Republicans tried to deflect criticisms that they were continuing Reconstruction for partisan political purposes.[38]

The actions of the Republicans, however, belied their public gestures toward civil service reform and ending Reconstruction. The chairman of the Texas Republican Executive Committee asked William E. Chandler, the secretary of the Republican National Executive Committee, to send the United States Army to Texas to help carry the fall election. "If we could have United States troops stationed at four or five control points, the effect would be great," the Texan explained to Chandler, and "in fact, it would go largely toward carrying the state. The rebels have a horror of the power of the U.S. Government, and are convinced that we are supported by it and backed by U.S. troops." The administration used its power in key states such as North Carolina, with a paper there reporting that the budget of the Department of Justice in the state increased from $5,000 in 1871 to $250,000 in 1872. In preparation for the important spring elections in New England, the National Republican Executive Committee organized patronage and money on a massive scale to thwart the Liberal Republicans' momentum. The administration authorized patronage projects for the Portsmouth, New Hampshire, shipyards and gave federal employees who could vote in New England leave and transportation to return there for the election. Government workers were also expected to contribute a percentage of their salary to the Republican Party.[39]

Another source of money for the Republicans was wealthy businessmen. Financier Jay Cooke complained that the party was wasting money and that "little New Hampshire isn't bigger than one of our wards, and I know I could carry a ward for $10,000!!" A week before the election, however, he assured Chandler that "we will do everything we can for Mr. Delano and Gen. Grant and all our folks in Washington. If necessary for you to have more money of course you shall have it."[40]

Money and patronage helped the Republican Party win the New England spring elections and secure Republican state organizations throughout the country for Grant's renomination. Aware that having federal employees serve as delegates to the Republican Convention would give the appearance of impropriety, the National Republican Committee asked about the number of such employees in each state delegation and urged their removal. Many state committees responded that it was necessary to include federal workers in their delegations; over 40 percent of Georgia's delegation worked for the federal government. Republican State Committees from across the nation reported to Chandler that they had secured their states' delegations for Grant well before the state conventions. Over two weeks before Florida's state convention Chandler learned that "the delegates are already mostly chosen and are almost if not quite unanimous for gen Grant's renomination."[41]

The predictions made to Chandler proved true, as the Republican Convention in Philadelphia easily renominated Grant for a second term on June 5. The convention continued the Republican Party's appropriation of Liberal Republican issues. While over a decade of shared party experience would naturally make the Republican and Liberal Republican platforms somewhat similar, the number of parallels in content and language was remarkable. The Liberal Republican platform decried the abuse of the patronage system as a danger to republican government, insisting that "honesty, capacity, and fidelity constitute the only valid claim to public employment." The Republicans had a similar plank on civil service reform, asserting that "any system of the civil service under which the subordinate positions of the Government are considered rewards for mere party zeal is fatally demoralizing." Even the language was alike, as the Republicans planned to "make honesty, efficiency, and fidelity the essential qualifications for public positions." For every plank in the Liberal Republican platform, the Republicans had a response. The Liberal Republicans called for amnesty, arguing "that universal amnesty will result in complete pacification in all sections of the country," and the Republicans praised their own past efforts at enacting amnesty, declaring that "we heartily approve the action of Congress in extending amnesty to those lately in rebellion, and rejoice in the growth of peace and fraternal feeling throughout the land." The Liberal

Republicans declared their goals: "for the individual the largest liberty consistent with public order; for the State, self-government, and for the nation a return to the methods of peace and the constitutional limits of power." The Republicans responded with a plank assuring that "the Republican party proposes to respect the rights reserved by the people to themselves as carefully as the powers delegated by them to the State and Federal Government. It disapproves of the resort to unconstitutional laws for the purposes of removing evils, by interference with rights not surrendered by the people to either the State or National Government."[42]

Nor did the Republicans confine themselves to taking from the Liberal Republicans such major issues as civil service reform, amnesty, and states' rights. Where the Liberal Republican platform insisted that "a speedy return to specie payments is demanded alike by the highest considerations of commercial morality and honest government," the Republicans predicted in their platform that "we confidently expect that our excellent national currency will be perfected by a speedy resumption of specie payment." The Republicans copied almost verbatim the Liberal Republican plank on land grants, which read, "We are opposed to all further grants of lands to railroads or other corporations. The public domain should be held sacred to actual settlers"; the Republican plank announced, "We are opposed to all further grants of the public land to corporations and monopolies, and demand that the national domain be set apart for free homes for the people." The *Cincinnati Commercial* accurately stated that "the principles professed by the opposing platforms are almost identical, differing in only a few cunning phrases and rhetorical padding." There were a few exceptions, such as the Republicans' boasting about their crackdown on the Ku Klux Klan, but the Republican platform essentially replicated all of the major, and even most of the minor, issues raised in the Liberal Republican platform.[43]

While the Republicans could match the Liberal Republicans' platform, the Liberal Republicans could not hope to equal the Republicans' monetary and patronage resources during the campaign. Various Republican campaign committees exacted money from federal workers as far away as Turkey, with the Republican National Committee sending a circular to employees and officials of foreign consulates "suggesting" a $50 contribution. At one point the secretary of the Illinois Union State Central Committee complained to the secretary of the Republican National Committee that "it does seem like an imposition for so many Eastern Committees to draw money from our office holders which of course prevents our Committee from getting anything from them." Despite some confusion over which Republican campaign committee was to shake down which civil servant, the money came pouring in. The clerk whom the financier Jay Cooke had placed in charge of recording "donations" to the Republican National Committee asked Chandler for a raise. He explained that "we receive from twenty to twenty five hundred dollars every day, but they are all in ten, twenty, and fifty dollar lots which give me no little trouble. I work hard at them all day and very often have to buy my dinner and stay late in order to get all the receipts for the day." Clerks were literally becoming worn out counting the money flowing into Republican coffers.[44]

The fact that Jay Cooke's bank was handling the Republican Party's money was not a coincidence, demonstrating another advantage the established party enjoyed—close ties to business. Cooke provided money to the Republican Party for the 1872 campaign and took a mortgage on Republican Speaker of the House James G. Blaine's Washington home. William Chandler had worked for Cooke before becoming secretary of the National Republican Committee, and while serving as secretary he held retainers from four railroad companies. Republican Congressman Grenville M. Dodge was likewise enmeshed in the railroad business. He advised Edwin Morgan, chairman of the National Republican Committee, that "I have had interviews with most of the RR interests of the west and as a general thing they are all right + with us. We must when the election comes make that interest felt on our side. They have great power when wielded quietly."[45]

The Republicans used their money and patronage power in a variety of ways during the campaign. While Congressman James G. Blaine demanded $20,000 for speakers in Maine, Morgan "felt disposed to promise $5000 from the committee for the state of Maine." Blaine pleaded to Chandler that Maine was not getting enough money and that "with $20,000 we can have 15,000 majority." The Soldiers and Sailors Convention in Pennsylvania, sponsored in part by the National Republican Committee, cost an estimated $25,000, including $2,500 for fireworks and another $2,500 for torches and oil for visiting clubs. Even when the Republicans ran low on money they still had resources unavailable to the Liberal Republicans. For example, many of the Republicans' campaign documents were sent out franked, saving the party the cost of postage. When the Union Republican Congressional Committee could not find the money to support a German newspaper, it still promised that "the committee desires to endow the work in question with all its moral support" and "will aid it in obtaining any legitimate Government or party patronage." Dodge saw the entire federal government as part of the Republican campaign. He complained to Morgan about George S. Boutwell, secretary of the Treasury: "Boutwell must either place in our hands his Department or someone else should take it. It is no use for us to undertake to force our friends to wake up in this fight, to spend their money and their time unless the Government and the ones directly involved in this fight use the power that they have."[46]

*   *   *

The Republicans constituted just part of the Liberal Republicans' trouble in 1872. Knowing that the Liberal Republican organization in Missouri had used Democratic support to capture control of the state in 1870, the national liberal republican movement had realized it would need the Democratic Party's endorsement to win. The nomination of Horace Greeley at the Cincinnati Convention complicated the task of procuring that endorsement, since Greeley had been an enemy of the Democratic Party for decades. While the Democratic leadership accepted Greeley's nomination with resignation and at least half-heartedly kept their promises to work with the Liberal Republicans, Democratic voters had made no such bargain, and they spurned Greeley. Most historians consider the obstinacy of the Democratic rank and file a sign of strength, both for the party and organizational politics. The refusal of Democratic voters to follow their leaders' orders and go for Greeley, however, indicates that the time of Gilded Age organizational politics had not yet fully arrived by 1872. Halfway through the campaign the *Cincinnati Commercial* asserted that "the Democrats have never been equaled in the tact with which they managed their canvasses," but complained, "Where is it today? Where is its splendid organization, that has always been its boast and the envy of its opponents? It ceased with the Baltimore Convention." Democratic voters' display of independence in refusing to follow their leaders' orders to support Greeley helps explain why the Liberal Republicans lost and suggests that the machine politics of the Gilded Age was still in the process of forming.[47]

Schurz began negotiating for support with August Belmont, national chairman of the Democratic Party, in early April 1872. Following a series of meetings and letters, the two agreed that Belmont would have the Democratic National Committee meet after the Cincinnati Convention, and the national Democratic Convention would convene a few weeks after the Republican Convention in early June, thus increasing the chances that the Democrats would endorse the Liberal Republican candidate nominated at Cincinnati. Belmont promised Schurz that "if you make a good national platform denouncing the abuse + corruption of the Grant administration, the military despotism in the South, the centralization of power + the subordination of the civil power to the military rule and declare boldly for genuine amnesty + a Revenue Tariff you will find every Democrat ready for your candidates," but he qualified his promise by adding, "provided you name men our Convention can endorse." Belmont indicated his strong preference for Charles Francis Adams, telling Schurz that "Adams is no personal friend of mine, but I cannot impress upon you enough the importance of selecting him as the head of your ticket." He explained that he found "an overwhelming desire for Ch. F. Adams," and warned that "with Adams + Trumbull or Adams + Brown *success is sure;* with any other combination the result would be doubtful." A month before the Cincinnati Convention, Thomas F. Bayard, a Democratic senator from Delaware, received corroboration of Belmont's prediction from a Democratic correspondent, who insisted that "the only chance for the Liberal Republicans to make their movement at Cincinnati a success, would be to nominate Hancock + Adams." The writer foresaw, however, that "they will nominate some sore headed Republicans and then if the Democratic Convention endorses their actions, I with thousands of others will consider ourselves released from all party fealty, and at liberty to support Grant if we please."[48]

The nomination of Greeley at Cincinnati destroyed Schurz's and Belmont's carefully laid plans to have the Democratic Party support the Liberal Republican presidential candidate. Since the 1840s Greeley had continually savaged Democrats in print. Upon the death of Andrew Jackson in 1845, Greeley vilified the former president and founder of the Democratic Party in the *New York Tribune* by calling him "a jobber in human flesh" and accusing him of "covert, rapacious treachery to Mexico." Personal attacks on political opponents were common in mid-nineteenth-century politics, but not attacks on recently deceased presidents. One of Greeley's biographers acknowledges that "Greeley's partisanship was often vindictive" and that "Greeley went to extreme lengths in attacking Democrats." There was also a personal feud between Greeley and Belmont that dated back to the early 1850s, begun by Greeley's public accusation that Belmont, a foreign-born Jew, had used "Jew gold" to buy votes in the 1852 election. Belmont considered the Liberal Republicans' nomination of Greeley "one of those stupendous mistakes which it is difficult even to comprehend," but wrote to an Ohio Democrat that "so much am I impressed with the fatal consequences in store for our common country by the reelection of Grant that I would willingly vote for my deadliest enemy in order to avoid such a catastrophe." Belmont was forced to support one of his deadliest enemies. He had made promises to Schurz, and nominating a separate Democratic candidate with Greeley already in the field would only assure Grant and the Republicans of victory. "The nomination is not what you and I wanted," Belmont told Bowles shortly after the Cincinnati Convention, "but the blunder is made."[49]

The Liberal Republicans counted on the Democrats to nominate Greeley, even if grudgingly, at their national convention. They realized that if the Democrats made it a three-way presidential race by nominating another candidate, most Republicans would support Grant rather than risk a Democratic victory. Bowles told Reid less than a week after the Cincinnati Convention that "the whole thing rests now with the democratic convention. With its endorsement there will be no trouble in getting republican votes for Greeley, nor in making sure of a triumphant election." At the same time Bowles confidently predicted to Wells that "the democrats are going it with a rush. Belmont is clearly for it." Belmont did his part when the Democratic National Committee met at his house on May 8. In accordance with his promise to Schurz, he used his influence to arrange for the Democratic Convention to be held a few weeks after the Republican Convention on June 5, thus increasing the chances that the Democrats would endorse Greeley. By late May Reid reassured Trumbull that "the hesitating democrats are gradually but surely coming up to the work."[50]

Belmont and the Liberal Republicans did see some signs of Democratic support, particularly in the South, where endorsing a former Republican like Greeley would help to signal to Northerners that Southern whites had accepted the results of the war. In addition, many Southern Democrats fatalistically accepted Greeley as a means of addressing their primary concern, ending Reconstruction. According to one Virginian, "what we want in the South more than anything else is to have the supremacy of the civil law returned. We cannot afford to quarrel about minor matters until the bayonet is first taken from our throats." Daniel M. Barringer, chairman of the North Carolina Democratic State Executive Committee, explained to congressional candidate David M. Carter that "Greeley's stock is rising here & encouraging opposition to a straight out De. ticket at Balt. The truth is we of the South cannot afford to be beaten again + further oppressed, if not utterly ruined by another four years of Grant radicalism." The acceptance of Greeley as the only option did not equate to enthusiasm, though. The letters to Carter support historian Daniel E. Sutherland's finding that "Greeley was less than popular in the South, even among Southerners who voted for him." A Virginia Democrat concluded, "I hate Greeley: I wish some one else had won the nomination at Cincinnati. But he is the man, and, for one, I can vote for him with a hearty good will, as against Grant." There were many reports of dissatisfaction with Greeley in the South. Chandler heard from Alabama that "if Greeley is endorsed by the Baltimore Convention there are 10,000 old Slave-owners who will not vote at all," and a Texan wrote to his brother that "since my return home I have seen some of my democratic friends. I think one half of them at least will not vote for Greeley. They say they will not go to the polls unless a straight out democrat is run."[51]

Many Democrats in the North, lacking the political desperation of Southern Democrats, were more adamantly opposed to Greeley. Belmont pressured Democratic papers like the *New York World* and the *New York Herald* to endorse Greeley, but such endorsements were a façade. Many Northern Democrats wanted their convention to nominate a Democratic candidate to run against both Grant and Greeley. Democratic Congressman Daniel W. Voorhees of Indiana publicly called Greeley "the most odious man to the Democratic Party" and asked, "Could I look the Democrats of my district in the face and support a man who is in favor of every villainy for which I ever denounced the Radical party?" Northern Democrats were even more adamant in private. In the months before the Democratic Convention, dozens of Northern Democrats wrote to Senator Bayard declaring they would never support Greeley. Some Northern Democrats feared endorsing Greeley would only weaken the Democratic Party and ensure Grant's victory. A Pennsylvanian informed Bayard that "H.G. will make a poor candidate here. Sure defeat awaits him," and a Bostonian asked, "How can the main body of Democrats be induced to follow such a lead? To me it seems that Greeley's success would utterly demoralize the party."[52]

The majority of letters, however, did not consider pragmatic political concerns in denouncing Greeley. "To the surprise and astonishment of every true Democrat, we find the Southern, so called Democracy idolizing the Cincinnati platform," proclaimed an outraged Philadelphian, "and the man, Horace Greeley, their nominee for the Presidency, who led the wicked hosts of abolitionists to plunge the Country into the late war, for no other purpose, but to overthrow the states and place them under an Absolute Monarch." He insisted that "Greeley has spit and stamped upon every principle of Democracy during his entire political life. I shall not support either of the Monarchical nominees now in the field." Many of the correspondents insisted that they would rather lose with a true Democrat than win with Greeley. A Pennsylvanian asserted that "it would be better a thousand times to be beaten this fall with a true Democrat heading us than to succeed with H. G.," while a writer from Delaware argued that "we had better be defeated ten times over with good sound Democrats than to sell our principles for such a thing as Greeley." He pleaded with Bayard, "Do not leave us to the alternative of choosing the least of two *Evils. Greeley* is an Evil not small enough for me to choose."[53]

Despite the unrest among many rank-and-file Democrats, the party leaders pushed Greeley's nomination at the Democratic Convention on July 9. Belmont recalled to the delegates the "violent attacks against myself, individually, which from time to time appeared in his journal," and acknowledged that Greeley "is not entitled to sympathy or preference at my hands." Still, the chairman of the National Democratic Committee announced that if the Baltimore delegates "decide to pronounce in favor of the Cincinnati candidates, I for one shall bury all past differences and vote and labor for their election." With few other options, 674 of the 732 delegates voted to adopt the Liberal Republican platform and make Greeley the presidential candidate for the Democratic Party. This was the only time in United States history that one of the two major parties endorsed the candidate and platform of a third party. The Liberal Republicans knew that the full support of the numerous and well-organized Democrats was essential to their success. Congressman Nathaniel Banks, a newly converted Liberal Republican, confided to his wife during the campaign that among the Liberal Republicans "the managers here have little force or experience. The democrats are the wisest + most active." By mid-September White was explaining to Reid that "the philosophy of the campaign is just here. If the Democratic vote can be held for Greeley there are Liberal Republicans to elect him."[54]

The Democratic Convention's nomination of Greeley proved a pyrrhic victory, however, to both the Democratic leaders and the Liberal Republicans. A Democrat had warned Schurz before the convention that "our state delegation—is as you are aware a unit for Greeley—but their Constituents are not." While the convention was meeting in Baltimore, a Democrat from the city wrote to Bayard that "Horace Greeley is the worst man in this country, and has said and done more bad things than any other man in the land. A Convention may nominate him, but 'God Almighty' could not make a good man out of him. . . . His nomination ought not be submitted to." Bayard, the son and father of Democratic senators from Delaware (his grandfather was also a senator, but a Federalist; in 1797 the Democratic Party had not yet formed), may have become troubled with the increasing dissatisfaction many of his constituents expressed with the Democratic leaders' support of Greeley. One Democrat from Delaware who planned to vote for Greeley warned Bayard that "the rank and file, the working class of our party—in Kent—have lost the confidence of our leaders," explaining that "our trouble is but one and that is Greeley. A great many of the voters say they cannot support him." Another constituent opposed to Greeley insisted, "I can count within an area of three miles around me five Democrats out of 60 or 70 who openly say they will vote for Greeley, while to the contrary I can count 40 or more who say openly and defiantly that they will not be sold for a price;—though the party leaders and shysters may surrender the principles of the party, yet they will not be a party to the contract."[55]

Many local Democratic leaders likewise decided that despite the decision of the national convention, they could not support Greeley. Immediately after the Baltimore Convention nominated Greeley, a small group of Democrats met, denounced the action, and called for a convention to meet in Louisville on September 3. In preparation, Democrats in New Jersey advertised this Louisville Convention as a mass meeting for "those Democrats who are unwilling to become Greeley Republicans or to march under the banners of a Life-long

Enemy to the music of Charles Sumner's Orders," called for the purpose of choosing electors for a straight-out Democratic ticket. Carl Schurz had worried about the Democrats as early as June, confiding to Grosvenor that "the opposition in the Democratic ranks is becoming more determined every day" and that "we can scarcely hope to make up by gains from the Rep. ranks what is thus lost on the Dem. side." By late August Schurz thought the campaign looked "promising enough," but warned Reid that "the Louisville movement threatens to become stronger than we anticipated—let us not deceive ourselves about that."[56]

The leaders of the Republican campaign also perceived the weakness of Democratic support for Greeley and saw it as an advantage for the coming election. Chandler received accounts from across the country commenting on Democratic dissatisfaction. An agent in West Virginia reported that "there are many Democrats who will not support Greeley," and a Georgia operative explained, "It is to be hoped that the Louisville Convention may prove a success, and give the Democrats, who have any principle or self respect left, candidates of some national reputation, in which case, thousands who are now ready to adopt the Baltimore Ticket, from party necessity, will wheel into the Democratic Rut." The discussion of how the Democrats opposed to Greeley could influence the election reached the highest levels of the Republican Party. Congressman Dodge informed Morgan, the chair of the Republican National Executive Committee, that after a tour of the South "I have found considerable disaffection there among the Democrats; they are very quiet however." The National Executive Committee met in Washington during mid-August to discuss the party's prospects, and Chandler reported their analysis to President Grant. "In addition to the improved general prospect," he noted, "there are two special causes from which I anticipate much help," one of which was the Louisville Convention. Just four days before Schurz warned Reid of the dangers associated with the convention, Chandler explained to Grant that "the Louisville Convention will tend to divide the democracy," for some "democrats will want to have off from Greeley who are not ready to go for Grant + Wilson and they can go only to Louisville."[57]

Many Republicans were not content just to observe the split in the Democratic ranks and began actively trying to encourage the Democrats opposed to Greeley. The chairman of the Delaware Republican State Central Committee wrote to Chandler, "If the present commotion in the Dem ranks continues, it cannot fail to yield the fruit which we are so anxious to reap." He thought that the Democrat in Delaware who was leading the charge for the Louisville Convention "is playing his card admirably for us," but advised that "it would be bad policy for us to give publicity to their doings at least for the present. We think we are doing well by letting them alone, and that they are doing more among themselves, than we can possibly do with the same material." The letter demonstrates that Republican leaders saw nothing wrong with helping the Democrats who were organizing the Louisville Convention, and only hesitated from fear that if discovered they would diminish the strength of the dissident Democrats.[58]

Republican leaders soon decided that the advantages of secretly helping the dissident Democrats outweighed the risk of discovery. Dodge instructed Morgan that "good men should be selected, funds placed in their hands, + one sent into each state and they should be instructed to work up full delegations for the Louisville Convention." Chandler received a similar letter from another Republican reporting that "I am encouraging the Louisville movement in N.C. + V.A. + making much progress. We are moving systematically." Proving the adage that politics makes strange bedfellows, he informed Chandler that "we are about to start a 'straight-out' Democratic paper in Raleigh, to be edited by Maj. Hearne, a[n] . . . old line Democrat, + violent Confederate + member of the Ku Klux." A third correspondent notified Chandler of "a nice little quarrel, the breach of which may be easily widened in this state," explaining that the "project of the Louisville Convention can be used effectively to keep Democrats from joining Greeley." According to the writer the dissident Democrats "have no money to operate with," but it appeared to him that "something might be done with it, if the money can be spared and judiciously used." The Republican National Committee found the money to support the Louisville Convention, providing funds for delegates' traveling costs and a brass band. James M. Edmunds of the Republican National Committee even arranged for Republican senators to frank 25,000 circulars for the Louisville Convention, sending them through the mails for free. Many Republicans in positions of power were willing to help the Democrats, even if it meant the continuation of the Democratic Party. Third parties in the nineteenth-century United States had a hard enough time achieving success, without the two major parties actively cooperating against them.[59]

Many Democrats did not need any encouragement from the Republicans to maintain their own party and run a third ticket. *The Nation* reported that in Georgia, a Democratic state that Greeley needed, "The local Greeley Republicans have received a very severe snub, the Democracy practically telling them that it will have nothing to do with them." A Republican agent in Georgia told Chandler the same news in stronger language, stating that "the fight here is a square one between Reps + Democrats. The Democratic party has ignored the liberal Rep. element in this state, and proposes to run the state election . . . on purely Democratic principles." Five hundred Atlanta Democrats held a meeting on August 1 to organize a delegation for the Louisville Convention. A month later the convention met and nominated its own candidates for the presidential contest. The candidates refused to accept the nomination, but the "straight-out" Democrats still placed them on the ballot in twenty-three states. They organized a new Democratic National Committee and tried running a campaign, though most of it consisted of attacks on Greeley. For instance, the letterhead of the "new" Democratic National Executive Committee mentioned neither their candidates nor Grant. Under headings like "Greeley's Love" and "Degradation of Southern Women," the letterhead carried Greeley quotes designed to inflame Southern Democrats, such as "I hope that the time will soon come when there will be actual Social Equality between the races," and "Democrats are Murderers, Adulterers, Drunkards, Cowards, Liars, Thieves, Assassins, Pugilists, Blacklegs, Burglars, and Felons."[60]

Even when the Democrats attempted to cooperate with the Liberal Republicans, they insisted on maintaining their own organization. In North Carolina, one of the key states for the Liberal Republicans because of its early election date and large Democratic population, the two parties tried to work together, but never became integrated. While Daniel Barringer, chairman of the North Carolina Democratic Party's Executive Committee, helped arrange Schurz's speaking tour in the state, his receipts for campaign expenses reveal the true separation between the Liberal Republicans and Democrats. Records indicate that during the month of July Barringer distributed over $20,000 for the campaign. Of the sixteen receipts that list party affiliation, only seven mention either the "Democratic Republican Party" or the "Republican Democratic Party." An equal number of receipts mention only the "Democratic Party" or the "Democratic Conservative Party," and another two name only the "Liberal Republican Party." The appearance of "Democrat" or "Liberal Republican" alone on a majority of the receipts indicates that where things mattered most, such as money, the Liberal Republican and Democratic parties were still separate entities. A similar situation occurred in Illinois, another important state for the new party because of its numerous prominent Liberal Republicans. The Illinois Liberal Republican Executive Committee and Democrat Cyrus McCormick, the principal source of funds for the Liberal Republican campaign in Illinois, could not agree on who would run the campaign. According to Michael Robinson's study of the 1872 election in Illinois, the inability of the Liberal Republicans and leading Democrats to work together "destroyed any chance of creating a viable campaign machine."[61]

The first test for the Liberal Republican–Democratic coalition occurred in the North Carolina state elections on August 1, which many saw as a barometer for the entire campaign. Several weeks before the election, a member of the

Kentucky Republican State Committee told Chandler "that a victory for the Republicans in North Carolina will be worth thousands of votes to us in this state. Scores of Democrats are uncommitted in this district, waiting to see the motion of the country. They will come out against Greeley if North Carolina votes for us." He considered North Carolina so important that he advised Chandler to spend money there that could otherwise be spent in Kentucky, arguing that "millions expended for speakers, documents, etc., in N.C. to win a success will be worth the cost." Chandler agreed, worrying that if the Republicans lost North Carolina, "it will give an impetus to Greeleyism that I should almost despair of saving Penn. & Indiana; & losing them we are pretty certain to lose the November election." Republican fears evaporated when their gubernatorial candidate beat his Democratic opponent by a small margin. A Republican exclaimed to Chandler, "Glorious victory. Our whole State Ticket elected. Majority nearly Two Thousand. State safe for Grant + Wilson in November. Rejoice!" The Democrats shared a similar interpretation with different emotions. Barringer learned from a Democrat that "what ruined us in this county was the great number of Conservatives that did not vote." Little room for optimism existed, as the report continued that "considerable opposition among Dem here to Greeley. I hope it can be remedied before the Nov. Election yet I . . . confess I have fears to the contrary."[62]

The situation did not improve for the Liberal Republicans in the state elections in Maine and Vermont, held in September. Some Republicans worried about the results, with Dodge insisting to Morgan that "we must not lose Maine," and the chairman of the Indiana Republican State Committee warning Chandler that "unfavorable returns from maine will hurt us badly." The win in North Carolina, combined with the traditional Republican strength in New England, however, gave the party huge majorities in both elections. In Vermont, for example, the Republicans won every seat in the state senate, and their gubernatorial candidate received more than double the number of votes received by his Democratic opponent. "We have met the enemy and have achieved a glorious victory," declared the secretary of the Vermont Republican Committee. He exulted that "Greeleyism has mewled out a puny existence, and we have now quietly laid it away in its little grave!" The Boston postmaster agreed, telling Chandler that "the elections in North Carolina, Vermont and Maine have decided the Greeley campaign two months in advance." A new political party could not suffer early defeats and still hope to win.[63]

The final blow came in the October state elections in the key presidential states of Pennsylvania, Ohio, and Indiana, where the Liberal Republicans had some of their last and best chances to change the campaign's momentum. Ohio was an original Liberal Republican stronghold and had hosted the Cincinnati

Convention. The Democrats controlled the legislature in Indiana and some Democrats in the state had been cooperating with the liberal republican movement for years. In Pennsylvania the recent investigation of the Republican gubernatorial candidate for corruption, Greeley's protectionist history, and the defection of the popular former governor, Republican Andrew Curtin, led Grant to determine in late August that the Liberal Republicans would probably win the state. According to contemporaries on both sides, however, the results of the elections in North Carolina, Vermont, and Maine had irreversibly swung the momentum solidly behind the Republicans. Just before the Vermont election, Democratic Congressman Kerr of Indiana reported to Trumbull that there was "a manifest change in the popular feeling going on. The tide is not so clearly with us as it was." By the night of the Vermont election, the chairman of the Indiana State Republican Committee had told Chandler that "I am sanguine of carrying the state," and with the victories in New England secured, Chandler thought the "political outlook encouraging." The Republicans did crush the Liberal Republicans and Democrats in the October elections, winning almost every important office in the three states except the governorship of Indiana. The *Chicago Tribune* acknowledged defeat. Just after the October elections the *Tribune* insisted that although "defeated now, the Liberal party is coming to power. Though overwhelmed at present, it is the means destined in the next four years to rescue the Government." The *Cincinnati Commercial* shared the *Tribune's* judgment, explaining that "taking yesterday's elections altogether, the conclusion is forced that the luck of General Grant, in politics as in war, is likely to be confirmed by his reelection to the Presidency. The Liberal and Democratic organization is not so compact that it can withstand the shock of repeated defeats."[64]

Banks had little doubt of the reason behind the Republican victory. "The elections are against us," he wrote his wife in October, and "I think the democrats must have failed us." Democratic voters certainly deserted Greeley and the Liberal Republicans in the national elections in November. In Pennsylvania over 100,000 Democrats decided to stay home, as the 317,760 votes for the Democratic gubernatorial candidate in October turned into only 211,961 votes for Greeley in November. A similar situation occurred in North Carolina, where Greeley received only 70,094 votes in November compared to the 96,234 votes for the Democratic gubernatorial candidate in September. The results were just as clear nationally. Greeley garnered 43.9 percent of the vote, a lower percentage than the Democrats would receive in any other election between 1848 and 1904, excluding the four-party election of 1860. The Democrats had done better on their own in 1868, receiving three more percentage points of the popular vote and twenty more Electoral College votes. The *Cincinnati Commercial* concluded that "the influence of their ablest leaders were not sufficient to bring them to a man to the support of Mr. Greeley at the polls. In summing up and analyzing the vote, it will be discovered that a host of Democrats abstained from voting."[65]

The disadvantages of a third party took their toll on the Liberal Republicans, eventually leading to their defeat in November 1872. Internal divisions distracted them for the first crucial months of the campaign, when they had the initiative, and eventually robbed them of many of their original leaders. The Republicans learned how to enjoy the benefits of being an established, entrenched party by appropriating the Liberal Republicans' issues and bludgeoning them with money, power, and patronage. Despite orders and pleas from their national leaders, Democratic voters refused to support a longtime political enemy. As the November results came in, Greeley lamented to a friend that "I was the worst beaten man that ever ran for that high office."[66]

9   The Lasting Effect of 1872 Campaign Rhetoric

After rejoicing that "the elections in North Carolina, Vermont and Maine have decided the Greeley campaign two months in advance," Boston Postmaster William Burt lamented that "if they would only be content to accept the result it would save us much later, and much disagreeable political talking and writing." As Burt feared, the Liberal Republicans did not concede the election in September, and the campaign increasingly degenerated into virulent personal attacks. According to Earle Ross, "The campaign of 1872 was primarily one of personalities. Probably no previous campaign had been conducted so largely on the basis of personal abuse and misrepresentation." The Republicans ridiculed Horace Greeley so much that at the end of the campaign he wailed to a friend, "I have been assailed so bitterly that I hardly know whether I was running for President or the penitentiary." Though the Republicans won in 1872, their attacks on Greeley oddly had less historical impact than the campaign rhetoric of the Liberal Republicans. During the campaign the new party repeatedly denounced Reconstruction, President Ulysses S. Grant, and the original members of the liberal republican movement who were opposed to Greeley. The attacks had special power because many members of the Liberal Republican Party had been Radical Republicans and leading advocates of Reconstruction in the late 1860s. Their 1872 campaign rhetoric helped create the lasting historical constructions of the "Tragic Era," "Grantism," and the "Best Men."[1]

The dynamics of the campaign dictated the focus of Liberal Republican rhetoric. At its inauguration in 1870, the national liberal republican movement had decided to devote its efforts to civil service reform and free trade. According to David M. Tucker, "None of the David Wells correspondents wrote of Reconstruction and African Americans; they were preoccupied with the troubles created by the war: tariff subsidies, greenbacks, and patronage. Corruption stemming from misguided government policy was their obsession." The surprise nomination at Cincinnati of Horace Greeley, long apathetic about civil service reform and opposed to free trade, stripped the new party of its principles and drove away many of the movement's most passionate members. As Carl Schurz recognized, "The difficulty really consists in there being no harmony between our candidates and the true spirit of the movement; and the worst of it is that this cannot be denied." In a campaign speech for Greeley, one of the original liberal republicans confessed that "Mr. Greeley may be a protectionist, and one of the worst protectionists at that," and that "the kind of civil service reform which . . . I am in favor of, will not be given us by Mr. Greeley." The removal of civil service reform and free trade as issues forced the Liberal Republican Party to concentrate on Reconstruction, a secondary issue for many of the liberal republicans at the inception of their movement. *The Nation* remarked that "the prominence which the wants and woes of the South are taking in the Presidential canvas is exciting the surprise of a good many of those who remember that in the Liberal Republican movement, as first started, the Southern grievances occupied only a subordinate position."[2]

Throughout the campaign of 1872 the *Cincinnati Commercial* commented on how the Liberal Republican Party's emphasis on Reconstruction had replaced the liberal republican movement's primary interest in civil service reform and free trade. Early in the campaign, when still optimistic, the newspaper reported, "The Cincinnati movement has taken a shape, and has brought about results which its originators never contemplated. Its original purpose was mainly to take ground in favor of civil service reform and revenue reform, and against administrative corruption and incapacity. . . . These reforms have not been lost sight of, but Charles Sumner has probably hit the mark in saying that the watchword of the campaign is Reconciliation." A month later the *Commercial* reiterated that "civil service reform was the original mainspring of the Liberal movement." By the time the election had been decided and the need to attract white Southern votes had passed, it declared, "The Liberal Republican movement began with an effort to bring into conspicuity reforms in our tariff and civil service systems. A more liberal policy toward the States and people of the South were primarily incidental." The willingness of the liberal republicans to publicly discuss the replacement of their original issues during the middle of a presidential campaign indicates their ambivalence in supporting Greeley, for such admissions could only hurt them at the polls. The politically damaging nature of these comments, combined with similar private statements, also shows that the liberal republicans were honest about how Greeley's nomination at the Cincinnati Convention had betrayed the agenda of their movement.[3]

The actions of regular Republicans, disgruntled liberal republicans, and Democrats only intensified the tendencies of the Liberal Republican Party to attack Reconstruction, Grant, and the original movement. Even before the Cincinnati Convention the regular Republicans had begun appropriating Liberal Republican issues, and in their own national convention adopted a platform almost identical to that of the Liberal Republican Party. The two parties' similar positions on issues forced much of the attention onto the personalities of the candidates. According to a Liberal Republican speaker, "The platform adopted at the [Republican] Philadelphia convention is, in all essential articles a copy of its Cincinnati predecessor." *The Nation* complained that "as it is, both the Cincinnati and Philadelphia platforms have ceased to represent anything, or to have any vitalizing and proselytizing power, and we are given over, from now till November, to a barren interchange of personalities, growing more and more bitter and vituperative, and only serving to reveal the extent of the rottenness of our politics." Meanwhile, the Democrats' nomination of Greeley led the Liberal Republicans to court the white Southern vote. The new party decided that personal attacks on Grant, the former Union Army commander, and the disparagement of Northern efforts to reconstruct the South would have the greatest appeal to white Southerners. According to Daniel Sutherland, Liberal Republican campaigners in the South "did not stress issues, such as tariffs or war debts during the campaign, nor the Liberal concern with civil service reform," but "kept the amnesty and reconciliation issue constantly in the fore." David W. Blight similarly notes that because of Greeley's nomination at the Cincinnati Convention, "The central cause around which a reform coalition could be held together was the contest between Reconstruction and reconciliation," and "Greeley beat the only drum he and his strange coalition possessed."[4]

Reconciliation was a common theme in Liberal Republican campaign speeches. Schurz put the issue into historical context, explaining during a campaign speech that Grant had failed because in 1869 he had not realized that "the Civil war was over. Its logical results, the abolition of slavery and the organization of free labor society in the South, were just being reduced to political form and embedded in the Constitution of the Republic. It remained to fortify those results by reconciling to them the minds of the Southern people." Most speakers, though, preferred a simpler appeal to white Southerners and Democrats. Longtime Republican John Farnsworth told a crowd in Illinois that it was "the most gratifying spectacle that I have seen since the conclusion of the war, that men of the North and the South, loyal men and rebellious men, Democratic men and Republican men, from all parts of the country, are ready to bury past differences and issues, and standing shoulder to shoulder, shake hands, as Greeley says, 'Over the Bloody Chasm of the War.'" Greeley's call to "clasp hands over the bloody chasm" became the Liberal Republicans' signature campaign slogan. Alexander K. McClure, a Pennsylvania Republican who had been responsible for placing seventeen regiments into the field for the Union while serving as U.S. assistant adjutant general in 1862, likewise rejoiced that "the war ended in 1865, and enemies are now friends." He predicted, "Men who have differed in the conflicts of politics, of statesmanship and of arms must often become allies and friends, unless enlightened progress is to perish from the earth." The regular Republicans saw the image of hands clasped over a bloody chasm as a double-edged weapon that could be turned against the Liberal Republicans. Thomas Nast, editorial cartoonist of the Republican *Harper's Weekly,* regularly portrayed Greeley reaching across the graves of Union soldiers or dead freedmen to shake hands with former Confederates.[5]

The Liberal Republican appeals for reconciliation were a natural counter to the Republicans' references to the Civil War, often called "waving of the Bloody Shirt." Since the election of 1864, Republicans had told Northerners, particularly veterans, to vote the way they had shot during the war. The Republicans used such references for the next several decades, since the veterans of the Grand Army of the Republic remained a major base of Republican political power. In contrast to this waving of the Bloody Shirt, the Liberal Republicans used the phrase "the Blue and the Gray" to signify the similarities between Confederate soldiers and Union soldiers, between Southerners and Northerners. George Julian, a longtime abolitionist and Radical Republican, declared, "When I see the Democracy of the North and South joining hands, and asking us to join with them out of the graveyard of dead issues, I am inclined to join them." He insisted that "not withstanding the declaration of the Grant Republicans, this is not the old fight between the boys in blue and the boys in gray." John M. Palmer, the Republican governor of Illinois, likewise argued that "if you elect General Grant, you retain in power men who, like Morton, insist that there is still a fight between the boys in blue and the boys in gray . . . but if you elect Horace Greeley . . . the people will shake hands over this period of blood, and we shall be brethren again." Historian David Blight comments that "although the Liberal Republican campaign failed, it is a compelling measure of the degree and character of the reconciliationist impulse in America during Reconstruction."[6]

Some of the Liberal Republicans' remarks strained the limits of reconciliation and fed into the growing myth of the Lost Cause being promulgated by former Confederate General Jubal Early and other Southerners. According to Gary W. Gallagher, one of the leading scholars of Southern memory of the Civil War, "The architects of the Lost Cause acted from various motives. They collectively sought to justify their own actions and allow themselves and other former Confederates to find something positive in all-encompassing failure." While the Liberal Republicans had often been Union soldiers or officials during the war, the motivation to secure white Southern votes now led them at times to obscure the causes of the war, so that no one was accused of being at fault, and to praise the bravery and skill of Confederate soldiers. Alexander McClure was obviously pandering for votes when he told an audience of North Carolinians that "the evil days of sectional war came upon you, and you ridged the plains and hill-sides of the South with the nameless graves of your sons." Though McClure had run Lincoln's 1860 campaign in Pennsylvania, he now described the war as "coming upon" the South, seemingly casting no blame upon it for the sectional crisis. As if that were not enough, McClure proclaimed, "Your history is replete with illustrious names in the annals of the forum and of the field, and with the noblest achievements in war and peace." It seems unlikely that McClure would have expressed similar sentiments just a few years earlier.[7]

More surprising than McClure's pandering for votes in North Carolina, though, were other Liberal Republicans' articulations of Lost Cause themes in the North. Cassius M. Clay, an abolitionist and a founder of the Republican Party, told a crowd in Columbus, Ohio, that "the people of the South have accepted the situation. They had property in slaves; they were allowed to hold this property by the Constitution of 1787. When we thought they were not willing to carry out the letter and spirit of that contract as there made, rather than submit to our version they made war as a people, for what they deemed their rights." While this was not exactly Jefferson Davis's defense of the legality of secession, Clay presented the causes of the Civil War as an honest difference of opinion between countrymen. He praised the Confederates, for "they fought gallantly, and I rejoice to know that they did. They are our own blood, they were standing up for what they believed to be their rights, and we ought to be proud to say that they fought gallantly, though, as I think, it was in a bad cause." Palmer likewise praised the efforts of Confederate soldiers to an audience in Decatur, Illinois. After recounting his years in the Union Army, he explained, "I quit with very great respect for our antagonists. . . . They are first class fighters." Unknowingly anticipating the reconciliationist effect of the Spanish-American War in 1898, Palmer stated, "I propose if we have a war with a foreign country, to blow the bugle south of the Ohio, and we will bring into the field the men who will compare with any soldier on God's earth."[8]

Liberal Republicans emphasized their long history as Republicans and abolitionists to legitimize their calls for reconciliation and their attacks on Reconstruction. Much of the attention naturally focused on Greeley, as the standard-bearer of the new party. A campaigner insisted that "Mr. Greeley is a Republican, an old Republican, and a good Republican." The *Cincinnati Commercial* explained that "all colored voters of the South ought to be intelligent enough to know that Horace Greeley was the champion of emancipation for twenty years before it took place." But the Liberal Republican campaigners also stressed their own Republican and antislavery credentials. "It is not those who voted against General Grant four years ago who denounce him," argued a Greeley campaign document, but "his accusers are the men who made the Republican Party, and in whom the men of the party have the most confidence." In commenting on the speakers at a Liberal Republican rally, the *Commercial* observed that "most of them had rarely been seen at any but strict Republican meetings during the last twelve years." A few weeks later under the headline "The Big Truth," the *Commercial* reiterated, "We find that the real fathers of and founders of the Republican party stand squarely by the Greeley flag." The Liberal Republicans even invoked the name of Lincoln, with one speaker at an Ohio rally declaring, "Here are men who have been earnest Republicans ever since the standard of 'Free soil, free speech, free men,' was raised by Lincoln and Trumbull."[9]

Many Liberal Republican campaigners began their speeches by recounting their connections to the birth of the Republican Party. William Grosvenor's first words to a campaign rally in Orono, Maine, were "I am a Republican and cast my first vote for Fremont in '56 and have never cast any other than a Republican vote." In the first moments of his speech in Springfield, Illinois, Lyman Trumbull likewise reminisced about his long history with the Republican Party. Roeliff Brinkerhoff waited longer than most, until the fourth paragraph of his address, to remind the audience that "as a delegate to the Convention which met at Pittsburg, on the 22nd of February, 1856, I helped to create that [Republican] party, and from that day to the present have never scratched its ticket." Establishing their heritage as Republicans and antislavery advocates gave more power to the Liberal Republicans' condemnation of Reconstruction. John Farnsworth started one speech by explaining that "some twenty-five or six years ago, I was denounced because I left an old Pro-Slavery party, and united with a little handful, an unpopular handful, of Anti-Slavery men." He recounted his activity in the Union Army and insisted that "the Rebels deserved all they got during the war." Farnsworth told how "during the existence of the Reconstruction Committee in the House of Representatives, I was a member of it, and assisted in framing the various bills that were passed. I gave my hearty concurrence to the bills that were framed and passed for the original reconstruction of the Rebel States." After listing all of his Republican and Union credentials, Farnsworth blasted Reconstruction.[10]

Some Liberal Republicans were not content merely to demonstrate their Republican and abolition history, but wanted to prove how much they had suffered during the fight against slavery and the Confederacy. John Palmer started his Decatur speech with the standard recounting of his presence at the first Republican Convention at Philadelphia; a little ways into his address he contended, "All over the land men may be found who assailed me years ago for abolitionism and black republicanism. If they serve the Republican party ten years longer, faithfully, they will not have served the party as long as I have." By the end of the speech his theme had become the injuries he was willing to forgive: "If there were reasons for hating these men, I have as many as anybody else. From the very first until the last day of the war, I was in the field, separated from all I loved. . . . I went over the home of my childhood desolated by war. I saw my kindred in the South, and my kindred in the North, shot down in battle." Asa Mahan, a former abolitionist and president of Oberlin College, made one of the most impassioned statements proclaiming his right to critique Reconstruction. "If any person has occasion to entertain ill will toward the South," contended Mahan, "I am certainly the one. My only son met his death from injuries received from a Southern bullet." He explained that depression over his son's death had also cost him "a blooming daughter" and "the wife of my youth." Liberal Republicans made clear that in advocating reconciliation and attacking Reconstruction and Grant, they were Republicans and abolitionists, not Democrats or ex-rebels.[11]

*   *   *

In the late 1920s historian Claude G. Bowers coined the phrase "the Tragic Era" as a description of Reconstruction and used it to title his book on the period. Though his interpretation has long since been discredited, *The Tragic Era: The Revolution after Lincoln* helped popularize the view of Reconstruction that would be dominant for generations. Bowers portrayed Reconstruction as a tragic mistake in which corrupt Republicans oppressed white Southerners and imposed on the South an ill-conceived experiment in interracial equality. His depiction of Reconstruction as the Tragic Era was not new, however, as white Southerners had advanced the same view during the 1870s; Eric Foner finds the interpretation "originating in the anti-Reconstruction propaganda of southern Democrats." But another source for the Tragic Era portrayal exists—the Liberal Republicans. Bowers mentioned in his preface how "invaluable . . . has been my access to the unpublished diary of George W. Julian." Describing Julian as "an old abolitionist, with extreme views on universal suffrage, but with an inveterate hate of jobbery and corruption," he used Julian's critique of Reconstruction to help legitimize his own interpretation. Bowers regularly quoted from many other Liberal Republican sources, such as *The Nation,* the *New York Tribune, The Education of Henry Adams* (1918), Carl Schurz's *Reminiscences* (1908), Horace White's *The Life of Lyman Trumbull* (1913), and George Merriam's *The Life and Times of Samuel Bowles* (1885). The Liberal Republicans thus became a source for the Tragic Era portrayal.[12]

Liberal Republican campaigners railed against the corruption in the South that they associated with Reconstruction. Though historians have since shown that the Southern states' greater need for government-financed services after the Civil War, such as the establishment of public schools for newly created citizens and the distribution of artificial limbs to veterans, caused most of the states' increased debt, Liberal Republicans argued that the growing government expenditures were proof of corruption. In addition, while the whole era seemed corrupt, North and South, they concentrated on what they considered corruption in the South. Judge J. R. Spaulding mentioned the "organized pillage at the South" in his campaign remarks, and vice-presidential candidate B. Gratz Brown declared that "the ruin wrought by unjust, despoiling taxation has been so great in many regions that its evil effects will be felt for many long years to come." Grosvenor argued, "Those rule with absolute power whose successful robbery has yielded the largest means of corruption." The section of Grosvenor's campaign speech detailing the debt and corruption of Republican-run Southern states filled almost three entire newspaper columns. Cassius Clay and Asa Mahan similarly expounded on state debts in the South. "The debts of those states have increased from $76,000,000 to upwards of $291,000,000," according to Mahan, "and no man living can show a solitary benefit which these states have received." He insisted, "Every well informed man of the South and the North knows that four-fifths of the money actually raised goes, not into the Treasury, but into the pockets of the robber carpet-bag men." During a campaign speech Schurz condemned "that system of wholesale robbery and misrule prevailing in the South," and his German-language newspaper predicted that the continuation of Reconstruction would mean "a new bloom and crop of corruption, not alone in the custom houses of New York and New Orleans, but in the whole country."[13]

Liberal Republican campaigners blamed much of the corruption in Southern states on "carpet-baggers," Northerners who had moved to the South after the Civil War. While Richard Nelson Current has discovered that most of the Northerners who moved there after the war went in search of legitimate economic opportunities and were generally honest, the Liberal Republicans stereotyped them as corrupt, politically motivated despots. Grosvenor lamented that "the most unscrupulous and desperate carpet-baggers [were] given control of the party." A huge debt, according to Alexander McClure, had been "loaded upon the Southern states by the rule of imbecile and characterless men, who were strangers to the people they so pitilessly oppressed." He predicted, "The reign of the carpet-bagger will stand out in our history of treason, perfidy and war as wholly exceptional in the degree of its unmingled wrongs against mankind." As evidenced by McClure and others, the carpetbaggers theme inspired rhetorical excess. Another Liberal Republican described "those **Carpet-Baggers, Festering with Corruption**, til their stench loads the very atmosphere with disgusting, sickening odors," and Mahan argued, "These men are swarming over those states, as clouds of vampires, lighting upon and sucking the blood of the body politic." Schurz maintained that there was no honor among these thieves, insisting to a crowd at St. Louis, "You must know that 'carpet-baggerdom' is exceedingly faithful to the party, except, perhaps when its leading spirits, quarreling over the spoils, fall out among themselves."[14]

Many Liberal Republicans also ascribed some of the difficulties of Reconstruction to the political rights that had been given to African Americans. Most of the campaigners had favored passage of the Fifteenth Amendment in the late 1860s, and the Missouri Liberal Republicans had pushed black suffrage more strongly than the state's Radical Republicans. Campaigning for Grant in September 1868, Schurz discussed the Republican plank supporting the Fifteenth Amendment, which had recently passed in Congress. He asked a Chicago crowd, "Was not the vote given to the colored man in the South that he might render us all a great service at the ballot-box?" and he argued that in black suffrage lay "the only safe and durable basis for national peace, good understanding and prosperous development." But during the campaign of 1872, while still insisting that "only by the exercise of political rights can the free laborer maintain his independence," Shurz regretted that "the colored voters, untutored and inexperienced, fell under the leadership of unscrupulous adventurers." Though in his view "the rule of unprincipled and rapacious leaders at the head of the colored population has resulted in a government of corruption and plunder," he maintained that "I will not throw the blame upon the colored people, who entered the political field without experience and a just understanding of their true interests."[15]

The Liberal Republicans followed Schurz's model of simultaneously castigating and excusing African Americans' voting behavior. Grosvenor, who had served as an officer to a black regiment during the Civil War and had pushed for the Fifteenth Amendment as a Missouri Liberal Republican, charged that "the colored voters are ignorant and inexperienced. It is not their fault, but their misfortune." Roeliff Brinkerhoff lamented that "the political fortunes of those [Southern] States, with all the delicate requirements of statesmanship, were thrown into the hands of freedmen, with no experience even in the government of their own families, and with no education except that of the cotton field. As a matter of course these people, in their ignorance, fell into the hands of scoundrels and carpet-baggers." Although the longtime antislavery advocates often partly excused the perceived failure of African Americans to vote for honest and qualified candidates as due to a lack of experience that could be corrected, their depictions of the ignorance and incapacity of black voters helped create a lasting racist image.[16]

Some discussions of African Americans in politics were blatantly racist. The *Cincinnati Commercial* ran an article entitled "The Colored Vote" that questioned why African Americans were not supporting Greeley, as he had a much longer antislavery record than Grant. The newspaper concluded, "This does not speak well for the intelligence of the colored voters of the South." The *Springfield Republican* offered some of the most detailed discussions of African American voting, asserting that "the negro in politics will unquestionably prove a trial," since "as a whole, he is ignorant, debased and abased, and even in his freedom and his voting will be the frequent victim of cunning and vulgar men." Playing to racist stereotypes, the newspaper explained, "His first intelligence will be an impulse and an instinct rather than a conviction." In an astounding argument that could be seen as either encouraging or depressing, the paper assured readers that "the country will survive this new burden of ignorance and impulse as it has others and severer. The negro element is hardly worse than the Irish element was, and every one can see that the latter has already greatly improved." The *Republican* concluded, "Anyhow, 'Sambo' is trumps in politics, this year."[17]

The complaint about African Americans in politics soon turned into general complaints of electoral corruption. In an address entitled "Self Government and Its Duties," Grosvenor concentrated on how Republicans used corruption to maintain power. "The methods of the dominant party are as dangerous and wicked as its policy," he said, because "the agents of power are loaded with vulgar cash, and sent out to hunt for venal votes." B. Gratz Brown contended that the election laws themselves exacerbated the problem of ignorant and inexperienced African American voters, for the Republicans had rigged the system. He addressed a speech entitled "Crimes Against Suffrage" to an Illinois crowd; did they find it acceptable, he asked, "that the very foundations of our Republican system shall be destroyed by tolerating a giant crime against all free suffrage that strikes down the will of the Nation, of the States, of the people, in one fell crusade?" Brown maintained that "the electoral laws of nearly all the Southern States were so framed as to give in perpetuity absolute control of affairs to a meager minority of the population." He thus ironically turned an earlier antislavery argument into a racist appeal to white Northerners. Before the Civil War, Brown and other antislavery advocates had railed against the Slave Power system, in which slaveowners' votes counted more in terms of congressional representation than the votes of white Northerners. Brown adapted the argument to 1872, titling a section of his speech "One Negro Vote South Equal to Four Whites at the North" and contended that the corruption of the electoral process gave African Americans political power at the expense of white Northerners.[18]

Much of the discussion of voting laws in the South focused on the perception that Grant and the Republicans were using the military to affect the outcome of elections. The 1871 Ku Klux Klan Act had given President Grant the

authority to declare martial law and suspend the writ of habeus corpus to protect African Americans' civil rights and lives in the South, but to many Liberal
Republicans the Act represented a great threat to liberty. For Roeliff Brinkerhoff, "One of the most dangerous of these inroads upon the rights of the States
is doubtless in the way of interference in elections. Whenever the ballot box is
interfered with, or voters intimidated, or elections controlled, you put a dagger
at the heart of liberty." John Dean Caton, former chief justice of the Supreme
Court of Illinois, likewise considered, "This is the very essence of despotic
power. The Czar of Russia can possess no more unrestrained power over the
meanest of his subjects." According to McClure, "The civil authority has been
suspended, bayonets have usurped the ballot, and despotism has sunk deep into
the policy of the Government." Spaulding described Grant's powers as "disgraceful to a free people, dangerous to our liberties, fit only for the order-book
of a conqueror," asking, "What are they but brands of shame and chains of
servitude for a whole people?"[19]

It may seem that claims that such legislation as the Ku Klux Klan laws was
creating a despotic central government for both the North and the South would
have sounded hyperbolic even in 1872, but some Liberal Republicans in fact
warned their audiences about the encroachments of military government in the
North. McClure proclaimed, "I am here to protest against military rule, not
only in the South, but in Pennsylvania, where the gleam of the bayonet has
been tried to make our elections a mockery and a fraud." John M. Palmer spent
almost a tenth of a campaign speech discussing what he termed the "military
occupation of Chicago" immediately after the Great Chicago Fire of 1871. He
charged that President Grant, General Sherman, and General Sheridan had
acted unconstitutionally by sending federal troops to Chicago to act as police
without the permission of the governor of Illinois—Palmer himself. During the
speech he insisted, "My political is very brief. It is that the only safety for popular liberty is in the observance of constitutions and laws," and "nothing is more
dangerous than to concede that a President or a Governor may violate your
laws." A Liberal Republican campaign book explained, "The plain issue presented to the American people now, is this. Shall we return to a government of
law; or shall we continue to submit to the rule of the oligarchy of military politicians, brought into existence by the Civil War?"[20]

*   *   *

Of course Grant, in the Liberal Republican Party's lexicon, was the chief "military politician" oppressing the South and endangering the nation's liberties. In
The Tragic Era, Claude Bowers discussed the events that "set Grant's feet in the
path he was to follow for eight years as the militant champion of Radicalism at
its worst," and at one point concluded, "Grant had crushed the rising of the

people." He also portrayed Grant's administration as one of the most corrupt in history. Other writers have questioned Grant's military ability, calling him a butcher who had simply had more men at his command than Robert E. Lee. In his 1981 biography of Grant, historian William S. McFeely commented that Grant's descendants had been forced to endure a long decline in his reputation, for "not only did Grant hold a low rank in ratings of the presidents, but even his military star dimmed." While Grant's military reputation improved during the later twentieth century, Brooks D. Simpson noted in 1990 that although Grant is now "celebrated as one of the Republic's greatest generals, he is denigrated as one of its worst presidents." Liberal Republican campaigners in 1872 were some of the first to develop the stereotypes of Grant as a threat to the republic, a corrupt, inept president, and an overrated general—and even to use the term "Grantism."[21]

Like many of the Liberal Republican assertions that Reconstruction posed a danger to liberty, the party's portrayals of Grant as a tyrant were filled with the rhetoric of classical republicanism. This use of republican language raises several important questions. First, republicanism had motivated the liberal republicans for decades, so wherein did the Liberal Republican Party differ from the movement? While the party's use of republican language appears similar to that of the liberal republican movement, it is significant that the original liberal republicans had expressed their concerns about dangers to republican institutions for decades, in both public and private, while the Liberal Republicans were invoking republican concerns during the heat of a presidential campaign. Second, how was the Liberal Republican Party's use of such rhetoric any different from the practice of other campaigners during the nineteenth century? Michael F. Holt and Mark E. Neely Jr. have demonstrated that portraying a political opponent as a danger to the republic was common in nineteenth-century politics, but the difficulty lay in convincing the voters that the danger was real. While in 1860 the Republican Party had been successful in convincing the North that the Slave Power threatened the liberties of white Northerners, in 1872 the Liberal Republicans could not persuade the majority of the electorate that Grant was really a danger to republican government. White Southerners living through Reconstruction, though, had little trouble seeing Grant as a tyrant, and the powerful imagery used in the 1872 campaign helped to tarnish Grant's image for generations.[22]

The Liberal Republican speakers used many traditional republican tropes in portraying Grant as a tyrant. While the *Cincinnati Commercial* used analogies particularly suited to Grant, such as "Grant wields his party like an army," most of the campaigners relied on common historical allusions, such as references to European monarchs. McClure described how Grant had created "a measure of

Executive usurpation that no monarch of Europe could have practiced with impunity." Of course King George III, the villain in the American Revolution, was the nation's most hated European monarch. Whereas George Washington was often compared to Cincinnatus, the Roman general who after saving the Republic returned to his farm rather than becoming a dictator, the Liberal Republicans compared Grant to George III. William Springer argued that the Liberal Republican platform "is almost a second Declaration of Independence. It arraigns Grant, as our fathers did George III, for his many crimes against the liberties of the people." Asa Mahan kept to the same theme in his speech, sections of which were given subtitles such as "The Kingly Grant" and "Grant's George the III Policy." In the section with the latter subtitle, Mahan contended, "The British soldiers of George III, you will remember, prior to our first Revolution, were quartered in this country," and "in a similar way, in this time of peace, Grant would quarter his soldiers in the subjected states."[23]

Despite the resonance of these American Revolution analogies, the most popular strategy seemed to be comparing Grant to Caesar and his policies to Roman imperialism. The *Cincinnati Commercial* argued that Grant wanted the Democrats to endorse Greeley, because "like the Roman tyrant, he would that his enemies have but one neck, that he may inflict a mortal wound at a single stroke." Later in the season the newspaper mocked a Grant campaigner's words, "Long Live Ulysses Grant," with the headline "Long Live Caesar!" Roeliff Brinkerhoff compared Grant's control of the United States Senate to Julius Caesar's taming of the Roman Senate: "As with Caesar the First, at Rome eighteen hundred years ago, the first encroachment upon the liberties of the Republic was through the subservience of the Senate. 'Upon what meat does our Caesar feed, that he has grown so great?' It is very possible that as yet no permanent injury to the Republic is apparent from these encroachments of power, but . . . they are all continuous steps in the old beaten track of despotism, and when the people become regardless of them, the shadow of the man on horseback is not far off."[24]

In late summer, when the election was still undecided, the *Cincinnati Commercial* had praised speeches describing Grant as a tyrant and had indulged in some Caesar analogies of its own. But immediately after the October elections had made clear how unlikely it was that Grant would be defeated, the paper insisted, "As for ourselves, we have no doubt of the safety of the country under the Presidency of either Grant or Greeley. The American Republic does not seem to us so tender." By early November the newspaper declared, "With the same contempt that we have regarded the wild harangues about Greeley's dishonesty and treachery, we have looked upon the assertions that Grant's reelection means the loss of liberties of the people. No President could turn the

Nation from its appointed course." The *Commercial* concluded that "Grant is a safe sort of President," explaining, "There is no occasion for alarm just now about too great a development of Nationalism or Caesarism. Grant is not of the stuff that Caesars are made of." Deprecating Grant's ability to become a Caesar, particularly on the grounds of insufficient intelligence or energy, had been an alternate Liberal Republican tactic since early in the campaign. Grant, according to Carl Schurz, "does not mean to be a despot, but he wants to have his will. Such is the character of his personal government. We should be doing it too much honor by calling it Caesarism." Schurz expounded, "It is not inspired by any grand, lofty and long-headed ambition, by the insatiable desire of genius to do brilliant deeds and to fill the world with the splendor of a great name, like that of Julius Caesar and Napoleon. It is absolutely barren of ideas and originality, bare of striking achievements, void of noble sentiments and inspiring examples. It is simply dull and heavy, stupid and stubborn in its selfishness."[25]

The Liberal Republicans certainly did not allow the scandals and corruption associated with the Grant administration to go unmentioned. J. D. Caton asked, "If a man occupying a place of trust, which he might abuse to his own advantage, becomes suddenly rich, beyond any known means of acquiring wealth, you naturally ask, **How Has He Made His Money?**" The answer, according to Caton, was "**Grant's Gift Taking**" and his acceptance of "bribes," which he detailed at great length. Asa Mahan charged, "Our President has an insatiable greed for gifts," while William Springer explicitly stated that several of Grant's patrons "had purchased his favor." Carl Schurz contended that Grant "has rewarded with influential and lucrative offices men who had acquired his favor by valuable presents." B. Gratz Brown likewise accused Grant of selling public offices. According to the Liberal Republican vice-presidential candidate, "General Grant has received lands, moneys, homes, and presents of value from men who are aspiring to high public office, and he has afterward appointed those men to those offices." Brown also insisted that Grant "has appointed relatives, and friends, and family connections in a degree unprecedented in the history of this country, to the high offices of the Nation." The *Cincinnati Commercial* agreed that "there has never been, in all the odious history of the distribution of patronage in this country, anything so shameful as this," and McClure argued, "Incompetency, venality and shame have been the logical results of unblushing nepotism, and the appointment of unscrupulous men who had found the way to the favor of the throne." Lyman Trumbull, John Farnsworth, and William Springer all devoted large portions of their campaign speeches to discussing various scandals during Grant's first administration, including kickbacks at the New York Customs House, the sale of arms to

France, and Grant's relations with the wealthy New York financier Jay Cooke. One Liberal Republican speaker assured his audience, "I could stand here and talk from now til sundown, and show you the **Most Unmitigated Corruption and Extravagance** in disbursing the public moneys in the last two years of this Administration."[26]

Some Liberal Republicans argued that Grant was not really corrupt, he was just too stupid to be an effective president. "Had Grant been intelligent and honest, he would have exhausted his official authority to restore the South to order and prosperity," McClure told a group of North Carolinians, but the question was "whether he is to be excused for incompetence, or charged with deliberate complicity in the unexampled wrongs of your State." Caton had no doubts, insisting that Grant, "when thus brought to appreciate his own weakness—his utter inability to run the Government himself—and that he must call to his aid the politicians . . . chose to place himself under the control and practically surrender the reins of government into the hands of the **Corruptest, Most Licentious, and the Wickedest** cabal of politicians who ever ran an Administration in this country or any other." John M. Palmer, the governor of Illinois, theorized that the reason Grant had not reprimanded the military for intervening during the Chicago Fire was because he knew nothing about the Constitution. He read a passage from a letter he had received concerning the affair, in which the correspondent argued, "Grant probably cares nothing for the constitution and perhaps knows no more about it than Nicodemus did of the new birth." Palmer agreed with the correspondent's interpretation, concluding, "I thought that the ignorance of Grant was his only excuse." The Liberal Republican press similarly questioned the incumbent's abilities as president. The *Springfield Republican* detailed Grant's "lack of intelligence and delicacy in the administration of civil affairs," while the *Cincinnati Commercial* declared, "His blunders were numerable and palpable, and his incapacity for the presidency was apparent."[27]

The charge of ignorance seems mild compared to the Liberal Republican charges of laziness and drunkenness. The *Cincinnati Commercial* suggested that "the fact that Grant neglects the business of the Government for his own pleasure, should be put into the proper shape for circulation." Palmer entitled one section of a speech "Our Idle President." After dramatically asking, "Do you remember that Abraham Lincoln left home in February, 1861, and never again returned to the prairies until his remains were carried through your cities draped with all the habiliments of mourning and woe?" he recounted that with Grant, "We have had travels and journeys. We have had the seaside residence and the visit to New York, and to Boston, and to the West, and all over the country, as though there were no duties for the President at Washington." In case anyone missed the point, Palmer stated, "Industry is one of the cardinal virtues." Though hardly a fair comparison—for Lincoln, after all, was a wartime president—accounts of Grant vacationing more than his predecessor reinforced the charges of laziness. Roeliff Brinkerhoff likewise referred to the "trait of President Grant, which carries him away to watering-places and junket with boon companions at the sea-side." The mention of watering places was not accidental, for it rekindled the rumors of Grant as a drunk that had circulated during the Civil War. The *Commercial* explicitly encouraged such tactics, arguing that "the kind of documents to circulate are not relating to foreign affairs or to finance," and suggesting that "there is no charge that will have more weight among the honest farmers and country people than that the President is a habitual drinker and habitually becomes intoxicated."[28]

Even Grant's military accomplishments were not sacred. Some Liberal Republicans refused to touch Grant's military record, one campaigner assuring the crowd that "I do not intend to disparage his great service as a soldier." Others cautiously picked at Grant's performance during the Civil War, often stating how much they respected his military accomplishments—just before questioning some aspect of his generalship. In discussing Grant's military qualities, Palmer remarked, "Nobody, during this canvas, will charge me with improperly deprecating General Grant. I served under him during the war, and I regard him in many respects as its most eminent soldier." The caveats of "improperly deprecating" and "in many respects" left Palmer room to maneuver. He explained that Grant was not a Napoleon and during battle displayed resolution, not courage. J. D. Caton likewise said "I would not wish to see the feeblest ray in his military star dimmed of its luster," yet still insisted that "much of the credit which has been awarded him is justly due to his able subordinates and brave soldiers." John Farnsworth likewise declared, "I am not disposed to pluck one laurel from his brow," just before insisting that "at the same time, I am not disposed to concede what is very often said by his admirers, that he saved the Nation. There were many other successful military heroes." He concluded that "the men who did not ride on horseback, nor wear epaulettes upon their soldiers, they saved the Nation's life."[29]

Other Liberal Republicans were less circumspect in attacking Grant's military record. Horace White published a letter to Charles Sumner noting that "the late Secretary [of War] Stanton not once merely, but several times, expressed to me substantially the same opinion of General Grant that he did to you, with the addition that General Grant had been greatly overrated as a military commander." The *Cincinnati Commercial* contended, "If there was one man to whom, more than any other, this Nation is indebted for the trampling out of the Southern Confederacy, Edwin M. Stanton is unquestionably his name. Grant was a weapon in Stanton's hand." Asa Mahan took the attacks on Grant's military ability to another level, arguing that "as a military commander, while I give him credit for honest intention, I regard him as one of the most ignorant, erring and reckless mortals that ever led an army." Standing in the Oberlin College chapel, one of the cathedrals of abolitionism, Mahan insisted, "I hold myself ready, when the proper time comes, to demonstrate that the war of rebellion ought to have ceased at least a year before the period of Lee's surrender; that, from no want of good intention, but wholly to his ignorance, do we owe to General Grant a needless protraction of the war for at least one year, and a needless sacrifice of one hundred thousand lives." During the Civil War, Democrats and Confederates had impugned Grant's military skills, but he nevertheless emerged from the conflict as one of the most respected generals. Having former Union generals and longtime Republicans insinuate that he was overrated and make the outright charge that he was responsible for the unnecessary deaths of one hundred thousand soldiers probably added to the decline of Grant's reputation as a general.[30]

Greeley certainly took a beating during the campaign of 1872, but Grant did not emerge unscathed. To a large extent the Liberal Republicans were reviving stories about Grant that had circulated since he had become a public figure a decade earlier, as all good politicians would do. Still, the fact that they attacked Grant's ethical, military, political, and intellectual abilities for seven months in countless newspapers, pamphlets, and speeches had an impact. The Liberal Republicans literally coined the term "Grantism" and helped to create its still-powerful negative connotations.

*   *   *

The Liberal Republican appeals to the South and attacks on Reconstruction and Grant during the 1872 campaign did more than provide fodder and legitimacy for the construction of the Tragic Era, Grantism, and the Lost Cause. Given the common conflation of the liberal republican movement and the Liberal Republican Party, the extreme campaign rhetoric of the party led historians to the conclusion that the liberal republican movement had been eager to abandon Reconstruction and was virulently anti-Grant, even though most members of the movement had already returned to the Republican Party by the time the campaign was in full swing. Moreover, at the same time the Liberal Republican campaigners were assailing Reconstruction and Grant, they were also dismissing as amateur politicians and unrealistic reformers those liberal republicans who had returned to the Republican Party. Their campaign rhetoric—denouncing Reconstruction, Grant, and the original liberal republicans—helped create the image of the liberal republicans that still dominates modern scholarship.

John G. Sproat, author of *"The Best Men,"* seemed to reflect the 1872 campaign rhetoric in his insistence that the liberal reformers "gave up the struggle for equality and justice in the South with remarkable alacrity" and that the liberal republican movement was primarily concerned with defeating Grant. He also promoted the image of liberal republicans as ineffectual reformers overly committed to principles, insisting that "he was rather an abstract philosopher." Sproat repeatedly showed his disdain, declaring that "the liberal's intellectual arrogance and unreasoning fear destroyed his own good influence" and that "above all, the liberal reformer lacked the humility that comes with true intellectual and moral superiority." This image of the "Best Men" became so accepted in the historical imagination that in his 1988 overview of Reconstruction Eric Foner, citing Sproat, referred to the liberal republicans as "these self-styled 'best men.'" The men who launched the liberal republican movement, however, did not so style themselves; rather, Liberal Republican Party campaigners and historians constructed this image for them.[31]

Soon after the Cincinnati Convention, the Liberal Republican press began characterizing their former allies in the liberal republican movement as politically naive ideologues. Probably lost on the editors was the irony that it was actually the newspaper men involved in the Quadrilateral who deserved much of the blame for handing the Cincinnati Convention to Greeley. With liberal republicans like Stanley Matthews and Edward Atkinson denouncing the outcome of the convention as a fraud, newspapers with a vested interest in the new party, such as the *Cincinnati Commercial* and the *Springfield Republican*, needed to undermine these men's reputations. The *Commercial*, for example, pointedly reported that "the Impression seems to have been made throughout the country that the Cincinnati Liberals are all bolters; that they have gone down the road with HOADLY, MATTHEWS, COX and STALLO. This is an inaccurate impression." To undermine those who had bolted from the Liberal Republican Party, the newspaper printed a letter written by Matthews proclaiming that since "the nomination was the result, evidently[,] of bargain and intrigue . . . I am not ashamed to say that I repudiate it," and editorialized, "The judge would, we think, under the circumstances, find it difficult to show that he is not chargeable with inconsistency, which he might fairly claim is sometimes a masculine virtue, though [it] is in politics a dreadful sin." Similarly, the *Republican* explained, "Some of the gentlemen who were earliest and most zealous in the liberal movement, find its first fruits very bitter and unpalatable. They believe in the doctrine of free trade with an almost religious fervor." While understanding the outrage of the liberal republicans over the convention's abandonment of free trade, the paper advised, "They should mix reason and common sense with it."[32]

The abuse increased when the liberal republicans opposed to Greeley left the Fifth Avenue conference of June 20, 1872, and nominated their own ticket. The *Springfield Republican* reported, "A somewhat surprising bit of news reaches us from New York. The free-trade 'irreconcilables' have definitely broken with the great body of their friends, and set up in politics for themselves." In attacking the "irreconcilable" liberal republicans, the paper insisted that "practical men could not help seeing that the time was unpropitious for the propagation of their pet dogma," and that "all together they represented very little political experience, wisdom, or power." The *Republican* demonstrated its own agenda in describing the outcome of the Fifth Avenue conference. The paper commented that "it is to be hoped that we have heard the last about the 'frauds' at Cincinnati; about the 'trickery' and 'bargaining' to which it has been the fashion heretofore in some quarters to refer to Mr. Greeley's nomination." Ironically, the *Republican* also hoped that "the result of the New York conference ought to put to an end to all such trifling with the truth of history," even while its own editorial was creating the false historical image of the "Best Men."[33]

The press attacks continued as many of the original liberal republicans started actively campaigning for Grant. After Matthews, George Hoadly, and others from Cincinnati made speeches endorsing Grant, the *Cincinnati Commercial* characterized them as politically naive elites. According to the newspaper, "It was the unhappiness of the May Convention to be assembled in Cincinnati, the city that contained the largest known assortment of amateur politicians, whose ability as lawyers and respectability as citizens gave them nationality of reputation; whereas they were actually quite incapable of engineering substantial results." Foreshadowing Sproat's portrayal of the liberal republicans' unsuitability for politics, the paper reported that "the impression that our distinguished friends made upon us in the Cincinnati Convention, was that they were quite too good to be of vital service in the rough and hard conflicts of this rude and wicked world." The *Commercial* concluded that "a more impolitic and inconsequential nest of distinguished gentlemen than Cincinnati is blessed with never adorned and afflicted another city."[34]

The Liberal Republican campaign speakers also dealt harshly with the members of the liberal republican movement who decided to support Grant. Alexander McClure wrote an entire speech titled "The Grant Investment in Bolters." Its first two pages parodied the liberal republicans at the Cincinnati Convention and their subsequent deliberations in New York. McClure described a mystery man who presided at the convention, "but the idol of his faith was free trade, and, as the convention bolted free trade, he was left shivering outside, and he bolted by the mere force of political gravitation. (Great laughter.) Having thus bolted, he at once became a patriot in the estimation of

the administration he had just denounced as a running sore of corruption."
After several more sentences of ridicule, he concluded, "Judge Stanley Matthews, of Ohio, will recognize this portrait." While there were other groups at
the Cincinnati Convention who had refused to support Greeley's nomination,
McClure concentrated on mocking the liberal republicans in the first part of
his speech, explaining, "There were some honest bolters from the Cincinnati
bolt, and all men were not for sale. The result was that honesty bolted again
from the bolting bolters (laughter), and the remnant again bolted from each
other." The liberal republican meeting in New York City during June had many
comic elements, which McClure did a nice job of summarizing: "A small remnant made a declaration of principles and nominated Mr. Grosenbeck for President; I forget who for Vice-President. A Committee was appointed to notify
the nominees, but the committee bolted before they found the candidates, and
the candidates bolted over to Greeley (Great applause.) So ended the bolt of the
Cincinnati bolters."[35]

   While McClure mocked them, many of the liberal republicans' former allies
heaped scorn on their political abilities and even their manliness. One of the
original members of the Ohio Central Republican Association argued that
"although the Club, with such men as Cox, Hoadly, Kittredge, Sage, Burnett,
Matthews, Stanton, Clark, contained the intellectual cream of the Republican
party of this county, the judgment of the politicians was that it amounted to
nothing, that it was all brains and no muscle; that there was—you will pardon
the expression—'no hell in it,' that the 'boys' were not with it; in short, that it
was not worth while to be troubled about it. And the politicians were right."
Grosvenor similarly went after Stallo, who campaigned for Grant. According to
Grosvenor, "There is another set of gentlemen who can not support Mr. Greeley," that "claim to be the original and only true reformers." He insisted, "This
is not a class of voters, but a class of talkers. . . . It is an army of major generals."
He declared, "I do not question the sincerity of Judges Stallo, Matthews,
Hoadly, et al., but in practice they resemble Mr. Pecksniff's horse, 'of wonderful promise, but no performance; it was always going to go, but never went.'"
In response to Stallo's charges of trickery at the Cincinnati Convention, Grosvenor answered, "Let them not accuse those of fraud or infidelity to principle
who prefer to do some live work in the live world of ours."[36]

   It must be admitted that during the campaign of 1872 the liberal republicans
themselves certainly contributed to their characterization as elitists. Disappointed with the results of the Cincinnati Convention and in the midst of
organizing the Fifth Avenue conference, many of them both privately and publicly denigrated the value of popular political conventions. Soon after the convention *The Nation* declared that the first lesson it had taught was "the

completeness with which nominating conventions have ceased to be, what they profess to be, deliberative bodies." *The Nation* added, "The only remedy we can suggest . . . is the disuse of large, excitable, frantic, ill-governed mass-meetings as even an ostensible means of selecting candidates or drawing up platforms, and the reduction of conventions to the forty or fifty men who would do the real work, as they do it now." Schurz agreed, privately suggesting to Godkin in mid-May that "the best thing to be done is that proposed by the Evening Post: to make another nomination, and to resort to that end not to the dangerous machinery of a convention, but to get up a meeting of 'notables.'" With the organization of the Fifth Avenue conference complete, the *New York Evening Post* declared, "Let it be understood that the Reformers will have nothing more to do with politicians. Let the public understand why it is that we will hold no more conventions. As we said the other day, the convention has ceased to be a deliberative assembly, and has become a mere place of political machinery." The liberal republicans' words appear to substantiate the "Best Men" stereotype, but clearly they had had enough faith to organize a popular convention in Cincinnati and now needed to attack the idea of conventions to justify their conference.[37]

Many liberal republicans who campaigned for Grant, needing some way to defuse the issue of having left the Republican Party only to return after the Cincinnati Convention, made self-deprecating comments that also may have fueled the stereotype. Hoadly told a crowd that "having bolted already twice this year—once from the Republican party into the Cincinnati Convention and then out of the Cincinnati Convention—I am not in a condition to advise anybody to vote the regular ticket without scratching." Discussing the founding principles of the liberal republican movement, Matthews reflected, "Such an idea. It is said it was utopian. So, it seems, the result has proven." Charles Francis Adams Jr. declared to a gathering at his hometown of Quincy, Massachusetts, "We may not be successful politicians, but we can at least try to be honest men."[38]

Some of the liberal republicans also contributed to their "Best Man" image in later decades. Historians have used Edwin Godkin's 1896 *Problems of Modern Democracy* and Henry Adams' 1907 *Education of Henry Adams* to portray the liberal republicans, and the many who later became mugwumps, as elitists who were pessimistic toward equality and republican institutions. The problem with using such later sources to understand the liberal republicans is that these sources do not necessarily reflect their writers' attitudes during the late 1860s and early 1870s, when many were sanguine about the United States' democratic political system. Sproat himself acknowledges that "early in the Gilded Age most liberals were optimists." Just a few years before helping to organize the liberal republican movement, Henry Adams had rejoiced at the reelection of Abraham Lincoln during wartime, telling his brother, "Systems of Government are secondary matters, if you've only got your people behind them. I never yet have felt so proud now of the great qualities of our race, so confident of the capacity of men to develop their faculties in the mass." Godkin likewise contradicted the perception that liberal republicans were too good for politics, writing in 1867, "I do not remember any case in which a man of culture and refinement, who wanted to get into politics, and was willing to work for it, has been kept out of it by popular dislike of his peculiar characteristics." By the late 1870s some liberal republicans had become more pessimistic and began to declare democracy a failure. David M. Tucker identifies the year 1878, in which Adams began his savage satire *Democracy*, as the turning point, but he still finds, "They never really gave up hope, except for the Adams brothers and Godkin, who finally abandoned hope in the 1890s." Many other liberal republicans became mugwumps, reformers who optimistically believed, notes Tucker, "that citizens would exercise republican virtue in political affairs." He shows that Sproat's depictions of the Gilded Age mugwumps as racist and antidemocratic elitists are inaccurate. Lyman Trumbull, for instance, became a Populist in the 1890s, and Carl Schurz published a defense of African American civil rights in 1904. Most liberal republicans never became the stereotype that history conferred on them, and for those few who did, the resemblence developed years after the liberal republican movement had ended.[39]

Political necessity drove the Liberal Republican Party's campaign rhetoric against Reconstruction, Grant, and the liberal republicans who returned to the Republican Party. Without civil service reform and free trade, the new party needed an issue, and unfortunately attacking Reconstruction seemed best suited to Greeley's strengths and to attracting white Southerners and Democrats. After establishing their bona fides as longstanding Republicans, the Liberal Republicans assailed Reconstruction's purported corruption, terrible carpetbaggers, ignorant black voters, and tyranny. They also portrayed Grant as a lazy, incompetent, tyrannical drunkard unfit for the presidency, as a man who had not even been that good a general during the Civil War. The defection of many disgruntled liberal republicans to the regular Republican Party made it imperative for the Liberal Republican Party to discredit the founders of the liberal republican movement, whom they belittled as elite ideologues with no political experience. The Liberal Republican campaign speakers and newspapers tried to portray these issues and people in ways that would influence the voters in 1872, but the attempt failed miserably. They did, however, influence generations of historians to accept their characterizations of Reconstruction as the Tragic Era, the practices of the Grant administration as Grantism, and the liberal republicans as the Best Men. In recent years scholars have reexamined Reconstruction and Grant and come to see them in a new light. The convention of the liberal republicans as Best Men, as "querulous aristocrats," however, has lingered.[40]

D espite losing control of their movement and enduring an invective-filled campaign, most liberal republicans remained in surprisingly good spirits after Grant's reelection in 1872. In postmortem correspondence, Schurz acknowledged to Horace White, "We designed it to be a campaign of ideas, and it became a campaign of personalities. We wanted it to become a fight for positive principles, and it became a mere fight against an Administration." He explained, "We want the civil service and the revenue system reformed: we want economy and honest government secured; we want a policy of reconciliation adopted with regard to the South; we want centralization prevented. We do not care who does it, provided it be done." Political pressure had forced Grant to adopt some of the liberal republican positions during the 1872 campaign, such as continuing the funding of the Civil Service Commission, lowering some tariff rates, and passing the Amnesty Bill of 1872. Happy that the liberal republican agenda was being advanced in an unexpected way, Schurz told Edwin Godkin, "Grant has made a good beginning in which we must certainly support, and if our support is superfluous, applaud him. But the true test is still to come."[1]

The coming test was whether Grant would continue on his new course and whether the liberal republicans could continue to exercise any influence. To maintain their advantage, Schurz suggested that "we should maintain our entire independence of the old organized parties," for "the Republic has entered upon a new period of its history. What the country now stands most in need of, is parties without records." Notwithstanding the recent election debacle, Schurz and others still thought the existing political parties were in the process of breaking up. "Attempts will be made to reorganize the old Democratic party, but I believe such attempts will fail," Schurz declared, because "one of the great and most beneficial results of the last Presidential campaign, consists in the fact that there is no national party in existence now that has not distinctly recognized the results of the war as embodied in the Constitution." The *Cincinnati Commercial* agreed that the 1872 election had settled the issues of the Civil War. In an article that appeared one day before Schurz's letter to White, the paper predicted that the tariff would be the only issue that remained to be addressed during the second Grant administration. According to the

Commercial, Congress would take care of civil service reform, and "in matters touching reconstruction and the removal of all disabilities from the people of the South, there need be no surprise should the action of the party in power be liberal and generous. Strong as it is, it would not care to provoke another schism in the Republican ranks, as will certainly happen if it be not done before 1876."[2]

The liberal republicans' experience of fighting the Slave Power for two decades probably accounted for much of their expectation that new political parties would emerge, and for their optimism about eventually accomplishing their goals. Most of them had experienced the political tumult of the late 1840s and 1850s, when the longstanding Whig Party had disappeared and new parties had emerged, only to die after a few fall elections. During the antebellum period, new parties were formed to deal with single issues—such as the Know-Nothings with their emphasis on nativism. A majority of the liberal republicans old enough to have been active in politics at the time had left their existing parties to create the Free Soil Party in 1848 to combat the expansion of slavery. Though the Free Soil Party lasted less than a decade and achieved little tangible success, its members saw this as a temporary setback and quickly helped to form the Republican Party in the mid-1850s. With the election of Abraham Lincoln in 1860, passage of the Thirteenth Amendment abolishing slavery five years later, and victory in the Civil War preserving the Union in 1865, the Republican Party and its liberal republican members had accomplished the party's original goals, and those of the Free Soil Party. While modern historians often criticize the Republicans for not securing racial equality for African Americans after the Civil War, that had not been part of their original agenda. Even committed abolitionists like William Lloyd Garrison believed their job was finished after the passage of the Thirteenth Amendment. After three decades of struggle against slavery Garrison ceased publication of the abolitionist newspaper *The Liberator* in 1865 and focused his reform efforts on temperance and women's suffrage. The liberal republicans were right in concluding that the Republican Party had achieved its objectives; and sometimes success can be more confounding than defeat for a political party.

The search for a new agenda coincided with a transition in the party's leadership. After spending decades in an idealistic crusade against slavery, the scandals and polices of the first Grant administration alienated many of its founders. Robert F. Engs and Randall M. Miller note that "by 1872 the first generation of Republicans were passing from the scene, weary of wrangling over issues of who got the franchise and the reward of office," and "a new generation of Republicans, in many cases indifferent to the reform interests of the party's founding generation, stood ready to take command." While the liberal republicans were no longer primarily concerned with the plight of African Americans, they did want to reform government and society, thus putting them at odds with the Republican Party's new leaders, men like Roscoe Conkling, Oliver P. Morton, and James G. Blaine, who since 1860 had worked their way up through the ranks. The political isolation of the few remaining founders of the party was accentuated in 1872. Lyman Trumbull became tired of being ineffective in the Senate after the Grant administration had ostracized him for joining the liberal republican movement; anticipating defeat for reelection that year, he expressed little concern. After being defeated as expected in 1873 he completely abandoned politics for the next three years. Charles Sumner also felt marginalized, as his attempts to influence the Republican Party during the Santo Domingo affair had been rewarded by his being stripped of his Senate Foreign Relations Committee chairmanship. Disappointment with the direction of the Republican Party had led some of its founders, such as Edward Atkinson, William Cullen Bryant, Jacob Cox, Trumbull, and Horace White, to create the liberal republican movement. Later, more of the original Republicans who felt alienated from the party they had helped organize, such as Cassius M. Clay, Horace Greeley, George Julian, and Charles Sumner, joined the Liberal Republican Party. Driving away such experienced, dedicated, and ideologically driven men only hastened the changes in the composition and nature of the Republican Party.[3]

Nature and time also played a part in the diminishing role of the Republican Party's founders. Thaddeus Stevens had died during the 1860s; more leaders felt the affects of age in the 1870s. Trumbull had spent eighteen years in the Senate and was sixty when he returned to private life—probably part of the reason he seemed to have little regret about leaving active politics. Though Bryant was still involved with politics in the summer of 1876, he was growing weary. He wrote to a friend, "I have nearly done with politics. What need a man of eighty one concern himself with these strifes? I long more and more to get away from them." Greeley, having lost both his wife and the election in 1872, died soon after, at age sixty-one. Charles Sumner's death in early 1874 was perhaps the event most symbolic of a transition from one generation to another. Sumner had been an abolitionist, a Free Soiler, and a founder of the Republican Party. He was considered one of the most outspoken opponents of slavery, and his name became a rallying cry of the new party in 1856 when South Carolina Congressman Preston Brooks viciously attacked him in the Senate for giving a powerful speech against slavery and against Senator Andrew P. Butler of South Carolina. The Republican campaign slogan for 1856 was "Bleeding Kansas and Bleeding Sumner." In many ways he had been the idealistic and abolitionist soul of the party.[4]

The city of Boston invited Carl Schurz to deliver the eulogy at Sumner's memorial meeting. Schurz used the opportunity not just to praise his friend and fellow senator, but to discuss the past, present, and future of the Republican Party. While recounting Sumner's contributions to ending slavery, Schurz declared, "The anti-slavery movement is now one of the great chapters of our past, the passions of the struggle having been buried in thousands of graves, and the victory of Universal Freedom standing as firm and unquestionable as the eternal hills." Besides settling the issue of slavery, Schurz argued that the Civil War had also created problems, for "no great civil war has ever passed over any country, especially a republic, without producing wide-spread and dangerous demoralization and corruption." Part of the problem, in his view, was that "the ascendancy of no political party in a republic has ever been long maintained without tempting many of its members to avail themselves for their selfish advantage of the opportunities of power and party protection, and without attracting a horde of camp followers, professing principle, but meaning spoil." Two years after the disaster at the Cincinnati Convention, Schurz still perceived dangers to the nation's republican institutions, such as the spoils system, legal tender, and protective tariffs.[5]

No eulogy for Sumner could be complete, however, without touching upon Reconstruction, and Schurz tread delicately on the subject, for the Massachusetts senator's last wish had been the enactment of his Civil Rights Bill, which many liberal republicans, including Schurz, opposed. Schurz reminded the audience of Sumner's "earnest and pathetic plea for universal peace and reconciliation" in 1872 before skillfully linking the civil-rights legislation to another of Sumner's last measures, a resolution removing the names of Civil War battles from the regimental colors and register of the United States Army. In Schurz's hands one of the most defiant advocates of African American rights became a symbol of reconciliation. He praised the fallen senator's independence in fighting corruption in the Republican Party and seeking a fair end to Reconstruction. "Let the American people never forget that it has always been the independent spirit . . . which gave the American colonies their sovereignty and made this great Republic; which defied the power of slavery, and made this a Republic of freedmen; and which—who knows?—may again be needed some day to defy the power of ignorance, to arrest the inroads of corruption, or to brake the subtle tyranny of organization in order to preserve this Republic!"[6]

Schurz's call for independent action during Sumner's eulogy was not accidental, as the memorial meeting served as a rendezvous for liberal republicans. Most of them had remained in contact, and even before Sumner's death had discussed creating a formal league. Less than two months before the present occasion Samuel Bowles had written to a friend in London, explaining that "politically things are going to pieces, which is right. A few impatient people, like Schurz and Charles F. Adams and David Wells, are eager to begin reconstruction, but there is nothing to reconstruct yet." When he learned that Schurz was to give Sumner's eulogy, Henry Adams asked Bowles to extend to him an invitation to stay with the Adams family while in Boston. In the correspondence Adams also mentioned the coming "of the three wise men of the West," referring to the other three members of the Quadrilateral at the Cincinnati Convention, Horace White of the *Chicago Tribune,* Henry Watterson of the *Louisville Courier-Journal,* and Murat Halstead of the *Cincinnati Commercial.* The local newspapers presumed that the famous journalists had come for political purposes, and despite claims that they were only there to hear Schurz's funeral oration for Sumner, it is likely that they planned and plotted politics, for in the next year another liberal republican organization with an almost identical membership rose from the ashes of 1872.[7]

Unlike in 1872, momentum from Missouri and national politics did not help the liberal republicans in 1875. Schurz faced a difficult reelection to the Senate; changing circumstances had made his positions a political liability, particularly in Missouri. The collapse of Jay Cooke's bank after its failed speculation in the Northern Pacific Railroad, a type of activity the liberal republicans had long warned against, started the Panic of 1873, which soon engulfed the nation's entire economy. While some historians have overstated how the panic affected the liberal republicans, arguing that the economic depression "pushed reformers' elitist hostility to political democracy and government activism . . . to almost hysterical heights," the Panic of 1873 did reinforce their belief that economic issues were the most important questions of the day. Charles Francis Adams Jr. and Schurz, for instance, corresponded about starting a Hard Money League in early 1874, as the liberal republicans began to consider a return to specie payments a more immediate concern than free trade in light of the recent depression. Unfortunately for Schurz's political fortunes, these long-held economic principles conflicted with the immediate needs of western farmers. The most pressing issue for them was Greenbacks. While the liberal republicans had been wary of legal tender during the Civil War and wanted a return to hard money as soon as possible afterward, western farmers suffering through the depression wanted an expansion, not a contraction, of the money supply. In a major election speech in St. Louis, Schurz spent approximately a third of his time advocating hard money, even though he admitted, "I have been asked by political and personal friends, for my own sake, either to abstain entirely from expressing my opinions on the financial question in this campaign, or at least to compromise a little by declaring myself, for instance, for specie payments in an indefinite future, but for some expansion at present. I cannot do that."[8]

The apparent success of the liberal republicans in working toward reconciliation also backfired on Schurz. In 1870 the Liberal Republicans in Missouri had won by enticing Democrats to join them on a platform of amnesty and universal suffrage. Now back in power, many Democrats in Missouri had little use for Schurz or for measures helping African Americans. Such attitudes in Missouri were symbolic of what was happening nationally. After winning reelection in 1872 by adopting Liberal Republican positions such as amnesty for former Confederates, Grant increasingly showed little inclination to use federal force in the South, to which many white Southerners responded with greater militancy and demands for power. Much of Schurz's St. Louis speech dwelt on the South, and he despaired that "it is one of the great misfortunes of our situation that we can scarcely attempt to engage the attention of the people in other subjects of legislation without being disturbed again and again by what may be called the Southern problem, reinflaming party spirit and distracting the popular mind." Still, he realized the need to address the problem. The first part of Schurz's analysis of the "Southern problem" probably pleased the Democrats in the audience, for he castigated the federal government's military intervention in Louisiana. Then, though he was relying on the votes of Democrats for reelection, Schurz displayed his propensity for political mistakes by insisting, "Nor was that the only wrong committed in the South. There was another, and on the other side. It was when bands of lawless ruffians infested the Southern country spreading terror by cruel persecution and murder." Assailing "lawless ruffians" in Missouri, with its history of proslavery border ruffians in the 1850s and guerrilla conflict during the Civil War, was not calculated to win the hearts and minds of white Democratic voters, particularly when the carpetbagger from Germany declared, "We know also that there is a ruffianly element in the South which, unless vigorously restrained by all the power of society, will resort to bloody violence."[9]

Schurz's speech demonstrated the liberal republicans' fundamental, continuing, and insoluble dilemma with Reconstruction. As in 1870, Schurz and his fellow liberal republicans wanted to see a republican, free-labor society in the South, with political and economic freedom for both races. That Schurz, during a campaign speech in a former slave state, would chastise white violence and endorse the use of "all the power of society" to stop it demonstrates at least some continued commitment to African Americans in 1874. Yet the refusal of white Southerners to embrace the liberal republican vision for the South left federal military intervention as the only way to protect African Americans, which in itself defeated the goal of creating republican institutions there. The liberal republicans had agreed to military governments as a temporary expedient in 1867, but now seven years had passed, and little progress could be seen.

If anything, white Southerners were becoming more intransigent. The willingness of both Southern whites and the federal government to use force in
advancing their agendas (though the government's will was declining) made it
difficult for Schurz to see a solution. He asked, "Is there no remedy for all this
except the employment of force? There must be, if our republican institutions
are to stand." The Missouri senator suggested, "The National Government and
the dominating party can do something far better for the colored man than
pass laws of doubtful Constitutionality or send troops for their protection. Let
them openly and severely discountenance those corrupt partisans in the South
who have misled the colored people into an organized support of robbery and
misgovernment." Schurz asked his fellow Missourians to once again display
their political independence, for "how much easier would it be to solve such
problems, how much easier to avert the dangers to our republican institutions
they bring with them, if but for a short period that partisan spirit could be
dispelled which blinds our patriotic impulse to do what is right." A majority of
Missourians disagreed with Schurz, and the Democrats won the legislature by
a large majority, thus ending Schurz's senatorial career.[10]

While the Missouri voters cared little for political independence anymore,
the liberal republicans, just as they had four years earlier after the election in
Missouri, wasted little time in gathering again. Instead of the New York–based
Free Trade League, the new Commonwealth Club of Boston hosted the meeting
in December 1874. Though the ostensible purpose of the meeting was to hear
Schurz lecture on educational problems, many of the participants were the
same as in 1872, and politics was clearly the main topic. Afterward Henry
Adams explained to a close friend in England, the aristocrat Charles Milnes
Gaskell, "I have been carrying on no end of political intrigues. . . . Just now I
am engaged single-handed in the slight task of organising a new party to contest
the next Presidential election in '76. As yet I have only three allies; a broken
down German politician [Schurz]; a newspaper correspondent [Horace White],
and a youth of twenty [Henry Cabot Lodge] who is doing all the work. With
these instruments I propose to do no less than decide the election of 1876. You
will see." Though few, the allies were impressive. Schurz was still the most powerful German-American politician and would become a cabinet secretary in
1877. White had just become a wealthy man by selling his share of the *Chicago
Tribune,* and at age forty was touring Europe with his beautiful young bride,
who was still in her twenties. He was so content that over the next few years he
turned down offers from Godkin to buy out *The Nation,* from Henry Adams
to run a Boston daily newspaper, and from Parke Goodwin to purchase William Cullen Bryant's interest in the *New York Evening Post.* While certainly the
most junior of the triumvirate, Lodge came from a privileged background; his

great-grandfather George Cabot had represented Massachusetts in the United States Senate from 1791 to 1796. Lodge also had some ability; he had just received his law degree from Harvard and would eventually spend over twenty years in the Senate, where his son and namesake would also spend a quarter of a century. With this talented, wealthy, and privileged threesome Adams got to work quickly, helping to arrange a dinner at Delmonico's in New York in honor of the departing senator in April 1875. Once again there were ulterior motives. Adams wrote to Schurz, "You know already that I want organisation and consider the New York meeting only valuable as it leads to and facilitates organisation. Would it not be well to arrange beforehand for a small interior meeting, the day of the dinner, to discuss policy?" The guests included such liberal republicans as the Adams brothers, Edwin Godkin, Samuel Bowles, and David Wells.[11]

The Boston and New York meetings, just like those four years earlier, produced a small movement whose members thought they could influence the 1876 presidential election. Henry Adams updated Gaskell: "My new party thrives. It consisted then [February 1875], I think of four men. Now it has reached more than that. It would not surprise me if I had as many as forty coadjustors." He displayed an oddly buoyant fatalism for a descendant of the Puritans, prattling, "We shall go ahead and you will need not be surprised to hear that we have covered ourselves with eternal ridicule by some new absurd failure, or have subsided into nothing for sheer feebleness, or have actually effected a brilliant *coup*, brought our man in as President, and are the rulers of forty million people. Such is the chaotic condition of our whole politics that any of these results is possible." Most observers in 1872 had expected continued party transformation; Adams and the liberal republicans believed that to some extent that environment still existed going into 1876. According to Adams, "My scheme is to organise a party of the centre and to support the party which accepts our influence most completely. But I doubt whether we can absolutely overthrow both parties as many of our ardent friends seem almost inclined to try doing." The reference almost certainly included the eternally optimistic Schurz, with whom Charles Francis Adams Jr. had been corresponding while Schurz was in Europe, telling him, "I am strongly persuaded that this year it may be well in your power to give the whole shape to the next year's Presidential issue." Schurz agreed that they could gain control of the Republican Party, for "in point of sentiment we Liberals have had a majority of the rank and file of the party with us for a considerable period, but the organization was controlled by the ringmasters." Thus he advised, "There are two ways in which we may expect to exercise a decisive influence upon the Presidential election of '76: either by appealing from the old parties directly to the people, or by imposing our terms as to men and policies upon one of those parties."[12]

Not only did the liberal republicans believe they were facing the same political environment and count on using the same strategy as in 1872, but even the details of the plan were eerily similar. Schurz wrote to William Grosvenor from Europe that "it seems quite likely, from the turn things have taken, that we shall be able to do substantially in '76 what we ought to have done in '72. . . . The main thing will be to get a machinery of action sufficiently strong." Schurz had not learned the vital importance of grassroots machinery, however, as at the same time he told Charles Francis Adams Jr., "Why should I hurry home then? The preparatory work of organization can, I think, just as well be done without me. All that is needed is some money to keep [W. M.] Grosvenor at work,"—the exact same man who had been responsible for the liberal republican organizing efforts for 1872! At this point the liberal republicans even desired the same unattainable candidate, Charles Francis Adams. Schurz wrote, "Adams is not too old yet for another trial. . . . Moreover, Adams is the name for 1876." Samuel Bowles mentioned to Murat Halstead the increasing prospects of getting the senior Adams elected president in 1876 and asked, "Wouldn't [it] be sweet, in view of 'Seventy-two,' to have that happen?" Of course, just as in 1872, Charles Francis Adams had no desire to run for president. The emerging similarities of the liberal republicans' plans for 1872 and 1876 should have been blazingly obvious to them and equally disturbing, considering that they seemed to be working toward recreating what was widely regarded as one of the most colossal failures in American political history.[13]

The Ohio gubernatorial election in 1875 unexpectedly affected both the liberal republicans' short- and long-term tactics. The Democrats had nominated Greenbacker William Allen to run against Ohio Republican Rutherford B. Hayes, who had many connections to the Cincinnati liberal republicans, such as having attended Kenyon College with his kinsman Stanley Matthews and Harvard Law School with George Hoadly Jr. Most observers considered German Americans to be the crucial swing voters in the Ohio contest. Many of the liberal republicans, including Murat Halstead, Charles Nordhoff, and David Dudley Field, wrote to the vacationing Schurz, begging him to return and secure the German American vote for the hard-money Hayes. Charles Francis Adams Jr. also wrote to Schurz, "Allen's election will be our destruction; his renomination on the rag-money issue was a defiance and insult to us, and his success would render us contemptible. If we don't kill him, he will kill us. The weapon with which to kill him is the German vote,—it is the only effective weapon at hand, and you are its holder. You must come back to strike." Always susceptible to flattery, Schurz quickly made his way back to the United States, and his presence encouraged both the liberal republicans and Hayes. "Our politics are getting lively. As yet we independents hold the balance of power and gain strength," Henry Adams wrote to Gaskell during the campaign, "but before this letter reaches you, we may be smashed to flinders. We called Schurz back from Germany to fight the democrats in Ohio. If he succeeds in beating them there, my friends will pretty surely control the next presidential election." While he had remained with the Republican Party in 1872, Hayes also thought Schurz's presence in the campaign was vital and asked him to give speeches in a number of key cities. Schurz obliged Hayes' request and gave a number of speeches concentrating on the battle for hard money. He hyperbolically insisted during one address that the Allen greenback and inflationist policy,

> if followed by the National Government, would discredit republican institutions the world over, expose the American people to the ridicule and contempt of civilized mankind, make our political as well as business life more than ever the hotbed of gambling and corruption and plunge the country into all those depths of moral and material bankruptcy and ruin, which, as all history demonstrates, never, NEVER fail to follow a course so utterly demented in its wickedness.

Although campaigning for a Republican, Schurz referred to the Liberal Republican Party of 1872, repeatedly addressed Democrats, and explicitly called for voters to be independent of political parties both in the Ohio gubernatorial contest and in the presidential election of 1876.[14]

Schurz's presence in Ohio was the decisive factor in Hayes's election as governor, according to many. The *New York Times*, which as a loyal Republican organ had abused Schurz during the 1872 campaign, rejoiced that "the coming of Mr. Schurz is an event of prime importance," for "he reaches the doubtful element—the German Liberals—who needed some good strong excuse for abandoning their Democratic allies and returning to the Republican camp." After the election Charles Francis Adams Jr. gloatingly wrote to Schurz, "I got home this morning, serene in the knowledge that 'old Bill Allen's' grey and gory scalp was safely dangling at your girdle." Schurz himself acknowledged his role in defeating Allen, but did not share the *Times*' assessment that he was leading the German Americans back into the Republican camp. "Looking over the whole field," he confided in his reply to Adams, "I find that the Independent voter is doing well and getting ready for the more important work for next year." Despite all their analysis, the liberal republicans seemed to have missed one aspect of the 1875 Ohio campaign that would play an important role in their plans for 1876: the first connection between Schurz and Hayes.[15]

As the New Year began, the liberal republicans increased their plotting to control the presidential election in 1876. Schurz informed Bowles in January that a number of friends in the West approved of holding a meeting to influence the coming campaign, and that he agreed with Bowles that circumstances were growing more propitious. As far as candidates went, Schurz still preferred Charles Francis Adams, asserting that "I not only consider him the best, but in the Centennial year also the strongest candidate." In early February, however, Schurz met with Henry Cabot Lodge—Henry Adams' lieutenant—to explain that support for Charles Francis Adams had not developed. Schurz and other liberal republicans began courting Secretary of the Treasury Benjamin H. Bristow, the one member of the Grant administration who was interested in reform. Compared to the other Republicans interested in the nomination, such as the notoriously corrupt James G. Blaine, Bristow certainly seemed preferable. Schurz told Bowles that "Bristow is our second choice, and right heartily too," while Bowles wrote to Murat Halstead, "It is the best thing to do,—to organize for Bristow." Schurz suggested to Bowles that they meet in a fortnight to "establish thorough concert of action. I shall by that time have elaborated a complete plan of operations and ought to have your judgment upon it." Soon after the meeting was to be held Schurz began corresponding with Bristow to gauge his interest, though the treasury secretary remained noncommittal. In the same month in which Schurz wrote to Bristow about running for president, Rutherford B. Hayes's private secretary sent Schurz a seventeen-page letter arguing that even though the governor of Ohio was not seeking the presidency, their common positions, such as hard money and reconciliation, made Hayes the exact man for which the liberal republicans were searching.[16]

While Schurz became more optimistic with the growing political commotion as the summer nominating conventions neared, Henry Adams became less sanguine. "Politics too are miserably out of joint," he confided to Gaskell, for

> our organisation has been secretly effected and is ready to act, but is in doubt what it ought to do and although we have unquestionably the power to say that any given man shall be President, we are not able to say that any given man shall be President. Our first scheme was to force my father on the parties. This is now abandoned, and we have descended to the modest plan of pushing one of the regular candidates or splitting the parties by taking one of their leaders. I am no longer confident of doing good and am looking with anxiety to the future. But things are getting beyond my capacity to influence or even measure.

While Adams' despondency might be construed as disappointment due to his father's waning chances at the nomination, in less than three weeks he would

instruct his close associate Henry Cabot Lodge "to lose no opportunity of putting your foot on any revival of the Adams scheme. We are well rid of it. Keep
it out of sight. We can do better by other tactics."[17]

After hearing of the weakening support for his father, Henry discussed with
Schurz his ideas for other tactics and his concerns about trying to force a candidate on one of the existing parties, explaining, "It is clear that your original
scheme must be abandoned. I am not sorry for it. I do not like *coups de main*.
I have no taste for political or any other kind of betting, and for us to attempt
to force ourselves on a party convention, necessarily entails the jockeying of
some-body. It would be the experience of '72 in a new shape, and successful or
not it would do no permanent good but rather permanent harm." He worried
that becoming involved with a party nominating convention would seemingly
condone the corrupt practices of the political parties they were fighting and
thus lose them the moral high ground. If they could not set up their own man,
the next alternative, according to Henry Adams, was "to attack in the flank" by
supporting "the man who comes nearest to our standard. This is Mr. Bristow."
Both Schurz and Adams recognized, however, that the liberal republicans could
do little to directly help Bristow, for they knew he would refuse their nomination and that in any event it would taint him in the eyes of the Republican
Convention meeting that summer in Cincinnati.[18]

The changing circumstances in early 1876 complicated the liberal republicans' plan for a grand meeting to decide on policy and affect the election. After
explaining why their original plans to dictate candidates to the conventions
would not work, Henry Adams suggested a new approach to Schurz. He recommended that Schurz and a few others write a circular letter to about two hundred "weighty and reliable friends" inviting them to meet after the Republican
Convention, "there to decide whether we will support the republican candidate
or nominate a candidate of our own." The goal was both to unite the liberal
republicans and to scare the Republican Convention. If the Republicans nominated someone like Bristow, then the conference would merely confirm their
action, but if the convention selected someone like Blaine, the conference
would nominate its own candidate. Adams described the worst-case scenario:
"We cannot vote the democratic ticket, for that would involve us in the support
of a party organisation which is a hopeless task to reform," he wrote to Schurz.
"But we can start a new party, and are content to bring the democrats into
power as the only means of reorganizing the parties. As I said before, I am
willing to sacrifice my father for such an object, if necessary. He used Van
Buren for a similar purpose in '48." Considering that many historians have
continued to describe the post–Civil War period as a time of entrenched political parties, Henry Adams' expectation of effecting major party reorganization

is significant. The reference to his father "using" Martin Van Buren's nomination as the Free Soil presidential candidate in 1848 to disrupt the existing parties also demonstrates that the environment in which Adams grew up during the mid-nineteenth century conditioned him to expect regular turnover among political parties.[19]

Always ready for a meeting, the loquacious liberal republicans decided to hold a conference before the Republican Convention, with the option of holding another if the Republicans did not nominate someone they found acceptable. The invitations went out in mid-April to several hundred men, inviting them to New York for a "conference to consider what may be done to prevent the National Election of the Centennial year becoming a mere choice of evils." Three of the five signers of the invitation were original liberal republicans— William Cullen Bryant, Horace White, and Carl Schurz—while all correspondence was to be directed to Henry Cabot Lodge, who at that time was essentially a proxy for the Adams family. Schurz explained the purposes of the conference in a private letter to a midwestern newspaper editor, insisting, "It is not confined to the Liberals of 1872," and "It is not intended to assume any attitude hostile to the Republican party, provided that party nominates men of character and ability as through reformers." He also wrote, "There is at present, as far as I can learn, no intention of making independent nominations at the meeting." The liberal republicans followed through on Schurz's plans when approximately two hundred leading reformers—including many liberal republicans—met at the Fifth Avenue Hotel in New York on May 15. After three days of talks the conference issued an "Address to the People" written by Schurz. The Address called for hard money, civil service reform, and reconciliation, repeatedly and explicitly discussing the neglect of these issues as threats to the nation's republican institutions. For instance, in summing up a section on corruption in government, the Address stated, "A corrupt monarchy may last by the rule of force; a corrupt republic cannot endure." Throughout the Address Schurz called for political independence, but suggested that if the Republican Party nominated a suitable candidate, "We shall sincerely rejoice to see the necessity of independent action avoided." Historian John Sproat judged the Fifth Avenue Hotel conference a failure and used it as another opportunity to mock the liberal reformers of the Gilded Age, insisting, because they did not nominate anyone, that "once assembled, the well-intentioned reformers actually did not know what to do." Henry Adams and Schurz, however, had never intended to nominate anyone, and had decided months beforehand to use the conference to pressure the Republican Convention to select a candidate they liked.[20]

Intrigue and plotting dominated the Republican Convention at Cincinnati in June. Two factions of the Republican Party battled over three leading candidates, Roscoe Conkling, Oliver P. Morton, and James G. Blaine, all of whom the liberal republicans despised. The liberal republicans' favorite, Bristow, received little support. The maneuvering took an unexpected turn when one of the Republican factions decided to wreck Blaine's candidacy by supporting the dark horse from Ohio, Governor Rutherford B. Hayes. Though the liberal republicans' preferred candidate was never a factor and they could claim little influence in the nomination of Hayes, at least one of the major spoilsmen had not been chosen. By accident, the Republicans had nominated a candidate with strong ties to the liberal republicans from Cincinnati.[21]

Hayes's nomination in 1876 split the liberal republican movement. Henry Adams saw the nomination as a failure of their efforts to influence the election. "We organized our party, and as usual have been beaten," he confided to Gaskell, for "after our utmost efforts we have only succeeded in barring the road to our opponents and forcing them to nominate as candidate for the Presidency one Hayes of Ohio, a third-rate nonentity whose only recommendation is that he is obnoxious to no one." Adams obviously had expected to effect the reorganization of the Republican and Democratic parties and realized that the Hayes nomination probably preserved the status quo. He bitterly told Gaskell, "I hope to enjoy the satisfaction of voting against him. The only good result of all the past eighteen months of work has been the savage hunting down of powerful scoundrels and the display of the awful corruption of our system." Still in a despondent mood a fortnight later, Adams informed Lodge that "politics have ceased to interest me. I am satisfied that the machine can't be smashed this time. As I feared, we have ourselves saved it by a foolish attempt to run it, which we shall never succeed in." After the seemingly disastrous defeat in 1872, Adams and his family had remained optimistic about changing the party structure and influencing politics, but the nomination of Hayes in 1876 turned them into pessimists.[22]

Carl Schurz, on the other hand, saw Hayes' nomination as an unexpected gift. Though they had not personally met, Schurz had approved enough of Hayes' policies to return from Europe to campaign for him in 1875, and already, months earlier, Hayes had indirectly solicited Schurz's support for his bid to become a presidential candidate. Upon Hayes's nomination Schurz immediately wrote to him, "I regret now more than ever that I did not have the pleasure of becoming personally acquainted with you last fall in the Ohio campaign, but . . . I desire to submit to you some suggestions concerning the contest." Schurz advised Hayes to embrace the liberal republican agenda of civil service reform, administrative reform, hard money, and reconciliation more energetically than did the party platform, in order to secure the independent vote. Two days later Schurz sent another unsolicited letter offering suggestions on campaign strategy. Hayes quickly responded, "I now think as you do—probably precisely as you do, on the civil service reform part of our platform. I want to make that *the* issue of the canvass." He then invited Schurz for his views on the subject, and while meeting in person the next week asked Schurz to write a paragraph for the civil service reform section of his letter of acceptance. Throughout the summer Schurz and Hayes continued to meet and exchange correspondence, much of which indicates that Hayes carefully listened to Schurz and accepted many of his suggestions. While Schurz had already seen Hayes as an acceptable candidate, the flattery of becoming intimate with the Republican presidential nominee certainly helped convince Schurz to support the governor of Ohio. When Charles Francis Adams Jr. wrote in early July about the possibility of holding another meeting of independents, Shurz replied that it would be too difficult, and that after having met Hayes several times, he felt that "unless I am very much mistaken, the [Republican] Cincinnati Convention has nominated our man without knowing it."[23]

The Adams clan did not take kindly to Schurz's endorsement of Hayes. Henry Adams complained to Lodge, "I cannot help laughing to think how, after all our labor and after we had by main force created a party for Schurz to lead, he himself, without a word or a single effort to keep his party together, kicked us over in his haste to jump back to the Republicans. If he had taken the least pains to hold his friends together, I feel sure we could have spoken with effect. . . . I am not angry with him, but of course his leadership is at an end." Adams' assessment was incorrect, however. With the exception of a few, such as the Adamses, David Wells, and Johann Stallo, who drifted toward the Democrats, most of the liberal republicans actively followed Schurz in supporting Hayes, some even enthusiastically. Most of the Ohio liberal republicans, such as Murat Halstead and Jacob Cox, naturally embraced their native son, and according to Schurz, "the man now nearest to him [Hayes] is Stanley Matthews." The liberal republican press, including the irascible Edwin Godkin, also advocated Hayes, and Schurz campaigned aggressively for the Ohio governor. Adams showed his astuteness as an observer when he described how "our principal leader [Schurz] has returned to his party traces" and "can hereafter buy power only by devotion to party." Though many liberal republicans would retain an independent streak and become mugwumps, they remained linked to the Republicans and no longer dreamed of starting a new party.[24]

While Hayes's nomination and election made a few liberal republicans like the Adamses pessimistic and inclined to avoid active politics in the future, for most of them 1876 was an opportunity to rejoin the Republican Party and exert some influence on its direction. To a large extent the party had co-opted the liberal republicans, moving toward their positions and eventually absorbing many of them back into its ranks. Schurz received his reward for supporting Hayes, after liberal republicans such as Halstead successfully lobbied the new president to appoint Schurz secretary of the interior—ironically, the same cabinet position Jacob Cox had held under Grant. Schurz enjoyed a much happier time in the Hayes cabinet than Cox had in Grant's, for the Republican Party began implementing many of the liberal republicans' policies. Hayes was already committed to hard money and made some efforts at civil service reform. Out of the ashes of defeat in 1872, the liberal republicans had finally achieved their objective of influencing the Republican Party in order to reform the nation and preserve its republican institutions.

Conclusion

The liberal republicans had been involved in the "Southern question" for three decades by the time Hayes became president in 1877. After helping to start the Free Soil Party in 1848, many of them had then helped organize the Republican Party in the 1850s. The goal of the liberal republicans in both parties was to end slavery and the Slave Power, both of which they thought endangered the nation's republican institutions. During the Civil War the liberal republicans fought against the Slave Power and for preservation of the Union's republican form of government, while becoming increasingly concerned about the effects of war measures such as a burgeoning civil service, protective tariffs, and Greenbacks. They actively supported Reconstruction for a few years after the war, trying to encourage free labor economies and republican governments in the Southern states. At the same time they began working to end the war measures that they felt threatened the nation's republican institutions. The continued intransigence of white Southerners prevented a quick and peaceable Reconstruction, however. The unsettled issue of Reconstruction both distracted the nation from problems the liberal republicans considered more important and left the Southern state governments in dubious condition. Pragmatically desiring to focus on other issues and still idealistically believing that laws could effect change, they argued that universal amnesty and universal suffrage would be a fair and just solution to Reconstruction for both blacks and whites in the South. The liberal republicans were trying to find a compromise to end Reconstruction so they could concentrate on other issues they thought more threatening to the existence of republican government.

The liberal republican movement met defeat at the Cincinnati Convention, as Horace Greeley's nomination meant that the campaign of 1872 would concentrate on Reconstruction and not the problems the liberal republicans considered more important. The 1872 election also became a fiasco for the Liberal Republican Party that had been created at the Cincinnati Convention. Yet in many respects the failure in 1872 had profound effects. According to Heather Cox Richardson, "The Liberal Republican movement failed, but its ideas flowed back into both the Republican and Democratic parties, creating a shared body of ideas." Whether it was due to their influence or they merely anticipated the political situation, by 1876 both major parties—and particularly the Republicans—had moved closer to the liberal republican positions of 1872. Rutherford B. Hayes embraced civil service reform and hard money, but he is best known for the electoral crisis of 1876 that led to the Compromise of 1877, in which the Republicans agreed to pull out federal troops and end Reconstruction in exchange for securing the presidency.[1]

The liberal republicans' active support of Hayes in 1876 directly tied them to the official end of Reconstruction. Hayes consulted with his kinsman Stanley Matthews on both his inaugural address and his cabinet appointments. The president-elect also asked Carl Schurz for advice on his inaugural address, and the liberal republican leader gave a detailed response. First, Schurz advised Hayes to address the campaign electoral crisis, explaining how its peaceful resolution was "a new proof of the inherent virtue of our republican institutions." The second part, Schurz advised, must discuss the material condition of the country and the importance of resuming specie payments, while the third section should concentrate on the importance of civil service reform. The fourth and final section in Schurz's outline was on "the Southern question," and he considered this "the most important in the inaugural."[2]

Schurz's view of Reconstruction had remained remarkably consistent with the liberal republican attitude ever since Grant's election in 1868. He suggested that Hayes begin his inaugural by alluding to "the inevitable confusion and perplexities which could not but follow a great civil war, and especially a sweeping revolution of the whole labor system of a country; the moral obligations of the National Government to fix the rights of the emancipated slaves and to protect them in the enjoyment of those rights." Then he counseled Hayes to elaborate: "that, while in duty bound and fully determined to protect the rights of all by the employment of every Constitutional power at your disposal, you are sincerely anxious to use every legitimate influence of the administration in favor of honest government in the Southern States." Amazingly, Hayes used several of the suggestions almost word for word, but even having a president speak his thoughts could not make Schurz's desires become reality. Schurz still wanted the seemingly impossible—to protect African Americans in the South without the permanent use of federal force. He concluded his advice by idealistically telling Hayes to "call upon all good citizens in the South to cast aside the prejudice of race and party and to cooperate with you in protecting the rights and promoting the interests of all." The problem was that twelve years of federal occupation had not convinced white Southerners to accept the realities of the Fourteenth and Fifteenth Amendments, and probably little short of military occupation for generations would have dramatically changed conditions and attitudes in the region. Military occupation of the South, however, would have meant the subversion of republican government. The liberal republicans were caught in a dilemma they could not solve, as they wanted republican governments in the South that were fair to both blacks and whites, yet they were not willing to use force indefinitely to create and uphold such governments. Ultimately, the liberal republicans did not know, and after a few years of trying did not particularly care, how to justly and peaceably bring Reconstruction to an end.[3]

Notes

Frequently cited manuscript repositories and government documents are identified in the Notes by the following abbreviations:

CG   *Congressional Globe*

CU   Butler Library, Columbia University
ISHL   Illinois State Historical Library
LC   Library of Congress
MHS   Massachusetts Historical Society

Introduction

1. Harold Francis Williamson, *Edward Atkinson: The Biography of an American Liberal, 1827–1905* (Boston: Old Corner Bookstores, 1934), 8–9; William M. Grosvenor, "The Law of Conquest the True Basis of Reconstruction," *The New Englander* 29 (January 1865): 126; Grosvenor, "The Rights of the Nation, and the Duty of Congress," *The New Englander* 29 (October 1865): 770.

2. Carl Schurz, *Speeches, Correspondence, and Political Papers of Carl Schurz*, Frederic Bancroft, ed. (New York: G. P. Putnam's Sons, 1913), 1:420, 444.

3. *Chicago Tribune*, January 20, 1862.

4. Richard Hofstadter, *The Age of Reform: From Bryan to F.D.R.* (New York: Vintage Books, 1955), 139; Ari Hoogenboom, *Outlawing the Spoils: A History of the Civil Service Reform Movement, 1865–1883* (Urbana: University of Illinois Press, 1961), viii, 33, 39–40, 100.

5. John G. Sproat, *"The Best Men": Liberal Reformers in the Gilded Age* (New York: Oxford University Press, 1968), 43, 281, 76, 277, 85. See William Gillette, *Retreat from Reconstruction, 1869–1879* (Baton Rouge: Louisiana State University Press, 1979), 61; Hoogenboom, *Outlawing the Spoils*, 100, viii; Michael E. McGerr, *The Decline of Popular Politics: The American North, 1865–1928* (New York: Oxford University Press, 1986), 55; Richard H. Abbott, *The Republican Party and the South, 1855–1877: The First Southern Strategy* (Chapel Hill: University of North Carolina Press, 1987), 218; and Mark W. Summers, *Party Games: Getting, Keeping, and Using Power in Gilded Age Politics* (Chapel Hill: University of North Carolina Press, 1987), 285, n. 8. Hoogenboom used the term "Best People" in 1961, but historians have adopted Sproat's 1968 term "Best Men." Neither Hoogenboom nor Sproat show any evidence that these were contemporary terms; Hoogenboom, *Outlawing the Spoils*, 33; Sproat, *"Best Men,"* vii, 7.

6. Hoogenboom, *Outlawing the Spoils*, viii, 50, 33.

7. Hans L. Trefousse, *Carl Schurz: A Biography* (Knoxville: University of Tennessee Press, 1982), 167–68; Schurz, *Speeches, Correspondence*, 1:458; Joseph Logsdon, *Horace White, Nineteenth-Century Liberal* (Westport, Conn.: Greenwood, 1971), 156; William Grosvenor to Edward Atkinson, April 5, 1872, Edward Atkinson Papers, MHS; Jacob D. Cox to William M. Grosvenor, Jacob D. Cox Papers, Oberlin College; Jacob D. Cox to Carl Schurz, April 5, 1872, Carl Schurz Papers, LC. Of the thirty to forty men at the meeting founding the national liberal republican movement on November 22, 1870, I

have been able to determine that in 1872 six supported Greeley while ten supported Grant.

8. Joel Silbey, *The American Political Nation, 1838–1893* (Stanford: Stanford University Press, 1991), 6, 130; William Nisbet Chambers and Walter Dean Burnham, eds., *The American Party Systems: Stages of Political Development* (New York: Oxford University Press, 1967).

9. Michael F. Holt, "Change and Continuity in the Party Period: The Substance and Structure of American Politics, 1835–1885," in *Contesting Democracy: Substance and Structure in American Political History, 1775–2000*, ed. Byron E. Shafer and Anthony J. Badger (Lawrence: University Press of Kansas, 2001), 106.

10. Carl Schurz to Margarethe Meyer Schurz, August 31, 1867, October 12 and 26, 1867, March 29, 1868, in *Intimate Letters of Carl Schurz, 1841–1869*, Joseph Schafer, ed. (Madison: State Historical Society of Wisconsin, 1928), 392, 407, 415, 431; Jacob D. Cox to David A. Wells, April 4, 1872, David A. Wells Papers, LC; Carl Schurz to Edwin Godkin, November 23, 1872, in Schurz, *Speeches, Correspondence*, 2:448. Richard Franklin Bensel has recently reinforced the idea of ethnocultural issues as the driving force in elections by arguing that party agents, not political ideologies, were pivotal in determining mid-nineteenth-century voting behaviors and election outcomes; see Bensel, *The American Ballot Box in the Mid-Nineteenth Century* (New York: Cambridge University Press, 2004).

11. Jean Harvey Baker, "Politics, Paradigms, and Public Culture," *Journal of American History* 84 (December 1997): 895; Mark Voss-Hubbard, "The 'Third Party Tradition' Reconsidered: Third Parties and American Public Life, 1830–1900," *Journal of American History* 86 (June 1999): 122.

12. Mark Voss-Hubbard, *Beyond Party: Cultures of Antipartisanship in Northern Politics Before the Civil War* (Baltimore: John Hopkins University Press, 2002), x, ix; Heather Cox Richardson, *The Death of Reconstruction: Race, Labor and Politics in the Post–Civil War North, 1865–1901* (Cambridge, Mass.: Harvard University Press, 2001), xii; Nancy Cohen, *The Reconstruction of American Liberalism, 1865–1914* (Chapel Hill: University of North Carolina Press, 2002), 11, 6.

13. Richardson, *Death of Reconstruction*, 276, 119; Cohen, *Reconstruction of American Liberalism*, 122. The discussion of the Liberal Republicans in David Herbert Donald et al., *The Civil War and Reconstruction* (New York: W. W. Norton, 2001), 617–21, is an anomaly, for it cites Sproat's *"Best Men"* as one of the few recommended readings for the period, but considers the election of 1872 a turning point in Reconstruction and the Liberal Republicans an important political force.

14. Gillette, *Retreat from Reconstruction*, 61; Sproat, *"Best Men,"* 80; Earle D. Ross, *The Liberal Republican Movement* (New York: AMS Press, 1919); Eric Foner, *Reconstruction: America's Unfinished Revolution, 1863–1877* (New York: Harper and Row, 1988); Robert W. Burg, "Amnesty, Civil Rights, and the Meaning of Liberal Republicanism, 1862–1872," *American Nineteenth-Century History* 4 (Fall 2003): 50.

15. *Cincinnati Commercial*, October 2, 1872.

16. Following Holt's suggestion in an earlier version of this project I changed all pre-1868 liberal republican references to either "future liberal republican" or "proto-liberal republican." As the scope of the project expanded more into the antebellum, Civil War, and early Reconstruction periods, though, it became increasingly awkward to use such phrases and I finally decided to use the term liberal republican throughout the work to increase readability.

17. Jacqueline Balk Tusa, "Power, Priorities, and Political Insurgency: The Liberal Republican Movement, 1869–1872," Ph.D. diss. (Pennsylvania State University, 1970), 78; Sproat, *"The Best Men,"* 7–8; Matthew T. Downey, "The Rebirth of Reform: A Study of Liberal Reform Movements, 1865–872," Ph.D. diss. (Princeton University, 1963), iv; Wil-

liam Gillette, "Election of 1872," in *History of American Presidential Elections, 1789–1968*, Arthur M. Schlesinger Jr., ed. (New York: Chelsea House, 1971), 2:1304. Robert W. Burg's article, "Amnesty, Civil Rights, and the Meaning of Liberal Republicanism, 1862–1872," starts during the Civil War but concentrates on the issue of amnesty until the late 1860s, not the background of liberal republicans. All but one of the monographs on the liberal republican movement begins with the end of the Civil War or Grant's becoming president in 1868; the exception is Wilbert Harrell Ahren's "Laissez Faire versus Equal Rights: Liberal Republicanism and the Negro, 1861–1877," Ph.D. diss. (Northwestern University, 1968). Since the only published monograph on the liberal republican movement is Earle Ross's *Liberal Republican Movement*, studies of the Gilded Age, such as Hoogenboom's *Outlawing the Spoils*, Sproat's *"Best Men,"* Michael E. McGerr's *The Decline of Popular Politics: The American North, 1865–1928* (New York: Oxford University Press, 1986), and David M. Tucker's *Mugwumps: Public Moralists of the Gilded Age* (Columbia: University of Missouri Press, 1998), have become the most influential work on the liberal republicans. Even works concentrating on Reconstruction tend to ignore the liberal republicans' political background and link them to Gilded Age politics. For example, in discussing the liberal republican movement Eric Foner contends that "with the decline of Radicalism, the ascendancy of organizational politics, and the emergence of liberal reform, party alignments now centered on attitudes toward Grant himself and the new politics of the Gilded Age" (Foner, *Reconstruction: America's Unfinished Revolution,* 499). One of the classic works on Gilded Age liberalism is Robert Kelly's *The Transatlantic Persuasion: The Liberal Mind in the Age of Gladstone* (New York: Knopf, 1969).

18. Foner, *Reconstruction*, 493. For more descriptions of civil service reform as a weapon to gain power see Hoogenboom, *Outlawing the Spoils*, ix, and Sproat, *"The Best Men,"* 259. For examples of the liberal republicans labeled as "insurgents," see Sproat, *"Best Men,"* 78; Hoogenboom, *Outlawing the Spoils*, 80; Tusa, "Power, Priorities, and Political Insurgency," 78. For examples of the portrayal of liberal republicans as elitists or inept politicians see Sproat, *"Best Men,"* 277–78, and Gillette, *Retreat from Reconstruction,* 61–62. Michael F. Holt argues that the Civil War era in which the liberal republicans lived was a period of considerable plasticity, where party realignment was a real possibility (Holt, "Change and Continuity in the Party Period," 93–116). For a good discussion of the historiography of the party system see Silbey, *American Political Nation,* 1–10, 125–40.

19. Robert E. Shalhope, "Toward a Republican Synthesis: The Emergence of an Understanding of Republicanism in American Historiography," *William and Mary Quarterly* 29 (January 1972): 72; Daniel T. Rodgers, "Republicanism: The Career of a Concept," *Journal of American History* 79 (June 1992): 38, 29; Bernard Bailyn, *The Ideological Origins of the American Revolution* (Cambridge, Mass.: Harvard University Press, 1967); J. G. A. Pocock, *The Machiavellian Moment: Florentine Political Thought and the Atlantic Republican Tradition* (Princeton: Princeton University Press, 1975). Gordon S. Wood authored a book in the late 1960s concerning republicanism that was just as influential as Bailyn's and Pocock's books; see *The Creation of the American Republic, 1776–1787* (Chapel Hill: University of North Carolina Press, 1969).

20. Jean Baker, "From Belief into Culture: Republicanism in the Antebellum North," *American Quarterly* 37 (Fall 1985): 534–35; William E. Gienapp, *The Origins of the Republican Party, 1852–1856* (New York: Oxford University Press, 1987), 4; Rodgers, "Republicanism," 38, 29. There is extensive literature on the liberalism and republicanism debate. Among the most important works are Rodger's "Republicanism"; Joyce Appleby, ed., "Republicanism in the History and Historiography of the United States," special issue, *American Quarterly* 37 (Fall 1985); Robert E. Shalhope, "Republicanism and Early American Historiography," *William and Mary Quarterly* 34 (April 1982); and J. G. A. Pocock,

"Between Gog and Magog: The Republican Thesis and the Ideologia Americana," *Journal of the History of Ideas* 48 (April–June 1987).

21. For examples of college letters, see Carl Schurz to Theodore Petrasch, April 3, 1847, in *Intimate Letters*, 37, and Henry Adams to Charles Francis Adams Jr., November 3, 1858, Adams Family Papers, MHS. Fred Bunyan Joyner, *David Wells: Champion of Free Trade* (Cedar Rapids, Iowa: Torch Press, 1939), 11.

22. Mark M. Krug, *Lyman Trumbull, Conservative Radical* (New York: A. S. Barnes and Company, 1965), 22.

23. Joyner, *David Wells*, 21–22; Carl Schurz to Gottfried Kindel, December 1, 1856, in Schurz, *Speeches, Correspondence*, 1:27–28; Henry Adams to Charles Francis Adams Jr., November 25, 1864, Adams Family Papers, MHS.

24. Henry Adams to Abigail Brooks Adams, May 22, 1850, Adams Family Papers, MHS.

1. Rehearsal in Missouri for the Liberal Republican Movement, 1865–1870

1. *CG*, 41st Cong., 3rd sess., 118–19; Mahlon Sands to Carl Schurz, November 10, 1870, Carl Schurz Papers, LC. The nomenclature of Missouri politics is confusing. The Republican Party was also known as the *Radical Party* in Missouri. Schurz's bolters called themselves *Liberals* or *Liberal Republicans*. The other Republicans were known as *Regular Republicans* or *Radical Republicans*. Another problem is the term *revenue reformer*, which many free traders used to refer to themselves. Revenue reformers wanted to use tariffs for revenue instead of protection and only gradually eliminate them, while free traders demanded an immediate end to all tariffs. Many revenue reformers, however, were in reality free traders who did not want to upset voters by appearing too radical, even though the majority of the electorate did not make any distinction between the two classifications. Since *free trader* describes their ultimate goal better than *revenue reformer*, I use the term *free trader*. In addition, the term *revenue reform* could be construed to encompass specie resumption, which was another goal of the liberal republicans, though they were clear in private correspondence and public discourse that their primary economic goal was tariff reduction. When liberal republicans spoke of revenue reform they were almost certainly referring to tariff policy. For instance, Carl Schurz regularly referred to the Free Trade League as revenue reformers, showing that he was using the term primarily in connection with tariff reform, not specie resumption.

2. Missouri politics before 1870, unfortunately, has not been integrated into an analysis of the liberal republican movement. Thomas Barclay and William E. Parrish have written monographs on Missouri politics after the Civil War, but both end with the victory of the Liberals in 1870, and the national liberal republican movement thus falls outside the scope of their works; see Thomas S. Barclay, *The Liberal Republican Movement in Missouri, 1865–1871* (Columbia: State Historical Society of Missouri, 1926) and William E. Parrish, *Missouri under Radical Rule, 1865–1870* (Columbia: University of Missouri Press, 1965). Historians specifically studying the liberal republican movement, meanwhile, have rushed past Missouri to reach the national phase of liberal republicanism. In Earle D. Ross's classic work, *The Liberal Republican Movement* (New York: AMS, 1919), the author acknowledges that "it was in Missouri . . . that factional strife led most directly to a national Liberal movement," and then spends one paragraph covering Missouri from 1865 to 1870 (28–29; 64–65). In subsequent studies Missouri has suffered a similar lack of attention, being considered only from the time of the bolt in 1870. Failure to examine Missouri in depth before the liberal republican movement became national in 1870 has led to numerous interpretive mistakes. The first is not recognizing the emergence of liberal republicanism before Grant took office and thus considering it only an anti-Grant movement. The second mistake is not defining accurately the membership

of the liberal republican movement, since political events in Missouri led to the first national meeting of the liberal republicans. Jacqueline Balk Tusa is one of the few historians who contends that the Missouri Liberal Republican bolt of 1870 did not represent "a 'microcosm' of national party discontent," or "convince reformers of the effect of direct political action." She begins her study with the election of Grant and relegates Missouri to a middle chapter, "Republican State Politics: The Erosion of Loyalties," even though she states in a footnote that "the new movement was inaugurated at the free trade caucus in New York, in November, 1870," immediately after the Missouri bolt. See Tusa, "Power, Priorities, and Political Insurgency: The Liberal Republican Movement, 1869–1872," Ph.D. diss. (Pennsylvania State University, 1970), vi–vii, 157 n. 9. Ironically, a year earlier, in an essay entitled "The Origins of Border State Liberal Republicanism," Tusa and Ari Hoogenboom contended that "in the border states the Liberal Republican movement was rooted not in the months immediately preceding 1872 but in the political turmoil which began with the election of 1860." The essay, though, stops at 1869, once again not integrating pre-1870 Missouri with the national liberal republican movement. See Tusa and Hoogenboom, "The Origins of Border State Liberal Republicanism," in *Radicalism, Racism, and Party Realignment: The Border States during Reconstruction*, ed. Richard O. Curry (Baltimore: John Hopkins University Press, 1969), 221.

3. Michael Fellman, *Inside War: The Guerrilla Conflict in Missouri during the American Civil War* (New York: Oxford University Press, 1989), 10; Norma L. Peterson, *Freedom and Franchise: The Political Career of B. Gratz Brown* (Columbia: University of Missouri Press, 1965), 161–62; James McPherson, *Battle Cry of Freedom: The Civil War Era* (New York: Ballantine Books, 1988), 290–92.

4. Parrish, *Missouri under Radical Rule*, 2–14.

5. Parrish, *Missouri under Radical Rule*, 25–27; Barclay, *Liberal Republican Movement in Missouri*, 13–19.

6. Parrish, *Missouri under Radical Rule*, 46–7, 20, 41–2, 29–30; Peterson, *Career of Brown*, 146–47.

7. Norma L. Peterson, "The Political Fluctuations of B. Gratz Brown: Politics in a Border State, 1850–1870," *Missouri Historical Review* 51 (October 1956), 30; Peterson, *Career of Brown*, 7.

8. Peterson, *Career of Brown*, 146–47, 150; Brown, in *Missouri Democrat*, April 28, 1865, quoted in Parrish, *Missouri under Radical Rule*, 38–9, 48; Barclay, *Liberal Republican Movement in Missouri*, 32–33.

9. Brown quoted in Peterson, *Career of Brown*, 152–54, 159–60; *Missouri Democrat*, September 27, 1865; Parrish, *Missouri under Radical Rule*, 66–72, 85; Brown quoted in *CG*, 39th Cong., 1st sess., 3450; Brown quoted in *Missouri Democrat*, July 2, 1866.

10. Barclay, *Liberal Republican Movement in Missouri*, 109–10; Peterson, *Career of Brown*, 161–63; Parrish, *Missouri under Radical Rule*, 100–1; *Missouri Republican*, December 1, 1866, quoted in Barclay, *Liberal Republican Movement in Missouri*, 110.

11. Enos Clarke to William A. Crane, August 19, 1916, William M. Grosvenor Papers, CU; Whitelaw Reid to Horace Greeley, March, 1872, Horace Greeley Papers, LC; Bingham Duncan, *Whitelaw Reid: Journalist, Politician, Diplomat* (Athens: University of Georgia Press, 1975), 72, 115.

12. Brown in *Missouri Democrat*, August 29, 1863 in Peterson, *Career of Brown*, 125, 140; Grosvenor, "The Law of Conquest the True Basis of Reconstruction," *New Englander* 29 (January 1865): 126; Grosvenor, "The Rights of the Nation and the Duty of Congress," *New Englander* 29 (October 1865): 767. See also Peterson, *Career of Brown*, 161–63; Barclay, *Liberal Republican Movement in Missouri*, 111; Parrish, *Missouri under Radical Rule*, 100–1; Peterson, "Political Fluctuations," 30. Peterson argues that Brown's abolitionism and later support of black suffrage were politically motivated, since before 1860 his antislavery speeches attacked the economic aspects of slavery and ignored the

humanitarian and moral objections. She contends that "for the most part Brown's actions were based on the expediency of the moment" and draws parallels between Brown's and Abraham Lincoln's positions on slavery before and during the Civil War.

13. Brown in *Missouri Democrat*, August 29, 1863, quoted in Peterson, *Career of Brown*, 125; Grosvenor, "Law of Conquest," 125, 127; Grosvenor, "Rights of the Nation," 756, 771.

14. Hans L. Trefousse, *Carl Schurz: A Biography* (New York: Fordham University Press, 1998), 96, 200, 299; Barbara Donner, "Carl Schurz as an Office Seeker," *Wisconsin Magazine of History* 20 (December 1936): 572–98.

15. *Speeches, Correspondence, and Political Papers of Carl Schurz*, Frederick Bancroft, ed. (New York: G. P. Putnam's Sons, 1913), 1:379, 378, 380, 288.

16. Schurz, *Speeches, Correspondence*, 1:379, 378, 380, 288, 318, 365; Carl Schurz, "The True Problem," *Atlantic Monthly* 19 (March 1867): 373; Trefousse, *Carl Schurz*, 154–62. Michael Les Benedict demonstrates that a conservative interpretation of the Constitution regarding federal-state relations constrained the efforts of many Republicans, and particularly Carl Schurz, with regard to Reconstruction; see Benedict, "Preserving the Constitution: The Conservative Basis of Radical Reconstruction," *Journal of American History* 61 (December 1974), 8.

17. Trefousse, *Carl Schurz*, 162–63, 167–68; Parrish, *Missouri under Radical Rule*, 230–31, 234–35.

18. Parrish, *Missouri under Radical Rule*, 241–42, 252–53; Charles Drake in *Missouri Democrat*, September 11, 1863, quoted in Parrish, *Missouri under Radical Rule*, 253–54.

19. Schurz, *Speeches, Correspondence*, 1:442, 422; *Address of the Radicals of Saint Louis to the People of Missouri* (Saint Louis: Missouri Democrat Book and Job Office, 1868), 7.

20. Parrish, *Missouri under Radical Rule*, 258–67; Enos Clarke to William A. Crane, August 19, 1916, Grosvenor Papers, CU.

21. Parrish, *Missouri under Radical Rule*, 258–67; Carl Schurz to Margarethe Schurz, January 10, 1869, in *Intimate Letters of Carl Schurz, 1841–1869*, Joseph Schafer, ed. (Madison: State Historical Society of Wisconsin, 1928), 462; *The Reminiscences of Carl Schurz* (New York: McClure, 1908), 3:296; Trefousse, *Carl Schurz*, 170–74; Barclay, *Liberal Republican Movement in Missouri*, 150–62.

22. Parrish, *Missouri under Radical Rule*, 271–72, 278; *Missouri Democrat*, March 1, 1869, June 5, 1869, quoted in Parrish, *Missouri under Radical Rule*, 278; *Westliche Post*, June 17, 1869, and the *Missouri Statesman*, July 16, 1869, quoted in Barclay, *Liberal Republican Movement in Missouri*, 173–74.

23. Marc Egnal, "The Beards Were Right: Parties in the North, 1840–1860," *Civil War History* 47 (April 2001), 55; *Missouri Democrat*, February 9, 1869, June 2, 1870; William M. Grosvenor, *Does Protection Protect? An Examination of the Effect of Different Forms of Tariff upon American Industry* (New York: D. Appleton, 1871); Carl Schurz to William Grosvenor, November 30, 1869, Grosvenor Papers, CU.

24. Parrish, *Missouri under Radical Rule*, 286–87; Trefousse, *Carl Schurz*, 182–83; Carl Schurz to James Taussig, April 18, 1869, in Schurz, *Speeches, Correspondence*, 1:483; Schurz, in *CG*, 41st Cong., 2nd sess., 237.

25. Parrish, *Missouri under Radical Rule*, 280–81, 286; Barclay, *Liberal Republican Movement in Missouri*, 204; *Missouri Democrat*, June 1, 1870.

26. Parrish, *Missouri under Radical Rule*, 286–89; *Missouri Democrat*, April 13 and 14, 1870, June 10, 1870. The delegate controversy was over how to determine representation for blacks. Every 150 Radical voters in a district were represented by one delegate, with a minimum of 50 voters to secure a delegate. Blacks were to have their own delegates at the convention, but the low number of black voters in the border districts meant that if they were held to the same minimum requirement of 50 voters for a delegate, they would be underrepresented. The Radicals demanded that any number of blacks in a district

deserved a delegate—a policy that would have both overrepresented blacks and increased the Radicals' strength at the convention, since their support came from the border districts. The Liberals argued that the rules for black delegates should be the same as for white delegates. For a full discussion of the apportionment issue see Parrish, *Missouri under Radical Rule*, 289–91, and Barclay, *Liberal Republican Movement in Missouri*, 213–16.

27. Parrish, *Missouri under Radical Rule*, 282–86; *Peoples' Weekly Tribune*, February 23, 1870, in Parrish, *Missouri under Radical Rule*, 284; Barclay, *Liberal Republican Movement in Missouri*, 229–30.

28. *Missouri Democrat*, September 3, 1870; Parrish, *Missouri under Radical Rule*, 292–97; Barclay, *Liberal Republican Movement in Missouri*, 233–46. One member of the platform committee did submit a third resolution that tried to avoid the subject of the amendments altogether, but the convention ignored it.

29. The first plank of the platform read, "That these are the vital principles of the Republican Party: That no citizen shall be deprived of his just share in the government which he helps to support for the benefit of others, and that no man shall be deprived of his earnings of his labor, or any part thereof, for the benefit of any other man." *Missouri Democrat*, September 4, 5, and 6, 1870; Parrish, *Missouri under Radical Rule*, 297–98; Barclay, *Liberal Republican Movement in Missouri*, 248.

30. Parrish, *Missouri under Radical Rule*, 304–9; Barclay, *Liberal Republican Movement in Missouri*, 255, 265; Trefousse, *Carl Schurz*, 191; Carl Schurz to David A. Wells, October 9, 1870, David A. Wells Papers, LC; "Address to the People of Missouri," *Missouri Democrat*, September 10, 1870; *Missouri Democrat*, September 11, 1870; Schurz, *Speeches, Correspondence*, 1:520.

31. Joanne Hartogs Reitano, "Free Trade in the Gilded Age: 1865–1895," Ph.D. diss. (New York University, 1974), 82–83, 114–15; Parrish, *Missouri under Radical Rule*, 69; Charles Nordhoff to William M. Grosvenor, March 5, 1870, Grosvenor Papers, CU; Carl Schurz to David A. Wells, October 9, 1870, Wells Papers, LC; *The Nation*, April 28, May, 1870; Henry Adams to Carl Schurz, October 27, 1870, Adams Family Papers, MHS.

32. *New York Tribune*, September 6 and 7, 1870; Charles Nordhoff to William M. Grosvenor, October 3, 1870, Grosvenor Papers, CU; *Chicago Tribune*, August 24, 1870, September 5, 1870; *Cincinnati Commercial*, September 9, 1870; *The Nation*, September 8 and 29, 1870; Parrish, *Missouri under Radical Rule*, 308.

33. "Address to the People of Missouri," *Missouri Democrat*, September 10, 1870; *Missouri Democrat*, October 10, 1870, November 4, 1870.

34. *Missouri Democrat*, November 4, 1870; Bernard Baylin, *The Ideological Origins of the American Revolution* (Cambridge, Mass.: Harvard University Press, 1967); John Palmer, quoted in Andrew L. Slap, "'The Strong Arm of the Military Power of the United States': The Chicago Fire, the Constitution, and Reconstruction," *Civil War History* 47 (June 2001): 149.

35. "Address to the People of Missouri," in the *Missouri Democrat*, September 10, 1870; *Missouri Democrat*, October 10, 1870, November 4, 1870. For more examples see *Missouri Democrat*, September 22, 1870, October 23 and 28, 1870, November 1, 1870; Parrish, *Missouri under Radical Rule*, 308–9; Barclay, *Liberal Republican Movement in Missouri*, 264–65.

36. *Missouri Democrat*, November 1, 1872; "Address to the People of Missouri," in the *Missouri Democrat*, September 10, 1870; Parrish, *Missouri under Radical Rule*, 305–7.

37. Barclay, *Liberal Republican Movement in Missouri*, 265, 269–70; Parrish, *Missouri under Radical Rule*, 309–14; Barclay, *Liberal Republican Movement in Missouri*, 270–73; *Missouri Democrat*, November 15, 1870; Carl Schurz to William Grosvenor, December 13, 1870, Schurz Papers, LC; B. Gratz Brown to Carl Schurz, November 26, 1870, in *Speeches, Correspondence*, 1:521; *CG*, 41st Cong., 3rd sess., 126; Carl Schurz to William M. Gros-

venor, January 1871, Schurz Papers, LC; *Missouri Statesman*, December 2, 1870, quoted in Parrish, *Missouri under Radical Rule*, 312.

38. Barclay, *Liberal Republican Movement in Missouri*, 273; Parrish, *Missouri under Radical Rule*, 313–14; *CG*, 41st Cong., 3rd sess., 128; *The Nation*, December 15, 1870; *Cincinnati Commercial*, December 16, 1870; *Springfield Weekly Republican*, December 2, 1870.

39. Mahlon Sands to Carl Schurz, November 10, 1870, Charles Nordhoff to Carl Schurz, December 21, 1870, Schurz Papers, LC; Mahlon Sands to William M. Grosvenor, November 5, 1870, Horace White to William M. Grosvenor, November 9, 1870, Grosvenor Papers, CU. Henry Adams reported "twenty or more present" at the meeting while Edwin Godkin said "there were about forty present." See Henry Adams to Jacob D. Cox, 28 November, 1870, Adams Papers, MHS, and Edwin L. Godkin to Fanny Godkin, December 1, 1870, in *Life and Letters of Edwin Lawrence Godkin*, Rollo Ogden, ed. (New York: Macmillan, 1907), 2:100.

40. Henry Adams to Jacob D. Cox, 28 November, 1870, Adams Family Papers, MHS; Edwin L. Godkin to Fanny Godkin, December 1, 1870, in Godkin, *Life and Letters*, 2:100; Jacob D. Cox to Charles Nordhoff, December 3, 1870, Jacob D. Cox to Carl Schurz, December 27, 1870, Schurz Papers, LC; Carl Schurz to Jacob D. Cox, February 3, 1871, in Schurz, *Speeches, Correspondence*, 2:176–77; Charles Nordhoff to Carl Schurz, December 21, 1870, Schurz Papers, LC.

41. See correspondence among participants, such as Mahlon Sands to William M. Grosvenor, February 20, 1871, Grosvenor Papers, CU; William Grosvenor to Edward Atkinson, December 12, 1871, Edward Atkinson to William Grosvenor, December 26, 1871, Atkinson Papers, MHS. Ross and Tusa are primarily interested in the political implications of liberal republicanism and, working backward from the Cincinnati Convention in May 1872, consider all members of the Liberal Republican Party to be liberal republicans. Historians such as Downey, Sproat, and Gerber, on the other hand, are primarily interested in the intellectual aspects of liberal republicanism and acknowledge the difference between the movement and the party, but conclude that "the liberal reform program was almost fully developed by 1869." Both historiographical schools dismiss the importance of Missouri and thus misconstrue the meaning of the movement. See Ross, *Liberal Republican Movement*; Tusa, "Power, Priorities, and Political Insurgency"; Gerber, "Liberal Republican Alliance"; Sproat, *"The Best Men"*; Downey, "The Rebirth of Reform," iv.

42. Carl Schurz to Horace Greeley, May 6, 11, and 18, 1872, in Schurz, *Speeches, Correspondence*, 2:361–62, 370–77; Carl Schurz to Whitelaw Reid, May 20, 1872, Whitelaw Reid Papers, LC; *Springfield Republican*, May 10, 1872; Charles Francis Adams Jr. in *Cincinnati Commercial*, October 2, 1872.

2. The Liberal Republican Conception of Party, 1848–1872

1. *Springfield Weekly Republican*, February 29, 1868; *Springfield Republican*, April 23, 1872.

2. The nine liberal republicans with Free Soil lineage are Charles Francis Adams, Edward Atkinson, Jacob Brinkerhoff, William Cullen Bryant, George Hoadly, Stanley Matthews, Horace White, David Dudley Field, and Don Piatt. The three liberal republicans active in politics in 1848 but not Free Soilers are Lyman Trumbull and Johann B. Stallo, both Democrats, and Samuel Bowles, a Whig. All thirteen of the liberal republicans whose political activity in 1856 is discernible were Republicans. Many of the liberal republicans active in politics during the late 1840s and early 1850s started their political lives as Democrats, joining the Republican Party directly in the mid-1850s or first passing through the Free Soil Party. The experiences of the former Democratic liberal republicans do not mesh with Eric Foner's generally bleak assessment of Democratic-Republicans, as he reduces them to the Blairs and blames them for the worst in the

Republican Party. In 1970, Foner argued that "during the 1850s, the former Democrats took the lead in racist appeals. They represented in the most extreme degree the racism from which no portion of the Republican party could claim total freedom." Almost two decades later he reiterated that "Democratic-Republicans . . . as a group, had always been the most racist element in the Republican coalition." Foner also dismissed many Democratic-Republicans' strict construction of the Constitution, insisting that some "had a penchant for reducing complex political questions to matters of supposedly 'plain and simple' constitutional interpretation." Examining the political careers of liberal republicans with Democratic origins at least partially redeems the reputation of the Democrats who came into the Republican Party. See Foner, *Free Soil, Free Labor, Free Men: The Ideology of the Republican Party Before the Civil War* (New York: Oxford University Press, 1970), 150, 267, and Foner, *Reconstruction: America's Unfinished Revolution, 1863–1877* (New York: Harper and Row, 1988), 218–19.

3. Joel Silbey, *The American Political Nation, 1838–1893* (Stanford: Stanford University Press, 1991), 126.

4. Foner, *Free Soil,* 151.

5. Charles H. Brown, *William Cullen Bryant* (New York: Scribner's, 1971), 330–31, 339–40; Martin Duberman, *Charles Francis Adams, 1807–1886* (Stanford: Stanford University Press, 1960), 124, 122; Stephen E. Maizlish, *The Triumph of Sectionalism: The Transformation of Ohio Politics, 1844–1856* (Kent, Ohio: Kent State University Press, 1983), 73–74, 78; John Niven, *Salmon P. Chase, A Biography* (New York: Oxford University Press, 1995), 100–4.

6. Brinkerhoff, quoted in Maizlish, *Triumph of Sectionalism,* 104; Duberman, *Adams,* 111, 113, 134; William Cullen Bryant to John Howard Bryant, February 7, 1848, in *The Letters of William Cullen Bryant,* ed. William Cullen Bryant II and Thomas G. Voss (New York: Fordam University Press, 1975–92), 2:516–17.

7. Brown, *Bryant,* 340–42; Kinley J. Brauer, *Cotton versus Conscience: Massachusetts Whig Politics and Southwestern Expansion, 1843–1848* (Lexington: University of Kentucky Press, 1967), 230–31, 237; Duberman, *Adams,* 138.

8. Niven, *Chase,* 105–7; Maizlish, *Triumph of Sectionalism,* 104. For a comprehensive discussion of events in May and June 1848 leading to the Buffalo Convention see Joseph G. Rayback, *Free Soil: The Election of 1848* (Lexington: University of Kentucky Press, 1970), 186–217.

9. Oliver Dyer, *Phonographic Report of the Proceedings of the National Free Soil Convention at Buffalo, N.Y.* (Buffalo, New York: G. H. Derby, 1848), 7, 19. For the best discussion of "the Slave Power," see Leonard L. Richards, *The Slave Power: The Free North and Southern Domination, 1780–1860* (Baton Rouge: Louisiana State University Press, 2000).

10. Dyer, *Free Soil Convention,* 7–8, 26–27, 19; Duberman, *Adams,* 133.

11. Michael F. Holt, *The Rise and Fall of the American Whig Party: Jacksonian Politics and the Onset of the Civil War* (New York: Oxford University Press, 1999), 28–31; Mark Voss-Hubbard, "The 'Third Party Tradition' Reconsidered: Third Parties and American Public Life, 1830–1900," *Journal of American History* 84 (December 1997): 129, 132; Mark W. Summers, *The Plundering Generation: Corruption and the Crisis of the Union, 1849–1861* (New York: Oxford University Press, 1987), 303.

12. Duberman, *Adams* 147, 133; Rayback, *Free Soil,* 223, 225–26; Dyer, *Free Soil Convention,* 19–20; *Proceedings of the Liberal Republican Convention* (New York: Baker and Godwin, 1872), 19–20.

13. Rayback, *Free Soil,* 281; Duberman, *Adams,* 157–58; Bryant, quoted in John Mayfield, *Rehearsal for Republicanism: Free Soil and the Politics of Antislavery* (Port Washington, N. Y.: Kennikat Press, 1980), 141, 190.

14. Henrik Boomraem V, *The Formation of the Republican Party in New York: Politics and Conscience in the Antebellum North* (New York: New York University Press, 1983), 14; *New York Evening Post*, March 14, 1850; Duberman, *Adams*, 179; Maizlish, *Triumph of Sectionalism*, 149, 155; Rayback, *Free Soil*, 310.

15. George W. Julian, *Political Recollections, 1840 to 1872* (Chicago: Jansen, McClurg and Company, 1884), 337; Edward Atkinson to Ned Wild, December 27, 1848, Edward Atkinson Papers, MHS. The Free Soil origins of many delegates at the Cincinnati Convention is discussed in Matthew T. Downey, "Horace Greeley and the Politicians: The Liberal Republican Convention in 1872," *Journal of American History* 54 (March 1967):730–31.

16. Michael F. Holt, *The Political Crisis of the 1850s* (New York: John Wiley and Sons, 1978), 170.

17. Eugene David Schmiel, "The Career of Jacob Dolson Cox, 1828–1900: Soldier, Scholar, Statesman," Ph.D. diss. (Ohio State University, 1969), 38–41; George S. Merriam, *The Life and Times of Samuel Bowles* (New York: Century Co., 1885), 1:80, 95; Foner, *Free Soil*, 19, 205–6; Holt, *American Whig Party*, 348–49.

18. Duberman, *Adams*, 197–98; Charles Francis Adams diary, November 14 and 24, 1854, Adams Family Papers, MHS; William E. Gienapp, *Origins of the Republican Party, 1852–1856* (New York: Oxford University Press, 1987); John G. Sproat, *"The Best Men": Liberal Reformers in the Gilded Age* (New York: Oxford University Press, 1968), 230–31, 250–51.

19. Duberman, *Adams*, 173, 188; Edward Atkinson to Ned Pluebrick, February 25, 1850, Subscription List for Kansas, 1856, Edward Atkinson Papers, MHS; Williamson, *Atkinson*, 4; Logsdon, *White*, 28–31; Foner, *Free Soil*, 104, 113–14.

20. Trumbull, in appendix to *CG*, 34th Congress, 1st sess., 861; Daun van Ee, "David Dudley Field and the Reconstruction of the Law," Ph.D diss. (The Johns Hopkins University, 1974), 131; William Cullen Bryant to John Howard Bryant, February 15, 1856, in Bryant, *Letters*, 3:379; Murat Halstead, *Trimmers, Trucklers, and Temporizers: Notes of Murat Halstead from the Political Conventions of 1856* (Madison: State Historical Society of Wisconsin, 1961).

21. Foner, *Free Soil*, 168, 180, 145; Charles Francis Adams, *The Republican Party a Necessity: Speech of Charles Francis Adams of Massachusetts* (Washington, D.C., 1860), 2–3; Schurz, *Speeches, Correspondence*, 1:132. Earlier in this chapter I argued that Foner paints a bleak picture of Democratic-Republicans on racial issues and that this view needs some revision. I agree much more with Foner's view of the Democratic-Republicans' attitudes toward economic policy, the Constitution, and federal power.

22. Schurz, *Speeches, Correspondence*, 1:65–67; Adams, *Republican Party*, 3, 6.

23. Carl Schurz to Edward L. Pierce, April 30, 1859, in Schurz, *Speeches, Correspondence*, 1:74, 131; Ee, "Field," 134–35; Summers, *Plundering Generation*, 269; William Cullen Bryant to Edwin D. Morgan, April 11, 1860, in Bryant, *Letters*, 4:146.

24. William Cullen Bryant to John Bigelow, February 20, 1860, in Bryant, *Letters*, 4:140.

25. David M. Potter, *The Impending Crisis, 1848–1861*, Don E. Fehrenbacher, ed. (New York: Harper and Row, 1976), 491, 523–26; Duberman, *Adams*, 227–29; Congressman from Arkansas quoted in Duberman, *Adams*, 228; Henry Adams to Charles Francis Adams Jr., December 13, 1860, Adams Family Papers, MHS.

For many historians the Republican victory in 1860 initiated the stabilization phase of the third, or Civil War, party system. Joel Silbey argues that the election completed party realignment, and that "by 1860 the electorate had become locked in"; Dale Baum agrees with this view. See Joel H. Silbey, *A Respectable Minority: The Democratic Party in the Civil War Era, 1860–1868* (New York: W. W. Norton, 1997), 157, and Dale Baum, *The Civil War Party System: The Case of Massachusetts, 1848–1876* (Chapel Hill: University of

North Carolina Press, 1984). Richard L. McCormick sees the Civil War as establishing Republican hegemony for the rest of the nineteenth century, asserting that during the war "leaders instilled in their supporters a lifelong passion for Republicanism"; Richard L. McCormick, *The Party Period and Public Policy: American Politics from the Age of Jackson to the Progressive Era* (New York: Oxford University Press, 1986), 168. Considering Civil War politics part of a stable party system, however, misses the plasticity of the era that the participants experienced. According to Michael F. Holt, "Those who lived during the nineteenth century never knew they were experiencing the realigning or stable phase of a party system. . . . That permanence can only be measured in hindsight." He explains, "Neither northern voters nor politicians living during the Civil War, in sum, could be sure that either the voter alignments of 1860 or the existing political parties that had contested the political election would endure." The liberal republicans' words and actions during the Civil War conform to Holt's analysis. See Holt, "Northern Politics during the Civil War," in *Writing the Civil War: The Quest to Understand,* ed. James M. McPherson and William J. Cooper Jr. (Columbia: University of South Carolina Press, 1998), 126. Some historians, such as Paul Kleppner, consider the Civil War as part of the realignment phase of the party system. While ascribing some flexibility to the time period, though, they still see it primarily in terms of a two-party system. Paul Kleppner, *The Third Electoral System, 1853–1892: Parties, Voters, and Political Cultures* (Chapel Hill: University of North Carolina Press, 1979).

26. Carl Schurz to Margarethe Meyer Schurz, December 17, 1860, in Schurz, *Speeches, Correspondence,* 1:168; Potter, *Impending Crisis,* 531, 547; William Cullen Bryant to Abraham Lincoln, December 25, 1860, in Bryant, *Letters,* 4:187–88; Samuel Bowles to Henry L. Dawes, February 26, 1861, in Merriam, *Bowles,* 1:318.

27. Mark E. Neely Jr., *The Union Divided: Party Conflict in the Civil War North* (Cambridge, Mass.: Harvard University Press, 2002), 9–10, 21, 23; Chester McArthur Destler, *Henry Demarest Lloyd and the Empire of Reform* (Philadelphia: University of Pennsylvania Press, 1963), 23.

28. William Cullen Bryant to Abraham Lincoln, January 4, 1861, in Bryant, *Letters,* 4:198; Krug, *Trumbull,* 165–66; Logsdon, *White,* 69; *Cincinnati Commercial,* June 24, 1861, quoted in Donald W. Curl, *Murat Halstead and the Cincinnati Commercial* (Boca Raton: University Presses of Florida, 1980), 25; Summers, *Plundering Generation,* 294.

29. Neely, *Union Divided,* 26–29; William Cullen Bryant to Frances F. Bryant, September 7, 1864, William Cullen Bryant to Abraham Lincoln, February 25, 1861, in Bryant, *Letters,* 4:403–4, 206; Bryant, in *New York Evening Post,* quoted in *Charles Sumner: His Complete Works,* George Frisbie Hoar, ed. (Boston, 1900), 2:281.

30. Curl, *Halstead,* 33; William M. Armstrong, *E. L. Godkin: A Biography* (Albany: State University of New York Press, 1978), 67; Ee, "Field," 153; Logsdon, *White,* 79–80; Fred Nicklason, "The Civil War Contracts Committee," *Civil War History* 17 (September 1971): 232.

31. *Springfield Weekly Republican,* October 26, 1861; *Springfield Republican,* March 7, 1863, April 8, 1865.

32. Potter, *Impending Crisis,* 423; Heather Cox Richardson, *The Greatest Nation on Earth: Republican Economic Policies during the Civil War* (Cambridge, Mass.: Harvard University Press, 1997), 5, 7; Leonard P. Curry, *Blueprint for Modern America: Nonmilitary Legislation of the First Civil War Congress* (Nashville: Vanderbilt University Press, 1968).

33. *New York Evening Post,* March 20, 1862; Trumbull, in *CG,* 37th Cong., 2nd sess., 2833, 2654, 2835.

34. Curry, *Blueprint,* 196–97; Logsdon, *White,* 31; *Chicago Tribune,* January 20, 1862; *New York Evening Post,* February 3, 1862, January 31, 1862; William Cullen Bryant to Charles Sumner, February 13, 1862, in Bryant, *Letters,* 4:255–56.

35. *Springfield Republican,* February 15, 1862; *Chicago Tribune,* February 14, 1862; *New York Evening Post,* February 14, 1862; Curry, *Blueprint,* 192; Brown, *Bryant,* 438.

36. Edward Atkinson to Anonymous, July 3, 1864, Edward Atkinson to Mary Atkinson, July 3, 1864, Edward Atkinson Papers, MHS; Charles Francis Adams Jr. to Charles Francis Adams, November, 18, 1864, January 30, 1865, Adams Family Papers, MHS.

37. Jeffrey B. Rutenbeck, "The Rise of Independent Newspapers in the 1870s: A Transformation in American Journalism," Ph.D. diss. (University of Washington, 1990), 4; Curl, *Halstead,* 39; Mark W. Summers, *The Press Gang: Newspapers and Politics, 1865– 1878* (Chapel Hill: University of North Carolina Press, 1994), 66; *Springfield Republican,* February 3, 1855; William Cullen Bryant to Abraham Lincoln, June 30, 1864, in Bryant, *Letters,* 4:369.

38. Logsdon, *White,* 84; Curl, *Halstead,* 34; Maizlish, *Sectionalism,* 233; Summers, *Press Gang,* 64–5; Harris L. Dante, "The Chicago Tribune's 'Lost' Years, 1865–1874," *Journal of the Illinois Historical Society* 58 (Summer 1965): 139–40; Armstrong, *Godkin,* 79; Godkin, *Life and Letters,* 1: 238.

39. Summer, *Press Gang,* 67.

40. *CG,* 41st Cong., 3rd sess., 126, 128; Appendix to *CG,* 41st Cong., 3rd sess., 77; Appendix to *CG,* 42nd Cong., 1st sess., 62; Appendix to *CG,* 42nd Cong., 2nd sess., 540.

41. *Cincinnati Commercial,* December 25, 1865, January 6, 1866, February 16, 1866.

42. *The Nation,* May 1, 1866; *Chicago Tribune,* quoted in *Springfield Weekly Republican,* November 18, 1870; *Cincinnati Commercial,* May 12, 1871; Schurz quoted in *Cincinnati Commercial,* May 1, 1872.

43. *The Nation,* August 18, 1869; *Cincinnati Commercial,* December 28, 1865; Schurz, *Speeches, Correspondence,* 2:305; *Springfield Republican,* April 23, 1872.

44. "Independence and Reform!!: Address of the Liberal Republican State Executive Committee and Other Prominent Liberals," January 1872, William M. Grosvenor Papers, CU; J. D. Cox to Carl Schurz, April 5, 1872, Schurz Papers, LC; Schurz, *Speeches, Correspondence,* 2:305; *Springfield Republican,* April 23 and 19, 1872; Trumbull, in appendix to *CG,* 42nd Cong., 2nd sess., 83.

45. Schurz quoted in *Cincinnati Commercial,* May 16, 1871, November 28, 1870, April 16, 1872; *The Nation,* May 29, 1866, September 9, 1869.

46. *Springfield Republican,* March 28 and 13, 1872; *Cincinnati Commercial,* March 29, 1872; J. D. Cox to Carl Schurz, April 5, 1872, Schurz Papers, LC.

47. David A. Wells to Francis Blair, December 22, 1871, Blair Papers, LC.

3. Preserving the Republic while Defeating the Slave Power, 1848–1865

1. Martin Duberman, *Charles Francis Adams, 1807–1886* (Stanford: Stanford University Press, 1960), 173–75; *The Letters of William Cullen Bryant,* William Cullen Bryant II and Thomas G. Voss, eds. (New York: Fordham University Press, 1975–92), 3:117; Eric Foner, *Reconstruction: America's Unfinished Revolution, 1863–1877* (New York: Harper and Row, 1988), 499; John G. Sproat, *"The Best Men": Liberal Reformers in the Gilded Age* (New York: Oxford University Press, 1968), 43.

2. Carl Schurz, *Speeches, Correspondence, and Political Papers of Carl Schurz,* Frederic Bancroft, ed. (New York: G. P. Putnam's Sons, 1913), 1:420, 444; Subscription List for Kansas, 1856, Edward Atkinson Papers, MHS; Harold Francis Williamson, *Edward Atkinson: The Biography of an American Liberal, 1827–1905* (Boston: Old Corner Bookstores, 1934), 4; Joseph Logsdon, *Horace White, Nineteenth-Century Liberal* (Westport, Conn.: Greenwood Publishing, 1971), 28–31.

3. Oliver Dyer, *Phonographic Report of the National Free Soil Convention at Buffalo, N.Y.* (Buffalo: G. H. Derby, 1848), 7, 19; Edward Atkinson to Ned Wild, December 27, 1848, Edward Atkinson Papers, MHS. For the best discussion of the Slave Power see

Leonard L. Richards' *The Slave Power: The Free North and Southern Domination, 1780–1860* (Baton Rouge: Louisiana State University Press, 2000).

4. Michael F. Holt, "Making and Mobilizing the Republican Party, 1856–1860," in *The Birth of the Grand Old Party: The Republicans' First Generation*, Robert F. Engs and Randall M. Miller, eds. (Philadelphia: Pennsylvania University Press, 2002), 43–4; William E. Gienapp, *The Origins of the Republican Party, 1852–1856* (New York: Oxford University Press, 1987), 364–65, 372.

5. *New York Evening Post*, January 12, 1850, March 2, 1850, May 29, 1851.

6. *New York Evening Post*, March 14, 1850, November 13, 1851. Bryant was so embittered about the national bank that when Nicholas Biddle, its former president, died in 1844, Bryan attacked other newspapers for publishing flattering eulogies. Bryant wrote in the *Post* that he would have preferred to have remained silent about Biddle's death, but the "praise of goodness bestowed upon bad men" was an "offence to morals." Charles H. Brown, *William Cullen Bryant* (New York: Scribner's, 1971), 291.

7. Mark Wahlgren Summers, *The Plundering Generation: Corruption and the Crisis of the Union, 1849–1861* (New York: Oxford University Press, 1987), 168, xii, 17; *New York Evening Post*, September 23, 1850, July 24, 1851, February 25, 1851, January 8, 1850.

8. Summers, *Plundering Generation*, xii, 24; Dyer, *Free Soil Convention*, 19.

9. Robert H. Wiebe, *The Search for Order, 1877–1920* (New York: Hill and Wang, 1967), 31.

10. *New York Evening Post*, February 15 and 28, 1851, November 29, 1850, April 3, 1851.

11. *New York Evening Post*, April 3, 1851.

12. *Springfield Republican*, February 8, 1854; Allan Nevins, *The Evening Post: A Century of Journalism* (New York: Russell and Russell, 1922), 250; Logsdon, *White*, 21; Carl Schurz to Gottfried Kinkel, January 23, 1855, in Schurz, *Speeches, Correspondence*, 1:16.

13. Schurz to Gottfried Kinkel, January 23, 1855, in Schurz, *Speeches, Correspondence*, 1:16; *Springfield Republican*, March 31, 1854. For examples of discussions about nativism among liberal reformers see Sproat,"*The Best Men,*" 230–13, 251–52. For the best study of the collapse of the Whig Party see Michael F. Holt, *The Rise and Fall of the American Whig Party: Jacksonian Politics and the Onset of the Civil War* (New York: Oxford University Press, 1999), and for the best examination of the rise of the Republicans see Gienapp, *Origins of the Republican Party.*

14. William Cullen Bryant to Edwin D. Morgan and Others, April 28, 1856, in Bryant, *Letters*, 3:117.

15. Schurz, *Speeches, Correspondence*, 1:59–60, 91.

16. Charles Francis Adams, *The Republican Party a Necessity: Speech of Charles Francis Adams of Massachusetts* (Washington, 1860), 1–2. Adams does not provide the number of Southern Congressmen in his speech, but I determined it by using the Congressional Globe for the First Session of the Thirty-Sixth Congress. I included the congressmen from the eleven states that seceded along with the border states of Delaware, Kentucky, Maryland, and Missouri.

17. Adams, *Republican Party a Necessity*, 2–3; William Cullen Bryant to Alfred Field, November 15, 1859, in Bryant, *Letters*, 4:125.

18. The major exception to the Free Soil Party's opposition to the Whig's economic agenda was their advocacy of a homesteading bill, which would have given land in the Western territories to settlers.

19. *Springfield Republican*, August 25, 1860; *Chicago Tribune*, December 22, 1860.

20. Edward Atkinson, "The Reign of King Cotton" (April 1861).

21. Adams, *Republican Party a Necessity*, 6; *Springfield Republican*, August 25, 1860; Carl Schurz to Margarethe Schurz, February 23, 27, 1860, in Carl Schurz, *Intimate Letters of Carl Schurz, 1841–1869*, Joseph Schafer, ed. (Madison: State Historical Society of Wis-

consin, 1928), 205–8; William Cullen Bryant to Abraham Lincoln, January 4, 1860, in Bryant, *Letters*, 3:198.

22. *Cincinnati Commercial*, May 6, 1862; December 9, 1861, April 3, 1862; *Springfield Weekly Republican*, July 2, 1864.

23. Phillip Shaw Pauldan, "War is the Health of the Party: Republicans in the American Civil War," in Engs and Miller, eds., *Birth of the Grand Old Party*, 64; *Springfield Weekly Republican*, August 1, 1863. The liberal republican attitudes toward emancipation during the war ranged from the *Cincinnati Commercial*'s advocacy of it solely as a war measure, to Henry Adams's desire for gradual emancipation, to William Cullen Bryant's and Carl Schurz's insistence on immediate emancipation. See *Cincinnati Commercial*, August 30, 1862; Henry Adams to Charles Francis Adams Jr., May 8, 1862; *New York Evening Post*, October 3, 1863; and Carl Schurz to Charles Sumner, November 14, 1861, in Schurz, *Speeches, Correspondence*, 1:197.

24. *Cincinnati Commercial*, February 11, 1862.

25. *Springfield Weekly Republican*, July 30, 1864, August 1, 1863, May 28, 1864, July 2, 1864.

26. *Springfield Weekly Republican*, September 5, 1863, August 1, 1863, March 26, 1864; *CG*, 37th Cong., 2nd sess., 2654, 2835. After the Senate rejected his amendment that would have allowed the federal government to sponsor the railroad only through federal territory, Trumbull eventually voted for the Pacific Railroad Act.

27. *Springfield Weekly Republican*, May 11, 1861, July 25, 1863.

28. *Springfield Weekly Republican*, September 10, 1864; *Cincinnati Commercial*, February 28, 1865.

29. *Springfield Weekly Republican*, March 21, 1863.

30. Mark E. Neely Jr., *The Fate of Liberty: Abraham Lincoln and Civil Liberties* (New York: Oxford University Press, 1991), 221; Trumbull, in *CG*, 37th Cong., 1st sess., 336, 392; Trumbull, in *CG*, 37th Cong., 2nd sess., 2972.

31. *Cincinnati Commercial*, March 18, 1863; *Springfield Weekly Republican*, March 23, 1863.

32. *Springfield Weekly Republican*, October 4, 1862, November 29, 1862; *Cincinnati Commercial*, November 4, 1862.

33. Trumbull, in *CG*, 37th Cong., 2nd sess., 18; *New York Evening Post*, April 17, 1862; *Springfield Weekly Republican*, March 21, 1863.

34. Neely, *Fate of Liberty*, 220–21; *Cincinnati Commercial*, July 12, 1862, August 30, 1862, December 31, 1864; Henry Adams to Charles Francis Adams Jr., May 8, 1862; Carl Schurz to Charles Sumner, November 14, 1861, in Schurz, *Speeches, Correspondence*, 1:197; Edward Atkinson to Ned Wild, May 20, 1862, June 10, 1862, Edward Atkinson Papers, MHS; Bryant, in *New York Evening Post*, October 3, 1863.

35. Heather Cox Richardson, *The Greatest Nation of the Earth: Republican Economic Policies during the Civil War* (Cambridge, Mass.: Harvard University Press, 1997), 116, 76, 82; Holt, "Making and Mobilizing the Republican Party," 51.

36. White, in *Chicago Tribune*, January 20, 1862; William Cullen Bryant to Charles Sumner, February 13, 1862, in Bryant, *Letters*, 4:255–56; *New York Evening Post*, January 15, 25, 1862, February 3, 1862; Bryant to John Bigelow, June 15, 1864, in Bryant, *Letters*, 4:363.

37. *Springfield Weekly Republican*, December 24, 1864; *Cincinnati Commercial*, December 9, 1861, February 4 and 5, 1862, June 18, 1862; Richardson, *Greatest Nation*, 66–72.

38. Richardson, *Greatest Nation*, 113, 136; *Cincinnati Commercial*, July 11, 19, 1861.

39. *Springfield Weekly Republican*, November 26, 1864, January 7, 1865; *New York Evening Post* quoted in *Cincinnati Commercial*, February 17, 1865.

40. *Cincinnati Commercial*, March 15, 1864; *New York Evening Post*, January 15, 1862; *Springfield Weekly Republican*, March 23, 1861.

41. *Cincinnati Commercial*, February 11, 1862, January 17, 24, 1862, March 8, 1864; *Springfield Weekly Republican*, January 23, 1864, May 14, 1864, March 15, 1865.

42. *The Nation*, June 12, 1866.

4. The Liberal Republican Dilemma over Reconstruction, 1865–1868

1. Carl Schurz to Frederick Althaus, June 25, 1865, in Carl Schurz, *Intimate Letters of Carl Schurz, 1841–1869*, Joseph Schafer, ed. (Madison: State Historical Society of Wisconsin, 1928), 341; Horace White to William P. Fessenden, October 9, 1865, Horace White Collection, ISHL.

2. *Springfield Weekly Republican*, February 27, 1864.

3. *Cincinnati Commercial*, August 16, 1865; *Springfield Weekly Republican*, April 29, 1865, May 27, 1865; *Cincinnati Commercial*, August 10, 1865.

4. Cox, in *Cincinnati Commercial*, July 18, 1865, June 15, 1865, August 10, 1865; *Springfield Weekly Republican*, June 26, 1865.

5. Edward Atkinson to Hugh McCulloch, January 3, 1866, Edward Atkinson Papers, MHS.

6. *Springfield Weekly Republican*, October 21, 1865; Edward Atkinson to Hugh McCulloch, November 27, 1865, Edward Atkinson Papers, MHS; Carl Schurz to Charles Sumner, August 2, 1865, Carl Schurz to Margarethe Schurz, August 27, 1865, in Schurz, *Speeches, Correspondence*, 1: 267–69.

7. William Cullen Bryant to William Dennison, October 3, 1865, in *The Letters of William Cullen Bryant*, ed. William Cullen Bryant II and Thomas G. Voss (New York: Fordham University Press, 1975–92), 5:51; *Springfield Weekly Republican*, November 25, 1865; *Cincinnati Commercial*, December 16, 1865.

8. Carl Schurz, *Report on the Condition of the South*, 39th Cong., 1st sess., Executive Document, No. 2: 20, 25, 41, 45–46; Carl Schurz to Frederick Althaus, June 25, 1865, in Schurz, *Intimate Letters*, 341.

9. Edward Atkinson to Hugh McCulloch, January 3, 1866, Edward Atkinson Papers, MHS.

10. *CG*, 39th Cong., 1st sess., 318, 320, 600. Just as contemporaries debated the radicalness of Trumbull's two bills, so have historians. Prior to the 1960s most historians considered the bills and subsequent Congressional Reconstruction to be a fundamental change from traditional interpretations of the Constitution and the role of the federal government; for a good, brief analysis of the pre-1960 interpretation of Republican constitutionalism, see Michael Les Benedict, "Preserving the Constitution: The Conservative Basis of Radical Reconstruction," *Journal of American History* 61 (December 1974): 65–67. Since the 1960s most historians have argued the opposite, that the traditional interpretations of the Constitution by congressman like Trumbull shaped Reconstruction in a fundamentally conservative fashion. For instance, Benedict insists, "Republicans never shook off their state-centeredness," and Harold Hyman contends that they were "ineluctably restrained by constitutional principles." See Benedict, "Preserving the Constitution," 89; Harold M. Hyman, *A More Perfect Union: The Impact of the Civil War and Reconstruction on the Constitution* (New York: Knopf, 1973), 490. Though Benedict and Hyman are correct that Trumbull and others tried to operate within the traditional governmental structures, Reconstruction legislation still represented a real growth in federal power. Eric Foner, who faults the legislation for being too conservative, acknowledges, "In normal times, the [Freedmen's Bureau] bill would have represented a radical departure in federal policy." The Civil Rights Bill, according to Foner, "combined elements of continuity and change," for "instead of envisioning continuous federal intervention in local affairs, it honored the traditional presumption that the primary

responsibility for law enforcement lay with the states, while creating a latent federal presence." See Eric Foner, *Reconstruction: America's Unfinished Revolution, 1863–1877* (New York: Harper and Row, 1988), 243, 245. While Reconstruction legislation was guided by adherence to the Constitution, and certainly did not go far enough to satisfy Radical Republicans or modern-day ideals, it did continue to expand both the actual and potential power of the federal government.

11. *New York Evening Post*, January 1, 1866; *The Nation*, January 18, 1866; Edward Atkinson to Hugh McCulloch, January 3, 1866, Edward Atkinson Papers, MHS; *Chicago Tribune*, quoted in Joseph Logsdon, *Horace White, Nineteenth-Century Liberal* (Westport, Conn.: Greenwood Publishing, 1971), 122; Foner, *Reconstruction*, 246.

12. *CG*, 39th Cong., 1st sess., 938, 941, 943.

13. *Chicago Tribune*, quoted in Logsdon, *White*, 123; *Springfield Republican*, March 1 and 3, 1866.

14. Donald W. Curl, *Murat Halstead and the Cincinnati Commercial* (Boca Raton: University Presses of Florida, 1980), 41; Eugene David Schmiel, "The Career of Jacob Dolson Cox, 1828–1900: Soldier, Scholar, Statesman," Ph.D. diss. (Ohio State University, 1969), 138, 164–70.

15. Jacob D. Cox to Andrew Johnson, March 22, 1866, Andrew Johnson Papers, LC.

16. Andrew Johnson, Veto of the Civil Rights Bill, in James Richardson, ed., *A Compilation of the Messages and Papers of the Presidents, 1789–1897* (Washington, 1869–1899), 6:405–13; William Cullen Bryant to Fanny Bryant Godwin, April 17, 1866, Bryant, *Letters*, 5:89; Trumbull, in *CG*, 39th Cong., 1st sess., 1756, 1760; *The Nation*, April 12, 5, 1866; *Springfield Republican*, April 4, 1866.

17. Schmiel, "Career of Cox," 171–77; Curl, *Halstead*, 41–42; *Cincinnati Commercial*, March 29 and 30, 1866, August 23, 1866, December 28, 1866.

18. *Cincinnati Commercial*, May 28, 1866.

19. William Cullen Bryant to Anna Q. Waterston, March 3, 1866, in Bryant, *Letters*, 5:79–80; Allan Nevins, *The New York Evening Post: A Century of Journalism* (New York: Russell and Russell, 1922), 330; *Cincinnati Commercial*, May 28, 1866.

20. *Chicago Tribune* in Logsdon, *White*, 126; *The Nation*, May 22, 1866; Schurz, *Speeches, Correspondence*, 1:403–4; *Springfield Weekly Republican*, June 9, 1866.

21. *Chicago Tribune*, in Logsdon, *White*, 126; *Springfield Weekly Republican*, June 9, 1866; Schurz, *Speeches, Correspondence*, 1:403–4; *Springfield Weekly Republican*, June 9, 1866.

22. Edward Atkinson to Henry Ward Beecher, June 25, 1867, Edward Atkinson Papers, MHS; *Springfield Weekly Republican*, April 7, 1866.

23. *Springfield Weekly Republican*, April 7, 1866; *The Nation*, May 22, 1866; Logsdon, *White*, 126; William E. Parrish, *Missouri under Radical Rule, 1865–1870* (Columbia, Missouri: University of Missouri Press, 1965), 100–1; Schurz, *Speeches, Correspondence*, 1:405–6.

24. John G. Sproat, *"The Best Men": Liberal Reformers in the Gilded Age* (New York: Oxford University Press, 1968), 38; Foner, *Reconstruction*, 499; Nancy Cohen, *The Reconstruction of American Liberalism, 1865–1914* (Chapel Hill: University of North Carolina Press, 2002), 77–78.

25. *The Nation*, May 22, 1866; Don E. Fehrenbacher, "Only His Stepchildren: Lincoln and the Negro," *Civil War History: A Journal of the Middle Period* 20 (December 1974), 301, 299. For one of the most thorough discussions of the liberal republicans and the amnesty issue see Robert W. Burg, "Amnesty, Civil Rights, and the Meaning of Liberal Republicanism, 1862–1872," *American Nineteenth-Century History* 4 (Fall 2003): 29–60.

26. Logsdon, *White*, 126, 129.

27. *New York Evening Post*, February 9, 1867; Henry Adams to Charles Adams, March 1, 1867, Adams Family Papers, MHS; *Springfield Weekly Republican*, March 2, 1867, February 16, 1867.

28. *Springfield Weekly Republican,* March 9, 1867; *The Nation,* March 23, 1867, February 14, 1867; Trumbull, quoted in Mark M. Krug, *Lyman Trumbull, Conservative Radical* (New York: A. S. Barnes, 1965), 250.

29. *Springfield Weekly Republican,* February 23, 1867, March 23, 1867.

30. *Chicago Tribune,* quoted in Logsdon, *White,* 141; *Springfield Weekly Republican,* March 23, 1867; *CG,* 39th Cong., 2nd sess., 1561.

31. Schurz, *Speeches, Correspondence,* 1:442.

5. Legacies of the Civil War Threaten the Republic, 1865–1872

1. *Cincinnati Commercial,* April 14, 1865; Leonard P. Curry, *Blueprint for Modern America: Nonmilitary Legislation of the First Civil War Congress* (Nashville: Vanderbilt University Press, 1968); Heather Cox Richardson, *Greatest Nation of the Earth: Republican Economic Policies during the Civil War* (Cambridge, Mass.: Harvard University Press, 1997); Richard Franklin Bensel, *Yankee Leviathan: The Origins of Central State Authority in America* (New York: Cambridge University Press, 1995); Jean Harvey Baker, "Defining Postwar Republicanism," in Robert F. Engs and Randall M. Miller, eds., *The Birth of the Grand Old Party: The Republicans' First Generation* (Philadelphia: University of Pennsylvania Press, 2002), 133.

2. *The Nation,* February 25, 1869; *Cincinnati Commercial,* July 4, 1866; Trumbull, in appendix to *CG,* 42nd Cong., 2nd sess., 83.

3. Mark W. Summers, *The Era of Good Stealings* (New York: Oxford University Press, 1993), 22.

4. Mark M. Krug, *Lyman Trumbull, Conservative Radical* (New York: A. S. Barnes, 1965), 244; *The Nation,* February 15, 1866.

5. Krug, *Trumbull,* 244–45; Joseph Logsdon, *Horace White, Nineteenth-Century Liberal* (Westport, Conn.: Greenwood Publishing, 1971), 126.

6. *Cincinnati Commercial,* December 13, 1865; Trumbull, in *CG,* 41st Cong., 2nd sess., 17. A few liberal republicans soon had personal reasons for opposing Senate control of patronage. On March 12, 1867, the Senate rejected the appointment of John Quincy Adams II to the Boston Custom House, a rejection which was presumably engineered by Massachusetts senators Charles Sumner and Henry Wilson. The Adams family differed with the Radical Sumner over Reconstruction, but they also had a longstanding political feud with him, going back to the 1850s. Henry Adams wrote to his brother Charles in November 1867 that the only reason he liked the Democrats' surprising success in the recent election in Massachusetts was "from the confident belief that Messrs Sumner and Wilson have received a distinct and dignified reprimand for the insult they thought proper to put upon us last summer in respect to the custom-house. I confess that rankled. I have not forgotten it, nor shall I." Henry Adams to Charles Francis Adams Jr., in *The Letters of Henry Adams,* J. C. Levenson et al., eds. (Cambridge, Mass.: Harvard University Press, 1982), 1:557–58.

7. Carl Schurz, "The Logical Results of the War," Philadelphia, September 8, 1866, in *Speeches, Correspondence, and Political Papers of Carl Schurz,* Frederic Bancroft, ed. (New York: G. P. Putnam's Sons, 1913), 1:398; *Cincinnati Commercial,* December 20, 1866; *The Nation,* May 28, 1868; Summers, *Era of Good Stealings,* 9; Edwin Godkin, "Commercial Immorality and Political Corruption," *North American Review* (July 1868): 265.

8. Carl Schurz to Margarethe Schurz, March 20, 1869, April 12, 1869, May 30, 1869, in *Intimate Letters of Carl Schurz, 1841–1869,* Joseph Schafer, ed. (Madison: State Historical Society of Wisconsin, 1928), 475–77.

9. Schurz, in appendix to *CG,* 41st Cong., 3rd sess., 73, 76–77.

10. Jacob D. Cox, "The Civil-Service Reform," *North American Review* 230 (January 1871): 82, 94, 97, 98; Eugene David Schmiel, "The Career of Jacob Dolson Cox, 1828–1900: Soldier, Scholar, Statesman," Ph.D. diss. (Ohio State University, 1969), 281.

11. Edward Atkinson to Edwin Godkin, June 3, 1867, Edward Atkinson Papers, MHS; *New York Evening Post,* May 25, 1872; *Cincinnati Commercial,* January 24, 1866; *Springfield Weekly Republican,* August 4, 1866; *The Nation,* May 30, 1867.

12. *The Nation,* February 25, 1869; *New York Evening Post,* January 20, 1866.

13. *Chicago Tribune,* January 29, 1866; Charles Francis Adams to E. G. Spaulding, October 13, 1869, Adams Papers, MHS; Edward Atkinson to Henry Ward Beecher, October 1, 1867, Atkinson Papers, MHS; *Cincinnati Commercial,* October 7, 1869; *Springfield Weekly Republican,* December 12, 1868; *The Nation,* February 17, 1870. One of the most recent and best analyses of the liberal republicans' attitudes toward making paper money legal tender is in David M. Tucker, *Mugwumps: Public Moralists of the Gilded Age* (Columbia: University of Missouri Press, 1998), 15–25.

14. Henry Adams to Charles Francis Adams Jr., February 16, 1867, Adams Family Papers, MHS; Edward Atkinson to Hugh McCulloch, October 27, 1867, Atkinson Papers, MHS; Tucker, *Mugwumps,* 19.

15. *New York Evening Post,* quoted in the *Springfield Republican,* December 9, 1865; William Grosvenor, "Political Protestantism," William Grosvenor Papers, CU; *The Tariff: As It Is and As It Should Be* (American Free Trade League, 1870), 3; *Cincinnati Commercial,* July 8, 1871.

16. Henry Adams, "The Session," *North American Review* 153 (April 1869), in Henry Adams, *The Great Secession Winter of 1860–1861 and Other Essays,* George Hochfield, ed. (New York: Sagamore Press, 1958), 70; Henry Brooks Adams to Edward Atkinson, February 1, 1869, Atkinson Papers, MHS; *The Nation,* May 30, 1867.

17. *Springfield Republican,* December 9, 1865; *New York Evening Post,* February 7, 1867; May 25, 1872; Central Republican Association of Hamilton County pamphlet, 1871, Schurz Papers, LC; *Cincinnati Commercial,* July 2, 1866; William M. Grosvenor, *Does Protection Protect? An Examination of the Effect of Different Forms of Tariff upon American Industry* (New York: D. Appleton, 1871), 359; "Atkinson on the Collection of Revenue," *North American Review* (July 1867): 286. See also Eric Foner, *Reconstruction: America's Unfinished Revolution, 1863–1877* (New York: Harper and Row, 1988), 233.

18. *Cincinnati Commercial,* July 2, 1866; *Chicago Tribune,* November 12, 1870; Schurz, in *CG,* 41st Cong., 3rd sess., 127; Edwin Godkin, "The Labor Crisis," *North American Review* 105 (July 1867): 212.

19. Edwin Godkin, "Commercial Immorality and Political Corruption," 255; Charles Francis Adams Jr., "The Railroad System," *North American Review* 104 (April 1867): 502–3; Charles Francis Adams Jr., "Railway Problems in 1869," *North American Review* 126 (January 1870): 126–27.

20. *Cincinnati Commercial,* June 19, 1871; appendix to *CG,* 41st Cong., 3rd sess., 77. For another example see *CG,* 41st Cong., 3rd sess., 127.

21. Charles Francis Adams Jr., "Railway Problems," 148–49; Henry Adams, "The New York Gold Conspiracy" in Hochfield, ed., *Secession Winter,* 189.

22. Charles Francis Adams Jr., "The Government and the Railroad Corporations," *North American Review* 230 (January 1871): 31.

23. *Springfield Weekly Republican,* June 5, 1869, June 3, 1870; *The Nation,* July 1, 1869, June 17, 1869.

24. *The Nation,* December 20, 1870; *Cincinnati Commercial,* March 17, 1870, April 22, 1870; James L. Huston, "The American Revolutionaries, the Political Economy of Aristocracy, and the American Concept of the Distribution of Wealth, 1765–1900," *American Historical Review* 98 (October 1993): 1080; Henry Adams, "The New York Gold Conspiracy" in Hochfield, ed., *Secession Winter,* 164.

25. *Springfield Weekly Republican,* June 5, 1869; *Cincinnati Commercial,* June 11, 1869; Charles Francis Adams Jr., "Railway Problems in 1869," 134, 149; *Springfield Weekly Republican,* January 20, 1871.

26. Henry Adams, "Gold Conspiracy," 164; Charles Francis Adams Jr., "Government and Railroad Corporations," 42–43.

27. *The Nation*, April 6, 1871.

28. *The Nation*, April 6, 1871; Charles Francis Adams Jr., "The Railroad System," 502–3; "The New Jersey Monopolies," *North American Review* 104 (April 1867): 429; Charles Francis Adams Jr., "Government and Railroad Corporations," 60.

29. *Springfield Weekly Republican*, May 6, 1870; *Springfield Republican*, July 1, 1871.

30. Charles Francis Adams Jr., "Government and Railroad Corporations," 47, 35. Henry Demarest Lloyd presented to the 1894 People's Party Convention a platform written by Lyman Trumbull, and it was adopted without any changes (Krug, *Trumbull*, 351).

31. Charles Francis Adams Jr., "Government and the Railroad Corporations," 49–50; *Springfield Weekly Republican*, January 13, 1870; *Springfield Republican*, July 1, 1871; C. F. Adams Jr., "Government and the Railroad Corporations," 50; Richardson, *Greatest Nation of the Earth*, 170–208.

32. Schurz, *Speeches, Correspondence*, 1:67; Schurz, in appendix to *CG*, 42nd Cong., 2nd sess., 74.

6. Grant and the Republic, 1868–1872

1. *Springfield Weekly Republican*, January 4, 1868; *The Nation*, December 9, 1867, January 16, 1868; Allan Nevins, *The Evening Post; a Century of Journalism* (New York: Russell and Russell, 1922), 389; Edward Atkinson to David A. Wells, February 12, 1868, Edward Atkinson Papers, MHS.

2. *The Nation*, June 25, 1868; Schurz, in *Speeches, Correspondence, and Political Papers of Carl Schurz*, Frederic Bancroft, ed. (New York: G. P. Putnam's Sons, 1913), 1:458; Joseph Logsdon, *Horace White, Nineteenth-Century Liberal* (Westport, Conn.: Greenwood Publishing, 1971), 156.

3. *Springfield Republican*, May 22, 1868; Edward Atkinson to Ginery Twitchell, July 1, 1868, Edward Atkinson Papers, MHS.

4. Schurz, *Speeches, Correspondence*, 1:421, 446, 432, 428.

5. Carl Schurz to Margarethe Schurz, August 2, 1868, in *Intimate Letters of Carl Schurz, 1841–1869*, Joseph Schafer, ed. (Madison: State Historical Society of Wisconsin, 1928), 441; see also Brooks D. Simpson, *Let Us Have Peace: Ulysses S. Grant and the Politics of War and Reconstruction, 1861–1868* (Chapel Hill: University of North Carolina Press, 1991), 252.

6. *The Nation*, January 28, 1869. The Adams family was an exception to liberal republican happiness with Grant's election. Henry Adams wrote to an English friend soon afterward, "Our elections as you can see, have passed off as everyone expected and we are approaching a new reign. Personally we have nothing to expect from it. My father is not in sympathy with the party in power, and my brother is a prominent opponent of it." Henry Adams to Charles Milnes Gaskell, November 5, 1868, Adams Family Papers, MHS.

7. Carl Schurz to Margarethe Schurz, March 20, 1869, in Schurz, *Intimate Letters*, 475; *Springfield Weekly Republican*, March 27, 1867; *New York Evening Post*, February 9, 1869; William Cullen Bryant to John Howard Bryant, February 10, 1869, in *The Letters of William Cullen Bryant*, ed. William Cullen Bryant II and Thomas G. Voss (New York: Fordham University Press, 1975–92), 5:306.

8. Horace White, quoted in Logsdon, *White*, 167–69; Edward Atkinson to S. C. Haskell, January 11, 1869, Edward Atkinson Papers, MHS; William Cullen Bryant to Ferdinand Field, June 8, 1869, in Bryant, *Letters*, 5:320.

9. *The Nation*, May 20, 1869, August 19, 1869; Horace White, quoted in Logsdon, *White*, 172–73; *Cincinnati Commercial*, June 2, 1869; Richard H. Abbot, *The Republican*

Party and the South, 1855–1877: The First Southern Strategy (Chapel Hill: University of North Carolina Press, 1987), 204–5.

10. Mark M. Krug, *Lyman Trumbull, Conservative Radical* (New York: A. S. Barnes, 1965), 272; Trumbull, in *CG*, 41st Cong., 2nd sess., 1361.

11. Eric Foner, *Reconstruction: America's Unfinished Revolution, 1863–1877* (New York: Harper and Row, 1988), 454–55; Trumbull, in appendix to *CG*, 41st Cong., 2nd sess., 290, 293.

12. Trumbull and Schurz, in *CG*, 42nd Cong., 1st sess., 578–79, 686–87, 690.

13. *The Nation*, March 23, 1871; *Springfield Weekly Republican*, April 21 and 14, 1871; *Cincinnati Commercial*, April 19, 1871, October 28, 1871.

14. *Springfield Weekly Republican*, April 17, 1869. As previously noted, historians such as Eric Foner, Nancy Cohen, and John Sproat have long considered racism a cause of the liberal republicans' reticence to support most Reconstruction measures after Grant's election. See Foner, *Reconstruction*, 499; Nancy Cohen, *The Reconstruction of American Liberalism, 1865–1914* (Chapel Hill: University of North Carolina Press, 2002), 77–78; John G. Sproat, *"The Best Men": Liberal Reformers in the Gilded Age* (New York: Oxford University Press, 1968), 38.

15. *Cincinnati Commercial*, June 13, 1869; *The Nation*, July 21, 1870.

16. *Cincinnati Commercial*, September 5, 1871.

17. Foner, *Reconstruction*, 494–95.

18. Schurz, in appendix to *CG*, 41st Cong., 3rd sess., 26–30, 33–34.

19. Jacob D. Cox to Carl Schurz, February 14, 1871, Schurz Papers, LC; *The Nation*, December 29, 1870.

20. Schurz, in appendix to *CG*, 42nd Cong., 1st sess., 60–61, 53; *Springfield Weekly Republican*, March 31, 1871, April 1, 1871.

21. *The Nation*, April 15, 1869; Schurz, in appendix to *CG*, 42nd Cong., 1st sess., 60.

22. *Springfield Weekly Republican*, December 16, 1870; Henry Adams, "Civil Service Reform," *North American Review* 225 (October 1869), 459; Trumbull, in *CG*, 42nd Cong., 2nd sess., 460.

23. Foner, *Reconstruction*, 444–45; *Chicago Tribune*, quoted in *The Nation*, May 6, 1869; *Chicago Tribune*, quoted in Logsdon, *White*, 173; *The Nation*, May 6, 1869.

24. *Springfield Weekly Republican*, June 12, 1869; *The Nation*, September 16, 1869.

25. Foner, *Reconstruction*, 494; Ari Hoogenboom, *Outlawing the Spoils: A History of the Civil Service Reform Movement, 1865–1883* (Urbana: University of Illinois Press, 1961), viii; Sproat, *"Best Men,"* 7–8; *New York Evening Post*, October 31, 1870; *Springfield Weekly Republican*, November 18, 1870.

26. *Springfield Weekly Republican*, November 25, 1870; *Cincinnati Commercial*, January 26, 1871, February 19, 1872, March 7, 1872; Hans L. Trefousse, *Carl Schurz: A Biography* (New York: Fordham University Press, 1998), 178–79; Schurz, in appendix to *CG*, 42nd Cong., 2nd sess., 540.

27. Schurz, in appendix to *CG*, 42nd Cong, 2nd sess., 540, 74.

28. Schurz and Trumbull, in appendix to *CG*, 42nd Cong, 2nd sess., 74, 87; Trefousse, *Schurz*, 178–79.

29. Schurz, in appendix to *CG*, 42nd Cong, 2nd sess., 532, 539, 523.

30. Henry Adams to Carl Schurz, April 25, 1871, Schurz Papers, LC; Schurz, *Speeches, Correspondence*, 2:292; *Springfield Weekly Republican*, November 18, 1870; Jacob D. Cox to David A. Wells, April 4, 1872, David A. Wells Papers, LC.

7. The National Phase of the Liberal Republican Movement, 1870–1872

1. Carl Schurz to Samuel Bowles, May 11, 1872, Samuel Bowles Papers, Yale University; Edward Atkinson to Harvey Kent, May 8, 1872, Edward Atkinson Papers, MHS;

Cincinnati Commercial, May 4, 1872; *Springfield Republican,* May 4, 1872; Samuel Bowles to Frederick Law Olmsted, May 15, 1872, Samuel Bowles Papers, Yale; Charles Francis Adams diary, May 18, 1872, Adams Family Papers, MHS; Schurz to Samuel Bowles, May 11, 1872, Samuel Bowles Papers, Yale University. In an earlier letter to Olmsted, however, Samuel Bowles had written, "It is a mistake to suppose the intriguers were for him [Greeley] at Cincinnati. They had other schemes, and meant to beat Greeley. It was because those schemes were broken that they were forced to fall back on him" (Bowles to Olmsted, May 11, 1872, Samuel Bowles Papers, Yale). Horace White was one of the few liberal republicans to think that B. Gratz Brown's support and political machinations had done little to nominate Greeley. Immediately after the convention White wrote to Trumbull that "the so-called Gratz Brown Trick was simply a desperate throw of the dice—the gambler's last 'chip'—to humiliate Schurz. It had the least effect upon the convention" (White to Trumbull, May 4, 1872, Lyman Trumbull Papers, LC). In the *Chicago Tribune,* White contended that "the nomination of Mr. Greeley was accomplished by the people, against the judgment and strenuous efforts of the politicians" (*Chicago Tribune,* May 4, 1872).

2. J. D. Cox to Carl Schurz, April 5, 1872, Carl Schurz Papers, LC. Though unable to direct the outcome of the convention, the liberal republicans successfully pressed their interpretation of events into the history books. In his nine-volume history of the United States, James Ford Rhodes described Horace Greeley's victory as the triumph of wire-pulling politicians over naive reformers, almost repeating the wording of Schurz's contention that "the convention had been made a dupe of those very methods against which its assembling protested." James Ford Rhodes, *History of the United States from the Compromise of 1850 to the Final Restoration of Home Rule in 1877* (New York: Macmillan, 1892–1919), 7:44–45. Earle D. Ross used the same explanation in the only full-length monograph on the liberal republican movement, even referring to Rhodes' work in his chapter "Reformers versus Politicians in the Cincinnati Convention." According to Ross, "This then is the real explanation [for Greeley's success]—the triumph of experienced political intriguers over inexperienced confident reformers." Earle D. Ross, *The Liberal Republican Movement* (New York: AMS Press, 1919), 95 n. 37, 102. For other examples of the politician-versus-reformer interpretation, see Horace Samuel Merril, *Bourbon Democracy of the Middle West, 1865–1896* (Baton Rouge: Louisiana State University Press, 1953), 72; Matthew Josephson, *The Politicos, 1865–1896* (New York: Harcourt and Brace, 1963), 160–63; Eric Goldman, *Rendezvous with Destiny: A History of Modern American Reform* (New York: Alfred A. Knopf, 1952), 21–22; and Donald Walter Curl, "The Cincinnati Convention of the Liberal Republican Party," *Bulletin of the Cincinnati Historical Society* 24 (April 1966): 162.

The politician-versus-reformer interpretation remained unchallenged until the 1960s, when historians such as Matthew T. Downey demonstrated that "it assumed a dichotomy which did not exist between reformers and politicians within the convention." Other historians agreed with Downey's argument that "a majority of the delegates at Cincinnati apparently preferred Greeley to Adams for the campaign against Grant that lay ahead." See Matthew T. Downey, "Horace Greeley and the Politicians: The Liberal Republican Convention in 1872," *Journal of American History* 53 (March 1967): 729, 750; Richard Allen Gerber, "The Liberal Republican Alliance of 1872," Ph.D. diss. (University of Michigan, 1967), 446; and Jacqueline Balk Tusa, "Power, Priorities, and Political Insurgency: The Liberal Republican Movement, 1869–1872," Ph.D. diss. (Pennsylvania State University, 1970), 259–60.

This revisionist interpretation of the Cincinnati Convention suffers from a number of methodological flaws, however. First, none of these historians perceive a difference between the longtime liberal republicans and those outsiders who had joined the movement only months before the convention—between the old liberal republican movement and the emerging Liberal Republican Party. To understand how and why the Cincinnati Convention nominated Greeley, the convention needs to be placed within the larger context of liberal republicans' efforts to transform their movement into a party. Second, the historians' uncritical use of sources such as newspaper accounts of the convention written months later, during the 1872 campaign, and of memoirs written sometimes more than forty years afterward, distorts the nature of the convention. While memoirs and later newspaper accounts can be valuable, the political pressures of the campaign, changed perspectives over time, and fading memories make such sources less accurate than contemporary primary sources. For example, Downey quotes an October 1872 issue of the *Springfield Republican,* which claimed "that the majority of the convention sincerely believed that he [Greeley] would prove the most popular candidate," to argue that the Cincinnati Convention nominated Greeley because the delegates thought he had the best chance against Grant (Downey, "Horace Greeley," 748–49). Downey does not cite the letter quoted in the first paragraph of this chapter, in which Samuel Bowles, editor of the *Republican,* confided to Frederick Law Olmsted just weeks after the convention that Greeley's nomination "was the work of fate and Frank Blair," indicating that in Bowles's private opinion Greeley's nomination was the result of a conspiracy, not popular sentiment (Bowles to Olmsted, May 11, 1872, Samuel Bowles Papers, Yale). Tusa, meanwhile, cites Roeliff Brinkerhoff's memoirs, written in 1904, to describe what the liberal republicans were thinking during the convention thirty-two years earlier, without acknowledging the distance of her source from the event (Tusa, "Power, Priorities, and Political Insurgency," 225). Most historians writing on the liberal republican movement regularly cite memoirs without acknowledging in the text that the accounts were written more than thirty years after the Cincinnati Convention. Among the memoirs most often cited are *Memoirs of Gustave Koerner* (Cedar Rapids, Iowa: Torch Press, 1909); Henry Watterson, *"Marse Henry": An Autobiography* (New York: George H. Doran, 1919); James G. Blaine, *Twenty Years at Congress: From Lincoln to Garfield* (Norwich, Conn.: Henry Bill Publishing Company, 1886); and Roeliff Brinkerhoff, *Recollections of a Lifetime* (Cincinnati: Robert Clarke Company, 1904).

3. According to William E. Gienapp, while sectional events were the most important cause of the Know-Nothings' decline in 1856, "other factors contributed to the erosion of the party's popular strength, however, including the inept record of its elected officials . . . and the Republicans' superior leadership." He shows the relationship between superior leadership and party success, explaining that "party leaders gave meaning to events, placed them in a larger context, established a party organization, reached out to groups of potential supporters, and presented policy alternatives to the voters." Ultimately, Gienapp concludes that "many new and obscure men were thrust into power by the Know Nothing movement," and that "superior leadership was vital to the success of the Republican party." William E. Gienapp, *The Origins of the Republican Party, 1852–1856* (New York: Oxford University Press, 1987), 441, 447. Michael F. Holt has also found poor leadership decisive in the demise of the Whig Party in the early 1850s. He argues that "the desperate decision during the 1852 presidential campaign to compete with Democrats for Catholic and immigrant votes was a colossal blunder," and that neither "did Whig leaders prove much more skillful in handling the other powerful and divisive new social issue that emerged in the early 1850s—prohibition." Holt also argues that "equally pernicious and divisive were the selfish ambition and dogmatic intolerance of so many Whig leaders, who often acted with heedless disregard for the party's welfare in order to advance their personal careers or simply humiliate Whig rivals." Michael F. Holt, *The Rise and Fall of the American Whig Party: Jacksonian Politics and the Onset of the Civil War* (New York: Oxford University Press, 1999), 956.

4. Mahlon Sands to Carl Schurz, November 10, 1870. For more discussion of the first meeting see also Charles Nordhoff to Carl Schurz, December 21, 1870, Carl Schurz

Papers, LC; Mahlon Sands to William M. Grosvenor, November 5, 1870, Horace White to William M. Grosvenor, November 9, 1870, William M. Grosvenor Papers, CU.

5. Henry Adams reported "twenty or more present" at the meeting, while Edwin Godkin said "there were about forty present." Henry Adams to Jacob D. Cox, November 28, 1870, Adams Family Papers, MHS; Edwin L. Godkin to Fanny Godkin, December 1, 1870, in *Life and Letters of Edwin Lawrence Godkin*, Rollo Ogden, ed. (New York: Macmillan Company, 1907), 2:100. For discussion of the meeting, see Jacob D. Cox to Charles Nordhoff, December 3, 1870, Jacob D. Cox to Carl Schurz, December 27, 1870, Charles Nordhoff to Carl Schurz, December 21, 1870, Carl Schurz Papers, LC; Carl Schurz to Jacob D. Cox, February 3, 1871, in *Speeches, Correspondence, and Political Papers of Carl Schurz*, Frederic Bancroft, ed. (New York: G. P. Putnam's Sons, 1913), 2:176–77. Without referring to the letters between Schurz, Cox, and Nordhoff, Jacqueline Tusa argues that the meeting demonstrated a desire to form a new party and that Carl Schurz "eschewed" the meeting (Tusa, "Power, Priorities, and Political Insurgency," 114–16). Carl Schurz did de-emphasize the role of free trade in the Missouri bolt during his speech before the Senate on December 15, 1870, but he explained in a letter to Grosvenor that he did so for political considerations and asked him "to think coolly about their bearing before expressing an opinion"; see *CG*, 41st Cong., 3rd sess., 123, and Carl Schurz to William M. Grosvenor, December 13, 1870, Schurz Papers, LC.

6. On liberal republican initial plans for direct action see Henry Adams to Jacob D. Cox, November 28, 1870, Adams Family Papers, MHS; On the liberal republicans' failure to organize the House see Ari Hoogenboom, *Outlawing the Spoils: A History of the Civil Service Reform Movement, 1865–1883* (Urbana: University of Illinois Press, 1961), 84; On Grosvenor's appointment see Mahlon Sands to William M. Grosvenor, February 20, 1871, William M. Grosvenor Papers, CU; On Brinkerhoff's activities see Roeliff Brinkerhoff, *Recollections of a Lifetime*, 205–11; On discussion of Grosvenor's organizing activities see Edward Atkinson to Carl Schurz, December 23, 1871, Edward Atkinson to William M. Grosvenor, December 26, 1871, Edward Atkinson to Mahlon Sands, December 27, 1871, Edward Atkinson Papers, MHS; William Grosvenor to David A. Wells, June 15, 1871, David A. Wells Papers, LC; Carl Schurz to Emil Preetorius, March 16, 1871, quoted in Tusa, "Power, Priorities, and Political Insurgency," 154. The National Revenue Reform Association was also formed at the New York meeting in November 1870, to elect tariff reformers to Congress, but its director was less ambitious than Grosvenor; see Joanne Reitano, "Free Trade in the Gilded Age: 1865–1895," Ph.D. diss. (New York University, 1974), 118–23.

7. Reitano, "Free Trade," 113; Ohio Free Trade League, May 1871, David A. Wells Papers, LC; On creation of Central Republic Association of Hamilton County see *Cincinnati Commercial*, March 22, 1871, April 6, 1871; Central Republican Association of Hamilton County, March 26, 1871, Carl Schurz Papers, LC.

8. Jacob D. Cox to Carl Schurz, March 27, 1871, April 4, 1871, and Carl Schurz to Edwin L. Godkin, March 31, 1871, Carl Schurz Papers, LC.

9. Tusa, "Power, Priorities, and Political Insurgency," 133–52; Carl Schurz to Edwin L. Godkin, March 31, 1871, Edwin L. Godkin to Carl Schurz, April 5, 1871, Carl Schurz Papers, LC; Edward Atkinson to David A. Wells, July 17, 1871, David A. Wells Papers, LC; *Springfield Republican*, January 13, 1871; *Cincinnati Commercial*, June 18, 1871.

10. Schurz, *Speeches, Correspondence*, 2:296; Carl Schurz to Charles Sumner, September 30, 1871, Carl Schurz to Jacob D. Cox, October 14 and 22, 1871, in *Speeches, Correspondence*, 2:310–15; Tusa, "Power, Priorities, and Political Insurgency," 171.

11. William Grosvenor to Edward Atkinson, December 21, 1871, Edward Atkinson to William Grosvenor, December 26, 1871, Edward Atkinson Papers, MHS; Lyman Trumbull to W. G. Flagg, January 10, 1872, Lyman Trumbull Collection, ISHL; Tusa, "Power, Priorities, and Political Insurgency," 178; Edward Chalfant, *Better in Darkness: A Biogra-*

phy of Henry Adams, His Second Life, 1862–1891 (Hamden, Conn.: Archon Books, 1994), 254.

12. "Address of the Liberal Republican State Executive Committee," 1872, "Resolutions of the Liberal Republican State Convention of Missouri," 1872, William M. Grosvenor Papers, CU; Willard L. King, *Lincoln's Manager, David Davis* (Cambridge, Mass.: Harvard University Press, 1960), 277; Tusa, "Power, Priorities, and Political Insurgency," 162.

13. Public letter in "Resolutions of the Liberal Republican State Convention of Missouri," 1872, William M. Grosvenor Papers, CU; *Springfield Republican*, February 1 and 13, 1872; *Cincinnati Commercial*, February 14, 1872; Lyman Trumbull to Hiram R. Enoch, February 29, 1872, Lyman Trumbull Papers, LC. For the initial reaction of the liberal republican press to the call for the Cincinnati Convention, see *The Nation*, February 1, 1871; *Chicago Tribune*, January 29 and February 6, 1872; *Springfield Republican*, February 6, 1872.

14. *CG*, 42nd Cong., 2nd sess., 1314, 1321–22; *Reports*, 42nd Cong., 2nd sess., vol. 3, no. 183, part 1, pp. 835–40; Tusa, "Power, Priorities, and Political Insurgency," 197–98, 205–7; for reports of Republican state committee chairmen see Edward Rollins to George Robeson, February 13, 1872; Edward Rollins to William E. Chandler, February 17 and 25, 1872; William Claflin to William E. Chandler, February 30, 1872; Eugene L. Sullivan to William E. Chandler, March 16, 1872; J. G. Tracy to William E. Chandler, March 14, 1872; Thomas B. Van Buren to William E. Chandler, March 29, 1872; M. M. Hale to William E. Chandler, March 25, 1872, William E. Chandler Papers, LC.

15. Samuel Bowles to Carl Schurz, March 22, 1872, in Schurz, *Speeches, Correspondence*, 2:353; *Springfield Republican*, March 4, 1872; *Cincinnati Commercial*, March 20, 1872, April 13, 1872.

16. Tusa, "Power, Priorities, and Political Insurgency," 160–68; Martin Duberman, *Charles Francis Adams, 1807–1886* (Stanford: Stanford University Press, 1960), 352–60.

17. For discussion of Trumbull and Adams as presidential candidates see Duberman, *Adams*, 352–61, and Mark M. Krug, *Lyman Trumbull, Conservative Radical* (New York: A. S. Barnes, 1965), 306–26.

18. O. P. Fitzgerald to Lyman Trumbull, January 4, 1871, James S. Whitmire to Lyman Trumbull, December 18, 1871, Walter B. Scates to Lyman Trumbull, April 15, 1872, Lyman Trumbull Papers, LC; W. M. Stroms to Charles Francis Adams, Adams Family Papers, MHS; William F. Bartlett to William Schouler, April 14, 1872, William Schouler Papers, MHS. Many more letters urging Trumbull to run for the presidency exist in both the Library of Congress and Illinois State Historical Library collections of his papers. For further examples of letters urging Adams to become a candidate, see John Danforth to Charles Francis Adams, April 19, 1872, Adams Family Papers, MHS. For examples of letters to Carl Schurz advocating Adams or Trumbull, see J. H. Caldwell to Carl Schurz, February 11, 1872, John Sullivan to Carl Schurz, March 9, 1872, and August Belmont to Carl Schurz, April 23, 1872, Carl Schurz Papers, LC.

19. Leonard Swett to Jesse W. Fell, April 1, 1872, Jesse W. Fell Papers, LC; O. M. Hatch to Lyman Trumbull, April 11, 1872, Lyman Trumbull Papers, LC; Frank P. Blair to Carl Schurz, March 15, 1872, Carl Schurz Papers, LC; Lyman Trumbull to Horace White, March 6, 1872, Horace White Collection, ISHL; Charles Nordhoff to Carl Schurz, April 17, 1872, Carl Schurz Papers, LC; Edward Atkinson to William Grosvenor, April 19, 1872, E. W. Kittridge to Edward Atkinson, April 8, 1872, Edward Atkinson Papers, MHS; Duberman, *Adams*, 357. The historical literature often contends that Adams' Anglophilia was a detriment to his nomination, as it would have cost the Liberal Republicans the Irish vote. No contemporary evidence, though, is given for this assertion. The liberal republican newspapers only mention Adams and the Irish a few times, once during the Cincinnati Convention, with the *Springfield Republican* reporting that "some of the local

Irish politicians are making a demonstration against him, but, on the other hand, the Catholic Telegraph—the organ of the Catholic church here, comes out, to-night, in a strong article in his favor" (May 2, 1872). The only letter I found discussing the issue is from a Democrat arguing for the nomination of David Davis (George W. Morgan to J. E. Harvey, April 26, 1872, David Davis Collection, ISHL). It is possible that Adams' nomination might have cost the Liberal Republicans the Irish vote, but that does not appear to have been a concern of the party in 1872. For discussion of Adams and the Irish-vote question in the historical literature, see Downey, "Horace Greeley and the Politicians," 749, and Duberman, Adams, 357.

20. Cincinnati Commercial, April 27, 1872; Springfield Republican, April 25, 1872; George W. Morgan to J. E. Harvey, April 26, 1872, David Davis Collection, ISHL; John A. McClerand to Lyman Trumbull, April 24, 1872, Horace White to Lyman Trumbull, April 25, 1872, Lyman Trumbull Papers, LC; Krug, Trumbull, 253.

21. Irving Katz, August Belmont: A Political Biography (New York: Columbia University Press, 1968), 197–98; David Black, The King of Fifth Avenue: The Fortunes of August Belmont (New York: Dial Press, 1981), 395–96; John Wentworth to Jesse W. Fell, April 26, 1872, David Davis Collection, ISHL; August Belmont to Carl Schurz, April 23, 1872, Manton Marble to Carl Schurz, April 23, 1872, Carl Schurz Papers, LC; Charles Francis Adams Diary, April 1, 1872, Adams Family Papers, MHS; John Wentworth to David Davis, April 16, 1872, David Davis Collection, ISHL; Jacob D. Cox to David A. Wells, March 16, 1872, David A. Wells Papers, LC; Cincinnati Commercial, March 29, 1872; Springfield Republican, April 25, 1872.

22. Edward Atkinson to Lyman Trumbull, March 13, 1872, Lyman Trumbull Papers, LC; William Grosvenor to Edward Atkinson, April 15 and 22, 1872, David A. Wells to Edward Atkinson, March 31, 1872, April 12 and 14, 1872, Edward Atkinson Papers, MHS; Chicago Tribune, April 26, 1872; Springfield Republican, April 25, 1872; Cincinnati Commercial, April 27, 1872. One might have expected the Chicago Tribune to have supported Trumbull's nomination much earlier, but Horace White waited until just a couple of weeks before the Cincinnati Convention to publicly endorse the liberal republicans' nomination of candidates; Joseph Logsdon, Horace White, Nineteenth-Century Liberal (Westport, Conn.: Greenwood Publishing, 1971), 208–9.

23. Lyman Trumbull to William Jayne, March 24, 1871, William Jayne Papers, ISHL; Lyman Trumbull to Joseph Brown, December 25, 1871, Gustave Koerner to Lyman Trumbull, April 5, 1872, Lyman Trumbull to John M. Palmer, April 8, 1872, John M. Palmer to Lyman Trumbull, April 13, 1872, Lyman Trumbull to Horace White, April 24, 1872, Lyman Trumbull Papers, LC; Krug, Trumbull, 16.

24. Charles Francis Adams diary, March 18, 1872, April 1, 1872, March 30, 1872, April 10, 1872, Charles Francis Adams to B. R. Wood, April 11, 1872, Adams Family Papers, MHS; David F. Musto, "Continuity across Generations: The Adams Family Myth," in New Directions in Psychohistory, Mel Albin, ed. (Lexington, Mass.: Lexington Books, 1980), 125; David F. Musto, "The Adams Family," Proceedings of the Massachusetts Historical Society 93 (1981): 57; Duberman, Adams, 358–59.

25. Charles Francis Adams to David A. Wells, April 18, 1872, David A. Wells Papers, New York Public Library; Charles Francis Adams diary, April 18, 1872, Adams Family Papers, MHS; Springfield Republican, April 25 and 26, 1872; Cincinnati Commercial, April 27, 1872; New York Tribune, April 27, 1872; Henry Adams to Charles Milnes Gaskell, April 27, 1872, Adams Family Papers, MHS; Charles Francis Adams diary, April 16, 1872, Adams Family Papers, MHS.

26. Glyndon Van Deusen, Horace Greeley, Nineteenth-Century Crusader (New York: Hill and Wang, 1953), 403; Cincinnati Commercial, November 10, 1870; D. E. Somes to Horace Greeley, October 18, 1871, W. B. Layphere to Horace Greeley, October 20, 1871, Horace Greeley Papers, LC.

27. *New York Tribune*, September 6 and 7, 1870; David A. Wells to Francis Blair, December 22, 1871, Blair Family Papers, LC; Van Deusen, *Greeley*, 137–38, 392; Bryant quoted in Godkin, *Life and Letters*, 1:167–68.

28. *New York Tribune*, January 18, 1870, June 8, 1869; *Springfield Republican*, January 27, 1872. For other examples of Bowles's criticism of Greeley, see *Springfield Republican*, January 13, 1871, June 2, 1871, September 14, 1871, and February 2 and 3, 1872.

29. *Cincinnati Commercial*, November 10, 1870, September 11, 1871, December 29, 1870; *Springfield Republican*, March 18, 1872, August 1, 1872.

30. Van Deusen, *Greeley*, 404; Schurz quoted in T. F. Randolph to Whitelaw Reid, February 20, 1872, Whitelaw Reid Papers, LC; Lyman Trumbull to Horace White, March 6, 1872, Horace White Papers, ISHL; Tusa, "Power, Priorities, and Political Insurgency," 184–86; A. W. Vitsch to Carl Schurz, March 24, 1872, Carl Schurz Papers, LC.

31. Edward Atkinson to Carl Schurz, March 20, 1872, Carl Schurz Papers, LC; Roeliff Brinkerhoff to Lyman Trumbull, March 23, 1872, Lyman Trumbull Papers, LC; George W. Nichols to Carl Schurz, March 28, 1872, Carl Schurz Papers, LC; Jacob D. Cox to William M. Grosvenor, March 23, 1872, William M. Grosvenor Papers, CU; S. K. Prime to Lyman Trumbull, March 29, 1872, Lyman Trumbull Papers, LC.

32. Van Deusen, *Greeley*, 403; *New York Tribune*, March 30, 1872; Edward Atkinson to Charles Sumner, April 3, 1872, Edward Atkinson Papers, MHS; J. D. Cox to Carl Schurz, April 5, 1872, Carl Schurz Papers, LC.

33. Whitelaw Reid to Henry Warmouth, March 12, 1872, Henry Warmouth Papers, Southern Historical Collection, University of North Carolina at Chapel Hill; Lyman Trumbull to Horace White, April 24, 1872, Lyman Trumbull Papers, LC; Whitelaw Reid to Horace Greeley, March 1872, Horace Greeley Papers, LC; William M. Grosvenor to Edward Atkinson, April 5, 6, 15, and 22, 1872, J. D. Cox to Edward Atkinson, April 11, 1872, Edward Atkinson Papers, MHS.

34. David Davis, quoted in King, *Davis*, 277–78.

35. King, *Davis*, 103, 107–8, 127, 172, 182, 184; Krug, *Trumbull*, 100, 168–69.

36. William M. Grosvenor, "The Rights of the Nation and the Duty of Congress," *New Englander* 29 (October 1865): 767, 772; Michael Les Benedict, "Preserving the Constitution: The Conservative Basis of Radical Reconstruction," *Journal of American History* 61 (December 1974): 8; *Chicago Tribune*, September 10, 1866; Mark E. Neely Jr., *The Fate of Liberty: Abraham Lincoln and Civil Liberties* (New York: Oxford University Press, 1991), 35, 175–76; King, *Davis*, 253–56, 263–64, 277, 280. The *Milligan* decision was unanimous, though Chief Justice Salmon P. Chase, who also briefly flirted with the liberal republicans, wrote the concurrent opinion for four justices, including himself.

37. Horace White to Lyman Trumbull, March 24, 1872, Lyman Trumbull to Gustave Koerner, March 9, 1872, Lyman Trumbull to John M. Palmer, April 8, 1872, Lyman Trumbull Papers, LC; Samuel Bowles to J. C. Collins, March 22, 1872, Samuel Bowles to Charles Sumner, March 30, 1872, Samuel Bowles Papers, Yale.

38. *Springfield Republican*, March 28, 1872; *Chicago Tribune*, March 30, 1872; Samuel Bowles to Carl Schurz, March 18, 1872, Carl Schurz Papers, LC; Lyman Trumbull to John M. Palmer, April 8, 1872, Horace White to Lyman Trumbull, March 21, 1872, Lyman Trumbull Papers, LC.

39. Jesse O. Norton to David Davis, March 6, 1872, John Wentworth to David Davis, April 13, 1872, David Davis Collection, ISHL; M. C. Kerr to Edward Atkinson, April 27, 1872, Edward Atkinson Papers, MHS; Lyman Trumbull to Gustave Koerner, March 9, 1872, Horace White to Lyman Trumbull, March 17, 1872, Lyman Trumbull Papers, LC; King, *Davis*, 277–78; *Cincinnati Commercial*, April 27, 1872.

40. Eric Foner, *Reconstruction: America's Unfinished Revolution, 1863–1877* (New York: Harper and Row, 1988), 478–79; King, *Davis*, 278–79; William M. Grosvenor to J. Warren Bell, March 4, 1872, David Davis Papers, ISHL; On Davis's preparations for the conven-

tion see *Springfield Republican*, May 10, 1872 and Koerner, *Memoirs*, 544, 548; *Cincinnati Commercial*, April 22, 1872.

41. Donald W. Curl, *Murat Halstead and the Cincinnati Commercial* (Boca Raton: University Presses of Florida, 1980), 63–64; Logsdon, *White*, 219–22; Henry Watterson, "The Humor and Tragedy of the Greeley Campaign," *The Century Illustrated Monthly Magazine* 85 (November, 1912): 29–31; Joseph Frazier Wall, *Henry Watterson: Reconstructed Rebel* (New York: Oxford University Press, 1956): 51–53, 96, 99–100; *Cincinnati Commercial*, April 29, 1872; *Springfield Republican*, April 29, 1872; *Chicago Tribune*, April 29, 1872; *Louisville Courier-Journal*, April 29, 1872. Watterson's article on the Cincinnati Convention, "The Humor and Tragedy of the Greeley Campaign," deserves greater weight than most remembered accounts because he sent copies of it to Whitelaw Reid and Horace White before publication. Reid pointed out some mistakes but found that "on the whole, it seems to me extremely fair and accurate"(43). White did not dispute the facts of Watterson's account but made note "that you have dwelt too much on the humorous side of the Cincinnati Convention, and that you have omitted the only features that gave it *raison d'être*"(45). Watterson decided not to revise his account, but did include Reid and White's reactions at the end of the article. Despite Watterson's published and corroborated account, most works covering the Cincinnati Convention still confuse the formation and activities of the Quadrilateral. Earle Ross and Matthew Downey both ignore the activities of the Quadrilateral on April 28, before Reid joined on the 29th, while Jacqueline Tusa has Reid joining the Quadrilateral on April 28. The result is that none of them fully explore the process by which Reid, and through him Greeley, joined forces with the liberal republicans at the convention. Ross, *Liberal Republican Movement*, 87; Downey, "Horace Greeley and the Politicians," 737; Tusa, "Power, Priorities, and Political Insurgency," 230–33.

42. Bingham Duncan, *Whitelaw Reid: Journalist, Politician, Diplomat* (Athens: University of Georgia Press, 1975), 19, 23–25, 37; James G. Smart, "Whitelaw Reid and the Nomination of Horace Greeley," *Mid-America: An Historical Review* 49 (October 1967): 233–35; *New York Tribune*, April 30, 1872; Watterson, "The Greeley Campaign," 31. Samuel Bowles was also indebted to Reid for arranging for *Springfield Republican* dispatches to be sent, at the *New York Tribune*'s expense, from Cincinnati to New York, whence they were then forwarded to Springfield. He was also friendly enough with Reid to have suggested in early April that they travel to Cincinnati together. Samuel Bowles to Whitelaw Reid, April 1 and 23, 1872, Reid Family Papers, LC.

43. Curl, *Halstead*, 64–65; *New York Tribune*, April 30, 1872; Watterson, "Greeley Campaign," 32–33; *Springfield Republican*, April 30, 1872; *Cincinnati Commercial*, April 30, 1872. See also the *Chicago Tribune* and the *Louisville Courier-Journal* for April 30, 1872.

44. Watterson, "Greeley Campaign," 33 (most historians take the same quote—"The Davis boom went down before it. The Davis boomers were paralyzed" from *"Marse Henry,"* 1: 247); Downey, "The Liberal Republican Convention," 737; King, *Davis*, 281–82; Jesse Fell to David Davis, April 30, 1872, James E. Harvey to David Davis, April 30, 1872, John Wentworth to David Davis, April 30, May 1 and 2, 1872, E. W. Stoughton to David Davis, May 8, 1872, David Davis Papers, ISHL. In addition to Downey, other historians who cite Watterson as their primary evidence to prove that the Davis movement ended on April 30 include Ross (*Liberal Republican Movement*, 87–88), Tusa ("Power, Priorities, and Political Insurgency," 233), Curl (*Halstead*, 65), and Wall (*Watterson*, 104). Logsdon (*White*, 224) misuses John Wentworth's May 2 telegram to David Davis—which mentions newspapers only once and not even the editorials of the 30th—to argue that the Quadrilateral killed the Davis movement on April 30.

45. Smart, "Whitelaw Reid," 238; John Wentworth to David Davis, May 2, 1872, David Davis Papers, ISHL.

46. Lyman Trumbull to Sinclair Tousey, April 27, 1872, Lyman Trumbull Papers, LC; William Grosvenor to Edward Atkinson, April 6, 1872, Edward Atkinson Papers, MHS; For discussion of the meetings between the liberal republicans and Greeley's representatives see the *Cincinnati Commercial*, April 30, 1872.

47. *Springfield Republican*, April 30, 1872, May 1, 1872; Horace Greeley to Whitelaw Reid (telegram), April 30, 1872, Horace Greeley Papers, LC.

48. Horace Greeley to Whitelaw Reid (telegram), April 30, 1872, Horace Greeley Papers, LC; *New York Tribune*, May 1, 1872; *Cincinnati Commercial*, May 1, 1872.

49. *Proceedings of the Liberal Republican Convention* (New York: Baker Godwin, 1872), 4–5; *Cincinnati Commercial*, May 2, 1872.

50. *New York Tribune*, May 2, 1872; *Springfield Republican*, May 2, 1872; *Proceedings*, 7–8, 13; *Cincinnati Commercial*, May 2, 1872; Smart, "Whitelaw Reid," 236–37. After the protest Theodore Tilton, an abolitionist and longtime friend of Greeley, convinced the rest of the New York caucus that since "there was a general feeling that this Convention was making a new departure in politics and ought not to adopt anything savoring of gag laws," New York delegates should be able to vote for any candidate. The compromise was meaningless, though, since only three of New York's sixty-eight delegates were free traders. *New York Tribune*, May 3, 1872.

51. *Proceedings*, 6–7; *Cincinnati Commercial*, May 2, 1872; *New York Tribune*, May 2, 1872; James E. Harvey to David Davis (telegram), May 2, 1872, David Davis Papers, ISHL; *New York Tribune*, May 3, 1872; *Springfield Republican*, May 2, 1872; Horace Greeley to Whitelaw Reid (telegram), May 1, 1872, Horace Greeley Papers, LC.

52. Clay and Matthews quoted in *Cincinnati Commercial*, May 3, 1872; For another account of Clay and Matthews's speeches see the *Springfield Republican*, May 3, 1872; Frank W. Bird to Charles Sumner, May 7, 1872, Charles Sumner Papers, Harvard; *Proceedings,*, 16–20.

53. *Proceedings*, 18–19.

54. Frank W. Bird to Charles Sumner, May 7, 1872, Charles Sumner Papers, Harvard; *Proceedings*, 16–21.

55. *Springfield Republican*, May 2, 1872; *Proceedings*, 12; Winslow Pierce to Charles Francis Adams, May 3, 1872, Adams Papers, MHS; *Cincinnati Commercial*, May 3, 1872.

56. *Cincinnati Commercial*, May 3 and 4, 1872; *Springfield Republican*, May 4, 1872; *New York Tribune*, May 4, 1872; *Louisville Courier-Journal*, May 4, 1872. Not surprisingly, the *Proceedings of the Liberal Republican Convention* uses the numbers from Greeley's *New York Tribune*. Historians have used different sources for voting results, some of which differ by up to fourteen votes for a candidate on a single ballot. Since it is impossible to know which vote counts are correct, and analyzing the important points of the balloting does not require such precision, I will only make arguments supported by all of the different sources.

57. *Springfield Republican*, April 29 and 30, 1872; *Cincinnati Commercial*, May 2, 1872; Winslow S. Pierce to Charles Francis Adams, May 3, 1872, Adams Papers, MHS.

58. *Cincinnati Commercial*, May 4, 1872; David Wells to Lyman Trumbull, May 8, 1872, Horace White to Lyman Trumbull, May 4, 1872, Lyman Trumbull Papers, LC.

59. *Cincinnati Commercial*, May 4, 1872; *Louisville Courier-Journal*, May 4, 1872. Smart thinks Reid's ability to keep the Greeley forces together in the face of Adams' growing strength was his most difficult and significant accomplishment in getting Greeley nominated; Smart, "Whitelaw Reid," 238–39.

60. *Proceedings*, 29–31; *Springfield Republican*, May 4, 1872; *Cincinnati Commercial*, May 4, 1872.

61. Koerner, *Memoirs*, 2:557.

8. The Experience of a Third Party in the Nineteenth Century

1. Earle Ross has contended that "the fundamental explanation of the 'tidal wave' of 1872 simmers down to this,—that the country had confidence in Grant," and Matthew Downey assures readers that "one need not delve too deeply for a sufficient explanation of Greeley's defeat. Popular though he was among the people, Greeley's opponent was Grant, the great war hero who saved the Union." Earle D. Ross, *The Liberal Republican Movement* (New York: AMS Press, 1919), 190; Matthew T. Downey, "The Rebirth of Reform: A Study of Liberal Reform Movements, 1865–1872," Ph.D. diss. (Princeton University, 1963), 593, 595. Other historians, such as William Gillette, blame Greeley's eccentric personality and blundering campaign; see Gillette, *Retreat from Reconstruction, 1869–1879* (Baton Rouge: Louisiana State University Press, 1979), 62–70. Michael Perman, in *The Road to Redemption: Southern Politics, 1869–1879* (Chapel Hill: University of North Carolina Press, 1984), finds that in 1872 "there was a growing sense that the parties were about to undergo a significant rearrangement" (152), but most historians have argued otherwise. In *The Liberal Republican Movement,* Ross concludes that "the formation of a new opposition party was out of the question" (239), and William Gillette's recent synthesis of the election argues that "as the Democratic party entered the 1872 campaign it was not in the most robust of health: yet its condition was scarcely terminal." Gillette, "Election of 1872," in Arthur M. Schlesinger and Fred L. Israel, eds., *History of American Presidential Elections, 1789–1968* (New York: Chelsea House, 1971), 2:1317.

2. *Springfield Republican,* March 28 and 13, 1872; *Cincinnati Commercial,* March 29, 1872, July 11, 1872; W. C. Flagg to Lyman Trumbull, July 25, 1872, Lyman Trumbull Papers, LC.

3. *Springfield Republican,* May 27 and 28, 1872; *Chicago Tribune,* June 13, 1872; John G. Sproat, *"The Best Men": Liberal Republicans in the Gilded Age* (New York: Oxford University Press, 1968); Julian in *Cincinnati Commercial,* May 6, 1872, July 20, 1872.

4. Frederick Law Olmsted to Samuel Bowles, May 11, 1872, Frederick Law Olmsted Collection, LC; Laura Wood Roper, *FLO: A Biography of Frederick Law Olmsted* (Baltimore: Johns Hopkins University Press, 1973), 287, 340; Samuel Bowles to Frederick Law Olmsted, May 11 and 21, 1872, Samuel Bowles Papers, Yale University; Samuel Bowles to Frederick Law Olmsted, May 15, 1872, Olmsted Collection, LC; Samuel Bowles to David A. Wells, May 21, 1872, Horace White to David A. Wells, May 17, 1872, Lyman Trumbull to David A. Wells, May 11, 1872, David A. Wells Papers, LC; William Cullen Bryant to Lyman Trumbull, May 8, 1872, in *Letters of William Cullen Bryant,* ed. William Cullen Bryant II and Thomas G. Voss (New York: Fordham University Press, 1975–92), 6:63; Lyman Trumbull to William Cullen Bryant, May 14, 1872, Trumbull Papers, LC.

5. Matthews and Hoadly, quoted in *Cincinnati Commercial,* August 3 and 26, 1872; *New York Evening Post,* May 24 and 4, 1872.

6. *The Nation,* May 9, 1872, June 20, 1872, July 18, 1872; Edwin L. Godkin to Carl Schurz, June 28, 1872, in *Speeches, Correspondence, and Political Papers of Carl Schurz,* Frederic Bancroft, ed. (New York: G. P. Putnam's Sons, 1913), 2:388.

7. Eugene David Schmiel, "The Career of Jacob Dolson Cox, 1828–1900: Soldier, Scholar, Statesman," Ph.D diss. (Ohio State University, 1969), 343; Jacob D. Cox to David A. Wells, May 23, 1872, July 22, 1872, David A. Wells Papers, LC; Jacob D. Cox to J. Q. Smith, August 6, 1872, quoted in Schmiel, "Career of Cox," 351.

8. *New York Times,* May 5 and 8, 1872, June 10, 1872; Grenville M. Dodge to Edwin D. Morgan, August 9, 1872, William E. Chandler to Edwin D. Morgan, July 11, 1872, Edwin D. Morgan to William E. Chandler, July 10, 1872, William E. Chandler Papers, LC.

9. *New York Times,* July 2 and 9, 1872; Volney Spalding to James Edmunds, July 12, 1872, Columbus Delano to "Sir," William E. Chandler Papers, LC.

10. Perman, *Road to Redemption,* 19–20, 126; *Savannah Morning News,* May 17, 1872, quoted in Daniel E. Sutherland, "Edwin DeLeon and Liberal Republicanism in Georgia: Horace Greeley's Campaign for President in a Southern State," *The Historian* 47 (November 1984): 50; Michael C. Kerr to Edward Atkinson, May 13, 1872, Atkinson Papers, MHS, quoted in Jacqueline Balk Tusa, "Power, Priorities, and Political Insurgency: The Liberal Republican Movement, 1869–1872," Ph.D. diss. (Pennsylvania State University, 1970), 265.

11. Cyrus McCormick to Daniel Cameron, quoted in Michael C. Robinson, "Illinois Politics in the Post–Civil War: The Liberal Republican Movement; A Case Study," Ph.D diss. (University of Wyoming, 1973), 180; *New York Herald,* May 5, 1872, June 11 and 21, 1872.

12. *New York Herald,* July 6, 1872; *New York Times,* May 8, 1872; Julian, in *Cincinnati Commercial,* May 20, 1872.

13. *New York Herald,* July 6, 1872.

14. Matthew Downey partially blames the Liberal Republicans for losing the election, asserting that "the reformers lost so decisively in 1872 partly because they neglected to cultivate and organize the voting masses" (Downey, "Rebirth of Reform," 593, 595). William Gillette agrees that the Liberal Republicans did not organize well enough, but proposes that "the root of the failure went deeper. Liberal Republicans had a way of their own. They wanted to play politics, but had no time or skill to learn the rules of the game. Instead of building a party with a broad base they conceived of a party of likeminded men who championed their own causes" (Gillette, "Election of 1872," 2:1329). Downey's and Gillette's analyses, though, do not distinguish between the liberal republican movement before the Cincinnati Convention and the Liberal Republican Party afterward. In addition, they and other historians cover the entire campaign in the same narrative, discussing the activities of the Liberal Republicans, Democrats, and Republicans in roughly chronological order.

15. Mark Voss-Hubbard, "The 'Third Party Tradition' Reconsidered: Third Parties and American Public Life, 1830–1900," *Journal of American History* 84 (December 1997); Joseph G. Rayback, *Free Soil: The Election of 1848* (Lexington: University of Kentucky Press, 1970), 301; Irwin Unger, *The Greenback Era: A Social and Political History of American Finance, 1865–1879* (Princeton: Princeton University Press), 337. In "The 'Third Party Tradition' Reconsidered," Voss-Hubbard notes that major parties could often crush their challengers "because third party movements, built on the antiparty appeal, lacked a durable culture of discipline and institutional loyalty"(148).

16. *Springfield Republican,* May 4, 1872; *Cincinnati Commercial,* May 4, 1872; *Chicago Tribune,* May 4, 1872; *New York Tribune,* May 6, 1872.

17. Charles Francis Adams Jr. diary, May 4, 1872, Charles Francis Adams II Papers, MHS; George Hoadly to Barney, May 13, 1872, Carl Schurz Papers, LC; David A. Wells to Edward Atkinson, May 11, 1872, Atkinson Papers, MHS; Edward Atkinson to Charles Sumner, June 1, 1872, Charles Sumner Papers, Harvard University; Petition to Carl Schurz, June 1, 1872, Schurz Papers, LC.

18. Memo to Carl Schurz, June 6, 1872, W. Sharpe to Carl Schurz, May 31, 1872, Edward Atkinson to Carl Schurz, Schurz Papers, LC; *The Nation,* June 6, 1872; Charles Francis Adams Jr. to Charles Francis Adams, June 15, 1872, Adams Family Papers, MHS.

19. William M. Grosvenor to Edward Atkinson, May 12, 1872, Mahlon Sands to Edward Atkinson, May 13, 1872, Edward Atkinson to R. B. Miniturn, May 13, 1872, Atkinson Papers, MHS; Mahlon Sands to Carl Schurz, May 14, 1872, Schurz Papers, LC; Jacob D. Cox to William Grosvenor, William M. Grosvenor Papers, CU; Chester McArthur

Destler, *Henry Demarest Lloyd and the Empire of Reform* (Philadelphia: University of Pennsylvania Press, 1963), 59–60.

20. Edward Atkinson to Charles Sumner, May 23, 1872, Atkinson Papers, MHS; Samuel Bowles to David A. Wells, May 28, 1872, David A. Wells Papers, LC; Samuel Bowles to Henry Demarest Lloyd, June 11, 1872, Samuel Bowles to Whitelaw Reid, June 11, 1872, Whitelaw Reid Papers, LC; *Springfield Republican*, May 4, 1872.

21. *Cincinnati Commercial*, May 6, 1872; Samuel Bowles to David Wells, May 28, 1872, David Wells Papers, LC; *Springfield Republican*, May 4, 1872, June 12, 1872.

22. *The Nation*, May 23, 1872; *New York Evening Post*, May 16, 1872.

23. Carl Schurz to Samuel Bowles, May 11, 1872, Carl Schurz to Horace Greeley, May 6, 1872, in Schurz, *Speeches, Correspondence,* 2:369, 361; Carl Schurz to Whitelaw Reid, May 20, 1872, Whitelaw Reid Papers, LC; Horace White to William Grosvenor, June 6, 1872, William M. Grosvenor Papers, CU.

24. Carl Schurz to Horace Greeley, May 6, 1872, in Schurz, *Speeches, Correspondence,* 2:361–63; Carl Schurz to William Grosvenor, June 5, 1872, William M. Grosvenor Papers, CU; Hans L. Trefouse, *Carl Schurz: A Biography* (New York: Fordham University Press, 1998), 206–7.

25. Horace Greeley to Carl Schurz, May 8, 1872, in *The Reminiscences of Carl Schurz* (New York: McClure, 1908), 3:350–51; Horace Greeley to Carl Schurz, May 20, 1872, in Schurz, *Speeches, Correspondence,* 2:377; Horace White to Carl Schurz, May 26, 1872, and William Grosvenor to Carl Schurz, May 26, 1872, Schurz Papers, LC; Hiram Barney to Carl Schurz, May 24, 1872, Schurz Papers, LC; Edwin Godkin to Carl Schurz, May 19, 1872, in Schurz, *Speeches, Correspondence,* 2:376; Carl Schurz to William Grosvenor, June 5, 1872, William M. Grosvenor Papers, CU; Carl Schurz to Edwin Godkin, May 20, 1872, in Schurz, *Speeches, Correspondence,* 2:377–79.

26. W. Sharpe to Carl Schurz, May 31, 1872, Schurz Papers, LC; Carl Schurz to William Grosvenor, June 5, 1872, William M. Grosvenor Papers, CU; Horace White to William Grosvenor, June 6, 1872, William M. Grosvenor Papers, CU.

27. Horace White to Lyman Trumbull, June 13, 1872, Trumbull Papers, LC; Lyman Trumbull to W. G. Flagg, January 10, 1872, Lyman Trumbull Papers, ISHL; Lyman Trumbull to William C. Bryant, May 10, 1872, Lyman Trumbull Papers, ISHL.

28. Trumbull and Wells quoted in *New York Herald*, June 21, 1872; S. L. Taylor to Edward Atkinson, June 24, 1872, Atkinson Papers, MHS. For another account of the conference see *Springfield Republican*, June 21, 1872.

29. *New York Evening Post*, June 21, 1872; *The Nation*, June 27, 1872.

30. The platform quoted in the *Springfield Republican*, June 22 and 24, 1872. For other accounts of the convention see the *New York Evening Post*, June 22, 1872; *The Nation*, June 27, 1872; Memo, June 21, 1872, Frederick Law Olmsted Papers, LC.

31. Edward Atkinson to Parke Goodwin, June 24, 1872, Edward Atkinson to George T. Bogley, August 16, 1872, Atkinson Papers, MHS; Schmiel, "Career of Cox," 351–52; Edwin Godkin to Carl Schurz, June 28, 1872, in Schurz, *Speeches, Correspondence,* 2:386; S. L. Taylor to Edward Atkinson, July 29, 1872, Edward Atkinson Papers, MHS; *Cincinnati Commercial*, October 2, 1872, August 3 and 26, 1872; Edwin Godkin to Edward Atkinson, October 31, 1872, Atkinson Papers, MHS.

32. Downey, "The Rebirth of Reform," 566; Ethan Allen to Nathaniel P. Banks, August 3, 1872, Nathaniel P. Banks Papers, LC; Ross, *Liberal Republican Movement,* 104; Summers, *Era of Good Stealings,* 210–13.

33. Samuel Bowles to Whitelaw Reid, June 11 and 18, 1872, Whitelaw Reid Papers, LC; Joseph Logsdon, *Horace White, Nineteenth-Century Liberal* (Westport, Conn.: Greenwood Publishing, 1971), 243–45; Horace White to Whitelaw Reid, June 27, 1872, July 1, 1872, Whitelaw Reid Papers, LC.

34. Horace Greeley to Carl Schurz, July 8, 1872, in Schurz, *Speeches, Correspondence,* 2:390; Horace Greeley to Whitelaw Reid, July 13, 1872, Samuel Bowles to Whitelaw Reid, June 18, 1872, Whitelaw Reid Papers, LC.

35. Lyman Trumbull to William C. Bryant, May 10, 1872, Trumbull Papers, ISHL.

36. Mark Voss-Hubbard describes how the major parties could beat back "third party challenges with party patronage and piecemeal reform." In his analysis of third parties in the nineteenth century, however, Voss-Hubbard intentionally flattens the differences among movements to "advance our interpretive approaches to them" (Voss-Hubbard, "Third Party Tradition," 148, 123). In "The Primacy of Party Reasserted," *Journal of American History* 84, no. 3 (December 1997), Michael F. Holt astutely observes that Voss-Hubbard's and others' decision "to treat the party period as a unit by largely ignoring spatial and chronological variations also forecloses the examination of interesting questions and limits the explanatory power of their analyses" (153). Mark W. Summers also argues, in *Party Games: Getting, Keeping, and Using Power in Gilded Age Politics* (Chapel Hill: University of North Carolina Press, 2004), that the Democrats and Republicans destroyed third parties in the same way from 1860 to the 1890s, insisting that "the means were all too ordinary, used for thirty years by one major party against the other, and by both against any intruder in the system" (x). I think the major parties' methods of dealing with third-party threats gradually evolved to fit the patterns Voss-Hubbard and Summers describe. The Democrats and Free Soilers formed coalitions in a number of states during the mid-1850s, but these remained local initiatives without the support of the national Democratic Party. See Eric Foner, *Reconstruction: America's Unfinished Revolution, 1863–1877* (New York: Harper and Row, 1988), 504.

37. Tusa, "Power, Priorities, and Political Insurgency," 197–98, 205–7; Ari Hoogenboom, *Outlawing the Spoils: A History of the Civil Service Reform Movement, 1865–1883* (Urbana: University of Illinois Press, 1961), 88, 90, 95, 107–8; *The Nation,* December 21, 1871.

38. Foner, *Reconstruction,* 504; *New York Times,* June 6, 1872; Samuel Bowles to David A. Wells, May 21, 1872, David A. Wells Papers, LC; *New York Times,* May 22, 1872; *New York Herald,* May 25, 1872; *The Nation,* August 22, 1872; Ross, *Liberal Republican Movement,* 176; James A. Rawley, "The General Amnesty Act of 1872: A Note," *Mississippi Valley Historical Review* 47 (December 1960), 480–84.

39. J. G. Tracy to William E. Chandler, March 14, 1872, Jay Cooke to William E. Chandler, February 26 and 29, Chandler Papers, LC. *CG,* 42nd Cong., 2nd sess., 1314, 1321–22; *Reports,* 42nd Cong., 2nd sess., vol. 3, no. 183, part 1, 835–40; Raleigh *News* quoted in J. G. De Roulhac Hamilton, "The Elections of 1872 in North Carolina," *South Atlantic Quarterly* 11 (April 1912): 148–49; Tusa, "Power, Priorities, and Political Insurgency," 197–98, 205–7.

40. Jay Cooke to William E. Chandler, February 26 and 29, 1872, March 2, 1872, Chandler Papers, LC.

41. Edward Rollins to George Robeson, February 13, 1872; Edward Rollins to William E. Chandler, February 17 and 25, 1872; William Claflin to William E. Chandler, February 30, 1872, Eugene L. Sullivan to William E. Chandler, March 16, 1872, J. G. Tracy to William E. Chandler, March 14, 1872, Thomas B. Van Buren to William E. Chandler, March 29, 1872, General Tichenor to William E. Chandler, April 8, 1872, Moses Hale to William E. Chandler, March 25, 1872, April 10, 1872, Chandler Papers, LC.

42. *Proceedings of the Liberal Republican Convention* (New York: Baker and Godwin, 1872), 19–21; *Proceedings of the National Union Republican Convention* (Washington: Gibson Brothers, 1872), 51–52.

43. *Proceedings of the Liberal Republican Convention,* 19–21; *Proceedings of the National Union Republican Convention,* 51–52; *Cincinnati Commercial,* October 14, 1872.

44. Tusa, "Power, Priorities, and Political Insurgency," 293; Daniel Shepard to William E. Chandler, July 29, 1872, Harry B. Brown to William E. Chandler, September 13, 1872, Chandler Papers, LC.

45. Margaret Susan Thompson, The "Spider Web": Congress and Lobbying in the Age of Grant (Ithaca: Cornell University Press, 1985), 169; Foner, Reconstruction, 467; Summers, Era of Good Stealings, 48, 234; Grenville M. Dodge to Edwin D. Morgan, July 27, 1872, Chandler Papers, LC.

46. James G. Blaine to William E. Chandler, July 20, 1872, Edmund D. Morgan to William E. Chandler, July 6, 1872, Jacob Reese to S. E. Dudley, September 2, 1872, James M. Edmunds to William E. Chandler, August 14, 1872, William E. Chandler to "The Friends of the Republican Cause and Candidates," May 11, 1872, Grenville M. Dodge to Edwin D. Morgan, August 9, 1872, Chandler Papers, LC.

47. For example, Foner contends, "The election of 1872 confirmed and reinforced the reign of organizational politics" (Foner, Reconstruction, 510); Cincinnati Commercial, September 4, 1872. Historians from Ross to Gillette have used Democrats' dissatisfaction with Greeley to help explain the Liberal Republican defeat. Gillette argues that "it was glib to expect loyal Democrats to furnish only the voters and dissident Republicans the candidates" (Gillette, "Election of 1872," 2:1329), while Ross argues that "the impossibility of reconciling large numbers of Democratic voters to Greeley's candidacy was probably decisive in bringing about the overwhelming defeat of the coalition ticket. Most of the Democratic leaders carried out their part of the compact faithfully, if not cheerfully, but the rank and file of the party recognized no such obligation" (Ross, Liberal Republican Movement, 188).

48. Irving Katz, August Belmont: A Political Biography (New York: Columbia University Press, 1968), 197–98; Augustus Belmont to Carl Schurz, April 23, 1872, Schurz Papers, LC; James T. Tall to Thomas F. Bayard, April 1, 1872, Thomas F. Bayard Papers, LC.

49. Glyndon Van Deusen, Horace Greeley, Nineteenth-Century Crusader (New York: Hill and Wang, 1953), 102–3; Augustus Belmont quoted in Katz, Belmont, 19–20, 202; George T. McJimsey, Genteel Partisan: Manton Marble, 1834–1917 (Ames: Iowa State University Press, 1971), 161.

50. Samuel Bowles to Whitelaw Reid, May 10, 1872, Whitelaw Reid Papers, LC; Samuel Bowles to David A. Wells, May 9, 1872, David A. Wells Papers, LC; Katz, Belmont, 202–3; Whitelaw Reid to Lyman Trumbull, June 2, 1872, Trumbull Papers, LC.

51. Perman, Road to Redemption, 110; James W. Hinton to Matt Whitaker Ransom, May 21, 1872, Matt Whitaker Ransom Papers, Southern Historical Collection, Wilson Library, University of North Carolina at Chapel Hill; Daniel M. Barringer to David Miller Carter, May 28, 1872, David Miller Carter Papers, UNC–Chapel Hill; Sutherland, "Edwin DeLeon," 40; H. G. Spruill to David Miller Carter, June 1, 1872, David Miller Carter Papers, UNC–Chapel Hill; Mark D. Brainard to William E. Chandler, May 28, 1872, Chandler Papers, LC; William D. C. Jones to George Washington Jones, June 13, 1872, George Washington Jones Papers, UNC–Chapel Hill.

52. McJimsey, Marble, 161; Katz, Belmont, 203; Sam H. Brinton to Thomas F. Bayard, May 29, 1872, George Lunt to Thomas F. Bayard, May 27, 1872, Thomas F. Bayard Papers, LC.

53. J. Belt Robinson to Thomas F. Bayard, June 14, 1872, George Lunt to Thomas F. Bayard, May 27, 1872, James Kanchy to Thomas F. Bayard, June 26, 1872, Thomas F. Bayard Papers, LC.

54. Katz, Belmont, 205–7; Logsdon, White, 246; Nathaniel P. Banks to Mary Theodosia Palmer Banks, August 14, 1872, Nathaniel P. Banks Papers, LC; Horace White to Whitelaw Reid, September 15, 1872, Reid Family Papers, LC.

55. Barnes to Carl Schurz, May 27, 1872, Schurz Papers, LC; B. Grvoal (sp?) to Thomas F. Bayard, July 8, 1872, Robert Reynolds to Thomas F. Bayard, October 7, 1872, John C. Gooden to Thomas F. Bayard, October 18, 1872, Thomas F. Bayard Papers, LC.

56. Circular, August 20, 1872, Chandler Papers, LC; Carl Schurz to William M. Grosvenor, June 5, 1872, William M. Grosvenor Papers, CU; Carl Schurz to Whitelaw Reid, August 20, 1872, Reid Family Papers, LC.

57. A. G. Bowman to William E. Chandler, July 15, 1872, Volney Spalding to William E. Chandler, August 3, 1872, Grenville M. Dodge to Edwin D. Morgan, July 27, 1872, William E. Chandler to "The President," August 16, 1872, Chandler Papers, LC.

58. H. F. Pickles to William E. Chandler, August 22, 1872, Chandler Papers, LC.

59. Grenville M. Dodge to Edwin D. Morgan, August 9, 1872, John Pool to William E. Chandler, August 20, 1872, Mr. Hathaway to "Gentlemen of the Nat. Rep. Com.," July 17, 1872, Chandler Papers, LC; Summers, *Party Games*, 198–99.

60. *The Nation*, August 15, 1872; Volney Spalding to William E. Chandler, August 3, 1872, Chandler Papers, LC; Ross, *Liberal Republican Movement*, 146–47; Blanton Duncan to G. W. Wright, October 28, 1872, Thurlow Weed Papers, LC.

61. W. J. Yates to Daniel M. Barringer, July 22, 1872, Daniel M. Barringer, July Folder, Daniel M. Barringer Papers, UNC–Chapel Hill; Robinson, "Illinois Politics in the Post–Civil War," 169–70.

62. Jamie R. Smith to William E. Chandler, July 20, 1872, Chandler Papers, LC; William E. Chandler to Elihu B. Washburne, July 19, 1872, Elihu B. Washburne Papers, LC; J. J. Young to William E. Chandler, August 7, 1872, Chandler Papers, LC; W. H. Avera to Daniel M. Barringer, August 9, 1872, Daniel M. Barringer Papers, UNC–Chapel Hill; Hamilton, "Election of 1872," 150–51.

63. Grenville M. Dodge to Edwin D. Morgan, August 9, 1872, John W. Foster to William E. Chandler, September 3, 1872, George Nicols to William E. Chandler, September 4, 1872, William L. Burt to William E. Chandler, September 11, 1872, Chandler Papers, LC; Tusa, "Power, Priorities, and Political Insurgency," 313.

64. Ross, *Liberal Republican Movement*, 180–81; Edwin Stanley Bradley, *The Triumph of Militant Republicanism: A Study of Pennsylvania and Presidential Politics, 1860–1872* (Philadelphia: University of Pennsylvania Press, 1964), 364, 413; Michael C. Kerr to Lyman Trumbull, Trumbull Papers, ISHL; John W. Foster to William E. Chandler, September 3, 1872, Chandler Papers, LC; William E. Chandler to Elihu B. Washburne, September 16, 1872, Elihu B. Washburne Papers, LC; *Chicago Tribune*, October 10, 1872; *Cincinnati Commercial*, October 9, 1872.

65. Nathaniel P. Banks to Mary Theodosia Palmer Banks, October 9, 1872, Nathaniel P. Banks Papers, LC, Bradley, *Triumph of Militant Republicanism*, 414; Hamilton, "Elections of 1872," 150–51; William Gillette, "Election of 1872," 1328; *Cincinnati Commercial*, November 7, 1872.

66. Horace Greeley to Mrs. Jennie Mason, November 8, 1872, Horace Greeley Papers, New York Public Library.

9. The Lasting Effect of 1872 Campaign Rhetoric

1. William L. Burt to William E. Chandler, September 11, 1872, William E. Chandler Papers, LC; Earle D. Ross, *The Liberal Republican Movement* (New York: AMS Press, 1919), 150; Horace Greeley to Mrs. Jennie Mason, November 8, 1872, Horace Greeley Papers, New York Public Library.

2. David M. Tucker, *Mugwumps: Public Moralists of the Gilded Age* (Columbia: University of Missouri Press, 1998), 57; Carl Schurz to William Grosvenor, June 5, 1872, William M. Grosvenor Papers, CU; *Cincinnati Commercial*, September 19, 1872; *The Nation*, August 1, 1872.

3. *Cincinnati Commercial*, July 19, 1872, August 15, 1872, November 7, 1872.

4. *Cincinnati Commercial*, August 22, 1872; *The Nation*, July 11, 1872; Daniel E. Sutherland, "Edwin DeLeon and Liberal Republicanism in Georgia," *The Historian* 47 (November 1984): 44; David W. Blight, *Race and Reunion: The Civil War in American*

Memory (Cambridge, Mass.: Harvard University Press, 2001), 124, 126. See also Earle D. Ross, "Horace Greeley and the South, 1865–1872," *South Atlantic Quarterly* 16 (October 1917): 324–338.

5. Carl Schurz, *Speeches, Correspondence, and Political Papers of Carl Schurz,* Frederic Bancroft, ed. (New York: G. P. Putnam's Sons, 1913), 2:393; John F. Farnsworth, "Speech of Hon. John F. Farnsworth," in *Chicago Tribune Campaign Documents* (Chicago: Rand, McNally and Company, 1872), document no. 4, 14; Alexander K. McClure, "Liberalism vs. Grantism!," in *The Speeches of A. K. McClure* (Philadelphia, 1872), 1; *Harper's Weekly,* September 21, 1872, October, 19, 1872.

6. *Cincinnati Commercial,* July 20, 1872; John M. Palmer, "Opening Speech of the Campaign at Decatur, May 25, 1872," 15, John M. Palmer I Papers, ISHL; Blight, *Race and Reunion,* 125.

7. Gary W. Gallagher, "Introduction," *The Myth of the Lost Cause and Civil War History,* Gary W. Gallagher and Alan T. Nolan, eds. (Bloomington: University of Indiana Press, 2000), 1; McClure, "Grant Rule in the South," in McClure, *Speeches,* 14.

8. *Cincinnati Commercial,* July 7, 1872; Palmer, "Opening Speech of the Campaign," 16.

9. *Cincinnati Commercial,* September 19, 1872, July 7 and 13, 1872, September 14, 1872, August 1, 1872; J. C. Thompson, *One Hundred Reasons Why General Grant Should Not Be Re-elected President of the United States* (Philadelphia: J. C. Thompson, 1872), 10.

10. *Bangor Commercial,* September 5, 1872, in William M. Grosvenor Papers, CU; Lyman Trumbull, "Senator Trumbull's Springfield Speech," *Chicago Tribune Campaign Documents* (Chicago: Rand, McNally and Company, 1872), document no. 3, 1; Brinkerhoff in *Cincinnati Commercial,* July 7, 1872; Farnsworth, "Speech of Hon. John H. Farnsworth," 1, 14, 7.

11. Palmer, "Opening Speech of the Campaign," 1, 3, 16; *Cincinnati Commercial,* August 22, 1872.

12. Claude G. Bowers, *The Tragic Era: The Revolution after Lincoln* (New York: Houghton Mifflin, 1929), 198, 282, 442, 340; Eric Foner, "Reconstruction Revisited," *Reviews in American History* 10 (December 1982): 82.

13. *Cincinnati Commercial,* August 1, 1872, September 25, 1872, October 25, 1872, August 22, 1872, July 7, 1872; Carl Schurz, "Why Anti-Grant and Pro-Greeley," in Schurz, *Speeches, Correspondence,* 2:412; *Westliche Post,* translated and quoted in *Springfield Republican,* June 19, 1872.

14. Richard N. Current, *Those Terrible Carpetbaggers: A Reinterpretation* (New York: Oxford University Press, 1988); *Bangor Commercial,* September 5, 1872; McClure, "Liberalism vs. Grantism!," in McClure, *Speeches,* 7; J. D. Caton, in "Speeches by Hon. J. D. Caton and Hon. Wm. M. Springer," *Chicago Tribune Campaign Documents* (Chicago: Rand, McNally and Company, 1872), document no. 5, 2; *Cincinnati Commercial,* August 22, 1872; Schurz, "Why Anti-Grant and Pro-Greeley," in Schurz, *Speeches, Correspondence,* 2:412; *Springfield Republican,* June 19, 1872.

15. Schurz, *Speeches, Correspondence,* 1:446–47; 2:396, 437–38.

16. *Cincinnati Commercial,* September 25, 1872, July 7, 1872.

17. *Cincinnati Commercial,* July 13, 1872; *Springfield Republican,* June 11 and 20, 1872.

18. *Cincinnati Commercial,* September 25, 1872, October 25, 1872.

19. *Cincinnati Commercial,* July 7, 1872, August 1, 1872; Caton, in "Speeches by Caton and Springer"; McClure, "The Finances and the Labor Interests—Secretary Boutwell and his Failures—The Syndicate," in McClure, *Speeches,* 6.

20. McClure, "Grant Rule in the South," in McClure, *Speeches,* 6; Palmer, "Opening Speech of the Campaign," 13–14; Thompson, *Why General Grant Should Not Be Re-elected,* 7. For a discussion of debate surrounding federal intervention during the Chicago Fire of 1871, see Andrew L. Slap, "'The Strong Arm of the Military Power of the

United States': The Chicago Fire, the Constitution, and Reconstruction," *Civil War History* 47 (June 2001), 146–63.

21. Bowers, *Tragic Era*, 279, 441; William S. McFeely, *Grant: A Biography* (New York: W. W. Norton, 1981), 521–22; Brooks D. Simpson, *Let Us Have Peace: Ulysses S. Grant and the Politics of War and Reconstruction, 1861–1868* (Chapel Hill: University of North Carolina Press, 1991), xiii; *Cincinnati Commercial*, August 1, 1872.

22. Mark E. Neely Jr., *The Union Divided: Party Conflict in the Civil War North* (Cambridge, Mass.: Harvard University Press, 2002), 55, 58; Michael F. Holt, "Making and Mobilizing the Republican Party, 1856–1860," in *The Birth of the Grand Old Party: The Republicans' First Generation*, Robert F. Engs and Randall M. Miller, eds. (Philadelphia: University of Pennsylvania Press, 2002), 40–44.

23. *Cincinnati Commercial*, June 7, 1872; McClure, "Liberalism vs. Grantism!," in McClure, *Speeches*, 5; Springer, in "Speeches by Caton and Springer," 9; Mahan quoted in *Cincinnati Commercial*, August 22, 1872.

24. *Cincinnati Commercial*, June 20, 1872, September 23, 1872, July 7, 1872.

25. *Cincinnati Commercial*, July 7, 1872, August 22, 1872, October 14, 1872, November 5, 1872; Schurz, *Speeches, Correspondence*, 2:424.

26. Caton, in "Speeches by Caton and Springer," 6–7; Springer, in "Speeches by Caton and Springer," 10–1; Schurz, *Speeches, Correspondence*, 2:389; *Cincinnati Commercial*, August 22, 1872, October 25, 1872, August 11, 1872; McClure, "Liberalism vs. Grantism!" in McClure, *Speeches*, 4; Trumbull, "Senator Trumbull's Springfield Speech," 2–8; Farnsworth, "Speech of Hon. John H. Farnsworth," 7; Springer, in "Speeches by Caton and Springer," 10–5.

27. McClure, "Grant Rule in the South," in McClure, *Speeches*, 9; Caton, in "Speeches by Caton and Springer," 4–5; Palmer, "Opening Speech of the Campaign," 14; *Springfield Republican*, May 22, 1872; *Cincinnati Commercial*, July 19, 1872.

28. *Cincinnati Commercial*, November 5, 1872; Palmer, "Opening Speech of the Campaign," 7; Brinkerhoff in *Cincinnati Commercial*, July 7, 1872.

29. *Cincinnati Commercial*, September 19, 1872; Palmer, "Opening Speech of the Campaign," 5; Caton, in "Speeches of Caton and Springer," 6–7; Farnsworth, "Speech of Hon. John H. Farnsworth," 2.

30. *Cincinnati Commercial*, June 10, August 22, 1872; McFeely, *Grant*, 521–22.

31. Sproat, *"Best Men,"* 281, 43, 76, 277, 280; Eric Foner, *Reconstruction: America's Unfinished Revolution, 1863–1877* (New York: Harper and Row, 1988), 488.

32. *Cincinnati Commercial*, July 1, 1872, May 24, 1872; *Springfield Republican*, May 10, 1872.

33. *Springfield Republican*, June 22 and 24, 1872.

34. *Cincinnati Commercial*, August 22, 1872.

35. Alexander K. McClure, "The Grant Investment in Bolters," in McClure, *Speeches*, 2–3.

36. *Cincinnati Commercial*, September 19 and 25, 1872.

37. *The Nation*, May 16, 1872; Carl Schurz to Edwin Godkin, May 20, 1872, in Schurz, *Speeches, Correspondence*, 2:378; *New York Evening Post*, June 1, 1872.

38. *Cincinnati Commercial*, August 26 and 3, 1872, October 2, 1872; *North American Review* 115 (October 1872), 408.

39. Sproat, *"Best Men,"* 273, 6; Henry Adams to Charles Francis Adams Jr., November 25, 1864, Adams Family Papers, MHS; Godkin, *Life and Letters of Edwin Lawrence Godkin*, Rollo Ogden, ed. (New York: Macmillan Company, 1907), 1:316; Tucker, *Mugwumps*, 71, 124.

40. Sproat, *"Best Men,"* 281.

10. The Liberal Republicans Try Again, 1872–1876

1. Carl Schurz to Horace White, November 15, 1872, in *Speeches, Correspondence, and Political Papers of Carl Schurz*, Frederic Bancroft, ed. (New York: G. P. Putnam's Sons, 1913), 2:444–45, 448.

2. Schurz, *Speeches, Correspondence*, 2:445–46; *Cincinnati Commercial*, November 14, 1872.

3. Robert F. Engs and Randall M. Miller, eds., *The Birth of the Grand Old Party: The Republicans' First Generation* (Philadelphia: University of Pennsylvania Press, 2002), 81, 101; Mark M. Krug, *Lyman Trumbull, Conservative Radical* (New York: A. S. Barnes, 1965), 339–41.

4. William Cullen Bryant to Leonice M. S. Moulton, May 17, 1876, in *The Letters of William Cullen Bryant*, ed. William Cullen Bryant II and Thomas G. Voss (New York: Fordham University Press, 1975–92), 6:304.

5. Schurz, *Speeches, Correspondence*, 3:18, 49–50.

6. Schurz, *Speeches, Correspondence*, 3:55, 58, 63; Hans L. Trefousse, *Carl Schurz: A Biography* (New York: Fordham University Press, 1998), 220–21.

7. Samuel Bowles to George W. Smalley, February 3, 1874, in George S. Merriam, *The Life and Times of Samuel Bowles* (New York: Century Co., 1885), 2:335; Schurz, *Speeches, Correspondence*, 3:1; Henry Adams to Samuel Bowles, April 23, 1874, in J. C. Levenson et al., eds., *The Letters of Henry Adams*, vol. 2, *1868–1885* et al., eds. (Cambridge, Mass.: Harvard University Press, 1982), 191–92.

8. Eric Foner, *Reconstruction: America's Unfinished Revolution, 1863–1877* (New York: Harper and Row, 1988), 512, 518; Schurz, *Speeches, Correspondence*, 3:97; Trefousse, *Carl Schurz*, 221–22.

9. Trefousse, *Carl Schurz*, 221–22; Foner, *Reconstruction*, 528; Schurz, *Speeches, Correspondence*, 3:79, 74, 79–83.

10. Schurz, *Speeches, Correspondence*, 3:83, 93, 97; Trefousse, *Carl Schurz*, 222–23.

11. Henry Adams to Carl Schurz, December 26, 1874; Henry Adams to Charles Milnes Gaskell, February 15, 1875; Henry Adams to Frederick Law Olmsted, April 7, 1875; Henry Adams to Carl Schurz, April 12, 1875, in *Letters of Henry Adams*, 2:214–18, 221–22; Joseph Logsdon, *Horace White, Nineteenth-Century Liberal* (Westport, Conn.: Greenwood Publishing, 1971), 269.

12. Henry Adams to Charles Milnes Gaskell, May 24, 1875, in *Letters of Henry Adams*, 2:225–26; Charles Francis Adams Jr. to Carl Schurz, July 16, 1875; Carl Schurz to Charles Francis Adams Jr., July 22, 1876, in Schurz, *Speeches, Correspondence*, 3:157–60.

13. Carl Schurz to William M. Grosvenor, July 16, 1876; Carl Schurz to Charles Francis Adams Jr., July 16, 1875; Carl Schurz to Charles Francis Adams Jr., July 22, 1876, in Schurz, *Speeches, Correspondence*, 3:155–60; Samuel Bowles to Murat Halstead, October 19, 1875, in Merriam, *Samuel Bowles*, 2:348.

14. Trefousse, *Carl Schurz*, 225; Charles Francis Adams Jr. to Carl Schurz, July 16, 1875; Carl Schurz to Charles Francis Adams Jr., July 22, 1875, August 18, 1875, in Schurz, *Speeches, Correspondence*, 3:156–61; Henry Adams to Charles Milnes Gaskell, October 4, 1875, in *Letters of Henry Adams*, 2:239–40; Schurz, "Honest Money," September 27, 1875, in Schurz, *Speeches, Correspondence*, 3:161–66.

15. *New York Times*, quoted in Trefousse, *Carl Schurz*, 225; Charles Francis Adams Jr. to Carl Schurz, October 13, 1875; Carl Schurz to Charles Francis Adams Jr., October 15, 1875, in Schurz, *Speeches, Correspondence*, 3:156–66.

16. Carl Schurz to Samuel Bowles, January 16 and 4, 1876; Carl Schurz to Benjamin H. Bristow, February 15, 1876; Benjamin H. Bristow to Carl Schurz, February 18, 1876, in Schurz, *Speeches, Correspondence*, 3:217–22; Trefousee, *Carl Schurz*, 226–27.

17. Henry Adams to Charles Milnes Gaskell, February 9, 1876; Henry Adams to Henry Cabot Lodge, February 27, 1876, in *Letters of Henry Adams*, 2:246–51, 256–58.

18. Henry Adams to Carl Schurz, February 14, 1876, in *Letters of Henry Adams*, 2:249–51.

19. Henry Adams to Carl Schurz, February 14, 1876, in *Letters of Henry Adams*, 2:249–51.

20. "Circular Call of the Fifth Avenue Hotel Conference," April 6, 1876; Carl Schurz to L. A. Sherman, April 15, 1876; "Address to the People," in Schurz, *Speeches, Correspondence*, 3:228–31, 240–48; John G. Sproat, *"Best Men": Liberal Reformers in the Gilded Age* (New York: Oxford University Press, 1968), 91; Trefousse, *Carl Schurz*, 227–28.

21. Sproat, *"Best Men,"* 92–93.

22. Henry Adams to Charles Milnes Gaskell, June 14, 1876; Henry Adams to Henry Cabot Lodge, June 24, 1876, in *Letters of Henry Adams*, 2:274–79.

23. Carl Schurz to Rutherford B. Hayes, June 21 and June 23, 1876; Rutherford B. Hayes to Carl Schurz, July 5, 1876; Carl Schurz to Charles Francis Adams Jr., July 9, 1876, in Schurz, *Speeches, Correspondence*, 3:248–60.

24. Henry Adams to Henry Cabot Lodge, September 4, 1876; Henry Adams to Charles Milnes Gaskell, September 8, 1876, in *Letters of Henry Adams*, 2:290–92.

Conclusion

1. Heather Cox Richardson, *The Death of Reconstruction: Race, Labor, and Politics in the Post–Civil War North, 1865–1901* (Cambridge, Mass.: Harvard University Press, 2001), 119.

2. C. Vann Woodward, *Reunion and Reaction: The Compromise of 1877 and the End of Reconstruction* (New York: Oxford University Press, 1966), 169, 222–23; Carl Schurz to Rutherford B. Hayes, January 25, 1877, in *Speeches, Correspondence, and Political Papers of Carl Schurz*, Frederic Bancroft, ed. (New York: G. P. Putnam's Sons, 1913), 3:366–76.

3. Carl Schurz to Rutherford B. Hayes, January 25, 1877, in Schurz, *Speeches, Correspondence*, 3:366–76.

Bibliography

Primary Sources

Manuscript Collections

Adams Family Papers, Massachusetts Historical Society
Charles Francis Adams II Papers, Massachusetts Historical Society
Edward Atkinson Papers, Massachusetts Historical Society
Edward A. Atkinson Papers, New York Public Library
John C. Bagby Papers, Illinois State Historical Library
Nathaniel P. Banks Papers, Library of Congress
Daniel M. Barringer Papers, Southern Historical Collection, Wilson Library, University of North Carolina at Chapel Hill
Thomas F. Bayard Papers, Library of Congress
Francis W. Bird Papers, Houghton Library, Harvard University
Blair Family Papers, Library of Congress
Samuel Bowles Papers, Manuscripts and Archives, Yale University
Frederick G. Bromberg Papers, Southern Historical Collection, Wilson Library, University of North Carolina at Chapel Hill
Orville H. Browning Papers, Illinois State Historical Library
David Miller Carter Papers, Southern Historical Collection, Wilson Library, University of North Carolina at Chapel Hill
William E. Chandler Papers, Library of Congress
Roscoe Conkling Papers, Library of Congress
James D. Cox Papers, Oberlin College
Richard Henry Dana Papers, Massachusetts Historical Society
David Davis Papers, Illinois State Historical Library
Anna E. Dickinson Papers, Library of Congress
Thomas Drew Papers, Massachusetts Historical Society
Endicott Family Papers, Massachusetts Historical Society
Jesse W. Fell Papers, Library of Congress
Joseph S. Fowler Papers, Southern Historical Collection, Wilson Library, University of North Carolina at Chapel Hill

Edward L. Godkin Papers, New York Public Library

Zephaniah N. Gooding Papers, Special Collections, Perkins Library, Duke University

Horace Greeley Papers, Library of Congress

Horace Greeley Papers, New York Public Library

William M. Grosvenor Papers, Butler Library, Columbia University

Risley Hanson Papers, Special Collections, Perkins Library, Duke University

Ozais M. Hatch Papers, Illinois State Historical Library

George F. Hoar Papers, Massachusetts Historical Society

Joseph Holt Papers, Library of Congress

William Jayne Papers, Illinois State Historical Library

George Washington Jones Papers, Southern Historical Collection, Wilson Library, University of North Carolina at Chapel Hill

Edward Kinsley Papers, Massachusetts Historical Society

Amos A. Lawrence Papers, Massachusetts Historical Society

Hugh McCulloch Papers, Library of Congress

Massachusetts Reform Club Papers, Massachusetts Historical Society

Frederick Law Olmsted Papers, Library of Congress

John M. Palmer I Papers, Illinois State Historical Library

John M. Palmer II Papers, Illinois State Historical Library

William M. Piatt Papers, Special Collections, Perkins Library, Duke University

Matt Whitaker Ransom Papers, Southern Historical Collection, Wilson Library, University of North Carolina at Chapel Hill

Reid Family Papers, Library of Congress

William Schouler Papers, Massachusetts Historical Society

Carl Schurz Papers, Library of Congress

Thomas Settle Papers, Southern Historical Collection, Wilson Library, University of North Carolina at Chapel Hill

William D. Simpson Papers, Southern Historical Collection, Wilson Library, University of North Carolina at Chapel Hill

Francis Elias Spinner Papers, Library of Congress

Charles Sumner Papers, Houghton Library, Harvard University

Charles Sumner Papers, Special Collections, Perkins Library, Duke University

J. C. Thompson Papers, Special Collections, Perkins Library, Duke University

Lyman Trumbull Papers, Illinois State Historical Library

Lyman Trumbull Papers, Library of Congress

John C. Underwood Papers, Library of Congress

Henry Clay Warmouth Papers, Southern Historical Collection, Wilson Library, University of North Carolina at Chapel Hill

Elihu Washburne Papers, Library of Congress

Thurlow Weed Papers, Library of Congress
David A. Wells Papers, Library of Congress
David A. Wells Papers, Massachusetts Historical Society
David A. Wells Papers, New York Public Library
Horace White Papers, Illinois State Historical Library
George Fred William Papers, Massachusetts Historical Society
Henry Wilson Papers, Library of Congress
George Washington Wright Papers, Library of Congress

Government Records and Publications

Congressional Globe
Congressional Record
Haines, Elijah M. *The Military Occupation of Chicago, Complete Vindication of Governor Palmer. Speech of Hon. E. M. Haines, of Lake, in the House of Representatives of Illinois, Wednesday, January 31, 1872.* Springfield, Ill.: State Journal Steam Print, 1872.
Journal of the Senate of the Twenty-Seventh General Assembly of the State of Illinois, at the Adjourned Session, Begun and Held at Springfield, November 15, 1871. Springfield, Ill.: State Journal Steam Print, 1872.
Palmer, John M. *Message of His Excellency John M. Palmer, Governor of Illinois, to the Twenty-Seventh General Assembly, Convened January 4th, 1871.* Springfield, Ill., 1871.

Periodicals

Atlantic Monthly
Bangor Commercial
Chicago Tribune
Cincinnati Commercial
Louisville Courier-Journal
Missouri Democrat
Missouri Republican
The Nation
New Englander
New York Evening Post
New York Herald
New York Times
New York Tribune
North American Review

Springfield Republican
Springfield Weekly Republican

Published Documents and Other Contemporary Publications

Adams, Charles Francis. *The Republican Party a Necessity: Speech of Charles Francis Adams of Massachusetts.* Washington, D.C., 1860. ·

Adams, Charles Francis Jr. "The Government and the Railroad Corporations." *North American Review* 112 (January 1871): 31–61.

———. *The Great Secession Winter of 1860–1861 and Other Essays.* Edited by George Hochfield. New York: Sagamore Press, 1958.

———. "Railway Problems in 1869." *North American Review* 110 (January 1870): 116–50.

———. "The Railroad System," *North American Review* 104 (April 1867): 476–511.

Adams, Henry [Brooks]. "Civil Service Reform." *North American Review* 109 (October 1869): 443–75.

Address of the Radicals of Saint Louis to the People of Missouri. Saint Louis: Missouri Democrat Book and Job Office, 1868.

American Free Trade League. *American Industry and the Tariff: An Abridgement of Commissioner Wells's Report for 1869.* New York: American Free Trade League, 1869.

———. *How the High Tariff Oppresses the Poor.* New York: American Free Trade League, 1870.

———. *Is this Protection?* New York: American Free Trade League, 1870.

———. *The Tariff: As It Is and As It Should Be.* New York: American Free Trade League, 1870.

———. *What the Farmers Say about the Tariff.* New York: American Free Trade League, 1870.

Atkinson, Edward. "Free Trade—Revenue Reform." *Atlantic Monthly* 28 (October 1871): 460–80.

———. *Inefficiency of Economic Legislation.* Cambridge, Mass.: Riverside Press, 1871.

Chicago Tribune Campaign Documents. Chicago: and, McNally and Company, 1872. Copy owned by the Illinois State Historical Library.

Cox, Jacob D. "The Civil Service Reform." *North American Review* 112 (January 1871): 81 113.

Curtis, George William. *Orations and Addresses of George William Curtis.* 3 vols. Edited by Charles Eliot Norton. New York: Harper and Brothers, 1894.

Dyer, Oliver. *Phonographic Report of the National Free Soil Convention at Buffalo, N.Y.* Buffalo, N.Y.: G. H. Derby, 1848.

Godkin, Edwin L. "Aristocratic Opinions of Democracy." *North American Review* 100 (January 1865): 194–232.

———. "Commercial Immorality and Political Corruption." *North American Review* 107 (July 1868): 248–66.

———. "Co-operation." *North American Review* 106 (January 1868): 150–75.

———. "The Labor Crisis." *North American Review* 105 (July 1867): 177–213.

———. "The Prospects of the Political Art." *North American Review* 100 (April 1870): 398–419.

Grosvenor, William M. *Does Protection Protect? An Examination of the Effect of Different Forms of Tariff upon American Industry.* New York: D. Appleton, 1871.

———. "The Law of Conquest the True Basis of Reconstruction." *New Englander* 29 (January 1865): 111–31.

———. "The Rights of the Nation, and the Duty of Congress." *New Englander* 29 (October 1865): 755–77.

Halstead, Murat. *Trimmers, Trucklers, and Temporizers: Notes of Murat Halstead from the Political Conventions of 1856.* Madison: State Historical Society of Wisconsin, 1961.

Hodgskin, J. B. "The Financial Condition of the United States." *North American Review* 108 (April 1869): 517–41.

McClure, Alexander K. *The Speeches of A. K. McClure.* Philadelphia, 1872.

Newcom, Simon. "The Labor Question." *North American Review* 111 (July 1870): 123–55.

Nordhoff, Charles. "The Misgovernment of New York,—A Remedy Suggested." *North American Review* 113 (October 1871): 321–43.

Proceedings of the Liberal Republican Convention. New York: Baker and Godwin, 1872.

Proceedings of the Republican National Union Convention. Washington, D.C.: Gibson Brothers, 1872.

Schurz, Carl. "The True Problem." *Atlantic Monthly* 19 (March 1867): 371–78.

Thompson, J. C. *One Hundred Reasons Why General Grant Should Not Be Reelected President of the United States: Which Will Be Sufficient to Prevent Every Sensible and Honest Man from Voting for Him.* Philadelphia: J. C. Thompson, 1872.

Wells, David A. "The Meaning of Revenue Reform." *North American Review* 113 (July 1871): 104–53.

Published Letters and Autobiographical Works

Adams, Henry. *The Education of Henry Adams.* Boston: Houghton Mifflin, 1918.
————. *The Letters of Henry Adams.* Edited by J. C. Levenson, Ernest Samuels,
   Charles Vandersee, and Viola Hopkins Winner. 6 vols. Cambridge, Mass.:
   Harvard University Press, 1982.
Blaine, James G. *Twenty Years at Congress: From Lincoln to Garfield.* 2 vols. Nor-
   wich, Conn.: Henry Bill Publishing Company, 1886.
Bryant, William Cullen. *The Letters of William Cullen Bryant.* Edited by William
   Cullen Bryant II and Thomas G. Voss. 6 vols. New York: Fordham Univer-
   sity Press, 1975–92.
Clay, Cassius M. *The Life of Cassius Marcellus Clay: Memoirs, Writings, and
   Speeches.* Cincinnati: J. Fletcher Bennan, 1886.
Godkin, Edwin L. *Life and Letters of Edwin Lawrence Godkin.* Edited by Rollo
   Ogden. 2 vols. New York: Macmillan Company, 1907.
Julian, George. *Political Recollections, 1840 to 1872.* Chicago: Jansen, McClurg
   and Company, 1884.
Koerner, Gustave. *Memoirs of Gustave Koerner, 1809–1896.* Edited by Thomas J.
   McCormack. 2 vols. Cedar Rapids, Iowa: Torch Press, 1909.
Palmer, John M. *Personal Recollection of John M. Palmer: The Story of an Earnest
   Life.* Cincinnati: Robert Clarke Company, 1901.
Schurz, Carl. *Intimate Letters of Carl Schurz, 1841–1869.* Edited by Joseph
   Schafer. Madison: State Historical Society of Wisconsin, 1928.
————. *The Reminiscences of Carl Schurz.* 3 vols. New.York: McClure, 1908.
————. *Speeches, Correspondence, and Political Papers of Carl Schurz.* Edited by
   Frederick Bancroft. 3 vols. New York: G. P. Putnam's Sons, 1913.
Sumner, Charles. *Charles Sumner: His Complete Works.* Edited by George Fris-
   bie Hoar. 20 vols. Boston: Lee and Shepard, 1900.
Watterson, Henry. "The Humor and Tragedy of the Greeley Campaign." *Cen-
   tury Illustrated Monthly Magazine* 135 (November 1912): 26–45.
————. *"Marse Henry": An Autobiography.* 2 vols. New York: George H.
   Doran, 1919.

Secondary Works

Books

Abbot, Richard H. *The Republican Party and the South, 1855–1877: The First
   Southern Strategy.* Chapel Hill: University of North Carolina Press, 1987.
Albin, Mel, ed. *New Directions in Psychohistory.* Lexington, Mass.: Lexington
   Books, 1980.

Appleby, Joyce Oldham. *Liberalism and Republicanism in the Historical Imagination.* Cambridge, Mass.: Harvard University Press, 1992.

Armstrong, William M. *E. L. Godkin: A Biography.* Albany: State University of New York Press, 1978.

Bailyn, Bernard. *The Ideological Origins of the American Revolution.* Cambridge, Mass.: Harvard University Press, 1967.

Baker, Jean Harvey. *Affairs of Party: The Political Culture of Northern Democrats in the Mid-Nineteenth Century.* New York: Fordham University Press, 1998.

Barclay, Thomas S. *The Liberal Republican Movement in Missouri, 1865–1871.* Columbia: State Historical Society of Missouri, 1926.

Baum, Dale. *The Civil War Party System: The Case of Massachusetts, 1848–1876.* Chapel Hill: University of North Carolina Press, 1984.

Bensel, Richard Franklin. *Yankee Leviathan: The Origins of Central State Authority in America.* New York: Cambridge University Press, 1995.

Black, David. *King of Fifth Avenue: The Fortunes of August Belmont.* New York: Dial Press, 1981.

Blight, David W. *Race and Reunion: The Civil War in American Memory.* Cambridge, Mass.: Harvard University Press, 2001.

Boomraem, Henrik V. *The Formation of the Republican Party in New York: Politics and Conscience in the Antebellum North.* New York: New York University Press, 1983.

Bowers, Claude. *The Tragic Era: The Revolution after Lincoln.* New York: Houghton Mifflin, 1929.

Bradley, Edwin Stanley. *The Triumph of Militant Republicanism: A Study of Pennsylvania and Presidential Politics, 1860–1872.* Philadelphia: University of Pennsylvania Press, 1964.

Brauer, Kinley J. *Cotton versus Conscience: Massachusetts Whig Politics and Southwestern Expansion, 1843–1848.* Lexington: University of Kentucky Press, 1967.

Brown, Charles H. *William Cullen Bryant.* New York: Scribner's, 1971.

Chalfant, Edward. *Better in Darkness: A Biography of Henry Adams, His Second Life, 1862 1891.* Hamden, Conn.: Archon Books, 1994.

Chambers, William Nisbet and Walter Dean Burnham, eds. *The American Party Systems: Stages of Political Development.* New York: Oxford University Press, 1968; 2nd ed. 1975.

Cherny, Robert W. *American Politics in the Gilded Age, 1868–1900.* Wheeling, Ill.: Harlan Davidson, 1997.

Cohen, Nancy. *The Reconstruction of American Liberalism, 1865–1914.* Chapel Hill: University of North Carolina Press, 2002.

Curl, Donald W. *Murat Halstead and the Cincinnati Commercial.* Boca Raton: University Presses of Florida, 1980.

Current, Richard N. *Those Terrible Carpetbaggers: A Reinterpretation.* New York: Oxford University Press, 1988.

Curry, Leonard P. *Blueprint for Modern America: Nonmilitary Legislation of the First Civil War Congress.* Nashville: Vanderbilt University Press, 1968.

Curry, Richard O., ed. *Radicalism, Racism, and Party Realignment: The Border States during Reconstruction.* Baltimore: Johns Hopkins University Press, 1969.

Destler, Chester McArthur. *Henry Demarest Lloyd and the Empire of Reform.* Philadelphia: University of Pennsylvania Press, 1963.

Donald, David. *Lincoln Reconsidered.* New York: Alfred A. Knopf, 1965.

Donald, David Herbert, Jean Harvey Baker, and Michael F. Holt. *The Civil War and Reconstruction.* New York: W. W. Norton, 2001.

Duberman, Martin. *Charles Francis Adams, 1807–1886.* Stanford: Stanford University Press, 1960.

Duncan, Bingham. *Whitelaw Reid: Journalist, Politician, Diplomat.* Athens: University of Georgia Press, 1975.

Dunning, William A. *Reconstruction, Political and Economic, 1865–1877.* New York: Harper and Brothers, 1907.

Engs, Robert F. and Randall M. Miller, eds. *The Birth of the Grand Old Party: The Republicans' First Generation.* Philadelphia: University of Pennsylvania Press, 2002.

Fellman, Michael. *Inside War: The Guerrilla Conflict in Missouri during the American Civil War.* New York: Oxford University Press, 1989.

Ferleger, Herbert Ronald. *David A. Wells and the American Revenue System, 1865–1870.* Ann Arbor, Mich.: Edward Brothers, 1942.

Foner, Eric. *Free Soil, Free Labor, Free Men: The Ideology of the Republican Party Before the Civil War.* New York: Oxford University Press, 1970.

———. *Reconstruction: America's Unfinished Revolution.* New York: Harper and Row, 1988.

Gallagher, Gary W. and Alan T. Nolan, eds. *The Myth of the Lost Cause and Civil War History.* Bloomington: University of Indiana Press, 2000.

Gienapp, William E. *The Origins of the Republican Party, 1852–1856.* New York: Oxford University Press, 1987.

Gillete, William. *Retreat from Reconstruction, 1869–1879.* Baton Rouge: Louisiana State University Press, 1979.

Goldman, Eric. *Rendezvous with Destiny: A History of Modern American Reform.* New York: Knopf, 1956.

Hess, Earl J. *Liberty, Virtue, and Progress: Northerners and Their War for Union.* New York: Fordham University Press, 1997.

Hofstadter, Richard. *The Age of Reform: From Bryant to F.D.R.* New York: Vintage Books, 1955.

Holt, Michael. *The Political Crisis of the 1850s.* New York: John Wiley and Sons, 1978.

———. *The Rise and Fall of the American Whig Party: Jacksonian Politics and the Onset of the Civil War.* New York: Oxford University Press, 1999.

Hoogenboom, Ari. *Outlawing the Spoils: A History of the Civil Service Reform Movement, 1865–1883.* Urbana: University of Illinois Press, 1961.

Hyman, Harold. *A More Perfect Union: The Impact of the Civil War and Reconstruction on the Constitution.* New York: Knopf, 1973.

Josephson, Matthew. *The Politicos, 1865–1896.* New York: Harcourt and Brace, 1963.

Katz, Irving. *August Belmont: A Political Biography.* New York: Columbia University Press, 1968.

Kelly, Robert Lloyd. *The Transatlantic Persuasion: The Liberal-Democratic Mind in the Age of Gladstone.* New York: Knopf, 1969.

King, Willard L. *Lincoln's Manager: David Davis.* Cambridge, Mass.: Harvard University Press, 1960.

Kleppner, Paul. *The Third Electoral Party System, 1853–1892: Parties, Voters, and Political Cultures.* Chapel Hill: University of North Carolina Press, 1979.

Krug, Mark M. *Lyman Trumbull, Conservative Radical.* New York: A. S. Barnes, 1965.

Logsdon, Joseph. *Horace White, Nineteenth-Century Liberal.* Westport, Conn.: Greenwood Publishing, 1971.

Maizlish, Stephen E. *The Triumph of Sectionalism: The Transformation of Ohio Politics, 1844–1856.* Kent, Ohio: Kent State University Press, 1983.

Mayfield, John. *Rehearsal for Republicanism: Free Soil and the Politics of Antislavery.* Port Washington, N.Y.: Kennikat Press, 1980.

McCormick, Richard L. *The Party Period and Public Policy: American Politics from the Age of Jackson to the Progressive Era.* New York: Oxford University Press, 1986.

McFeeley, William S. *Grant: A Biography.* New York: W. W. Norton, 1981.

McGerr, Michael E. *The Decline of Popular Politics: The American North, 1865–1928.* New York: Oxford University Press, 1986.

McInerney, Daniel. *The Fortunate Heirs of Freedom: Abolition and Republican Thought.* Lincoln: University of Nebraska Press, 1994.

McJimsey, George T. *Genteel Partisan: Manton Marble, 1834–1917.* Ames: Iowa State University Press, 1971.

McPherson, James M. *Battle Cry of Freedom: The Civil War Era.* New York: Oxford University Press, 1988.

McPherson, James M. and William J. Cooper Jr., eds. *Writing the Civil War: The Quest to Understand.* Columbia: University of South Carolina Press, 1998.

Merriam, George S. *The Life and Times of Samuel Bowles.* 2 vols. New York: Century Co., 1885.

Merril, Horace Samuel. *Bourbon Democracy of the Middle West, 1865–1896.* Baton Rouge: Louisiana State University Press, 1953.

Montgomery, David. *Beyond Equality: Labor and the Radical Republicans, 1862–1872.* New York: Alfred A. Knopf, 1967.

Morgan, Wayne H., ed. *The Gilded Age: A Reappraisal.* Binghamton, N.Y.: Syracuse University Press, 1963.

————. *The Gilded Age: Revised and Enlarged Edition.* Syracuse, N.Y.: Syracuse University Press, 1970.

Neely, Mark E. Jr. *The Fate of Liberty: Abraham Lincoln and Civil Liberties.* New York: Oxford University Press, 1991.

————. *The Union Divided: Party Conflict in the Civil War North.* Cambridge, Mass.: Harvard University Press, 2002.

Nevins, Allan. *The Evening Post: A Century of Journalism.* New York: Russell and Russell, 1922.

Niven, John. *Salmon P. Chase: A Biography.* New York: Oxford University Press, 1995.

Palmer, George Thomas. *A Conscientious Turncoat: The Story of John Palmer, 1817–1900.* New Haven: Yale University Press, 1941.

Parrish, William E. *Missouri under Radical Rule, 1865–1870.* Columbia: University of Missouri Press, 1965.

Perman, Michael. *The Road to Redemption: Southern Politics, 1869–1879.* Chapel Hill: University of North Carolina Press, 1984.

Peterson, Norma L. *Freedom and Franchise: The Political Career of B. Gratz Brown.* Columbia: University of Missouri Press, 1965.

Potter, David M. *The Impending Crisis, 1848–1861.* Completed and edited by Don E. Fehrenbacher. New York: Harper and Row, 1976.

Rayback, Joseph. *Free Soil: The Election of 1848.* Lexington: University of Kentucky Press, 1970.

Reitano, Joanne. *The Tariff Question in the Gilded Age: The Great Tariff Debate of 1888.* University Park: Pennsylvania State University Press, 1994.

Rhodes, James Ford. *History of the United States from the Compromise of 1850 to the Restoration of Home Rule in 1877.* 9 vols. New York: Macmillan, 1892–1919.

Richards, Leonard L. *The Slave Power: The Free North and Southern Domination, 1780–1860.* Baton Rouge: Louisiana State University Press, 2000.

Richardson, Heather Cox. *The Death of Reconstruction: Race, Labor and Politics in the Post–Civil War North, 1865–1901.* Cambridge, Mass.: Harvard University Press, 2001.

———. *The Greatest Nation of the Earth: Republican Economic Policies during the Civil War.* Cambridge, Mass.: Harvard University Press, 1997.

Roper, Laura Wood. *FLO: A Biography of Frederick Law Olmsted.* Baltimore: Johns Hopkins University Press, 1973.

Ross, Earle D. *The Liberal Republican Movement.* New York: AMS Press, 1919.

Schlesinger, Arthur M. and Fred L. Israel, eds. *History of American Presidential Elections, 1789–1968.* Vol. 2, *1848–1896.* New York: Chelsea House, 1971.

Shafer, Byron E. and Anthony J. Badger, eds. *Contesting Democracy: The Substance and Structure of American Political History, 1775–2000.* Lawrence: University Press of Kansas, 2001.

Silbey, Joel. *The American Political Nation, 1838–1893.* Stanford: Stanford University Press, 1991.

Simpson, Brooks D. *Let Us Have Peace: Ulysses S. Grant and the Politics of War and Reconstruction, 1861–1868.* Chapel Hill: University of North Carolina Press, 1991.

Sproat, John G. *"The Best Men": Liberal Reformers in the Gilded Age.* New York: Oxford University Press, 1968.

Summers, Mark Wahlgren. *The Era of Good Stealings.* New York: Oxford University Press, 1993.

———. *Party Games: Getting, Keeping, and Using Power in Gilded Age Politics.* Chapel Hill: University of North Carolina Press, 2004.

———. *The Plundering Generation: Corruption and the Crisis of the Union, 1849–1861.* New York: Oxford University Press, 1987.

———. *The Press Gang: Newspapers and Politics, 1865–1878.* Chapel Hill: University of North Carolina Press, 1994.

Terrill, Tom E. *The Tariff, Politics, and American Foreign Policy, 1874–1901.* Westport, Conn.: Greenwood Press, 1973.

Thompson, Margaret Susan. *The "Spider Web": Congress and Lobbying in the Age of Grant.* Ithaca: Cornell University Press, 1985.

Trelease, Allen W. *White Terror: The Ku Klux Klan Conspiracy and Southern Reconstruction.* New York: Harper and Row, 1971.

Trefousse, Hans L. *Carl Schurz: A Biography.* New York: Fordham University Press, 1998.

Tucker, David M. *Mugwumps: Public Moralists of the Gilded Age.* Columbia: University of Missouri Press, 1998.

Unger, Irwin. *The Greenback Era: A Social and Political History of American Finance, 1865–1879.* Princeton: Princeton University Press, 1964.

Van Deusen, Glyndon. *Horace Greeley, Nineteenth-Century Crusader.* New York: Hill and Wang, 1953.

Wiebe, Robert H. *The Search for Order, 1877–1920.* New York: Hill and Wang, 1967.

Welch, Richard E. Jr. *The Presidencies of Grover Cleveland.* Lawrence: University Press of Kansas, 1988.

Williamson, Harold Francis. *Edward Atkinson: The Biography of an American Liberal, 1827–1905.* Boston: Old Corner Book Store, 1934.

Wood, Gordon S. *The Creation of the American Republic, 1776–1787.* Chapel Hill: University of North Carolina Press, 1969.

Woodward, C. Vann. *Reunion and Reaction: The Compromise of 1877 and the End of Reconstruction.* New York: Oxford University Press, 1966.

Articles

Appleby, Joyce. "Republicanism in Old and New Contexts." *William and Mary Quarterly* 43 (January 1986): 20–34.

———, ed. "Republicanism in the History and Historiography of the United States." Special issue, *American Quarterly* 37 (Fall 1985).

Atack, Jeremy. "The Agricultural Ladder Revisited: A New Look at an Old Question with Some Data for 1860." *Agricultural History* 63 (Winter 1989): 1–25.

Baker, Jean Harvey. "Politics, Paradigms, and Public Culture." *Journal of American History* 84 (December 1997): 894–99.

Banning, Lance. "Jeffersonian Ideology Revisited: Liberal and Classical Ideas in the New American Republic." *William and Mary Quarterly* 43 (January 1986): 3–19.

Benedict, Michael Les. "Reform Republicans and the Retreat from Reconstruction," in *The Facts of Reconstruction: Essays in Honor of John Hope Franklin.* Edited by Alfred Moss and Eric Anderson. Baton Rouge: Louisiana State University Press, 1991.

———. "Preserving the Constitution: The Conservative Basis of Radical Reconstruction." *Journal of American History* 61 (December 1974): 65–90.

Blodgett, Geoffrey. "A New Look at the American Gilded Age." *Historical Reflections* 2 (1974): 231–46.

Burg, Robert W. "Amnesty, Civil Rights, and the Meaning of Liberal Republicanism, 1862–1872." *American Nineteenth Century History* 4 (Fall 2003): 29–60.

Curl, Donald Walter. "The Cincinnati Convention of the Liberal Republican Party." *Bulletin of the Cincinnati Historical Society* 24 (April 1966): 150–63.

Dante, Harris L. "The Chicago Tribune's 'Lost' Years, 1865–1874." *Journal of the Illinois State Historical Society* 58 (Summer 1965): 139–64.

Diggins, John Patrick. "Republicanism and Progressivism." *American Quarterly* 37 (Fall 1985): 572–98.

Donner, Barbara. "Carl Schurz as an Office Seeker." *Wisconsin Magazine of History* 20 (December 1936): 127–42.

Downey, Matthew T. "Horace Greeley and the Politicians: The Liberal Republican Convention in 1872." *Journal of American History* 54 (March 1967): 727–50.

Egnal, Marc. "The Beards Were Right: Parties in the North, 1840–1860." *Civil War History* 47 (April 2001): 30–56.

Fehrenbacher, Don E. "Only His Stepchildren: Lincoln and the Negro." *Civil War History: A Journal of the Middle Period* 20 (December 1974): 301, 299.

Foner, Eric. "Reconstruction Revisited." *Reviews in American History* 10 (December 1982): 82–100.

Gerber, Richard A. "Liberal Republicanism, Reconstruction, and Social Order: Samuel Bowles as a Test Case." *New England Quarterly* 45 (September 1972): 393–407.

———. "The Liberal Republicans of 1872 in Historiographical Perspective." *Journal of American History* 62 (September 1975): 40–73.

Goodman, Paul. "The Emergence of Homestead Exemption in the United States: Accommodation and Resistance to the Market Revolution, 1840–1880." *Journal of American History* 80 (September 1993): 470–98.

Hamilton, J. G. de Roulhac. "The Election of 1872 in North Carolina." *South Atlantic Quarterly* 11 (April 1912): 143–52.

Hansen, Mary Eschelbach. "Land Ownership, Farm Size, and Tenancy after the Civil War." *Journal of Economic History* 58 (September 1998): 822–29.

Holt, Michael F. "Making and Mobilizing the Republican Party, 1856–1860," in *The Birth of the Grand Old Party: The Republicans' First Generation.* Edited by Robert F. Engs and Randall M. Miller. Philadelphia: University of Pennsylvania Press, 2002.

———. "The Primacy of Party Reasserted." *Journal of American History* 84 (December 1997): 151–57.

Houston, James L. "The American Revolutionaries, the Political Economy of Aristocracy, and the American Concept of the Distribution of Wealth, 1765–1900." *American Historical Review* 98 (October 1993): 1079–1105.

Kloppenberg, James T. "The Virtues of Liberalism: Christianity, Republicanism, and Ethics in Early American Political Discourse." *Journal of American History* 74 (June 1987): 9–33.

Maier, Pauline. "The Revolutionary Origins of the American Corporation." *William and Mary Quarterly* 50 (January 1993): 51–84.

Matson, Cathy and Peter Onuf. "Toward a Republican Empire: Interest and Ideology in Revolutionary America." *American Quarterly* 37 (Fall 1985): 496–531.

McGerr, Michael E. "The Meaning of Liberal Republicanism: The Case of Ohio." *Civil War History* 28 (December 1982): 307–23.

McPherson, James M. "Grant or Greeley? The Abolitionist Dilemma in the Election of 1872." *American Historical Review* 71 (October 1965): 43–61.

Musto, David F. "The Adams Family." *Proceedings of the Massachusetts Historical Society* 93 (1981): 40–58.

Nicklason, Fred. "The Civil War Contracts Committee." *Civil War History* 17 (September 1971): 232–44.

Peterson, Norma L. "The Political Fluctuations of B. Gratz Brown: Politics in a Border State, 1850–1870." *Missouri Historical Review* 51 (October 1956): 22–30.

Pocock, J. G. A. "Between Gog and Magog: The Republican Thesis and the Ideologia Americana." *Journal of the History of Ideas* 48 (April–June 1987): 325–46.

Rawley, James A. "The General Amnesty Act of 1872: A Note." *Mississippi Valley Historical Review* 47 (December 1960): 480–84.

Rodgers, Daniel T. "Republicanism: The Career of a Concept." *Journal of American History* 79 (June 1992): 11–38.

Ross, Earle D. "Horace Greeley and the South, 1865–1872." *South Atlantic Quarterly* 16 (October 1917): 324–38.

"A Round Table: Alternatives to the Party System in the 'Party Period,' 1830–1890." *Journal of American History* 86, no. 1 (June 1999).

"A Round Table: Political Engagement and Disengagement in Antebellum America." *Journal of American History* 84, no. 3 (December 1997).

Shalhope, Robert E. "Republicanism and Early American Historiography." *William and Mary Quarterly* 39 (April 1982): 334–56.

Slap, Andrew L. "'The Strong Arm of the Military Power of the United States': The Chicago Fire, the Constitution, and Reconstruction." *Civil War History* 47 (June 2001): 146–63.

Smart, James G. "Whitelaw Reid and the Nomination of Horace Greeley." *Mid-America: An Historical Review* 49 (October 1967): 227–43.

Sutherland, Daniel E. "Edwin DeLeon and Liberal Republicanism in Georgia: Horace Greeley's Campaign for President in a Southern State." *The Historian* 47 (November 1984): 38–57.

Voss-Hubbard, Mark. "The 'Third Party Tradition' Reconsidered: Third Parties and American Public Life, 1830–1900." *Journal of American History* 84 (December 1997): 121–50.

Winters, Donald L. "The Agricultural Ladder in Southern Agriculture: Tennessee, 1850–1870." *Agricultural History* 61 (Summer 1987): 36–52.

Dissertations

Ahern, William Harrell. "Laissez Faire versus Equal Rights: Liberal Republicans and the Negro, 1861–1877." Ph.D. diss., Northwestern University, 1968.

Downey, Matthew T. "The Rebirth of Reform: A Study of Liberal Reform Movements, 1865–1872." Ph.D. diss., Princeton University, 1963.

Ee, Duan van. "David Dudley Field and the Reconstruction of the Law." Ph.D. diss., The Johns Hopkins University, 1974.

Gerber, Richard Allen. "The Liberal Republican Alliance of 1872." Ph.D. diss., University of Michigan, 1967.

Reitano, Joanne. "Free Trade in the Gilded Age: 1865–1895." Ph.D. diss., New York University, 1974.

Robinson, Michael C. "Illinois Politics in the Post–Civil War: The Liberal Republican Movement; A Case Study." Ph.D. diss., University of Wyoming, 1973.

Rutenbeck, Jeffery B. "The Rise of Independent Newspapers in the 1870s: A Transformation in American Journalism." Ph.D. diss., University of Washington, 1990.

Schmiel, Eugene David. "The Career of Jacob Dolson Cox, 1828–1900: Soldier, Scholar, Statesman." Ph.D. diss., Ohio State University, 1969.

Tusa, Jacqueline Balk. "Power, Priorities, and Political Insurgency: The Liberal Republican Movement, 1869–1872." Ph.D. diss., Pennsylvania State University, 1970.

Index

Adams, Charles Francis
  background of, xxiii–xxiv, 51
  Cincinnati Convention and, 150–51,
    159–61, 162–63
  Conscience Whigs and, 27–29
  on corruption, 30, 61
  Free Soil Party and, 29–34, 52
  on free trade and tariffs, 31, 36
  political parties, conceptions of, 28–29,
    32, 35–37
  as potential nominee of the Cincinnati
    Convention, 126, 128, 134–41, 148, 150
  as potential presidential candidate after
    the Cincinnati Convention, 175, 178,
    188–89
  as potential presidential candidate in
    1876, 230, 232–33
  Republican Party and, 37, 58–60
  on Slave Power, 29, 36, 52, 58–61
Adams, Charles Francis Jr.
  background of, xxiii, xxiv, 19, 33, 51
  campaign of 1872 and, 181, 219
  on corruption, 105
  on currency issues, 44, 96, 226
  formation of liberal republican move-
    ment, xix, 22, 24, 128
  on Greeley, 173–74
  post 1872 activities of, 226, 229–31, 236
  on railroad monopolies, xii, 99–106
  on republican government, 100, 106
  on Slave Power, xii, 100
Adams, Henry. See also *North American
    Review*
  background of, xxiii–xxiv, 33
  campaign of 1872 and, 180
  on civil service reform, 120
  conservatism of, 68, 87, 125, 220
  on corruption, 98, 120
  on currency issues, 97, 125
  on democracy, 220
  formation of liberal republican move-
    ment, 17, 22, 128

  on free trade and tariffs, 97–98
  on Grant, 120
  liberal republican image and, 219
  post 1872 activities, 226, 228–236
  on Republican Party, 39
  source for Bowers, 205
African Americans
  blamed for Reconstruction problems,
    207–8, 220
  liberal republicans leave on their own,
    xiv, 77, 84, 86, 113, 116–17, 223–24
  liberal republicans seek to protect, 8,
    74–6, 80, 89, 92, 110, 227, 239
  liberal republicans support voting
    rights for, 8–12, 80, 83–6, 110, 207
  Radical Party in Missouri and, 5, 10–11
  Radical Republicans and, 77–8, 83–85
  republican government and, 73, 115–19
  suffrage and, 5–6, 12–13, 15, 82–6
  white South and, 75–76, 78, 113, 227, 239
Amnesty
  Election of 1872 and, 184–6, 188, 201,
    222
  liberal republican movement and, 1,
    86, 110, 115, 126, 130, 132, 147, 238
  Liberal Republican Party and, 158,
    185–6
  in Missouri, 1, 5–8, 10, 17–19, 126, 227
  Republican Party and, xiii, 86, 110, 184,
    222, 227
Atkinson, Edward
  background of, xi, 33, 35–36, 51–52, 112
  campaign of 1872 and, 216
  Cincinnati Convention and, 126, 136,
    138, 154, 157, 161, 175
  Cincinnati Convention fallout and,
    168, 170, 173–74, 179–81
  on corruption, 61, 95, 109
  formation of the liberal republican
    movement and, 22, 128–29, 131–32,
    224

on free trade and tariffs, 95, 112, 136,
    154, 157, 174
on Grant, 108–9, 112, 173
on Greeley, 144–45, 173, 179
on legal tender and currency, 44, 96–
    97, 112
Reconstruction and, 75, 77–9, 84, 86,
    112
on republican government, 61
on Slave Power, 35, 51–52, 61, 68

Baker, Jean Harvey, xvii, 90
Bailyn, Bernard, xxii, 19
Baltimore Convention (1872), 169–70,
    178, 188, 190–92
Banks, Nathaniel P., 33–34, 182, 197
Barclay, Thomas S., 20–21, 244n2
Bayard, Thomas F., 189, 191–92
Benedict, Michael Les, 147, 246n16, 255n10
Belmont, August, 137–38, 188–91
blacks. See African Americans
Blaine, James G., 129, 187, 224, 232–35
Blair, Francis P., 2, 126, 134, 162
Blight, David W., 201–2
Bowers, Claude, 205, 209
Bowles, Samuel. See also Springfield
    Republican
    background of, xxiv, 34, 39, 40, 56–57
    campaign of 1872 and, 181–82, 184,
        189–90
    Cincinnati Convention and, 126, 131,
        133, 143–44, 148, 150–52
    Cincinnati Convention fallout and,
        166, 172, 174–76
    formation of liberal republican move-
        ment, 21–22, 128
    journalism career and, 39, 45–6, 176
    on legal tender, 44, 70
    post 1872 activities of, 225–26, 229–30,
        232
    on republican government, 64–65
    source for Bowers, 205
Brinkerhoff, Jacob, 27–30, 33
Brinkerhoff, Roeliff, 27, 33, 35, 129, 144,
    172–73, 204, 207, 209, 211, 214
Bristow, Benjamin H., 232–33, 235
Brown, B. Gratz
    background of, 4
    campaign (1872) rhetoric of, 206, 208,
        212
    Cincinnati Convention and, 126, 134,
        150, 159–60, 162

Cincinnati Convention fallout and,
    172, 174–74, 189
formation of liberal republican move-
    ment and, 21–22, 128
Missouri and, 1, 4–9, 11, 13, 17, 19–21,
    132, 139
Bryant, William Cullen. See also New
    York Evening Post
    background of, xiv, 27, 51
    campaign of 1872 and, 180
    Cincinnati Convention fallout and,
        166–67, 173, 176, 178
    civil service reform and, 41, 96
    on corruption, 38, 40–41, 43, 56, 62, 111,
        116
    on federalism, 53, 69, 76, 96
    formation of the liberal republican
        movement, 17, 22, 128, 224
    on free trade and tariffs, 55–56, 71, 97,
        112
    Greeley and, 17, 142, 166, 178
    journalism career and, 45, 48, 176
    on legal tender, 44, 69, 96
    political activity before Reconstruc-
        tion, 27–28, 31–33, 35–41, 43
    post 1872 activities of, 224, 234
    on Reconstruction, 76, 81, 83
    on republican government, 53, 56
    on Slave Power, 36, 53, 62
Buren, Martin Van, 26–27, 31, 233–34
Burg, Robert, xix, 243n17

campaign rhetoric of 1872
    "Best Men" and, 199, 215–21
    "Grantism" and, 199, 209–215, 220–21
    "Tragic Era" and, 199–209, 220–21
Caton, John Dean, 209, 212–14
Chandler, William E., 133, 169, 184–85,
    187, 190, 193–94, 196–97
Chase, Salmon P., 27–29, 32, 70, 109, 134,
    150
Cincinnati Commercial. See also Halstead,
    Murat
    background of, 36, 45–6
    on campaign (1872), 186, 188, 197–8,
        200
    campaign rhetoric of (1872), 203–4,
        207–8, 211–14, 216–17
    on the Cincinnati Convention, 150–52,
        154–57, 159–63
    on the Cincinnati Convention and
        potential candidates, 131, 137–39, 141,
        143

on Cincinnati Convention prospects, 133–34, 149–50
on Cincinnati Convention results, 126, 175
on civil service reform, 92–93, 200
during the Civil War, 40, 62–63, 65–68, 70–72, 74
on corruption, 71–72, 93, 97
on currency and legal tender issues, 70–72, 97
on free trade and tariffs, 70, 90, 97–99, 143
on Missouri politics, 18
on monopolies, 100, 102
as part of liberal republican movement, 17–18, 54, 128
as part of Quadrilateral at the Cincinnati Convention, 150–52
on party reorganization potential, 47–48, 50, 164–65
on party tyranny, 49, 92
post 1872 activities, 226
on race, 115–16, 203, 207–8
ready to move past Civil War and Reconstruction, 90, 95, 112, 222–23
on Reconstruction, when supporting Andrew Johnson, 74, 80–82, 95
on Reconstruction, after breaking with Andrew Johnson, xi, 82–83, 115
on republican government, 62–63, 65, 74, 76, 82, 102
on Slave Power, 63
Cincinnati Convention
Brown scheme, 159–60, 162
comparisons to Free Soil Buffalo Convention, 31, 33, 48
compromise on tariff at, 145, 152, 154–57
conflict over outcome of, 23, 167–68, 172–76, 179, 182, 200, 219, 238
Democrats and, 137–38, 146–50, 188–90
Greeley and, 127, 134–35, 141–45, 150–63
historiography of, 260n1, 261n2, 264n19, 267n41
liberal republican mistakes at, 128, 151–56, 158–61, 163
outcome of, 24, 126–27, 163, 165
platform of, 157–59
potential candidates at, 128, 134–41, 146–50
preparation for, 132–34, 143–50
Quadrilateral and, 151–53, 155, 159

as threat to Republican Party, 126, 133–34
voting at, 159–63
Civil Rights Act (1866), xi, 7, 78–82, 95
civil service reform. See also patronage system; republican government
appropriated by Republican Party, xiii, 183–86
Free Soil Party and, 30–31, 55
historians interpretation of, xv, xvii, xix, xxi, 122
Greeley and, 31, 143, 182, 199–200
as issue in 1876, 234–37, 239
liberal republicans interest in after the Cincinnati Convention, 180, 223, 225
liberal republicans criticize Ulysses S. Grant for lack of, 110–11, 113, 120–22
liberal republicans' early interest in, xv, xxi, 13, 37, 40–42, 54–56, 71, 92–95, 106–7, 111
liberal republicans might benefit from, 22, 92, 94–95, 257n6
Liberal Republican Party's lack of interest in, 158, 200–1, 220
as means of limiting party power, 40
as means of limiting presidential power, 92–94
in Missouri Bolt, 1, 5, 12–13, 15, 18–19
as a primary issue for the liberal republican movement, xii, 1, 17–18, 22–24, 127–28, 132, 158, 163, 199–200
Clay, Cassius M., 157, 203, 206, 224
Cohen, Nancy, xviii, 86, 260n14
Conkling, Roscoe, 123–24, 131, 144, 224, 235
Cooke, Jay, 185, 187, 213, 226
Cox, Jacob Dolson
background of, xv, 22, 34, 80
campaign of 1872 and, 216, 218
Cincinnati Convention and, 48, 138, 144–46, 153–54, 157, 162
Cincinnati Convention fallout and, 168, 173–74, 178, 180
on civil service, 22–23, 94–95, 121–22
formation of liberal republican movement and, 22–23, 128–32, 224
Grant and, xvi–xvii, 22, 125, 127–28
on political parties, 50, 168
post 1872 activities, 236–37
racism of, 80, 86, 118
Reconstruction and, 80–82, 118

on republican government, 74, 80, 94,
    118
Current, Richard N., 206
Curry, Leonard P., 43
Curtin, Andrew, 134, 197
Curtis, George William, xx, 183

Davis, David, 23, 134–36, 138, 146–54, 157,
    159, 161
Democratic Convention in Baltimore
    (1872), 169–70, 178, 188, 190–93
Democratic Party. *See also* Baltimore
    Convention; Belmont, August; Lou-
    isville Convention
    before the Civil War, 26–33, 35–38, 56–
        58, 63, 146, 183
    Cincinnati Convention potential can-
        didates and, 136–38
    Davis and, 146–52
    demise of expected, 50, 148, 164–70,
        222, 235
    Greeley nominated by, 170–71, 188–92
    Greeley rejected by, 170, 177, 188–96
    Greeley supported by, 188–98
    Johnson and, 80–82
    liberal republican background in, 27–
        30, 35–38, 41, 43, 45, 48, 60, 64, 69,
        135, 142, 146
    liberal republicans weary of, 131, 134–
        35, 147–48, 167, 233
    liberal republican movement seeks
        support of, 1, 130–31, 137, 148, 163,
        188, 231, 233
    Liberal Republican Party appeals to,
        200–1, 220
    in Missouri, 1–4, 6, 8, 11, 14–24, 134, 159,
        227–28
    New Departure and, 50, 170
    possum policy of, 14, 16, 127
    post 1872, 227–28, 230–33, 235–36, 238
    in the South during Reconstruction,
        113, 130
    threat of holds Republican Party
        together, 15, 50, 148, 164–65
Downey, Matthew T., 261–62*n*2, 269*n*1,
    270*n*14
Drake, Charles D., 2–4, 6, 9–13, 18, 21,
Duberman, Martin, 140

Egnal, Marc, 12
Election of 1872. *See also*, campaign rhet-
    oric of 1872

Democratic Party Strategy in, 188–92
Democratic rank and file disaffection
    with Greeley in, 188, 190–95, 197–98
effects of, xiii–xiv, xvi
expectations for a political realignment
    in, 164–72
explanation of outcome, 164, 182, 192,
    195–98
intraparty struggles of the liberal
    republican movement during,
    172–81
Liberal Republican Party strategy in,
    181–82, 188–90
Louisville Convention (1872) and,
    193–95
Republican Party's strategy in, 182–88,
    192–95
voting in, 195–98

Farnsworth, John F., 201, 204, 212, 214
Fehrenbacher, Don E., 86
Fell, Jesse W., 146, 153
Fenton, Rueben, 131, 181–82
Field, David Dudley, xxiv, 17, 22, 33, 35,
    36, 41, 103, 128, 154, 230
Fifteenth Amendment, 12–13, 112, 158, 170,
    207, 239
Foner, Eric, xix, 26, 34–36, 86, 205, 216,
    243*n*17, 248–49*n*2, 250*n*21, 255*n*67
Force Acts, 113–14, 125
Fourteenth Amendment, 7, 82–83, 85–88,
    158, 170, 239
free labor ideology and liberal republi-
    cans, 10, 63, 73, 84–85, 89, 149, 201,
    207, 227, 238
Free Soil Party, xi–xii, xiv, 25–26, 29–35,
    47–48, 50–53, 55, 57, 60, 142, 172, 183,
    223–24, 234, 238
free trade. *See also* Free Trade League;
    tariffs, protective
    appropriated by Republican Party, 183,
        222
    Cincinnati Convention compromise
        about, 143–45, 150–59, 167, 174–75
    Cincinnati Convention potential nom-
        inee's and, 136
    Free Soil Party and, 36
    Horace Greeley against, 24, 31, 127, 142–
        45, 150, 174, 199
    liberal republicans' early interest in, xv,
        13, 36, 55, 71, 110, 112, 142

liberal republicans' commitment to,
145–46, 150, 154–57, 173, 180, 216–17
Liberal Republican Party's lack of
interest in, 200, 220
in Missouri Bolt, 1, 13, 15, 17–19, 126
as a primary issue for the liberal republican movement, xii, 1, 17–19, 22–24,
95, 107, 111–12, 126–30, 132, 177,
199–200
Free Trade League. *See also* free trade;
tariffs, protective
Cincinnati Convention and, 138, 143,
153–54, 156
Cincinnati Convention fallout and,
174–75
formation of liberal republican movement and, 1, 21–22, 128–29
founding of, xii, 17
on tariffs, 97
Freedmen's Bureau, 7, 78–82, 92, 95, 147

Gallagher, Gary W., 202
Garrison, William Lloyd, 155, 223
German Americans. *See also* Belmont,
August; Koerner, Gustave; Schurz,
Carl
background of liberal republicans,
xxiii, 8–10, 57
French Arms Sales and, 123
in Missouri, 1, 3–5, 8–12, 14, 23
Republican Party and, 187, 230–31
support for liberal republicans, 1, 23,
133, 154, 177, 206
Gienapp, William E., xxii, 52, 262n3
Gillette, William, xix, 269n1, 270n4,
273n47
Godkin, Edwin L. *See also* The Nation
background of, 46
campaign of 1872 and, 180–81
Cincinnati Convention and, 144
Cincinnati Convention fallout and,
167–68, 173, 176, 178
on civil service reform, 93
on corruption, 41, 96, 99
formation of liberal republican movement and, 17–18, 21–22, 128, 130–31
on legal tender, 96
liberal republican image, 219–20
post 1872 activities of, 219, 229
on Santa Domingo, 118
Grant, Ulysses S.
accused of party despotism, 123–24, 130

accused of tyranny, 119–20, 124–25, 158,
188
attacked by liberal republicans, 18–19,
125, 135
campaign of 1872 and, 164, 179–81, 183–
85, 188–91, 193, 195–97
campaign of 1872 and image of, xiii, xx,
199–203, 205, 208–15, 220–21
corruption and, 113, 117, 120–25, 135, 188
French Arms Sales and, 123–24
historiography of, xiv–xv, 122, 209–10
liberal republican support of before the
Cincinnati Convention, xiii–xvi, 16,
25, 93, 108–13, 125, 179
liberal republican support of after the
Cincinnati Convention, 167, 172–73,
180–81, 183
liberal republicans, difference with, xii,
xv, xvii, 22–25, 48, 94–95, 108, 120,
127, 130–34, 137–38, 142, 144
liberal republicans not anti-Grant
movement and, xvi, 23–24, 110, 127,
131, 145, 217, 219
Missouri politics and, 1, 16–19, 22–24,
123
post 1872 activities of, 222–24, 227
Reconstruction and, xiii–xiv, 122,
209–10
Santo Domingo and, 117, 119–20, 122
Greeley, Horace. See also *New York Evening Post*
after 1872 campaign, 224
in 1872 campaign rhetoric, 203–4, 217–
18, 220
campaign of 1872 and Liberal Republican Party and, 164, 181–84
campaign of 1872 and Democratic
Party and, 164, 168–72, 188–98, 201,
211
Cincinnati Convention and, 126–27,
150–63
Cincinnati Convention, potential
nominee of, 131, 134–35, 141–46, 150
image of, 199, 202, 211, 215
liberal republicans, antagonism
between, 6, 17–18, 127, 131, 142–45,
150, 177, 180
liberal republicans, *rapprochement*
between, 127, 131, 135, 143–45
liberal republicans opposition after
nomination of, 166–68, 172–81

Grosvenor, William. See also *Missouri Democrat*
  background of, 6–7, 19, 51
  campaign of 1872 and, 182, 193, 204, 206–8, 218
  Cincinnati Convention and, 138, 149, 145, 154–55
  Cincinnati Convention fallout and, 174, 177–78, 181
  formation of liberal republican party and, xv, 21–22, 128–29, 132, 136
  Missouri politics and, 6–8, 10–14, 16–21
  on Reconstruction, xi, 7–9, 11, 13–14, 18, 85, 147
  on tariffs, 12–13, 17, 97–98
  post 1872 activities of, 6, 230

Halstead, Murat. See also *Cincinnati Commercial*
  background of, xv, 36, 45, 68, 80
  campaign of 1872 and, 181
  Cincinnati Convention and, 126, 150–52, 174
  on corruption, 40, 41, 45
  formation of the liberal republican movement and, 18, 21
  Greeley as potential nominee and, 131, 143
  journalism career and, xv, 45–46, 175
  on legal tender, 70
  post 1872 activities, 226, 230, 236–37
  Reconstruction legislation and, 80–83
Hayes, Rutherford B.
  Election of 1876 and, 236–38
  liberal republican connections and, xxiii, 230–32, 236–37, 239
  liberal republican split over, 235–36
Hoadly, George Jr., xxiii, 29, 33, 129–30, 132, 151, 157, 167, 172–73, 180–81, 216–19, 230
Hofstadter, Richard, xiv
Holt, Michael F., xvi–xvii, 30, 32, 52, 69, 210, 242*n*16, 243*n*18, 251*n*25, 262*n*3, 272*n*36
Hoogenboom, Ari, xv, 245*n*2

Johnson, Andrew
  conflicts with liberal republicans, xvii, 8, 79, 81–82, 92–93, 95, 108, 122, 135
  friendships with liberal republicans, 80–81

Reconstruction and, 73–75, 77, 79–82, 87, 91–92, 129
Julian, George, xiii, xx, 33, 165–66, 171, 202, 205, 224

Kerr, Michael C., 170, 197
Know-Nothing Party, 33–35, 37, 48, 57, 127, 183, 223
Koerner, Gustave, 136, 139–40, 148, 162–63
Ku Klux Klan Act (1871), 114, 208–9

Legal Tender Act (1862), xii, 43–44, 69–71, 96–97
liberal republicans
  African Americans and, xiv, 8, 74–77, 80, 84, 86, 89, 92, 110, 113, 116–17, 223–24 , 227, 239
  background in Democratic Party, 27–30, 35–38, 41, 43, 45, 48, 60, 64, 69, 135, 142, 146
  civil service reform and, xv, xxi, 13, 37, 40–42, 54–56, 71, 92–95, 106–7, 111, 180, 223, 225
  free labor ideology and, 10, 63, 73, 84–85, 89, 149, 201, 207, 227, 238
  free trade and, xv, 13, 36, 55, 71, 110, 112, 142, 145–46, 150, 154–57, 173, 180, 216–17
  background, German, of xxiii, 8–10, 57
  Grant's differences with, xii, xv, xvii, 22–25, 48, 94–95, 108, 120, 127, 130–34, 137–38, 142, 144
  Grant supported by, xiii–xvi, 16, 25, 93, 108–13, 125, 167, 172–73, 179–82, 183
  Greeley, antagonism toward, 17–18, 127, 131, 142–45, 150, 177, 180
  Greeley, *rapprochemen*, 127, 131, 135, 143–45
  Republican Party and. See Republican Party
  Hayes and, xxiii, 230–32, 236–37, 239
  Johnson and, xvii, 8, 79, 80–82, 92–93, 95, 108, 122, 135
  mistakes at Cincinnati Convention, 128, 151–56, 158–61, 163
  racism of, 80, 86–87, 115–16, 118, 207–8
  Reconstruction and. See Reconstruction.
  republican ideology of. See republican government
liberal republican movement

civil service reform a primary issue of, xii, 1, 17–18, 22–24, 127–28, 132, 158, 163, 199–200

consider Civil War and Reconstruction issues settled, 8–9, 77, 101, 110, 199, 223, 238

Democratic Party, seeks support of, 1, 130–31, 137, 148, 163, 188, 231, 233

Democratic Party, weary of, 131, 134–35, 147–48, 167, 233

Election of 1872 and, 181–82, 188–90

formation of, xv, 17–18, 21–22, 128–29, 131–32, 136, 224

free trade a primary issue of, xii, 1, 17–19, 22–24, 95, 107, 111–12, 126–30, 132, 177, 199–200

German American support of, 1, 23, 133, 154, 177, 206

membership of, xx. See also Adams, Charles Francis; Adams, Charles Francis Jr.; Adams, Henry; Atkinson, Edward; Bryant, William Cullen; Bowles, Samuel; Brinkerhoff, Jacob; Brinkerhoff, Roeliff; Cox, Jacob Dolson; Field, David Dudley; Godkin, Edwin L; Grosvenor, William M.; Halstead, Murat; Hoadly, George; Lloyd, Henry Demarest, Nordhoff, Charles; Piatt, Don; Sands, Mahlon; Schurz, Carl; Stallo, Johann B.; Trumbull, Lyman; Wells, David Ames; White, Horace

newspapers of. See Chicago Tribune; Cincinnati Commercial; The Nation; New York Evening Post; Springfield Republican

not anti-Grant, xvi, 23–24, 110, 127, 131, 145, 217, 219

taking control of Republican Party primary strategy, xii, 1, 17, 21–25, 126–33, 148, 156, 229–35

Liberal Republican Party. See also Cincinnati Convention; Greeley, Horace

campaign rhetoric of, xiii–xiv, 199–218, 220

creation of, xiii, xv, xxv, 6, 33

Democrats and, 137–38, 170, 188–98

effects of, 238–39

expectations of party realignment, 164–67, 171

intraparty conflicts, 172–82

members of, xiii, xix–xx, 19, 23, 33, 224

Lincoln, Abraham
campaign of 1872, mentioned in, 204, 213–14
patronage and, xii, 40–42, 91, 120
liberal republicans and, 39–42, 44–45, 62, 66–69, 71–72, 146–48, 151, 220
Reconstruction and, 75

Lloyd, Henry Demarest, 40, 129, 156, 173–75

Lodge, Henry Cabot, 228–29, 232–36

Louisville Convention (1872), 192–95

Louisville Courier-Journal, 150–51, 162, 226. See also Watterson, Henry

Mahan, Asa, 205–6, 211–12, 215

McClure, Alexander K., 201–3, 206, 209–210, 212–13, 217–18

McCulloch, Hugh, 78, 97

McClurg, Joseph, 14–16, 19–20

McCormick, Cyrus, 170, 195

McFeeley, William S., 210

Missouri Democrat, 6, 11–12, 14, 17–19. See also Grosvenor, William

Missouri
African American suffrage and, 4–6, 8–15, 19
amnesty and, 1, 5–8, 10, 17–19, 126, 227
civil service reform and, 1, 5, 12–13, 15
Democratic Party and, 1–4, 6, 8, 11, 14–24, 159, 227–28
during Civil War, 2–5
Election of 1868, 10–12
Election of 1870, 1, 14–17, 20–21
free trade and, 1, 12–13, 15
German Americans and, 1, 3–5, 8–12, 14, 23
Liberal Party and, 1, 14–22
loyalty oaths and, 2–5, 9, 12–13, 17
origins of liberal republicanism in, 1–2, 21–24
Planter House Meeting and, 5–8
Radical Union Party and, 2–6, 9–16, 18, 20–21
Republican Party and, 1–2, 15–16
two party system of, 2, 24

Morton, Oliver, 123–24, 202, 224, 235

Musto, David F., 140

Nast, Thomas, 8, 202

Nation, The. See also Godkin, Edwin
on African American suffrage, 83–86
on campaign (1872), 184, 194, 200, 201

on Cincinnati Convention results,
218–19
on civil service reform, 91–93, 95,
119–20
on Civil War, exigencies of, 72
on corruption, 97–98, 101–2
on currency and legal tender issues, 90,
97
on free trade and tariffs, 95, 98
founding of, 46,
Grant, 108–110, 112, 121, 183
Greeley, 173, 176, 180
on Ku Klux Klan Act, 114–15
on Missouri politics, 18
as part of liberal republican movement, 17–18, 128
on party reorganization potential, 49,
167–68
on party tyranny, 49
on political parties, purpose of, 48
on race, 86, 116, 118
on railroad monopolies, 101–4
ready to move past Reconstruction, 95,
110, 112
on Reconstruction, xi, 78, 81, 83–85, 88
on republican government, 48, 83–84
source for Bowers, 205
on third parties, 47–48
Neely, Mark E. Jr., 40, 68, 210
New Political History, xvi–xviii, 172
New York Evening Post. See also Bryant,
William Cullen
on African American suffrage, 83
background of, 27, 45, 142
during campaign of 1872, 167, 176, 178–
80, 219
on civil service reform, 111
before the Civil War, 28, 31–32, 37–38,
48
during the Civil War, 41
on corruption, 37–38, 41, 43, 55–56, 71,
95, 111
on currency and legal tender issues, 44,
69, 71, 95–96
on federalism, 53–54
on free trade and tariffs, 55–56, 71, 95,
97–98
on Grant, 108, 111, 122, 180
on Greeley, 142, 167
on military encroachment, 54, 67, 83
on Missouri politics, 17, 122

as part of liberal republican movement, 17, 54, 128
on party tyranny, 122
on Reconstruction, xi, 78, 83, 87
on republican government, 53–54, 78,
83
on Slave Power, 53, 57
New York Times, 46, 169, 171, 183–84, 231
New York Tribune, 6, 17, 24, 135, 141, 143–
44, 150–53, 157, 160, 163, 173, 189, 205.
See also Greeley, Horace; Reid,
Whitelaw
Nordhoff, Charles, 17, 23, 33, 128, 136, 230
North American Review, 17, 27, 94, 98, 104,
128. See also Adams, Henry

Olmsted, Frederick Law, 166–67, 180

Palmer, John M., 19, 134, 136, 139–40, 148,
153, 178, 202–4, 209, 213–14
Parrish, William E., 11, 20
patronage system. See also civil service
reform; republican government
corruption and, 56, 71, 83, 93, 120
described, 13, 55
Grant's use of, 122–23
growth of, 55, 71, 183
Johnson's use of, 91–93
Lincoln's use of, xii, 40–41, 91
as basis of political parties, 40–41, 71
Radical Party's use of in Missouri, 18–
19, 21, 94, 122
republican government and, xvii, 18,
54, 94, 107, 185, 199, 225
Republican Party's use of in 1872, 133,
182–87, 198
Piatt, Don, xxiv, 17, 33, 35, 128
Preetorius, Emil, 9–11

Quadrilateral, 151–53, 155, 159, 174, 176,
216, 226

Radical Republicans, xiii, 36, 78, 83, 87,
92, 120, 147, 151, 199, 207
Reconstruction
Liberal Republican Party campaigns
against, xxv, 199–207, 210, 215, 220
Liberal Republican Party supports end
of, 142, 158, 184, 201
liberal republicans' support of, xi–xii,
7–11, 25, 73–84, 86–89, 95, 109–10

liberal republicans' problems with, 64,
68, 73, 76, 80, 87, 89, 111, 227–28
liberal republicans see dangers in, xii–
xiii, 73–74, 76, 87, 89, 114
liberal republicans think accomplished, seek end of, 84, 88–89, 109–
10, 112, 163, 180, 225, 227, 238–40
Republican Party ends, xiii–xiv, xxiii,
184, 222, 238–29
secondary issue for liberal republican
movement, xii–xiii, 24, 73, 95, 112,
116–17, 158
Reconstruction Act (1867), xi, 87–89
Reid, Whitelaw
campaign of 1872 and, 174–77, 181–82,
189–90, 192–93
Cincinnati Convention and, 6, 24, 145,
151–54, 157, 159, 161
republican government
African American suffrage and, 15, 73
definition of, xi, xxii
during war, 71–72, 74, 82
centralization threatens, 53–54, 64–67,
71–72, 78, 114
Civil War's effects on, xi–xii, 61–63,
65–67, 72, 82, 107, 158
corruption threatens, 31, 56, 60–61, 71–
72, 93–96, 98–99, 122–23
different races in, 115–19
Europe and, 65
as goal of Civil War, xxiv–xxv, 62,
116–17
as goal of Missouri Bolt, 15
as goal of Reconstruction, 73, 89,
238–40
Grant threatens, xvii, 95, 109–11, 113,
119, 122, 124–25, 158, 210
historians on, xxii, 19, 30
historical comparisons and, 19, 54, 61,
67, 109
Legal Tender Act threatens, 71, 96, 231
liberal republican disillusionment with
after 1872, 219
limits to Reconstruction and, 15, 20, 84,
88–89, 114, 117, 130, 227–28
military threats to, 19, 54, 76, 125, 239,
228
monopolies threaten, 99–103, 106–7
political parties in, 48, 57
post 1872 threats, 225, 228, 231, 234, 237,
239

Slave Power threatens, xi–xii, 51–54, 56,
58, 60–64, 72, 74, 89–90
spoils system threatens, 15, 18, 91, 93–
95, 158, 185
tariffs threaten, 56, 60, 95, 98
tyranny threatens, 92
workings of, 61, 113, 119
republican ideology. See republican
government
republican institutions. See republican
government
Republican Party
in 1876, 233–37
appropriates Liberal Republican issues,
xiii, 133, 182–88
background of Liberal Republicans in,
4, 19, 134, 145–48, 201, 203–5, 215
campaign of 1872 and, 164, 182–88, 193–
98, 200–5
changed by Civil War, 25, 39–45, 49, 52,
69–70
economic program of, 12, 42–45, 59–
60, 69–70, 98, 112
expectations of political realignment
and, xvi, 164–72
founded by liberal republicans, xi–xii,
xiv–xv, 23, 26, 33–36, 48, 51–53, 57–
58, 135
liberal republicans break with, xv,
131–33
liberal republicans early independence
in, 39–46, 70–71
liberal republicans return to, xvi, 180–
81, 215–20, 231
liberal republicans' membership in,
xxiv, 8, 10, 37–39, 109, 111, 130
liberal republican movement tries to
take control of and reform, xii, 1, 17,
21–25, 126–33, 148, 156, 229–35
loses original members, xiii, xxv,
223–24
in Missouri, 1–2, 4, 13–19, 21, 24, 94,
122–24
Missouri Liberals break with, 15–17
party discipline and, 47, 94, 122, 133–34,
208
Reconstruction and, 77–87, 91–93, 113–
14, 184, 237–38
revenue reform. See free trade
Richardson, Heather Cox, xviii, 238
Rodgers, Daniel T., xxii

Ross, Earle D., xix, 199, 242*n*2, 261*n*2, 269*n*1

Sandow, Robert, 19
Sands, Mahlon, 21–22, 128–29, 156, 173–74
Schurz, Carl
    background of, xv, xxiv, 8–9, 19, 35–36, 68
    campaign of 1872 and, 181–83, 188–90, 193, 195, 199, 201, 206–7, 212
    Cincinnati Convention and, 126, 150–52, 154–56, 158–63
    Cincinnati Convention potential nominees and, 136, 138, 148
    Cincinnati Convention fallout and, 173–74, 176–80, 219
    on civil service reform, 13, 93–94, 111, 125, 222, 236
    on corruption, 62, 93–94, 107, 125, 225
    Democrats and, 131, 137–38, 148, 188–90, 189, 199
    on federalism, 9–10, 77, 114, 222, 228
    formation of liberal republican movement and, 1–2, 21–24, 122, 126–33, 144–45
    on free trade and tariffs, 17, 99, 222
    French Arms Sales and, 123–24
    Grant and, xv, xvii, 109, 111, 114, 119–120, 122–23
    Greeley and, 144–45, 176–77, 180–82
    Missouri and, 1, 7–13, 15–17, 20–23, 226–27
    post 1872 activities of, 220, 222, 225–37, 239
    Reconstruction and, 8–13, 24, 73, 76–77, 84–86, 89, 101, 239
    Reconstruction, end of, and, 84, 225–28, 239
    Reconstruction, white Southern resistance to, and, 9, 20, 73, 75–76
    Reconstruction, universal amnesty and suffrage, and, 10–12, 15, 84–86, 110
    on republican government, xi, xvii, 8–9, 37, 57–58, 76–77, 94, 99–100, 109, 114, 118–19, 124, 225, 228, 239
    Republican Party and, 16–17, 21–23, 39, 46–49, 124, 229
    Santo Domingo, annexation of, and, 117–20
    on Slave Power, xi, 36–37, 51, 57–58, 109
    sources for Claude Bowers, 205
Shalhope, Robert E., xxii

Silbey, Joel H., xvi, 250*n*25
Simpson, Brooks D., 210
Slave Power, xii, 29, 36–37, 52–53, 55–56, 83, 89–90, 100, 102, 104, 107–9, 112, 208, 210, 223, 238
Spaulding, J. R., 206, 209
spoils system. *See* civil service reform; patronage system
Springer, William, 211–12
Springfield Republican. See also Bowles, Samuel
    on African American suffrage, 84, 208
    background of, 34, 42, 45–46
    campaign rhetoric of (1872), 208, 213
    on the Cincinnati Convention, 154, 160, 175
    on the Cincinnati Convention and potential candidates, 137–39, 141
    on Cincinnati Convention prospects, 133
    on Cincinnati Convention results, 126, 166, 172–73
    on civil service reform, 111, 120
    during the Civil War, 42, 44, 45, 49, 61–68, 70–71, 73
    on corruption, 42, 61, 71, 101
    on currency and legal tender issues, 44, 95, 97
    on federalism, 64–66
    on free trade and tariffs, 70, 95
    on Grant, 108–9, 111, 119–22, 125, 213
    on Greeley, 131, 143, 175–76
    on liberal republicans defecting after the Cincinnati Convention, 24, 180, 216–17
    on Missouri politics, 17
    as part of liberal republican movement, 54, 128
    as part of Quadrilateral at the Cincinnati Convention, 151–52
    on party reorganization potential, 25, 50, 148, 164–65
    on political parties, conception of, 25, 42
    on race, 87, 115, 208
    on railroad monopolies, 101–3, 106
    ready to move past Civil War and Reconstruction, 65–66, 70, 73
    on Reconstruction, xi, 74–76, 79–81, 85, 88–89, 95, 115
    on the Republican Party, 17, 25, 47, 49–50, 61, 81

on republican government, 56–57, 62–
    66, 74, 87, 106
on Slave Power, 60, 62–64
Sproat, John G., xiv–xv, xviii–xxi, 85, 165,
    216–17, 219–20, 234, 241n5, 242n13,
    260n14
Stallo, Johann B., xxiii, 132–33, 163, 179,
    180, 216, 218, 236
Steinway Hall Meeting, 173–74, 178
Summers, Mark W., 31, 45–6, 54, 93,
    272n36
Sumner, Charles, xiii, 13, 35, 58, 77, 83, 117,
    122, 134, 181, 193, 200, 224–26
Sutherland, Daniel E., 190, 201

tariffs, protective. See also free trade; Free
    Trade League
  civil service and, 56
  corruption and, xii, 12, 55–56, 59–60,
    71, 97–98
  Greeley supports, xiii, 17–18, 23, 127,
    142–43, 197
  instituted during Civil War, xii, 42, 62,
    70, 90, 95, 108, 238
  monopolies and, 18, 99, 107
  as part of Whig economic program, 12,
    36, 42, 59–60, 70, 112, 143
  republican government and, xvii, 12,
    19, 50, 56, 60, 71, 95, 97–98, 107
  Republican support of, 13–14, 42, 59–
    60, 98–99
  special interests and, 5, 55, 71, 98, 111
Thirteenth Amendment, 7, 51, 75, 77, 135,
    158, 170, 223
Trefousse, Hans L., 8, 16
Trumbull, Lyman
  background, xxiii, xxiv, 23, 36, 135,
    146–47
  campaign of 1872 and, 181–83, 204, 212
  Cincinnati Convention and, 150–51,
    153–54, 159–63
  Cincinnati Convention prospects and,
    131, 133, 144–45, 148–49
  Cincinnati Convention fallout and,
    166, 178–79
  on civil service reform, 93, 120
  Constitution and, 66–67, 88, 114
  on corruption, 40, 49, 91, 120, 124
  on federalism, 36, 43, 64, 78–79, 81, 113–
    14, 147
  formation of liberal republican move-
    ment and, 23

Grosvenor and, 7
post 1872 activities, 220, 224
as politician, 91–92
as potential presidential candidate, 126,
    128, 131, 134–41, 150, 189
Reconstruction legislation and, xi, 51,
    77–79, 81, 88–89, 114
Republican Party and, 23, 49, 124,
    132–33
source for Bowers, 205
Tucker, David M., 97, 199, 220
Tusa, Jacqueline Balk, xx, 245n2, 248n41

Voss-Hubbard, Mark, xviii, 30, 270n15,
    272n36

Watterson, Henry, 150–53, 226. See also
    Louisville Courier-Journal
Wells, David Ames
  background of, xxiii, 142
  Cincinnati Convention and, 142, 144,
    154–56, 161
  Cincinnati Convention fallout and,
    166–68, 173–75, 178, 179
  formation of liberal republican move-
    ment and, 16–17, 22, 50, 128–29, 132
  Grant and, xvii, 122, 125
  Greeley and, 143–44, 155, 166, 173, 179
  not interested in Reconstruction, 199
  post 1872 activities, 226, 229, 236
  supports Adams for nomination,
    138–41
Wentworth, John, 138–39, 153–54
Whig Party, 25–34, 36–38, 42–3, 48, 50, 57,
    59–60, 69–70, 127–28, 142–43, 146,
    165, 170–72, 183, 223
White, Horace
  background of, xxiii, 33, 35–36, 51, 228
  campaign of 1872 and, 166, 181–82, 192,
    214
  Cincinnati Convention and, 140, 148–
    52, 154, 156, 158, 161, 175
  Cincinnati Convention fallout and,
    176–79
  on corruption, 40–42
  formation of liberal republican move-
    ment and, 17, 22, 128–29, 131, 224
  Grant and, xv, 109–10, 158, 214
  journalism career and, 45–46, 176, 181,
    228
  on legal tender, xii, 44, 69

post 1872 activities, 226, 228, 234
on Slave Power, 57, 60
on Reconstruction 73, 79, 83–87, 112,
    147
source for Bowers, 205

on tariffs, 110–11, 155, 156
as Trumbull's political lieutenant, 92,
    137, 140, 140–52, 161, 179
Wiebe, Robert H., 55
Wilson, Henry, 35, 167

RECONSTRUCTING AMERICA SERIES
Paul A. Cimbala, series editor

1. Hans L. Trefousse, *Impeachment of a President: Andrew Johnson, the Blacks, and Reconstruction.*

2. Richard Paul Fuke, *Imperfect Equality: African Americans and the Confines of White Ideology in Post-Emancipation Maryland.*

3. Ruth Currie-McDaniel, *Carpetbagger of Conscience: A Biography of John Emory Bryant.*

4. Paul A. Cimbala and Randall M. Miller, eds., *The Freedmen's Bureau and Reconstruction: Reconsiderations.*

5. Herman Belz, *A New Birth of Freedom: The Republican Party and Freedmen's Rights, 1861 to 1866.*

6. Robert Michael Goldman, *"A Free Ballot and a Fair Count": The Department of Justice and the Enforcement of Voting Rights in the South, 1877–1893.*

7. Ruth Douglas Currie, ed., *Emma Spaulding Bryant: Civil War Bride, Carpetbagger's Wife, Ardent Feminist—Letters, 1860–1900.*

8. Robert Francis Engs, *Freedom's First Generation: Black Hampton, Virginia, 1861–1890.*

9. Robert F. Kaczorowski, *The Politics of Judicial Interpretation: The Federal Courts, Department of Justice and Civil Rights, 1866–1876.*

10. John Syrett, *The Civil War Confiscation Acts: Failing to Reconstruct the South.*

11. Michael Les Benedict, *Preserving the Constitution: Essays on Politics and the Constitution in the Reconstruction Era.*